Child Guidance Centres in Japan

> This book represents a Copernican change to our understanding of alternative care in Japan and answers the question of Japan's continued use of institutional care over foster care.
> – Tsuzaki Tetsuo

In contemporary Japan, 85 per cent of children in alternative care remain housed in large welfare institutions, as opposed to family-based foster care. This publication examines how Japan has been isolated from the global discourse on alternative care, urging a shift in social work and alternative care policies.

As the first ethnographic account from inside child guidance centres, it makes a key contribution towards understanding the closed world of Japan's social services, including the decision-making processes by which a child is removed from the family and placed into care. In addition, regional variation in policy implementation for alternative care is outlined, with reference to detailed case studies and a discussion around organisational cultures of the child guidance centres. Where foster care is constructed as anything other than professional, it is often seen as a threat to the child's family-bond with their natal parent and therefore not used. Child Guidance Centres in Japan destabilises this construction of the family-bond as singular and discrete, highlighting new practices in alternative care.

Child Guidance Centres in Japan: Alternative Care, Social Work, and the Family will be a vital resource for students, scholars of social work and Japanese studies, as well as practitioners and lobbyists involved in alternative care.

Michael Rivera King completed his doctorate in Social Policy at the University of Oxford. His research interests centre on Japan's alternative care system and the children and care-leavers whose lives are touched by this. Michael is the CEO of Ashinaga Association in the UK, a registered charity (number 1183750) promoting international access to higher education in the UK.

The Nissan Institute/Routledge Japanese Studies Series
Series Editors:

Roger Goodman, Nissan Professor of Modern Japanese Studies, University of Oxford, Fellow, St Antony's College

J.A.A. Stockwin, formerly Nissan Professor of Modern Japanese Studies and former Director of the Nissan Institute of Japanese Studies, University of Oxford, Emeritus Fellow, St Antony's College

The Dilemma of Faith in Modern Japanese Literature
Metaphors of Christianity
Massimiliano Tomasi

Understanding Japanese Society
Fifth edition
Joy Hendry

Japan and the New Silk Road
Diplomacy, Development and Connectivity
Nikolay Murashkin

The Liberal Democratic Party of Japan
The Realities of 'Power'
Nakakita Kōji

Japan's New Ruralities
Coping with Decline in the Periphery
Edited by Wolfram Manzenreiter, Ralph Lützeler and Sebastian Polak-Rottmann

New Directions in Japan's Security
Non-U.S. Centric Evolution
Edited by Paul Midford and Wilhelm Vosse

Child Guidance Centres in Japan
Alternative Care, Social Work, and the Family
Michael Rivera King

For more information about this series, please visit: www.routledge.com/Nissan-Institute-Routledge-Japanese-Studies/book-series/SE0022

Child Guidance Centres in Japan

Alternative Care, Social Work, and the Family

Michael Rivera King

LONDON AND NEW YORK

First published 2021
by Routledge
2 Park Square, Milton Park, Abingdon, Oxon OX14 4RN

and by Routledge
52 Vanderbilt Avenue, New York, NY 10017

Routledge is an imprint of the Taylor & Francis Group, an informa business

© 2021 Michael Rivera King

The right of Michael Rivera King to be identified as author of this work has been asserted by him in accordance with sections 77 and 78 of the Copyright, Designs and Patents Act 1988.

All rights reserved. No part of this book may be reprinted or reproduced or utilised in any form or by any electronic, mechanical, or other means, now known or hereafter invented, including photocopying and recording, or in any information storage or retrieval system, without permission in writing from the publishers.

Trademark notice: Product or corporate names may be trademarks or registered trademarks, and are used only for identification and explanation without intent to infringe.

British Library Cataloguing-in-Publication Data
A catalogue record for this book is available from the British Library

Library of Congress Cataloging-in-Publication Data
A catalog record has been requested for this book

ISBN: 978-1-138-36594-0 (hbk)
ISBN: 978-0-429-43054-1 (ebk)

Typeset in Times New Roman
by codeMantra

To Nina and my mum and dad

Contents

List of figures ix
List of tables xi
Series editor's preface xiii
Acknowledgements xv
List of abbreviations and technical terms xix

PART I
Introduction 1

1 Introduction 3

PART II
The context of alternative care 31

2 Alternative care 33
3 Child guidance centres 63
4 The family-bond 103

PART III
Regional variation of policy implementation 141

5 Regional variation of resources 143
6 Regional variation of norms 182
7 Regional variation of organisational cultures 215

PART IV
Conclusion **237**

8   Conclusion 239

Appendix one 255
Appendix two 257
Index 259

Figures

1.1	The foster care rate of each local authority. 2016–2017	8
1.2	Mapping the foster care rate. 2014	9
1.3	Mapping the foster care rate. 2004	12
1.4	Conceptualising the decision-making process	17
2.1	The foster care rate and the percentage of foster parents with a placement and the number of children in different care placements. 1955–2014	42
2.2	Mapping the change in the foster care rate. 2004–2014	46
3.1	The organisation of child protection (MHLW 2011)	65
3.2	The organisation of the Teru child guidance centre	73
3.3	The organisation of the Irifune child guidance centre	74
3.4	Teru child guidance centre consultation flow	81
3.5	Irifune child guidance centre consultation flow	82
4.1	A unique genogram (Irifune)	114
4.2	Two genograms: Yuno	115
4.3	Two genograms: Irifune	116
4.4	Four genograms: Teru	117
4.5	Age at time of placement into foster care or family home. Nationwide, in care on February 1st 2013	129
5.1	The capacity of BIWIs and CWIs, relative to child population, and the foster care rate. By local authority, 2014	149
5.2	The number of registered foster parents, relative to child population, and the foster care rate. By local authority, 2014	149
5.3	The child poverty rate (2012) and the total rate in care (2011). By prefecture	152
5.4	The rate of children in care, relative to child population, and the foster care rate. By local authority, 2011–2012	153
5.5	The occupancy rate of BIWIs and CWIs and the foster care rate. Teru, Irifune, Japan, 1997–2013	154

x *Figures*

6.1	Percentage of children of each age group, at time of placement, by care placement. Nationwide, in care February 1st 2013. Excludes mother and child supported living institutions	190
6.2	Marketing foster care. MHLW	194
6.3	Marketing foster care. Irifune	195
6.4	Marketing foster care. Teru	196
6.5	An overview of the spectrum of alternative care	203

Tables

2.1	An overview of alternative care	34
2.2	Costs of alternative care	48
5.1	The capacity of care providers, relative to child population. Teru, Irifune, Japan	148
6.1	Gilbert's orientations of alternative care systems	183

Series editor's preface

The Nissan Institute/Routledge Japanese Studies Series is now well past its 100th volume. It has published across a wide variety of areas relating to Japan, including political science, social anthropology, international relations, modern history, education, business, economics, religion, and the arts. The broad aim of the series is to inform readers of the many aspects of Japan and Japanese people, using objective, and where necessary, critical methodologies. We believe that the rest of the world can learn much from the experience of what is now the third largest economy in the world and is heir to sophisticated national traditions. The latest volume by Michael Rivera King rises to all the aspirations of the series admirably.

One of the things which we think we know about Japanese social policy is its focus on equality and equity. In the education system, for example, it is possible for students to transfer from any one part of Japan to any other with hardly any disruption to their educational experience. Not only will the curriculum and the teaching methodology be almost exactly the same, but even the school buildings, school events, even the school dinners will be virtually identical. This emphasis on uniformity and homogeneity is part of a conscious state policy to construct an ideology of meritocracy: success in life is dependent on an individual's effort not their background. It is something of a surprise therefore, as Michael Rivera King points out, to discover that there is considerable regional variation in the implementation of policy for children whose parents are unable to look after them. In some parts of Japan, for example, up to a third of such children are placed in foster placements; in other parts of Japan, almost all children are placed in large institutions. In order to explore this conundrum, Rivera King provides us with the first-ever detailed ethnography of the inner workings of Japan's child guidance centres (*jidōsōdanjo*). Japan does not have professional social workers but instead relies on local government bureaucrats working in these centres to make the placement decisions for children who come into care.

Rivera King's fascinating study shows how the bureaucrats in the child guidance centres operate on the ground. These mid-level bureaucrats are crucial in making decisions about both removing children from their families and the types of placements to then use. One thing they all have in common is a shared value around the importance of the family-bond. The decision on removing the child is made by evaluating the risk that doing so poses to the child's family-bond against the risk that not doing so poses to the child's physical or mental health. Where foster care, for example, is constructed as a replacement family, with care based upon the family-bond, it is often deemed as unsuitable for children for whom the ultimate goal of care is family reunification. In such cases, Child Welfare Institutions may be preferred mainly because they do not create attachments which threaten the family-bond. Understanding this key point gives us insight into two questions which have long puzzled western observers of Japan's child protection system: the low rate of children entering care and the low foster care rate in Japan. Caseworkers seem to assume that there can only be one family-bond at a time, that it is formed up to a certain age and that removing the child from the family risks cutting this bond. This explains why in Japan children are still quite often returned to parents who are known to be serious abusers.

Rivera King's study, however, goes beyond the shared context in the values of those implementing policy to show that there are also substantial differences in resources, norms, and organisational cultures and in how policy is implemented. Placement decisions balance staff's constructions of the goals of care, the functions of different care placements, and the threshold above which a child is seen as unsuitable for foster care. It is his study of the culture of these 'street level bureaucrats' which gives the lie to the idea that public officials in Japan are unable to interpret their remit in different ways. Indeed, the power of some of these mid-level managers that impact on the lives and the experiences of the children who come into their care is extensive.

In the course of exploring the work of the child guidance centres and the placements of children who come into care, Michael Rivera King introduces a raft of contemporary issues in Japan: family break-up, child abuse, gender relations. He also shows how Japan both changes and retains child welfare policies. At the centre of his analysis is the question of the rights of the child and his concern that these are not yet sufficiently recognised in Japan. As we said earlier, these are exactly the kinds of issues which the Nissan Institute/Routledge Japanese Studies Series was set up to explore and we are proud to include this volume as part of that project.

Roger Goodman
Arthur Stockwin
Series Editors

Acknowledgements

I have been engaged with the Japanese alternative care system for the last decade, as a volunteer, as a staff member of a charity, and as a researcher. It is almost impossible to acknowledge everyone who has helped guide, inspire, and support me through this period, and I can only apologise in advance to those I do not mention by name.

I must first thank all of those who engaged in this research process. Without Professor Tsuzaki's introduction to Mr Sano, the head of the Teru child guidance centre, and without Mr Sano's gracious offer to host me for six months, this research could never have been undertaken. I am equally grateful to Mr Suzuki, the head of the Irifune child guidance centre, and Mr Takahashi, the head of the Yuno child guidance centre, without whom the comparative research, from which much of the insight presented in this work emerged, could not have occurred.

My thanks extend beyond these three actors to all those working within these three child guidance centres. Their patience with my ignorance and engagement in my research was beyond what I could ever have imagined, and their dedication and heart was humbling. I am also incredibly grateful to the staff in the other child guidance centres who hosted me for day visits. These allowed me to understand better what was common and what was unique in each of my fieldwork sites.

I am also indebted to all the foster parents and staff of welfare institutions for their time and openness. I can only imagine that my experience volunteering in institutions and my desire to become a foster parent later in life contributed to the willingness of all my participants to speak frankly and fully with me. I am also grateful to all the bureaucrats within the Ministry of Health, Labour, and Welfare who were kind enough to grant me their time. There are two bureaucrats in particular who I wish I could name and express my thanks openly.

My respect for all those working within alternative care, which was already very high before I began my fieldwork, grew by the day during my stay. Even where I disagreed with a particular practice, I respected the dedication of everyone I met and their efforts to improve the systems in which they are working.

I must also thank all the academics I met along the way, with particular thanks to Kiyoko Miwa, Saki Yamazaki (nee Nagano), Kazuhiro Kamikado, Chiaki Shirai, Taishi Arimura, Hiroyasu Hayashi, Ichiro Matsumoto, Masashi Aizawa, Machiko Yamamoto, Shigeyuki Mori, Satoru Nishizawa, Kathryn Goldfarb, Judy Sebba, and everyone at the REES centre, and, once again, Tetsuo Tsuzaki. I would also like to thank Neil Gilbert for both his inspiring work and his kind permission to reproduce a table in this work. There are many other academics to whom also I am indebted, who I did not get the chance to meet in person. My reference list seems a spartan compliment to those who have inspired me so much. Special thanks also go to Glenda Roberts and Waseda University for hosting me and affording me the opportunity to present my work.

I must also express my deep gratitude to all the activists I have met, including Mamoru Watanabe of Key Assets Japan, Kanae Doi and Riyo Yoshioka of Human Rights Watch, Eriko Takahashi of The Nippon Foundation, Shihoko Fujiwara of Lighthouse: Center for Human Trafficking Victims, Katsumi Takenaka, and all the staff at SOS Children's Villages. The passion, drive, and perseverance of these actors are inspiring, and I am amazed at the changes they have been able to facilitate. Finally, among those who I met during my fieldwork, I wish to thank the children. While I didn't interview children, I volunteered in temporary care facilities, in classrooms for school-refusers, with foster children, and on day trips with juvenile delinquents. These were without doubt the most animated and fun parts of my fieldwork.

Stepping back in time a moment, I am grateful to the head of the first child welfare institution who allowed me and my friends to volunteer, to all those who supported me in setting up Smile Kids Japan, and to all those who volunteered with institutions around the country. Had you told me before setting off on the JET program that in a little over a decade I would be completing a book on Japanese alternative care I would have thought you were mad. To all those who opened doors and inspired me to go through them, thank you. I would like to extend special thanks to Mrs Yonezawa, who patiently taught me Japanese, without which these nothing else could have happened. I also want to thank Matthew Gilhool for his empathy and poker nights, Christopher Raine and Luke Happle for their kindness and Britishness, and Patrick Newell, who helped me learn how to think big.

Skipping back to the present, I am incredibly grateful for the supervision and support of Professor Roger Goodman, whose book on Japanese child welfare institutions inspired and enlightened me in equal measure. I am also incredibly grateful to Professor Martin Seelieb-Kaiser who, along with Roger, set high standards and pushed me to achieve them. I am grateful to all the students and staff, academic and administrative, in the Nissan Institute of Japanese Studies and the Department of Social Policy and Intervention who have taught me so much. It would be remiss here not to thank Jane Baker, for the tea and the friendly ear.

I am also greatly indebted to Mrs Teresa Smith and Professor Ito Peng for examining my doctorate. Their insights strengthened my work and their warmth and manner made the viva voce process a real pleasure, despite my initial nerves!

This work was supported by the Economic and Social Research Council (ESRC), grant number ES/J500112/1. I am fortunate to have been awarded a full research council scholarship, without which I could not have undertaken this research. While I question the impetus the ESRC place on impact later in this work, the comprehensive nature of this award undoubtedly strengthened my skills as a junior academic. Due to the sensitive nature of this research the data is not publicly available. Any researcher with questions on the data should email the author.

I am also grateful to Pembroke College and the Nissan Institute for additional funding during my Masters. I want to thank Pembroke College: the MCR and all the staff, with special thanks to Lynn Wilkinson, Giles Henderson, Lynne Brindley and all the porters for helping me find my *ibasho*, my place where I felt belonging, in Oxford. In particular, I want to thank Gabriel Schenk, William Badger, Jonathan Neve, Meghan Campbell, and Samuel Wills for their friendship, support, and bar nights.

Completing two masters, a doctorate, and this book has been a very long journey and I have loved almost every second of it. For this, I want to thank my friends and family for their love and support. In particular, my mum and dad, who always know what to say, and Peter Lower and Iain Wilson, who have been there for me since primary school. Finally, I want to thank Regina Rivera King for her patience, her support, and her love. You fill my heart and make me dream.

Abbreviations and technical terms

BIWI   Baby and Infant Welfare Institution. Tasked with providing alternative care for babies and infants under two years of age.

CGC   Child Guidance Centre. CGCs are the local government offices with responsibility for implementing policy on alternative care. This covers the decision on removing a child from their family/care provider and the decision on placement type, most commonly institutional care or foster care.

CPI   Child Psychotherapy Institution. Previously termed Short-Term Therapeutic Institution for Emotionally Disturbed Children. For children with more serious psychotherapy needs who are also in need of alternative care.

CSP   Common Sense Parenting. A parenting course offered by some child guidance centres.

CSRSI   Child Self-Reliance Support Institution. Tasked with providing alternative care for children at risk of becoming juvenile delinquents.

CUREC   Central University Research Ethics Committee. The University of Oxford Research Ethics Committee.

CVV   Children's Views and Voices. A care-leaver group started by Midori Nakamura.

CWI   Child Welfare Institution. Tasked with providing alternative care for infants and children aged between two and eighteen years old. This can be extended in exceptional circumstances up to 20 years of age.

FC   Foster care. Tasked with providing alternative care in a family setting. There are three types of foster care – regular foster parents, with a subcategory of specialist foster parents, foster parents wishing to adopt, and kinship foster parents.

FH   Family Home. Alternative care for up to six children provided by two 'foster parents' and an assistant, normally in a family setting. Categorised as foster care.

FICE	International Association of Residential Care.
HRW	Human Rights Watch.
ISPCAN	International Society for the Prevention of Child Abuse and Neglect
JaSPCAN	Japan Society for the Prevention of Child Abuse and Neglect
MCWI	Mother and Child Welfare Institution. Alternative care institution wherein the mother and child live in a self-contained small apartment with staff primarily working to support the mother.
MHLW	Ministry of Health, Labour, and Welfare. Responsible for alternative care.
MHLW SC	MHLW Specialist Committee for the Promotion of Placements into Foster Care.
NHK	Nippon Hōsō Kyōkai. Japan's national public broadcasting organisation.
NPO	Non-Profit Organisation.
OECD	Organisation for Economic Co-operation and Development
SRAH	Self-Reliance Assistance Home. Tasked with providing alternative care for youths who have left school, normally at 15 years of age.
TC	Temporary Care. An institution within child guidance centres tasked with providing protective custody for a child after they are removed from their family/care provider and before a formal placement into alternative care.
UN	United Nations.
UNCRC	United Nations Committee on the Rights of the Child
UNICEF	United Nations International Children's Emergency Fund
Zenshakyō	Japan National Council of Social Welfare

Note: Welfare Institutions are either publicly or privately run. Article 22 (1951) of the Social Welfare Service Law allows privately run welfare institutions, classified as *shakai fukushi hōjin*, to receive public funding provided the institution complies with government regulations (see Goodman, 2000: 50). This status exempts the institution from corporation and property tax, and tax on donations and gifts, as well as allowing them to access funds for building and administration costs. Public welfare institutions are run directly by the local authority.

Reference

Goodman, R. (2000). Children of the Japanese state: The changing role of child protection institutions in contemporary Japan. Oxford: Oxford University Press.

Part I
Introduction

1 Introduction

1 Personal connection

When reading academic work, I am always curious as to what led the researcher to the topic, what prompted them to dedicate time and energy to their question. My journey to this book started in 2006 when I began volunteering in a *jidōyōgoshisetsu*, a Child Welfare Institution (CWI),[1] while living in Japan. These institutions care for children who, whether due to abuse, bereavement, or other issues, cannot live with their parents. Over time, I set up a volunteering group, Smile Kids Japan, and then started work for a small non-profit organisation (NPO) supporting CWIs affected by the 2011 Tohoku earthquake and tsunami.[2]

I had never volunteered with children in care before and knew very little about social work in any context. Yet I was always puzzled as to the use of *nyūjiin*, Baby and Infant Welfare Institutions (BIWI), and CWI in Japan. Surely, I thought, in other OECD countries these children would be in foster care placements or adopted?

Over time this question troubled me. What if I was dedicating my time to incrementally improving a system that was fundamentally flawed? What if my efforts to improve the situation for these children in care were contributing in a tiny way to stabilising it against change? I did not assume the alternative care system was flawed but I realised that I could not assume that it wasn't. This led me to return to university to investigate this issue.

Without a comprehensive understanding of the mechanisms underpinning processes, any attempt to improve them risks both the quality of the research and creating unexpected or even undesirable outcomes (see Edin and Kefalas, 2005; Pfau-Effinger, 2005; Sellman et al., 2002). As such, I focused on understanding alternative care in Japan on its own terms. Where I did attempt to have an 'impact', something evangelised by the UK research councils, I always qualified my opinion with my doubts.

When compared with other OECD countries, Japan's alternative care system is an outlier in two significant regards. First, with 19 children per 10,000 (calculated from the Ministry of Health, Labour, and Welfare (MHLW), 2016), Japan takes half the number of children into care than the next lowest

4 *Introduction*

OECD country, Italy (Ainsworth and Thoburn, 2014: 18).[3] Second, with around 85 per cent of these children entering BIWI or CWI, Japan has the second-highest institutional care rate of all OECD countries, behind only Portugal (Carvalho et al., 2017).

The more I read, the more confused I became. OECD countries have long been de-institutionalising care (Colton and Hellincx, 1994; Gudbrandsson, 2004), a trend that is well supported (Cantwell et al., 2012; European Commission, 2013; European Expert Group on the Transition from Institutional to Community-Based Care, 2009; Everychild, 2011; Oswald, 2009; Save the Children, 2009; Stockholm Declaration, 2003; UN General Assembly, 2010; UNICEF, 2010; UNICEF and World Bank, 2003; World Health Organization, 2010).[4] Moreover, there is a long-standing move away from large institutions to smaller specialist facilities (Madge, 1994).

Arguments for family-based care often reference the 1989 UN Convention on the Rights of the Child, which states that 'the child should grow up in a family environment' (UN General Assembly, 1989, Article 20), or literature on the relationship between institutionalisation and developmental damage (see Barth, 2002; Bowlby, 1951, 1969; Browne, 2009; Browne et al., 2006; Goldfarb, 1945; Johnson et al., 2006; Nelson et al., 2007). Other factors contributing to de-institutionalisation include external pressure (Ainsworth and Thoburn, 2014; Courtney et al., 2009), abuse scandals (Bullock and McSherry, 2009; Gilligan, 2009; Stein, 2006, 2014), and financial considerations (Ainsworth and Hansen, 2009; Browne, 2008; EuroChild, 2012; Tobis, 2000).

This global discourse is embodied in the 2010 UN Guidelines for the Alternative Care of Children. This calls for residential care to be limited to 'specifically appropriate' cases (Article 21) and states that 'in accordance with the predominant opinion of experts, alternative care for young children, especially those under the age of 3 years, should be provided in family based settings' (Article 22).[5] So why, when Kasza argues that policy change in Japan has often been instigated to bring Japan in line with 'accepted standards of modernity' (2006: 166), has policy not changed here?

These concerns are not new in Japan: Ishii Juuji, a founding father of CWIs, argued for family-based alternative care in 1893 (Maus, 2006: 334), an argument repeated by the Welfare Ministry in 1954 (Kashiwame, 2010) and again in 1974 (Harada, 2013). Contemporary arguments for the de-institutionalisation of care focus on rights (Human Rights Watch (HRW), 2014; Shirai, 2015; UN Committee on the Rights of the Child (UN CRC), 1998, 2004, 2010), on the psychological, emotional, and developmental damage that institutionalisation can cause (Hennessy, 2013; HRW & The Nippon Foundation, 2014),[6] and on the higher cost of institutions (Takeuchi, 2014).

Kashiwame summarises domestic concerns neatly, writing, 'for children robbed of their upbringing in a home, providing a home for them to be raised in is obvious. Isn't the strange thing thinking that institutions are the norm?' (2010: 6).

So, why has de-institutionalisation not occurred? Does, as Tsuzaki (2006, 2009) argues, the configuration of alternative care represent a victory of vested interests over children's interests? Or is the situation more nuanced than this?

2 Current explanations

Japan's foster care rate, that is, the percentage of children in care who are in foster care, is receiving increasing attention, both domestically and abroad. One international comparative study that considers Japan is Ainsworth and Thoburn (2014). This divides alternative care systems into three types: Anglophone countries, which use residential care as a last resort; continental European countries, which see residential care as the most suitable placement for some children; and developing world and transition economies, which often believe large institutions are the only solution to overwhelming need and minimal resources. Residential care facilities in continental European countries are normally small, supported residential units run with a social pedagogical approach for older children with complex needs, which 'bear no resemblance to the large-scale institutional or congregate care facilities of the past that are still to be found in many developing and Eastern European 'transition' economies, and at which UNICEF's deinstitutionalisation policies are mainly aimed' (Ainsworth and Thoburn, 2014: 17).

Ainsworth and Thoburn offer tentative 'broad-brush partial explanations' (2014: 19) for Japan's low foster care rate, 'from the practical (the small size of most family homes) to the traditional (concern about taking a 'stranger' into the family...)' (2014: 19). Other international comparative work also draws on ideas of 'tradition' or *a* Japanese culture: Kendrick et al. write that 'traditional views of the family in Japan have led to the predominance of residential over foster care' (2011: 6), Bamba emphasises the importance of 'culturally embedded practices and beliefs' (2010: 12), and Kadonaga and Fraser argue that 'financed kinship care and foster family care have been viewed as incongruent with the blood-line values of Japanese culture' (2015: 13).[7]

Goldfarb challenges these explanations, stating that 'there are many reasons for contemporary welfare practices, and the notion that Japanese people are unwilling to care for unrelated children is not a central factor (2012: 25). Goldfarb argues that 'the culturalist explanations for welfare practice were both insufficient and misleading' (2012: 25).

Miwa's (2016) overview of the reasons given for Japan's low foster care rate highlights that cultural explanations were not common in Japanese academia until the 1980s. In the 1950s explanations focused on concerns over child labour and foster parents wanting to adopt (Yamamoto, 1952). Arguments in the 1960s acknowledged Bowlby's work on attachment (Tsuzaki, 2006) and focused on the shortage of foster parents. This was understood as being the result of low fees and limited support for foster parents (Miyoshi,

1963), and a lack of public awareness of foster care (Ogasawara, 1963). In the 1970s arguments focused on the lack of specialist knowledge in Child Guidance Centres (CGCs), which make both the decision to remove the child from their family and on the placement type, where foster care was still confused with adoption (Matsumoto, 1971, 1974).

Cultural explanations gained traction in the 1980s, including Iwasaki's (1986) work centred on the limited reach of Christianity in Japan. Other explanations focused on urbanisation, the nuclearisation of the family, a declining living environment, and a declining birth-rate (see Yoshizawa, 1987). The 1990s saw a focus on the lack of support for foster parents, which, combined with a discourse that increasingly saw childrearing as inherently challenging, led to the idea of a threshold of complexity of needs, above which children were not seen as suitable for foster care (see Sakurai, 1999; Shoji et al., 1998).

Much of the research on foster care in the 2000s rehashes existing themes. Exceptions include Miyajima (2001), who provides insight into the challenges CGCs face in using foster care, including gaining parental consent (see also Hasegawa, 1984), and Tsuzaki (2006, 2009), who considers macro-factors, including the lack of a social work profession.

The most original work since 2010 on Japan's foster care rate is by Miwa (2011, 2012, 2014, 2016). This argues that there is limited empirical evidence for the contemporary focus on the lack of foster parents. Instead, Miwa argues, the issues are a 'lack of children eligible to be fostered' (2016), the CGCs' lack of knowledge and heavy workload (2011, 2012, 2014), and the welfare institutions' negative attitude towards foster care (2016).

Existing relevant literature can be categorised into two groups. The first offers sweeping cultural explanations for the limited use of foster care. The second looks at specific factors inhibiting the use of foster care. Both groups of literature have their limitations.

There are two issues with the sweeping cultural explanations found in both Japanese and non-Japanese work. Goldfarb succinctly expresses the first, arguing that 'cultural explanations tend to neglect the capacity of policies and practices to shift and instead conflate current child welfare practice on the ground with an intransigent notion of timeless culture as a barrier to change' (2018: 183). Yet policy and practice have changed, change that in some local authorities[8] has been relatively rapid. The second issue is that explanations based upon a national culture cannot account for regional variation in policy implementation, visible in the different foster care rates of local authorities.

The group of literature that looks at specific issues has one major issue – none of it explains how the decision to place children into institutional care or foster care is made. Understanding factors such as the absence of social work as a profession, the issues around parental consent, and the lack of support for foster carers is important, but these all represent pieces of the puzzle, with the overall picture still missing.

Introduction 7

The key to understanding the big picture lies in understanding two things: the CGCs that implement policy, and the regional variation between local authorities in how alternative care policy is implemented.

The decision to remove the child from their family and the decision on the placement type, into institutional care or family-based care, are made in the CGCs. Yet the CGCs have remained closed to researchers. The few studies that exist are either survey-based (Kashiwame et al., 1995; Saimura et al., 2000, 2004, 2010; Ushijima and Yukawa, 1975) or are written by those 'inside' the CGCs and offer insight into narrow fields, including the construction of foster care (Miyajima, 2001; Sadaka, 2007) and the role of the judiciary (Kubo, 2012, 2014).

This book is the first to take us into this closed world, the first to explain how the decision to place a child is made, and the first to understand the bigger picture of why Japan's foster care rate is low. In doing so, this book offers a central argument on the contemporary construction of the Japanese family, as well as looking at the impact of resources, norms, and organisational culture on how policy is implemented.

3 Regional variation in policy implementation

As noted previously, there are two issues with the 'Japanese culture' explanation for the low foster care rate. The first is that they cannot explain the change seen over time in alternative care. The second is that they cannot explain why local authorities implement alternative care policy differently. Figure 1.1 shows the foster care rate of each local authority in 2016–2017.[9]

Sugimoto's *An introduction to Japanese society* (2010) gives different types of regional variation commonly used to explain differences in Japan. These include the eight regional blocs, the Eastern-Western divide, and a divide between the centre, in which half of the population lives, and the periphery, as well as between local industries, popular culture and language. The 2014 regional variation in the foster care rate, mapped in Figure 1.2, does not follow any of these divides.[10]

Examining this regional variation allows us to interrogate explanations based upon *a* national culture. This is particularly important in Japan, which is prone to being homogenised (Gjerde, 1996: 294).

Studying regional variation is also important because the uniform national legislation and guidelines on alternative care, the fact that the Constitution guarantees 'the provision of welfare to all Japanese citizens on an equal basis' (Goodman, 2000: 35), and the ideal of 'equal opportunities' found in the Children's Charter (1951), and Basic Act on Education (2006), make the gap between Miyagi's foster care rate of 37.5 per cent and neighbouring Akita's 6.1 per cent noteworthy. This 'postcode lottery' in service provision is even more surprising when compared with education, where policy is uniformly implemented in the content of what is taught, the timing

8 Introduction

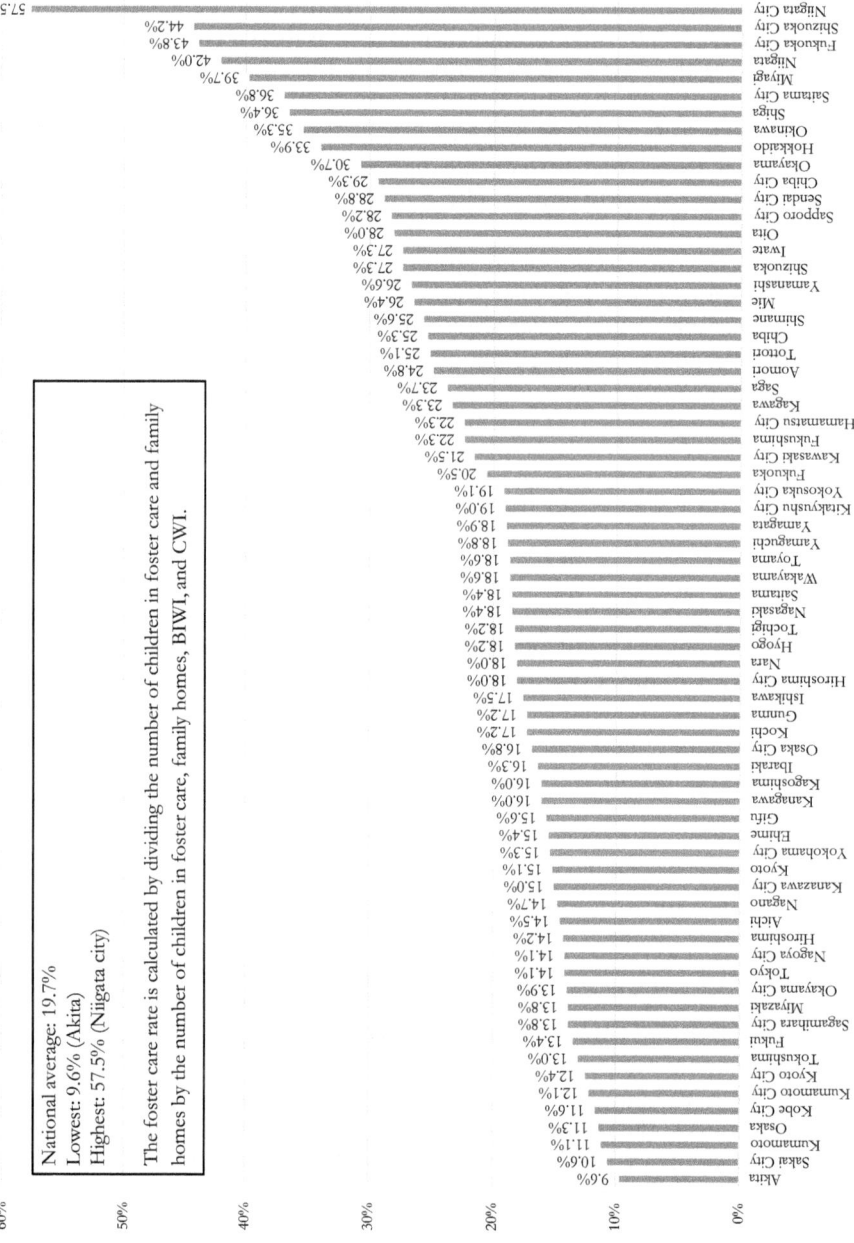

Figure 1.1 The foster care rate of each local authority, 2016–2017.
Data Source: MHLW, (2019: p24). Welfare administration reported cases, 2016–2017

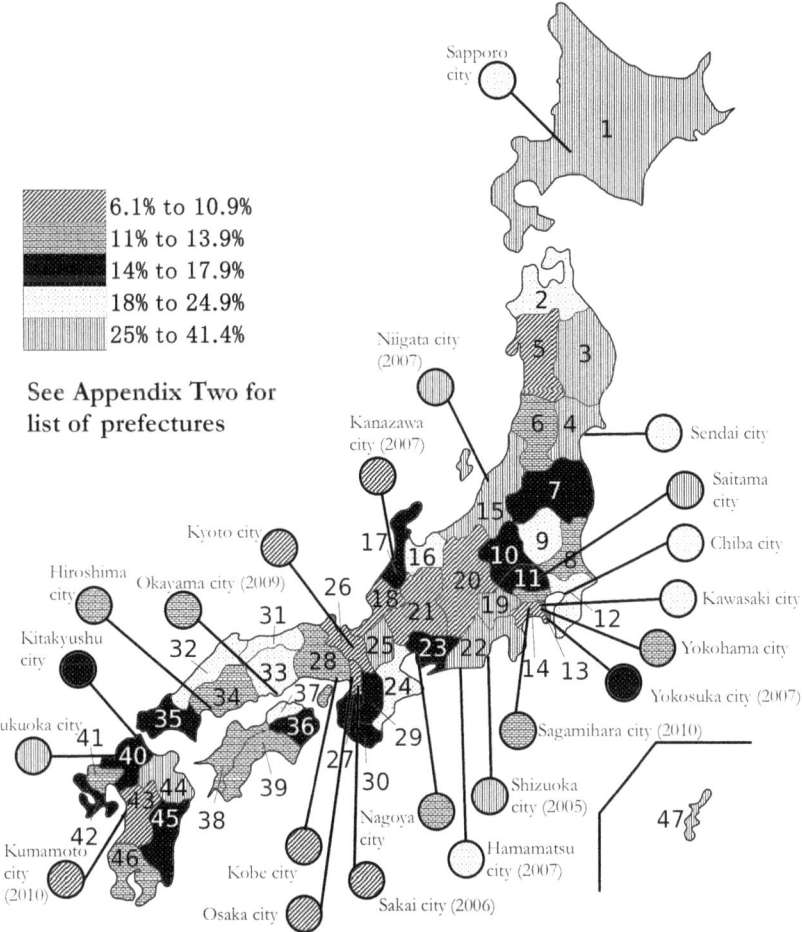

Figure 1.2 Mapping the foster care rate. 2014.

of when it is taught, and even the architecture of the schools in which it is taught (Aspinall, 2016; Cummings, 1980).

Wada et al. neatly summarise these concerns in their study on regional variation in temporary care institutions, stating that 'the Child Welfare Act is supposed to set national standards for child welfare, but we can see large differences between regions' (2013: 1). This reflects a fundamental tension between the ideals of equality and those of the decentralisation of power.

One possible reason for the regional variation is Kasza's argument that 'bureaucratic discretion marks the administration of Japan's public assistance program' (2006: 99; see also Seeleib-Kaiser, 1995). Goldfarb too, discussing children's rights in 'legal and policy initiatives' (2013: 166) on alternative care, argues that 'there remains a significant gap between laws and policies, and enforcement in daily practice' (2013: 166). This casts CGC caseworkers as powerful agents.

Yet Goldfarb (2013) also cites CGC staff defending themselves from accusations of negligence by arguing that they are constricted by systemic problems. This mirrors Rowe's observation that street-level bureaucrats 'talk of the rules that bind them. They bemoan the performance demands and scrutiny that comes with that. They readily cite financial constraints as a barrier to their work' (2012: 10). This speaks to a paradox that Lipsky (1980) explores, of street-level bureaucrats as powerful yet weak, as having agency yet being constrained. This book uses Lipsky's (1980: 3) definition of street-level bureaucrats:

> public service workers who interact with citizens in the course of their jobs, and who have substantial discretion in the execution of their work. Typical street-level bureaucrats are teachers... social workers... and many other public officials who grant access to government programs and provide services within them

The discretion of CGC staff lies at the heart of this tension between equality and decentralisation. This book uses Davis' broad definition of discretion: 'A public officer has discretion wherever the effective limits on his power leave him free to make a choice among possible courses of action and inaction' (1969: 4). While discretion is inevitable when street-level bureaucrats are faced with 'complex tasks for which elaboration of rules, guidelines, or instructions cannot circumscribe the alternative' (Lipsky, 1980: 15), its exercise raises concerns relating to democratic governance, fair and equitable treatment of citizens, and policy achievement (Meyers and Vorsanger, 2003). The extent to which the exercise of discretion is considered valid varies, for example across federal and 'strong centre' states (see Hill, 1997), or by the degree of professionalisation of those implementing policy (Evans, 2012; Freidson, 2001).

To understand the regional variation of policy implementation, we must shine a light into the CGCs and explore how discretion is exercised. Goodman notes that 'there is virtually nothing written in English, not only on the child welfare services but indeed on personal social services in Japan in general' (2000: 4). There is an absence of ethnographic work on CGCs, and an extremely limited amount of literature relating to the CGC's decision-making process (see Harada, 2010; Kurihara, 2011). The CGC caseworkers remain 'an important and understudied group' (Goodman, 2000: 36).

This book is not the first work to look at regional variation in policy implementation in alternative care in Japan. Wada et al. (2013) explore regional variation in temporary care, and Miwa (2012, 2016) and Matsumoto (1991) have touched tangentially on the regional variation of the foster care rate. Matsumoto (1991) suggested that CGCs with more expertise in foster care may have a higher foster care rate; Miwa (2012) found a correlation between a higher caseload of the CGC caseworkers and a lower foster care rate.

In their time-study of CGC staff, Kashiwame et al. found 'discrepancies between the centres in the way that they dealt with such issues as protective care, delinquency, truancy, the rearing of children and mental and physical disabilities', as well as 'differences in involvement of specialist staff, team approach, etc.' (1996: 173). These findings were replicated in later work by Saimura et al. (2007, 2014). Kashiwame et al. (1996) concluded their study by calling for further research here.

Other work includes Nabekura (2004), who highlights the large disparities between CWIs in educational attainment (see also King, 2017), and Hayashi et al. (2013), who studied regional variation in foster care recruitment and registration. The 2011 survey by the National Child Guidance Centre Directors' Committee also highlights regional variation in the structure of foster care service provision, though it does not explicitly problematise this (2011: 32). Finally, Hayashi (2015) has also highlighted regional variation in adoption practice: in 2012–2013, 39.6 per cent of CGCs had no cases of adoption (Asahi Shinbun, 2015), a figure that rose to 45 per cent in 2013–2014 (NHK, 2016).

This body of research describes regional variation but does not sufficiently address the 'why' questions: why are local authorities implementing uniform national legislation, policy, and guidelines differently? If expertise and caseload affect the foster care rate, why do some local authorities allocate more resources here than others? Nor does this research address whether the CGCs understand key constructions uniformly, including their role, the child, the family, the goals of care, and the function of different placements.

There is a tension between the desire for 'national standards for child welfare' (Wada et al., 2013) and the desire to devolve power and responsibility for alternative care to local authorities. This led Kashiwame et al. to argue: 'there is quite a wide range in the way the [child guidance] centres are operated and in order to guarantee the equality, fairness, and securing of children's rights, it is recognised that a certain set of guidelines should be produced' (1995: 141). This call was repeated in 2007 by an MHLW committee, which 'recommended that the national government provide a basic planning guideline to avoid disparity in foster care services among prefectures' (Harada, 2013: 19). This resulted in the 2011 Foster Care Guidelines (MHLW, 2011), which called for foster care to become the 'default' placement.

Despite these Guidelines, local authorities differ more now than they did in 2004; see Figures 1.2 and 1.3. This adds the questions: are practitioners problematising the increased diversity in policy implementation? Are there actors arguing for equality over the devolution of power?

12 *Introduction*

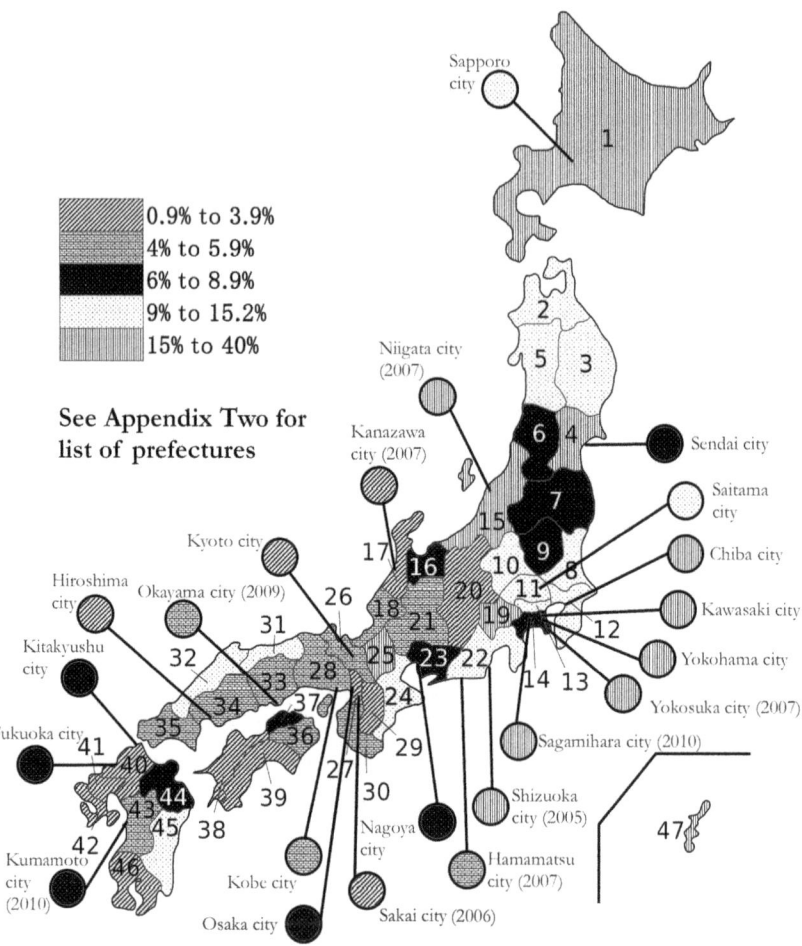

Figure 1.3 Mapping the foster care rate. 2004.

This book investigates this regional variation as a way to understand Japan's foster care rate. The unit of analysis is the CGC, rather than the local authority, partly as I could not collect rich data at the local authority hall or at every CGC in the local authorities where I conducted fieldwork. It is also due to the emphasis that my theoretical framework places on the organisational culture of the specific implementing organisation. The research question addressed in this book is thus,

What factors contribute to the regional variation in policy implementation on alternative care in Japanese child guidance centres?

Addressing this also allows us to understand the bigger-picture question of Japan's low foster care rate.

4 Research methods

4.1 Research design

This research centres on CGCs: where the state meets the family and where children become cases. Within this, the focal point is the decision-making process by which a child enters care and is placed into foster care or institutional care. In the absence of ethnographic research, this process has remained a black box, into which uniform policy and guidelines enter and diverse outcomes emerge.

This research began with a literature review of both the topic and the methodology. This resulted in a structure for analysis and, indeed, for this book. The first part of this is the context in which policy implementation occurs, here understood to include the values of those implementing policy. The remaining factors that contribute to regional variation of policy implementation are then grouped into resources, beliefs, and organisational culture.[11]

There is little data on alternative care, something Goodman describes as 'curious—and, in Japan, where statistics are kept on almost everything, probably significant' (2000: 13). The data that does exist is predominantly national aggregated data. This includes data on education progression, current placement length, and contact with natal parents. There are some aggregated data reported at the local authority level. This includes the foster care rate, the use of foster care and BIWIs for children of different ages, and the number of CGC foster care caseworkers. MHLW reports on alternative care included data by local authority on the rate of children entering care, per population, until 2012 when this graph was removed.[12] Since January 2016 these MHLW reports have included local authorities' self-set target foster care rates for 2029,[13] and the number of 'specialist counsellors for foster care support' in BIWIs and CWIs by local authority. This descriptive data is of limited value in understanding the mechanisms underlying policy implementation. For example, it is unclear why some local authorities have set their 2029 target for foster care significantly higher than others.

This research, centred on the CGCs, draws on academic work on street-level bureaucrats. This research can be grouped into evaluation and implementation studies. This study is not evaluative, in part because before evaluating these actors it is first necessary to establish the frameworks of how actors understand their actions and decisions, what a Bourdieuian scholar would term their 'habitus'.[14] In line with other implementation studies, this book utilises an anthropological case study approach (see Bobrow, 2008; Goodman, 2006; Hann, 1996; Shore and Wright, 1997) aimed at understanding processes.[15]

To understand this regional variation, I used a comparative research design 'in order to sort out the influence of different implementation variables' (Winter, 2003: 212). Case selection followed theoretical sampling focused on

14 *Introduction*

two variables: the foster care rate and the change in foster care rate between 2005–2006 and 2011–2012.[16] The second variable was included to maximise regional variation in practice. My plan was thus to research three sites: one with a high foster care rate that had seen a large increase in the foster care rate, one with a medium foster care rate that had seen a medium increase in the foster care rate, and one with a low foster care rate that had seen a small increase in the foster care rate.[17]

In reality, I could not quite fulfil these criteria exactly: Teru,[18] my first fieldwork site, had a high foster care rate and had seen a large increase in the foster care rate. Irifune, my second fieldwork site, had a low foster care rate and had seen a medium increase in the foster care rate. Yuno, my third fieldwork site, had a medium foster care rate and had seen a medium increase in the foster care rate.

While I conducted research and analysis on all three sites, this book primarily discusses Teru and Irifune. These represent the extremes of difference in policy implementation in my model.

4.2 The research process

The second most common question I am asked, after 'why do you study this?', is 'how were you able to study this?' Prior to this work, no CGC had granted access for ethnographic work. The most critical moment in this project came before I left for Japan, when Mr Sano, the head of the Teru CGC, agreed that I could conduct fieldwork in his CGC. There are four reasons why Sano may have granted me access. The first reason was an introduction from Professor Tsuzaki. The second was my experience with CWIs – Sano knew that I cared about the situation of children in care, and that I was sympathetic to CWI staff. The third reason was the confidentiality agreement I signed with the CGC, noting standard academic procedures on data protection and use.

The final reason is perhaps the most important: Sano's desire to question existing practice. Teru is considered a pioneering local authority for foster care practice, with Sano understood as being central to this. The ethical challenges this raised, in remaining an observer and not a participant, are discussed later.

I am also incredibly grateful to Mr Suzuki, the head of the Irifune CGC, and Mr Takahashi, the head of the Yuno CGC. A personal introduction from Sano to Suzuki, coupled with the fact that I was already conducting research in a CGC, secured access in Irifune.

My route to the Yuno CGC was facilitated by HRW and the Yuno Governor's office. I was concerned that this 'top-down' introduction would impact upon data collection but a personal introduction from Sano, who vouched for my character, along with a concerted effort to distance myself from both the governor and from HRW, meant that the data collection process was not affected in any significant way.

Introduction 15

I spent six months in the Teru CGC, three months in the Irifune CGC, and two months in the Yuno CGC. I employed multiple data collection techniques. In addition to participant observation, I interviewed CGC staff, attended meetings on policy and practice change, and training for staff and for registering foster parents. Most importantly, I attended all formal meetings on children who came into contact with the CGC. This involved attending 'acceptance' meetings covering over 3,000 children, 'ruling' meetings covering around 750 children, and 210 'division head' or 'aid objectives' meetings. I also attended 50 'emergency' meetings, which determine if immediate intervention is required. In addition, I was shown case files for over 50 children who were in foster care or whose cases the CGC staff felt were interesting or unusual.

I transcribed the discussions in all these meetings and made additional notes on things I did not understand or found interesting. Some CGCs allowed me to keep heavily redacted, anonymised versions of this paperwork.

I remained silent in these meetings to minimise the impact of my presence. There were three exceptions to this. The first was when I did not understand a word central to the case.[19] The second was when, despite having established that I have never studied or trained in social work, I was asked about social work or foster care in the UK. Here I deferred answering, researched the answer, and responded later to the questioner.

On one occasion I did speak about a case during a meeting. A child had been trafficked and was being 'adopted' by a holding agent to be sold into domestic or international adoption. During this discussion the Japanese terms for trafficking, '*jinsai baibai*' or '*jinshin torihiki*', had not been used. In a moment that I regret, though fortunately one that had no consequence, I asked: 'To clarify my understanding of this, this is a case of human trafficking, right?' The caseworker and senior manager replied together in the affirmative and the discussion continued.

Fears over the impact of my presence in meetings were quickly allayed. It is possible that the language used was slightly affected by my presence, particularly at the start of placements, but put simply, the weight of the decisions being made meant that the CGC staff did not change decisions because of my presence.

In all cases, I was struck by how hardworking, conscientious, and caring the CGC staff were. Some staff expressed concerns over resources or system limitations, and all were concerned to do the best that they could for the children for whom they were responsible.

During the course of my fieldwork I visited a further six CGCs in four local authorities. I conducted interviews in all of these and observed the decision-making process in five. I visited 12 CWIs, six BIWIs, two self-reliance assistance homes, two self-reliance support institutions, including for the annual 'culture day' festival in one, one mother and child welfare institution, and one juvenile detention centre.[20] I also visited *Musashinogakuen*, the national self-reliance support institution[21] which deals with

16 *Introduction*

children displaying the most challenging behaviours. I visited foster care recruitment events, local foster care association meetings, ten foster parents' homes, five family homes, an NPO providing foster care services, an NPO specialising in adoption, and a two-night summer camp for foster carers and foster children. I also attended various local NPO events,[22] many on foster care, which informed my understanding of the relationship between local government and civil society.

I also attended the annual conferences for the National Foster Care, CWI, and Family Home associations, the first Japan Foster Care Association[23] conference, and the annual public MHLW hearing on the direction of alternative care. These meetings helped me understand the nature of these bodies and the divisions and debates occurring within them.[24]

During my fieldwork I also met politicians, of the Upper and Lower houses, who were members of party and cross-party groups on alternative care, including Mr Fukuda, the secretary-general of the Liberal Democratic Party's 'Committee to think about the future of alternative care', the most influential political body on alternative care.

Towards the end of my fieldwork, I interviewed six MHLW bureaucrats, including a senior bureaucrat who is seen by academics as having laid some of the foundations for the promotion of foster care. I also met national journalists, one of whom had served as an advisor on alternative care to the MHLW, and academics, the majority of whom worked closely with the MHLW or one of the national care associations. I also met the two largest non-governmental organisations working to reform this field, HRW, and The Nippon Foundation.[25]

While I had been concerned about access, if anything, I faced the opposite problem. I attended almost everything and collected far richer data than anticipated. This window into a hitherto closed world is one of this book's most important contributions.

Ethical considerations meant I decided not to interview any children. This does not impact on my ability to address my research question, which is on policy implementation rather than on how the process of entering care is understood or experienced by children. The children's voice thus only emerges where it is given weight in the decision process by the CGC.

4.3 Data analysis

Data analysis focused on the meetings in which the decision-making process occurred.[26] I had assigned each case a unique reference number, allowing me to link redacted case files to my transcripts.

I grouped these cases based on where the child was before and after the meeting, resulting in, home to home, home to care, care to home, and care to care; a fifth category, other, covered miscellaneous cases. These included where the child was involved with the law, investigation of abuse within a CWI, and one case of fraud by a foster carer. I then coded cases for which

Introduction 17

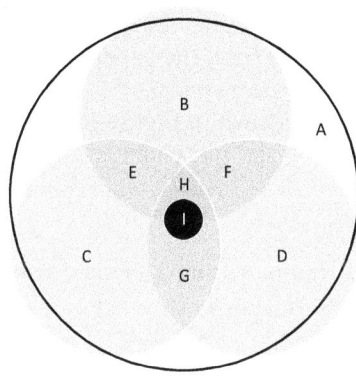

A model of decision-making for street-level bureaucrats

A: Organisational culture, values of street-level bureaucrats, broader context of policy implementation

B: Construction of problem
C: Construction of options
D: Construction of self

E: Construction of problem and options meet but believe unable to do
F: Construction of self and problem meet but believe unavailable

G: Construction of self and options meet but not seen as suitable
H: Construction of problems, options, and self meet

I: Future processing of case

Conceptualising the CGC decision-making process

A: Framework: Macro-context, organisational culture, caseworkers' values

B: Construction of the child's needs. Affected by the caseworker's 'norms' on the threshold of complexity of needs and the goals of care
C: Construction of available care placements. Affected by caseworker's 'norms' on the function of different care placements and by resources
D: Construction of the role of the CGC

E: Placement seen as suitable but outside the role of the CGC to provide
F: Placement seen as suitable and within the remit of the CGC but is unavailable

G: Possible placement but considered unsuitable
H: Possible placement. Suitable, available, and within the remit of the CGC

I: How the case transitions forwards

Figure 1.4 Conceptualising the decision-making process.

I had redacted files and transcripts within groups, for example all home to home cases, and across groups, for example comparing home to home cases with home to care cases, both within and across fieldwork sites.

I conducted this coding three times, each time building up a level in abstraction. Figure 1.4 shows the third model, alongside a more abstract model of decision-making by street-level bureaucrats. In this model, the decision is framed by the values of the caseworker, the organisational culture in which the caseworker is working, and the macro-context of policy implementation, shown by (A). The decision-making process is understood as an interaction between the constructions of the child's needs (B), of available placements (C), and of the CGC's role (D).

This model creates four possible outcomes. In the first two, placement decisions cannot be made: (E), where the care placement is seen as suitable but outside the CGC's role, for example, where the parent refuses consent, and (F), where the desired care placement is seen as being unavailable, for example, where the CGC does not think that available foster parents are suitable. In either of these scenarios the CGC must compromise, either not making a placement, or making a placement that is feasible but unsuitable – (G). These cases were often framed as, 'have no choice but to...', or as a provisional decision with hopes of moving the child later.[27]

The final possible outcome, (H), is where the placement is seen as suitable, available, and within the valid remit of the CGC. While represented as binary, the distinction between unsuitable placements (G) and suitable ones (H) is in fact a spectrum, with the nature of this work meaning that it is sometimes unclear what the best decision is. To help analysis I added two codes: (I) on how the case moved forwards after the decision, and (J) on policy and practice learning from individual cases.

I then tested this model against all the cases, not just those that I had redacted files for. I had basic descriptive data for all the transcripts, including the case type, child's age and gender, the local authority, and the 'purpose of the meeting', and a one-line explanation I had noted from the paperwork. I then coded all cases using NVivo 10 and manually, using paper.

This coding refined the decision-making model shown in Figure 1.4. The factors that were most important in determining the placement decision were:

Context (Chapters 2, 3, 4)
- Limited CGC power: in terms of context, Chapters 2 and 3. (This is also considered in relation to resources, Chapter 5)
- Values: The family-bond, Chapter 4

Resources (Chapter 5)
- Limited resources available to the caseworker, including expertise and time
- Care placements available to the caseworker (quantity and quality)

Beliefs / 'norms' (Chapter 6)
- CGC staff's 'norms' relating to the:
  - goals of care, with anticipated placement length important here
  - function of different placement types
  - threshold until which foster care was considered suitable – closely linked to age

Organisational culture (Chapter 7)
- Impact on the decision-making process: visible in the senior managers' role and in who attends meetings
- The willingness of the CGC to act against the guardian's initial wishes
- References to 'similar' cases to understand potential trajectories
- Willingness of CGC to accept 'positive risk'

I do not attempt to evaluate the relative strength of these factors. Instead, I attempt to specify 'the conditions under which these variables are important and the reasons we should expect them to be important' (Matland, 1995: 153).

5 Outline of the book

This book argues that the macro-context that underpins policy implementation is largely uniform, with 'values' on the family-bond of central importance, and that regional variation in resources, beliefs, most notably on the function of foster care, and organisational culture explain regional variation in policy implementation.

Introduction 19

The remainder of this book is organised into seven chapters. The following three chapters lay out the contextual factors that impact upon policy implementation. Chapter 2 introduces alternative care in Japan more fully, covering efforts to reform policy and practice to promote foster care. Chapter 3 introduces the role of the CGCs and outlines the decision-making process by which a child enters care.

Chapter 4 introduces the most important value that underpins the alternative care system in Japan, the construction of the family-bond between child and 'parent'. The chapter breaks down the components of the family-bond before looking at its three defining characteristics. The first is that a child can only have one family-bond. Forming a new family-bond weakens the existing (or potential) family-bond, and the formation of a new family-bond cuts the existing family-bond. The second is that removing a child from their parents risks destroying the existing family-bond. The final characteristic is that children are understood as being unable to form a family-bond after a certain age. The consequence of the discrete and singular nature of the family-bond is that where foster care is constructed as anything other than professional or semi-professional care in a family setting, it is seen as a threat to the existing family-bond. Indeed, institutional care is often used precisely because it does not create a new family-bond.

The subsequent three chapters focus on the impact of regional variation in resources (Chapter 5), beliefs (Chapter 6), and organisational culture (Chapter 7), on policy implementation. Chapter 5 divides resources into external resources, including the physical geography of the local authority, political attention, the capacity of the institutions and of foster care, the need for alternative care, the perceived quality of available care, and internal resources, the capacity of the child guidance centres themselves.

Chapter 6 examines the impact of beliefs on policy implementation. CGC staff make two decisions for each child that enters care. The first is whether to remove the child from their family. This is made by evaluating the risk this poses to the family-bond against the risk that leaving the child in the family poses to the child. The second decision is on the placement type. This centres on the CGC staff members' constructions of the goals of care, which are shaped by the assessment of the strength of the family-bond and the parents' present and future capacity to provide care, the functions of different care placements, and the threshold above which a child is seen as unsuitable for foster care. The most important of these beliefs in explaining regional variation is the construction of foster care. Foster care can be seen as a proxy for adoption or as professional care in a family setting.

Chapters 5 and 6 focus mainly on what differences exist between local authorities and the impact these have on policy implementation. Chapter 7 considers why these differences exist, focusing on the organisational cultures of the CGCs. The lack of social work as a profession increases the importance of the organisational culture of each individual child guidance centre. Differences in the decision-making process, the role and composition of senior management, and in how knowledge is acquired, retained, and used are central in explaining why differences occur.

Chapter 8 summarises the arguments proposed to explain the puzzle and the research question laid out in this chapter. It also shows how these arguments explain tangential questions, such as why Japan still uses BIWI, including one housing over 80 babies run by the Red Cross, and why children are returned with minimal oversight to parents who have tried to kill them. The book concludes with a consideration of the policy implications of the findings.

Notes

1 Goodman (2000) translates the term *jidōyō goshisetsu* as 'child protection institutions', 'children's homes', 'homes', and 'institutions', whereas Goldfarb (2012) uses the term 'children's homes'. I have used the word 'welfare' rather than protection, as this role is increasingly emphasised by the MHLW (MHLW, 2010). Welfare Institutions are either publicly or privately run. Article 22 (1951) of the Social Welfare Service Law allows privately run welfare institutions, classified as *shakai fukushi hōjin*, to receive public funding provided the institution complies with government regulations (see Goodman, 2000: 50). This status exempts the institution from corporation and property tax, and tax on donations and gifts, as well as allowing them to access funds for building and administration costs. Public welfare institutions are run directly by the local authority.
2 See (ITN, 2011; Maher King, 2011).
3 There is concern within Japan about the low rate of children entering care (Zenshakyō, 2008: 6).
4 These arguments are not unchallenged: In Southern and Central Europe, residential care is not a 'last resort' (Kendrick et al., 2011: 88) and some argue that for some children residential care should be 'a placement of first choice' (The College of Social Work, 2012; see Ainsworth and Hansen, 2009; Bryderup, 2008; Malmo Declaration, 1986; Peters, 2008; Sallnas, 2009; Social Work Services Inspectorate for Scotland, 1992). As a caveat within a caveat, residential care is usually small and used for older children. For an overview of these debates see Knorth et al. (2008) and Courtney and Hughes-Heuring (2009).
5 Exceptions are permitted

> in order to prevent the separation of siblings and in cases where the placement is of an emergency nature, or is for a predetermined and very limited duration, with planned family reintegration or other appropriate long-term care solution as its outcome.
>
> (UN General Assembly, 2010, Article 22)

6 The Nippon Foundation is very active in promoting foster care. They have translated summaries of the Bucharest Early Intervention Project (Nelson et al., 2013) and sponsored one of these authors, Fox, to be a keynote speaker at the 2014 International Society for the Prevention of Child Abuse and Neglect Conference (Fox, 2014).
7 Similar explanations are offered for Japan's low adoption rate. Hayes argues that 'aspects of Japanese culture combine to reinforce some of these preferences in a way that tends to make adoptive parents unusually selective' (2008: 90). Precisely what 'aspects of Japanese culture' is left unclear, and this argument does not consider the lengthy waiting lists of would-be adopters. It is worth noting that Kadonaga and Fraser's article contains factual errors.

8 I have used the terms governor, local authority, and local authority hall in relation to both cities and prefectures.
9 The label 'Source' is used where I have replicated the figure or table from a source. The label 'Data source(s)' is used where I have created a figure or table referencing data sources. On some figures, axes are intentionally left without numbers to protect the anonymity of the research sites.
10 Figure 1.2 maps the foster care rate for 2014, which is when I conducted my research.
11 The framework draws on the work of Meyers and Vorsanger (2003: 251–254), May and Winter (2007: 453–355), and Hill (2013: 223). See King (2017) for a fuller account of this process.
12 This can still be calculated manually.
13 Frustratingly, this graph combines data for some of the designated cities with the prefecture they are located in.
14 Okano summarises this concept neatly: 'Habitus creates one's preferences and perception of feasible options and influences the evaluation of the pros and cons of these options. It is defined as the strategy-generating principle that improvises all the thoughts, perceptions, expressions, and actions of agents' (1995: 33).
15 There is a slight tension between 'pure' ethnography and case study research. Meyer (2001: 331) argues that

> The key difference between the case study and other qualitative designs such as grounded theory and ethnography... is that the case study is open to the use of theory or conceptual categories that guide the research and analysis of data. In contrast, grounded theory or ethnography presupposes that theoretical perspectives are grounded in and emerge from firsthand data.

The resolution of this tension, 'according to Gummesson... is not to require researchers to have split but dual personalities: "Those who are able to balance on a razor's edge using their pre-understanding without being its slave" (p. 58)' (Meyer, 2001: 331). To achieve this, I followed Eisenhardt's advice to 'formulate a research problem and... specify some potentially important variables, with some reference to extant literature... [but] avoid thinking about specific relationships between variables and theories as much as possible, especially at the outset of the process' (1989: 536). As such, I did not attempt to consider the relationship between context, resources, beliefs, and organisational culture at this early stage.
16 This represents the range of data I had accessed at this time.
17 I excluded local authorities in the Tohoku region from my fieldwork as the rapid increase in the foster care rates here, which came after the 2011 Tohoku earthquake and tsunami, are likely to be underpinned by different theoretical mechanisms than change during 'normal' times.
18 Local authority names and all CGC staff names are anonymised.
19 On occasion this prompted peals of laughter, most memorably when I asked what *'deri-heru'* meant. *Deri-heru* is a shortening of term *delivery-health*, where sex workers are 'delivered' to your home. One caseworker joked that it is unclear what kind of health is being delivered.
20 While volunteering in and working with CWI prior to my research I visited 24 CWI and one BIWI.
21 The senior management of this institution are national bureaucrats who rotate back into positions in the MHLW. As such they are amongst the small number of national policymakers to have practical experience in alternative care. The other MHLW position where staff can have relevant practical experience are the *senmonkan*, the senior specialists, who are often local bureaucrats on one- to three-year placements in the MHLW.

22 *Introduction*

22 Perhaps the most unexpected of these was a pleasant Sunday spent picking citrus with juvenile delinquents.
23 This is a separate body from the national foster care association, with a focus on research.
24 I had not been aware of how much more influential the National CWI Association, which works closely with both bureaucrats and politicians, is than the National Foster Care Association. Nor had I been aware of the split on foster care within the National CWI Association: one faction argues that Japan places too few children into care and that foster care should help meet increased demand as numbers rise, while the second maintains that foster care is poorly supported, lacks professional knowledge, and is unsafe for vulnerable children.
25 I also met actors from UNICEF who explained that their primary role in Japan is fundraising and that this policy area is too politically sensitive to broach.
26 For a full account of the data analysis process see King (2017).
27 Many of these children never move. One of CGC's staff calls these *zuru-zuru* cases, cases that drift.

References

Ainsworth, F., & Hansen, P. (2009). Residential programs for children and young people: Their current status and use in Australia. In M. Courtney, & D. Iwaniec (Eds.), *Residential care of children: Comparative perspectives* (139–153). New York: Oxford University Press.

Ainsworth, F., & Thoburn, J. (2014). An exploration of the differential usage of residential childcare across national boundaries. *International Journal of Social Welfare*, 23, 16–24.

Asahi Shinbun. (2015, June 24). Yōshi chūkai jidō no 6-wari: Suishin e hatsu no honkaku chōsa [60 per cent of adopted children: First full-scale investigation for promotion]. *Asahi Shinbun*.

Aspinall, R.W. (2016). Children's rights in a risk society: The case of schooling in Japan. *Japan Forum*, 28(2), 135–154.

Bamba, S. (2010). The experiences and perspectives of Japanese substitute caregivers and maltreated children: A cultural-developmental approach to child welfare practice. *Social Work*, 55(2), 127–137.

Barth, R.P. (2002). *Institutions vs. foster homes: The empirical base for a century of action*. Report for UNC, School of Social Work, Jordan Institute for Families.

Basic Act on Education. (2006). Act number 120 of 2006, December 22.

Bobrow, D.B. (2008). Social and cultural factors: Constraining and enabling. In M. Moran, M. Rein, & R.E. Goodin (Eds.), *The Oxford handbook of public policy* (pp. 572–586). Oxford: Oxford University Press.

Bowlby, J. (1951). *Maternal care and mental health*. Geneva: World Health Organization.

Bowlby, J. (1969). *Attachment: Attachment and loss (Vol. 1)*. New York: Basic Books.

Browne, K. (2008). *The overuse of institutional care for young children in Europe*. (PowerPoint presentation). Second International Conference on Community Psychology. Lisbon. 2008, June 5.

Browne, K. (2009). *The risk of harm to young children in institutional care*. London: Save The Children.

Browne, K., Hamilton-Giachritsis, C., Johnson, R., & Ostergren, M. (2006). Overuse of institutional care for children in Europe. *British Medical Journal*, 332 (7539), 485–487.

Bryderup, I.M. (2008). *Summary for Denmark – Project Yippee.* (Young People from a Public Care Background Pathways to Education in Europe). n.p.: n.p.
Bullock, R., & McSherry, D. (2009). Residential care in Great Britain and Northern Ireland. In M. Courtney, & D. Iwaniec (Eds.), *Residential care of children: Comparative perspectives* (pp. 20–37). New York: Oxford University Press.
Cantwell, N., Davidson, J., Elsley, S., Milligan, I., & Quinn, N. (2012). M*oving forward: Implementing the 'Guidelines for the alternative care of children'.* U.K: Centre for Excellence for Looked After Children in Scotland.
Carvalho, J.M.S., Delgado, P., Benbenishty, R., Davidson-Arad, B., & Pinto, V.S. (2017). Professional judgments and decisions on placement in foster care and reunification in Portugal. *European Journal of Social Work*, 0 (0), 1–15.
Children's Charter. (1951). 1951, May 5.
Colton, M., & Hellincx, W. (1994). Residential and foster care in the European community: Current trends in policy and practice. *British Journal of Social Work*, 24, 559–576.
Courtney, M., Dolev, T., & Gilligan, R. (2009). Looking backward to see forward clearly: A cross-national perspective on residential care. In M. Courtney, & D. Iwaniec (Eds.), *Residential care of children: Comparative perspectives* (pp. 191–208). New York: Oxford University Press.
Courtney, M., & Hughes-Heuring, D. (2009). Residential care in the United States of America: Past, present, and future. In M. Courtney, & D. Iwaniec (Eds.), *Residential care of children: Comparative perspectives* (pp. 173–190). New York: Oxford University Press.
Cummings, W.K. (1980). *Education and equality in Japan.* Princeton: Princeton University Press.
Davis, K.C. (1969). *Discretionary justice: A preliminary inquiry.* Louisiana: Louisiana State University Press.
Edin, K., & Kefalas, M. (2005). *Promises I can keep: Why poor women put motherhood before marriage.* London: University of California Press.
Eisenhardt, K. (1989). Building theories from case study research. *The Academy of Management Review*, 14(4), 532–550.
EuroChild. (2012). De-institutionalisation and quality alterative care for children in Europe: Lessons learned and the way forward. *Eurochild Working Paper.* Brussels: EuroChild.
European Commission. (2013). *Investing in children: Breaking the cycle of disadvantage.* Commission recommendation of 20.2.2013, C(2013), 778 final.
European Expert Group on the Transition from Institutional to Community-Based Care. (2009). *Report of the ad hoc expert group on the transition from institutional to community-based care.* Directorate-General for Employment, Social Affairs and Equal Opportunities.
Evans, T. (2012). Organisational rules and discretion in adult social work. *British Journal of Social Work*, 43(4), 739–758.
EveryChild. (2011). Scaling down: Reducing, reshaping and improving residential care around the world. *Positive Care Choices, Working Paper 1.*
Fox, N. (2014). *Timing matters: How to think about the effects of early experience on brain and behavioral development.* Presentation at International Society for the Prevention of Child Abuse and Neglect Conference (ISPCAN). Nagoya. 2014, September 14–17.
Freidson, E. (2001). *Professionalism: The third logic.* London: Polity Press.

Gilligan, R. (2009). Residential care in Ireland. In M. Courtney, & D. Iwaniec (Eds.), *Residential care of children: Comparative perspectives* (pp. 3–19). New York: Oxford University Press.

Gjerde, P.F. (1996). Longitudinal research in a cultural context: Reflections, prospects, challenges. In D.W. Shwalb, & B.J. Shwalb (Eds.), *Japanese childrearing: Two generations of scholarship* (pp. 279–299). New York: The Guildford Press.

Goldfarb, K. (2012). *Fragile kinships: Family ideologies and child welfare in Japan.* (Doctoral dissertation). The University of Chicago.

Goldfarb, K. (2013). Japan. In P. Welbourne, & J. Dixon (Eds.), *Child protection and child welfare: A global appraisal of cultures, policy, and practice* (pp. 144–169). London: Jessica Kingsley Publishers.

Goldfarb, K. (2018). Beyond blood ties: Intimate kinships in Japanese foster and adoptive care. In A. Alexy, & E. Cook (Eds.), *Intimate Japan* (pp. 181–198). Honolulu: University of Hawaii Press.

Goldfarb, W. (1945). Effects of psychological deprivation in infancy and subsequent stimulation. *American Journal of Psychiatry*, 102, 18–33.

Goodman, R. (2000). *Children of the Japanese state: The changing role of child protection institutions in contemporary Japan.* Oxford: Oxford University Press.

Goodman, R. (2006). Thoughts on the relationship between anthropological theory, methods and the study of Japanese society. In J. Hendry, & D. Wong (Eds.), *Dismantling the East-West dichotomy: Views from Japanese anthropology* (pp. 22–30). London: Routledge.

Gudbrandsson, B. (2004). *Children in institutions: Prevention and alternative care. Working group on children at risk and in care, Council of Europe. Focus on children and families. CS-Forum in care (2003) final report as approved by the European Committee for Social Cohesion (CDCS) at its 12th meeting.* Strasbourg: Council of Europe.

Hann, C. (1996). Introduction: Political society and civil anthropology. In C. Hann, & E. Dunn (Eds.), *Civil society: Challenging Western models* (pp. 1–26). London: Routledge.

Harada, A. (2010). The Japanese child protection system: Developments in the laws and the issues left unsolved. *International Survey of Family Law*, Vol. 2010, pp. 217–236.

Harada, A. (2013). Children in need of permanent families: The current status of and future directions for the Japanese foster care system. *Illinois Child Welfare*, 6(1), 14–29.

Hasegawa, S. (1984). Wa ga kuni no satooya seido no mondaiten to Tōkyōto yōiku katei seido [Problems of foster parents in our country and the Tokyo foster care system]. *Atarashī Kazoku*, 4, 19–30.

Hayashi, H. (2015). *Jidōsōdanjyo ni okeru tokubetsu yōshi engumi e no torikumi* [The approach of child guidance centres to adoption]. Paper for presentation at Yokohama City social welfare centre. 2015, November 8.

Hayashi, H., Yamamoto, T., Ookubo, M., Sato, T., Niiro, T., Kurihara, A., ... Tanaka, H. (2013). Jidōsōdanjyo ni okeru satooya nintei ni kansuru chousa kenkyuu [A study on the approval process as foster parents in the child guidance centres]. *Nihon kodomo katei sōgōkenkyūsho*, 50, 1–29.

Hayes, P. (2008). Special adoption in Japan: Its problems and prospects. *Adoption Quarterly*, 11(2), 81–100.

Hennessy, S. (2013). *Akachan no nō no hattatsu ni oyobosu aichaku keisei ni tsuite* [Attachment formation and the development of babies' brains]. Presentation at The Nippon Foundation symposium Subete no akachan ni aijō to katei wo. Tokyo. 2013, May 24.
Hill, M. (1997). Implementation theory: Yesterday's issue? *Policy & Politics*, 25(4), 375–385.
Hill, M. (2013). *The public policy process*. London: Routledge.
Human Rights Watch (HRW). (2014). *Without dreams. Children in alternative care in Japan*. USA: Human Rights Watch.
Human Rights Watch & The Nippon Foundation. (2014). *Subete no akachan ga 'katei' de sodatsu shakai wo mezashite 'sekai kodomonohi' Kokuren kodomonokenrijōyaku saitaku 25 shūnenkinen shinpojiumu* [Symposium celebrating the 25th anniversary of the UN Convention of the Rights of the Child: Aiming at a society where all babies grow up in a 'home']. Tokyo. 2014, November 20.
Independent Television News (ITN). (2011). *Children of the tsunami*. [News documentary]. Retrieved from URL: https://www.youtube.com/watch?v=TjN8gCLZ-Bxw (last accessed 2017, August 28).
Iwasaki, M. (1986). Nihon ni okeru gurūpuhōmu, satooya yōshi seido no tenbō [The outlook for group homes, foster care, and the adoption system in Japan]. *Gekkanfukushi*, 69(16), 68–77.
Johnson, R., Browne, K., & Hamilton-Giachritsis, C. (2006). Young children in institutional care at risk of harm. *Trauma Violence Abuse*, 7(1), 34–60.
Kadonaga, T., & Fraser, M.W. (2015). Child maltreatment in Japan. *Journal of Social Work*, 15(3), 233–253.
Kashiwame, R. (2010). Kodomotachi ni atarimae no seikatsu wo [Towards a lifestyle that is obviously right for children]. *Shakai-teki yōgo to famirīhōmu*, 1, 6–9. 2010, June.
Kashiwame, R., Nakatani, S., Hayashi, S., & Amino, T. (1995). Jidōsōdanjyo no unnei bunseki [Analysis of Child Guidance Centres' Operations]. *Nihon sōgō aiiku kenkyū kiyō*, 32, 137–147.
Kashiwame, R., Nakatani, S., Amino, T., & Hayashi, S. (1996). Jidōsōdanjyo senmon shokuin no shitsumu bunseki [Analysis of the child guidance centres' office works]. *Nihon sōgō aiiku kenkyū kiyō*, 33, 173–194.
Kasza, G.J. (2006). *One world of welfare: Japan in comparative perspective*. London: Cornell University Press.
Kendrick, A., Steckley, L., & McPheat, G.A. (2011). Residential child care: Learning from international comparisons. In R. Taylor, M. Hill, & F. McNeill (Eds.), *Early professional development for social workers* (pp. 81–87). Birmingham: The British Association of Social Workers.
King (nee Rivera King), M. (2017). *Child guidance centres in Japan: Regional variation in policy implementation and the family-bond*. (Doctoral dissertation). The University of Oxford.
Knorth, E.J., Harder, A.T., Zandberg, T., & Kendrick, A. (2008). Under one roof: A review and selective meta-analysis on the outcomes of residential child and youth care. *Children and Youth Services Review*, 30, 123–140.
Kubo, K. (2012). Jidōsōdanjyo ni jōkin suru bengoshi no nichijō to bengoshi jōkin no yūyō-sei [Employment of full-time lawyer at child guidance centre: Daily job and its merit to child protection]. *Kodomo no gyakutai to negurekuto*, 14(3), 340–346.

Kubo, K. (2014). Gyakutai taiō ni okeru kadai to kon'nan: jidōsōdanjyo no bengoshi no tachiba kara [The difficulties and challenges in the corresponding abuse: From the standpoint of full-time lawyer of child guidance centre]. *Kodomo no gyakutai to negurekuto*, 16(3), 242–249.

Kurihara, N. (2011). Jidō fukushi-hō dai 28-jō tekiyō no genjō to kadai ni tsuite: jidōsōdanjyo no genjō to kadai [The current state and challenges around the use of Article 28 of The Child Welfare Act: The current state and challenges of the child guidance centres]. *Nihon Shakai Fukushi Gakkai*.

Lipsky, M. (1980). *Street-level bureaucracy: The critical role of street-level bureaucrats*. New York: Russell Sage Foundation.

Madge, N. (1994). *Children and residential care in Europe*. London: European Children's Centre and National Children's Bureau.

Maher King (nee Rivera King), M. (2011). *Against all odds*. Presentation at TEDxTokyo. Retrieved from URL: https://www.tedxtokyo.com/tedxtokyo_talk/against-all-odds/ (last accessed 2017, August 28). Tokyo. 2011, May 21.

Malmo Declaration. (1986). *Malmo declaration*. Passed by the delegates of the FICE-International at the 1986, August FICE Congress held in Malmo, Sweden.

Matland, R.E. (1995). Synthesizing the implementation literature: The ambiguity-conflict model of policy implementation. *Journal of Public Administration Research and Theory*, 5(2), 145–174.

Matsumoto, T. (1971). Satooya seido no un'yō ni kansuru hikaku kenkyū [Comparative research on the operation of the foster care system]. *Nihonjoshidaigaku kiyō bungakubu*, 21, 116–143.

Matsumoto, T. (1974). Hokkaidō no satooya seido—kurumi satooya-kai to Barō buraku [Hokkaido's foster care system—The Kurumi foster care association and the Baro community]. *Shakai fukushi*, 17, 2–18.

Matsumoto, T. (1991). *Satooya seido no jisshō-teki kenkyū* [Empirical study of the foster care system]. Tokyo: Kogyo.

Maus, T. (2006). *Ishii Juji, the Okayama orphanage and the Chausubaru settlement: A vision of child relief through communal labor and a sustainable local economy, 1887–1926*. (Doctoral dissertation). The University of Chicago.

May, P.J., & Winter, S.C. (2007). Politicians, managers, and street-level bureaucrats: Influences on policy implementation. *Journal of Public Administration Research and Theory*, 19, 453–476.

Meyer, C. (2001). A case in case study methodology. *Field Methods*, 13(4), 329–352.

Meyers, M.K., & Vorsanger, S. (2003). Street-level bureaucrats and the implementation of public policy. In B.G. Peters, & J. Pierre (Eds.), *Handbook of public administration* (pp. 245–256). Thousand Oaks: Sage.

MHLW. (2010). *Kodomo ~ kosodate bijyōn ~ kodomo no egao ga afureru shakai no tame ni* [Children and child rearing vision ~ In order to build a society overflowing with children's smiles].

MHLW. (2011). *Sato-oya itaku gaidorainu* [Foster care guidelines].

MHLW. (2016). *Shakai-teki yōgo no genjou ni tsuite (sanka shiryou)* [Current status of alternative care (reference)]. 2016, January.

Miwa, K. (2011). Satooya itaku to shisetsu itaku no kankei no chōki-teki dōtai 1953-nen -2008-nen no jikeiretsu dēta no bunseki kara [The longitudinal dynamics of the relationship between the foster care placement and the residential care: Time-series analyses of the macro data 1953–2008 Japan]. *Japanese Journal of Social Welfare*, 52(2), 43–53.

Miwa, K. (2012). 2000-Nen ikō no satooya itaku no zōka wo motarashita mono jidō gyakutai no zōka no chokusetsuteki kōka to kansetsu-teki kōka wo megutte [What has caused an increase of the placement in foster care after 2000: Direct and indirect effect of child abuse increase]. *Japanese Journal of Social Welfare*, 53(2), 45–56.

Miwa, K. (2014). *Satooya seido no chouki-teki doutai to tenbou* [The long-term dynamics and outlook of the foster care system]. (Doctoral dissertation). Tokyo Metropolitan University.

Miwa, K. (2016). Naze satooya itaku wa shinten shinai no ka? Satooya touroku-sha fusoku kasetsu to satooya itaku jidō gentei kasetsu [Why has family-based foster care not become more common in Japan? A lack of registered fostered carers and of children who are able to be fostered]. *Japanese Journal of Social Welfare*, 56(4), 1–13.

Miyajima, K. (2001). *Jidō gyakutai bōshi-hō shikōgo no jidōsōdanjyo to satooya seido no kongo ni tsuite* [On the child guidance centres and foster care system after the enforcement of the Child abuse prevention act]. Preliminary paper for dai 75-kai yōshi to satooya wo kangaeru kai kōjutsu-roku.

Miyoshi, A. (1963). *Satooya seido no kenkyū* [Research on the foster care system]. Tokyo: Nihon jidōfukushi kyōkai.

Nabekura, S. (2004). Jidō yōgo shisetsu ni okeru hi gyakutai jidō no kyōiku wo ukeru kenri no shomondai mensetsu chōsa oyobi san'yo kansatsu wo chūshin to shite [The problems of the right to education for the ill-treatment child in the child welfare institutions: Based on the interview investigation and the participatory observation]. *Bungaku kenkyū-ka kyōiku senkō hakushikōkikatei zaigaku*, 26, 261–276.

National Child Guidance Centre Directors' Committee. (2011). Zenkoku jidōsōdanjyo-chō-kai jidōsōdanjyo ni okeru satooya itaku oyobi iki jidō ni kansuru chōsa [Survey on abandoned children and foster care placements at child guidance centres]. *Zaidanhōjin zenkoku satooya-kai,* 91. 2011, July.

Nelson III, C.A., Zeanah, C.H., Fox, N., Marshall, P.J., Smyke, A.T., & Guthrie, D. (2007). Cognitive recovery in socially deprived young children: The Bucharest early intervention project. *Science*, 318, 1937–1940.

Nelson III, C.A., Fox, N.A., & Zeanah Jr., C.H. (2013). Chaushesuku no kodomotachi ikuji kankyō to hattatsu shōgai [Ceausescu's children: Child-care environment and developmental disorders]. *Nikkei Science*, 193, 114–119. 2013, August 22.

NHK. (2016). [Article on regional variation in adoption referencing Hayashi, H.]. Retrieved from URL: http://www.nhk.or.jp/kaisetsu-blog/sp/400/243880.html (last accessed 2016, October 11).

Ogasawara, H. (1963). *Satooya hogo—sono kenkyū to jissen* [Foster care—Research and practice]. Tokyo: Kawashima shoten.

Okano, K. (1995). Rational decision making and school-based job referrals for high school students in Japan. *Sociology of Education*, 68(1), 31–47.

Oswald, E. (2009). Because we care: Programming guidance for children deprived of parental care. *World Vision: Keeping children safe from abuse, exploitation and neglect*. California: World Vision International.

Peters, F. (Ed.). (2008). *Residential child care and its alternatives*. Stoke on Trent: FICE and Trentham Books.

Pfau-Effinger, B. (2005). Culture and welfare state policies. Reflections on a complex interrelation. *Journal of Social Policy,* 34(1), 3–20.

Rowe, M. (2012). Going back to the street: Revisiting Lipsky's street-level bureaucracy. *Teaching Public Administration*, 30(1), 10–18.

Sadaka, J. (2007). Jidōsōdanjyo ni okeru satooya seido un'ei ni kansuru kōsatsu zenkoku to Gifu ken no satooya itaku shien jōkyō ni chakumoku shite [Thoughts on the operation of the foster care system in the child guidance centres. Focusing on Gifu Prefecture and the nationwide picture of foster care placements and support]. *Nagoya-shi daigaku daigakuin bunka kenkyū-ka ningen bunka kenkyū*, 7, 93–109.

Saimura, J., Takahashi, S., Shoji, J., Kashiwame, R., Oyama, O., Saito, S., & Kato, H. (2000). Jidōsōdanjyo shokuin no gen'nin kenshūnado no arikata ni kansuru kenkyū [A study of training and supervision systems for staff of child guidance centres]. *Nihon-kodomo katei sōgōkenkyūsho kiyō*, 37, 181–198.

Saimura, J., Shibuya, M., Kashiwame, R., Shoji, J., Arimura, T., Aizawa, H., ... Yamamoto, T. (2004). Gyakutai taiō-tō ni kakaru jidōsōdanjyo no gyōmu bunseki ni kansuru chōsa kenkyū (2) [The analysis of actual quantity of works in child guidance centres (2)]. *Nihon-kodomo katei sōgōkenkyūsho kiyō*, 41, 129–174.

Saimura, J., Shoji, J., Arimura, T., Itakura, T., Nemoto, A., Abe, K., ... Honma, H. (2007). Jidōsōdanjyo ni okeru kazoku sai tōgō enjo no arikata ni kansuru kenkyū ~ jissen jirei no shūshū, bunseki [A study on the system for supporting family reintegration in child guidance centers: Gathering and analysis of pioneering practices]. *Nihon-kodomo katei sōgōkenkyūsho kiyō*, 44, 187–256.

Saimura, J., Arimura, T., Kashiwame, R., Yamamoto, T., Nagano, S., Tsuruoka, H., ... Yokoyama, T. (2010). Jidōsōdanjyo no gyōmu bunseki ni kansuru kenkyū (1) [Time-studies and incident-studies about social work for child abuse cases in child guidance centres]. *Nihon-kodomo katei sōgōkenkyūsho kiyō*, 47, 181–191.

Saimura, J., Arimura, T., Yamamoto, T., Kashiwame, R., Nagano, S., Kawamatsu, R., ... Yokoyama, T. (2014). Jidōsōdanjyo no jimu bunseki ni kansuru kenkyū (3) [The analysis of actual quantity of works in child guidance centres (3)]. *Nihon-kodomo katei sōgōkenkyūsho kiyō*, 49, 1–37.

Sakurai, N. (1999). Satooya yōiku no shien no arikata ni kansuru kenkyū—satooya seido no kassei-ka o motomete [A study on the ways to support foster parents—Seeking to activate the foster care system]. *Aichi tankidaigaku kenkyū kiyō*, 21, 11–20.

Sallnas, M. (2009). Swedish residential care in the landscape of out-of-home care. In M. Courtney, & D. Iwaniec (Eds.), *Residential care of children: Comparative perspectives* (pp. 38–53). New York: Oxford University Press.

Save the Children. (2009). *Keeping children out of harmful institutions: Why we should be investing in family-based care*. London: The Save the Children Fund.

Seeleib-Kaiser, M. (1995). The development of social assistance and unemployment insurance in Germany and Japan. *Social Policy & Administration*, 29(3), 269–293.

Sellman, E., Bedward, J., Cole, T., & Daniels, H. (2002). Thematic review: A sociocultural approach to exclusion. *British Educational Research Journal*, 28(6), 890–900.

Shirai, C. (2015). *Foster care and children's rights*. (Symposium). Shizuoka. 2015, January 1.

Shoji, J., Taniguchi, W., Andoh, A., Oyama, O., Takahashi, S., Suzuki, Y., ... Masuda, S. (1998). Satooya e no shien no arikata ni kansuru kenkyū [A study on the training of foster parents]. *Nihon kodomo katei sōgō kenkyū kiyō*, 35, 33–39.

Shore, C., & Wright, S. (1997). Policy: A new field of anthropology. In C. Shore, & S. Wright (Eds.), *Anthropology of policy* (pp. 3–39). New York: Routledge.
Social Work Services Inspectorate for Scotland. (1992). *Another kind of home: A review of residential care*. Edinburgh: Social Work Services Inspectorate for Scotland.
Stein, M. (2006). Missing years of abuse in children's homes. *Child and Family Social Work*, 11, 11–21.
Stein, M. (2014). *Igirisu no shakai-teki yōgo tōjisha no jinken yōgo undō-shi* [Care less lives: The story of the rights movement of young people in care]. (Tsuzaki, T. Trans.). Tokyo: Akashi Shoten.
Stockholm Declaration. (2003). *Stockholm declaration on children and residential care*. Delegates' statement following the Second International Conference on Children and Residential Childcare. Retrieved from URL: https://resourcecentre.savethechildren.net/node/2584/pdf/2584.pdf (last accessed 2017, September 7).
Sugimoto, Y. (2010). *An introduction to Japanese society*. Cambridge: Cambridge University Press.
Takeuchi, T. (2014). *Shōshika taisaku Nippon keizai e no meritto* [Countermeasures against the declining birth rate and the benefits to the Japanese economy]. Presentation at Human Rights Watch and The Nippon Foundation Subete no akachan ga 'katei' de sodatsu shakai wo mezashite 'sekai kodomonohi' Kokuren kodomonokenrijōyaku saitaku 25 shūnenkinen shinpojiumu. Tokyo, 2015, February 14.
The College of Social Work. (2012). *Briefing for Lord Listowel: Re: House of Lords debate, 11am, October 25: Looked after children and the government's response to changes in residential childcare in the light of child protection failures*. n.p.: The College of Social Work.
Tobis, D. (2000). *Moving from residential institutions to community-based social services in Central and Eastern Europe and the former Soviet Union*. Washington: The World Bank.
Tsuzaki, T. (2006). *The vested interests vs. children's rights: children's rights and foster care in Japan*. Presentation at Asia conference on children's rights and foster care. Retrieved from URL: http://www.geocities.jp/hokukaido/satooya/seoul2006/article/12-japan-tsuzaki-e.htm (last accessed 2017, August 22). Seoul. 2006, September 16.
Tsuzaki, T. (2009). *Kono kuni no kodomotachi: Yōhogo jidō shakai-teki yōgo no Nihonteki kōchiku; otona no kitoku ken'eki to kodomo no fukushi* [This country's children: Constructing social care for children in need of care; The vested interests of adults and children's welfare]. Tokyo: Nihon Kajo Shuppan.
United Nations Committee on the Rights of the Child (UN CRC). (1998). *Concluding observations of the committee on the rights of the child: Japan. Eighteenth session: Consideration of reports submitted by states parties under Article 44 of the convention*. CRC/C/15/Add.90 (June).
UN CRC. (2004). *Consideration of reports submitted by states parties under Article 44 of the convention: Concluding observations: Japan*. CRC/C/15/Add.231. 2004, February 26.
UN CRC. (2010). *Consideration of reports submitted by states parties under Article 44 of the convention: Convention on the Rights of the Child: Concluding observations: Japan*. CRC/C/JPN/CO/3. 2010, June 20.

United Nations General Assembly. (1989). *Convention on the rights of the child*. Document A/RES/44/25. 1989, December 12.

United Nations General Assembly. (2010). *Guidelines for the alternative care of children. Resolution adopted by the General Assembly 64/142*. A/RES/64/142*, on the report of the Third committee A/64/434.

UNICEF. (2010). *At home or in a home? Formal care and adoption of children in Eastern Europe and Central Asia*. Geneva: UNICEF.

UNICEF & World Bank. (2003). *Changing minds, policies and lives: Improving protection of children in Eastern Europe and Central Asia: Gatekeeping services for vulnerable children and families*. Florence: UNICEF & World Bank.

Ushijima, Y., & Yukawa, R. (1975). Jidōsōdanjyo ni okeru hantei no kinō oyobi kijun ni kansuru kenkyū [A study on the decision making function and standards of the child guidance centres]. *Nihon sōgō aiiku kenkyū kiyō*, 11, 305–331.

Wada, I., Yamamoto, T., Tsutsumi, C., Ookubo, M., Tamai, N., Bando, M., ... Kawamatsu, R. (2013). Ichijihogō no gaiyō haaku to nyūsho jidō no jittai chōsa [For the better shelter care facility at the child guidance centre. The study of the shelter care facility and the actual condition of placed children]. *Nihon kodomo katei sōgōkenkyūsho*, 50, 1–73.

Winter, S.C. (2003). Implementation perspectives: Status and reconsideration. In B.G. Peters, & J. Pierre (Eds.), *Handbook of public policy* (pp. 212–223). London: Sage.

World Health Organization. (2010). *Better health, better lives: Children and young people with intellectual disabilities and their families: Transfer care from institutions to the community*. EUR/51298/17/PP/3. Bucharest, Romania.

Yamamoto, M. (1952). Yōshi to satogo—minpō to jidōfukushihō to no kōsaku [Adopted children and fostered children: The intersection of civil law and the child welfare law]. *Kōbe hōgaku zasshi*, 2(1), 52–86.

Yoshizawa, E. (1987). Wa ga kuni ni okeru satooya seido no genjō to mondaiten [The situation and issues with the foster care system of our country]. *Tōyōdaigaku shakaigakubu kiyō*, 24(2), 157–193.

Zenshakyō. (2008). *Kodomo katei fukushi shakai-teki yōgo ni kansuru seido no arikata kentō tokubetsu iinkai hōkoku-sho* [On child and family welfare and alternative care. Report of the special committee for examination of the system]. 2008, May 8.

Part II
The context of alternative care

2 Alternative care

1 Alternative care in Japan

In 2017–2018 there were 44,354 children in alternative care. Table 2.1 (MHLW, 2019), shows that 5,424 children were cared for in 4,245 foster care households, with a further 1,434 children in 347 'family homes'. 2,706 babies and infants were in 140 BIWIs, with 25,282 children in 605 CWIs (MHLW, 2019: 2). The remainder of the children were cared for in specialist welfare institutions, with 6,346 children (in 3,789 households) in 227 mother and child living support institutions, *boshi seikatsu shien shisetsu*, 1,309 children in 58 child self-reliance support institutions, *jidō shiritsu shien shisetsu*, 573 children in 154 self-reliance assistance homes, *jiritsu enjo hōmu*, and 1,280 children in 46 child psychotherapy institutions, *jidō shinri chiryō shisetsu* (MHLW, 2019: 2).

Adoption plays a minimal but slowly growing role in Japan's alternative care system. From 2008 to 2017, between 309 and 616 children were adopted each year under special adoption legislation (MHLW, 2019: 101; Ministry of Internal Affairs and Communications, 2015).

There are three kinds of foster care: 'regular' foster parents, *yōiku satooya*,[1] with a subcategory of 'specialist' foster parents, *senmon satooya*; foster parents wishing to adopt, *yōshiengumi satooya*; and kinship foster parents, *shinzoku satooya*.[2] Specialist foster parents must complete a nationally run training programme after three years of fostering experience (MHLW, 2016b: 14). In most local authorities foster parents can be registered under multiple categories. In 2010, the MHLW created 'family homes'. These are run by two foster parents and an assistant and house up to six children.[3]

When children enter foster care there is an 'acclimatisation' period, *kōryuu*, in which they develop their relationship with the foster parents before the placement is made.[4] This process averages five months, with the longest reported lasting 15 years (National CGC Directors' Committee, 2011: 68). This is also done for adoptive placements and, very occasionally, when children will return to their parents. There is no acclimatisation period for institutional placements.

Table 2.1 An overview of alternative care

For the approximately 45,000 children who have no guardians, children who have been abused, and other children who cannot be raised in their home environment, the public takes responsibility and care is carried out socially

Foster parents	Division (includes multiple registrations)	Registered foster parents	Foster parents with children	Children in placements	Family homes	
		11,730 households	4,245 households	5,424	Home care carried out in the child-rearer's house (maximum 5~6 children)	
Child-rearing in a house. Placement with foster parents	Foster parent	9,592 households	3,326 households	4,134	Number of homes	347 buildings
	Specialist foster parent	702 households	196 households	221	Children in placements	1,434
	Foster parent wishing to adopt	3,781 households	299 households	299		
	Kinship foster parent	560 households	543 households	770		

Type of institution	Baby and Infant Welfare Institution	Child Welfare Institution	Child Psychotherapy Institution	Self-Reliance Support Institution	Mother and child living support institution	Self-Reliance Assistance Home
Targeted children	Babies (Where particular needs, includes infants)	Children with no guardian, children who have been abused, children who need protection for other environmental reasons (where particular needs, includes babies)	Children who have difficulty adjusting to life in society due to their family environment, friendships at school or other environmental reasons	Children who have done bad things, or who it is feared may do bad things, or children who for other reasons, including the environment of their house, need lifestyle guidance.	For women and children who do not have a partner or those who are in the same circumstances as this, and children who should be in the custody of that person	Children who have finished obligatory child-rearing period, children who have left Child Welfare Institutions etc.

Type of institution	Baby and Infant Welfare Institution	Child Welfare Institution	Child Psychotherapy Institution	Self-Reliance Support Institution	Mother and child living support institution	Self-Reliance Assistance Home
Number of Institutions	140	605	46	58	227	154
Capacity	3,900	32,253	1,892	3,637	4,648 households	1,012
Current number of children	2,706	25,282	1,280	1,309	3,789 households, 6,346 children	573
Total number of staff	4,921	17,883	1,309	1,838	1,994	687
Small scale group care	1,620 buildings					
Community small scale CWI	391 buildings					

Source (translated): MHLW (2019). Shakai-teki yōiku no suishin ni mukete (April 2019): 2

Note: Child Psychotherapy institutions were previously called 'Short-term Therapeutic Institution for emotionally disturbed children'. The 'targeted children' description has changed from Children who have mild emotional disturbances to the one above

* Data on the number of foster parents, family homes, and children in care, as well as the number of, the capacity, and the current number of children for: Baby and Infant Welfare Institutions; Child Welfare Institution; Short-term Therapeutic Institution for emotionally disturbed children; and Mother and child living support institution taken from the Social Welfare institutions etc survey report (*Fukushi gyōsei hōkoku rei*) (31st March 2018)
* Data on the number, the capacity, and the current number of children for Self-Reliance Support Institutions and Self-Reliance Assistance Homes, as well as the number of small-scale group care and community small scale CWI taken from Home Welfare Survey (*Katei fukushi-ka-chō*) (1 October, 2017)
* Data on the number of staff (excluding self-reliance assistance home) taken from Social welfare institutions etc survey report (*Shakai fukushi shisetsu-tō chōsa hōkoku*) (1st October, 2014)
* Data on the number of staff for self-reliance assistance homes taken from Home Welfare Survey (*Katei fukushi-ka-chō*) (1st March, 2017)
* The number of self-reliance support institutions includes two nationally run institutions

BIWIs cater for babies and infants from birth to two years old, though it is not uncommon to find older infants in BIWI or babies and infants aged under two in CWIs. CWIs care for children from 2 to 18 years of age, though this can be extended up to 20 years.[5] I use the term 'welfare institution' rather than residential care. This reflects a distinction made in Article 3 of the UN Guidelines for the Alternative Care of Children (UN General Assembly, 2010, emphasis added):

> While recognizing that residential care facilities and family-based care complement each other in meeting the needs of children, where large residential care facilities (*institutions*) remain, alternatives should be developed in the context of an overall deinstitutionalization strategy, with precise goals and objectives, which will allow for their progressive elimination.

I follow the Council of Europe's Recommendations on Childcare in adopting Mulheir and Browne's classification, with large institutions 'having 25 or more children living together in one building', small institutions 'housing 11 to 24 children', and 'family-like' homes accommodating '10 children or less' (2007: 13).

The average capacity of the BIWIs is 28, with the largest housing over 80. The most common size for CWIs is 41 to 50 children, though there are more children in CWIs housing over 100 than in CWIs housing under 30 (Calculated from MHLW, 2019: 144).[6] Despite a reduction in the number of large-scale units since 2008[7] (MHLW, 2016a: 2), the majority of children in CWIs in 2012 still lived in large dormitory-style CWIs.

Large-style CWIs normally have between four and twelve children in dormitory rooms, with a separate dining hall, playroom, bathrooms, and laundry stations (see MHLW, 2012a: 8). It is hard to visualise this, so the rarely published photographs (see for example HRW, 2014: Cover, 37) are invaluable in adding colour to the factual description given here. Small-style group care CWIs are meant to replicate a house and normally have a mixture of individual and twin rooms, with a living room, and bathroom. Some group care CWI have a kitchen in each unit, others have food bought in from a central kitchen. The staff-child ratio in BIWI and CWI was amended in 2013 to one staff member for every 1.6 children aged under 2, two children aged 2 to 3, four pre-schoolers aged over 3, and 5.5 children of school age (MHLW, 2016b: 11).[8]

The child self-reliance support institutions cater for children at risk of becoming juvenile delinquents (see Aizawa, 2011; Matsuura, 2011), with self-reliance assistance homes catering for those who have left school, often at 15 years of age, and who still need care (see Hoshi, 2012). The child psychotherapy institutions support children who 'have difficulty adjusting to life in society' (MHLW, 2019: 2) who also require alternative care. Until the 2016 revision of the Child Welfare Act these were named short-term therapeutic institutions for emotionally disturbed children, *jōshoshōaiji tanki chiryō shisetsu,* 'short-term' as placements were supposed to last for up to two years, though 41.2 per cent of current placements have lasted over two years (MHLW, 2019: 133).[9]

Mother and child living support institutions are seen as distinct from other institutions by most practitioners and policymakers (National Child Welfare Administration Division Head Meeting, 2015). This is because the child is living with their mother in an apartment and because support is aimed primarily at the mother. Families are placed into these institutions due to 'domestic violence from partner', 'inappropriate home environment', 'instability of the mother's body or mind', 'employment reasons', 'housing conditions' or 'economic conditions' (MHLW, 2016a: 77).

These are also reasons given for placements into other institutions. Other categories include 'child rearing problems', which includes the detention, hospitalisation, unemployment, or mental health issues of parents, the death of parents, divorce, discord between parents, and bankruptcy or economic issues (MHLW, 2016d: 3). While data on the number of children who enter care due to abuse is high (see MHLW, 2016d: 4), it underreports abuse, due to differences in how caseworkers label cases and because abuse sometimes only surfaces post-placement. My fieldwork would suggest that Goldfarb was correct when she wrote that 'almost all children in state care have experienced at least some degree of neglect in their families of origin' (2012: 28).

The children that entered care during my fieldwork were disproportionately from lower socio-economic status families, single parents, young pregnancies,[10] and families involved in organised crime, hostess work, or the sex trade. This echoes a 1990 study that estimated the average income of the families of children in care as 25 per cent of the national average (cited by Goodman, 2000: 55).

The ethnic composition of children in care reflects the relative lack of diversity in Japan. While data is not available for all children in alternative care, in 2011, 1.5 per cent of children in foster care were not Japanese nationals, with a further 0.4 per cent 'not registered' to a family registration (National Child Guidance Centre Directors' Committee, 2011); 1.6 per cent of children in foster care had a father who was not Japanese, while 4 per cent had a mother who was not Japanese.[11]

This data was collected in a one-off survey conducted by the National Association of CGCs and is not collected annually. This is indicative of a broader challenge for both academics and advocates: Japan publishes very little data on alternative care. Goodman terms this a 'glaring gap' (2000: 199) and Tsutsui and Otaga (2011) note that this inhibits the development of evidence-informed practice.

In the past six years there have been some attempts by local authorities to collect data on careleavers (Osaka, 2012; Tokyo, 2011a, 2011b, 2012).[12] In 2014 Nagano and Arimura analysed these and conducted two further surveys. This work found that careleavers are 18 to 19 times more likely than the national average to be on public assistance benefits, and that the most vulnerable group were those who left care under the age of 18.

The only careleaver data that the MHLW publishes is the progression rate to tertiary education. Here Japan appears to outperform all other OECD countries: in 2017, 16.1 per cent of children leaving CWIs after high school entered university, with a further 14.8 per cent of CWI high school graduates entering junior college. For foster care these figures rise to 28.3 per cent going to university and 17.4 per cent to junior college.[13] While higher than other countries,[14] these figures are below the national average of 52.1 per cent progressing to university and 21.7 per cent to junior college (MHLW, 2019: 71). Further, a small survey of careleavers in Kyushu and Okinawa found a drop-out rate of 46 per cent, over three times the national average (Bridge for Smile, 2005).[15]

Children in temporary care institutions, *ichiji hogo*,[16] within the CGC[17] are not captured in alternative care statistics as they do not enter under a 'placement order'. Wada et al. (2013) found that 45.7 per cent of children in temporary care had previously been in temporary care, with an average of 2.84 times.[18] Despite repeatedly entering temporary care, this group are never recorded as being in alternative care.

Children are placed into temporary care for their protection, to allow further assessment of their circumstances and current state, or, less frequently, prior to entering the judicial system.[19] Stays are supposed to last less than two months but can be much longer, with at least one child having stayed for over two years (HRW, 2014). Recent work shows that stays in temporary care are getting longer and suggests that limited capacity here may be limiting the number of children entering care (Abe and Ogiso, 2011; Ogiso, 2010; Yamamoto et al., 2013).[20] While in temporary care children do not attend school, which is sometimes seen as an abrogation of their rights (Abe and Ogiso, 2011; HRW, 2014; Ogiso, 2010; Suzuki, 1999; Wada et al., 2013).

While data on placement changes in alternative care is not recorded at a national level, or published at any level, there is a belief (which is probably correct) that there are fewer placement changes in Japan than elsewhere. This number would increase by one for all children if the stays in temporary care were defined as a placement. Yamamoto et al. (2009) argue that stays in temporary care should be considered as stays in institutional care. This number would also increase if breakdowns during the 'acclimatisation period', which are not considered to be a placement change even if the child has spent years getting to know the foster parents, were included. Finally, one CGC head argued that from the child's perspective staff turnover in CWIs is at times comparable to a placement change.

The official foster care rate only covers foster care, family homes, BIWIs and CWIs, and does not include specialist welfare institutions, even though these are part of the alternative care system.[21] Children in temporary care are also omitted from the calculation of the foster care rate.

The UN Guidelines for Alternative Care of Children provides a definition of residential care: 'care provided in any non-family-based group setting, such as places of safety for emergency care, transit centres in emergency situations, and all other short- and long-term residential care facilities, including group homes' (UN General Assembly, 2010, Article 29c). Under this admittedly circular definition, the foster care rate would include temporary care and specialist institutions, other than the mother and child facilities. If we used this definition, the foster care rate for 2017–2018 would fall from the official 19.7 per cent to 17.3 per cent. With this caveat noted, the term 'foster care rate' in this book refers to the official foster care rate.[22]

2 The development of alternative care

Perhaps the most surprising feature of Japanese alternative care is the lack of change. An Associated Press photo from 1951 (see King, 2017: 30) shows the dining room of an 'orphanage' in Osaka that housed 160 children, with children sitting neatly in rows. The largest CWI today houses 159 children, and the communal dining room is still the norm in large-style CWIs. This stability has led Kashiwame to argue that contemporary practice 'continues from the past, with distortions unsuited to the present day' (2010: 8) and call for a 'change [to] the foundations of the child welfare system' (Kashiwame, 2011: 2). To understand this continuity, we must first outline relevant policy over this period.

Prior to World War II, fostering in Japan was informal and privately arranged (Murata, 2006). The formal foster care system began with the 1947 Child Welfare Act, which also established the CGCs. This act remains the basis of alternative care, with Kashiwame arguing that the 'basic tenets of alternative care have not changed since the war' (2010: 7). Japan's approach to foster care can be split into three periods: the first decade post-war, 1950s–2002, and 2002 to present. This section focuses on the most recent of these periods.

In the immediate post-war period there was 'great support for strengthening foster care' (Miwa, 2016: 1), and the use of foster care peaked in 1958. Despite support for the idea of foster care, foster parents received minimal state support in this period (Goodman, 2000). This is perhaps due to the construction of foster care, as close to adoption (see Dower, 1999; Goodman, 2000; Kumasaka and Aiba, 1968).

After this initial enthusiasm, the government took an 'ambiguous, passive approach to foster care' (Miwa, 2016: 10) until 2002. This can be seen in statements that promoted foster care by the Welfare Ministry in 1954 (Kashiwame, 2010) and 1974 (Harada, 2013) but that lacked corresponding reforms (Kashiwame, 2010). Miwa argues that this ambiguity is likely to 'have affected the CGCs' understanding of foster care' (2016: 10).

Nakagawa attributes this lack of engagement to the fact that 'the public has very little consciousness of alternative care' (2010: 46). Harada states that 'simply put, foster care was long considered a less urgent policy issue than those affecting the general population' (2013: 19). Goodman too, addressing the lack of change in CWI for 50 years states, 'the simple answer is that there was no pressure—either internally or externally—for them to alter the way they operated' (2000: 13).

During this period, there were four key government initiatives. The first was a 1987 memorandum that, in Goodman's words (2000: 142)

> attempted to increase the number and improve the image of foster-parents and parenting by reducing the amount of investigation potential foster-parents had to go through before registration; by utilizing non-government organizations to publicize the activities of and train foster-carers; and by simplifying the standards expected of foster-parents... to simply having an understanding of child care and offering a stable family life.

The second initiative was the introduction of 'special' adoption in 1988. This was framed as adoption 'for the sake of the child' (Goldfarb, 2013: 152), in contrast with 'normal' adoption of a known person to continue family lineage (Bryant, 1990; Krogness, 2014) or for economic reasons (Mehrotra et al., 2013).

The third action was the 1994 ratification of the UN Convention on the Rights of the Child, though, despite cyclical UN reports criticising Japan's alternative care system (see UN CRC 1998, 2004, 2010), this ratification had little effect on policy for the first 15 years (Goldfarb, 2012).

The final initiative was the (2000) Child Abuse Prevention Act, which followed the 'discovery' of child abuse (Goodman, 2000: 160–174). This discovery led to an explosion in the reporting and investigation of abuse, from 1,101 consultations in 1990 to 133,778 cases in 2017 (MHLW, 2019: 5), which in turn led to an increase in the number of children entering care.

The Child Abuse Prevention Act categorised abuse into physical, sexual and psychological abuse, and neglect. Under this act, anyone knowing of child abuse now had a legal obligation to report it. Goodman (2012: 116) argues that the increased awareness of child abuse has:

> radically altered the relationship between the state and parents in giving much greater powers to state authorities to intervene in a context that had been seen as the exclusive and private domain of the family... Parents were no longer seen as being 'naturally' and unquestionably good... families were no longer considered sacrosanct... The stability of the family – seen by many in the 1980s as one of Japan's greatest strengths... was no longer seen as necessarily superior to the rights of its individual members, particularly women and children.

Subsequent amendments, in 2004 and 2007, strengthened the 'capacity of local authorities to intervene into family affairs' (Kadonaga and Fraser, 2015: 236) and increased the role of the police and family court (Yamamoto and Sato, 2008). This included a change to anyone suspecting, as opposed to knowing, child abuse having to report it (Goodman, 2006).

The third period in post-war foster care, from 2002, marked a shift towards a 'positive approach to foster care in government' (Miwa, 2016: 9–10).[23] Miwa (2016) notes that the upswing in foster care, starting in the early 1990s, predates this government attention and suggests that political attention may have contributed to, rather than triggered, change.

The 2002 revision of the Child Welfare Act introduced formal kinship foster care, specialist foster care (MHLW, 2016b: 13), and respite care (Aizawa, 2011), as well as higher minimum standards for foster parent registration (MHLW, 2002). A 2004 amendment to the Child Welfare Act allowed cities other than 'designated cities'[24] to establish CGCs. This amendment also allowed foster parents to hold certain parental rights, though this 'changed little at the level of practice' (Goldfarb, 2012: 104). The year 2004 also saw the creation of an expert committee (Cabinet Office, 2009) to review cases where children had died following abuse.

2005 saw an amendment to Article 2 of the Enforcement Order of the Child Welfare Act, increasing the number of caseworkers from one per 100,000 to 130,000 people to one per 50,000 to 80,000 people (Miwa, 2012). Miwa argues that 'this was not done to increase the foster care rate, but the effect it had on this is undeniable' (2014: 146).

While not a legal change, the 2007 'Report on measures to improve the alternative care system' by the MHLW 'Special Committee on Alternative Care' was influential (Harada, 2013). This called for the expansion of family-like care, which at this point included smaller CWIs, and an overhaul of CWI functions, including supporting foster parents (Harada, 2013). The report also called for the rights of children in care to be protected (Harada, 2013), though the Child Welfare Act still does not define what children's rights are. This report 'also recommended that the national government provide a basic planning guideline to avoid disparity in foster care services among prefectures' (Harada, 2013: 21).

The subsequent 2008 reform to the Child Welfare Act introduced 'foster care with a view to adopt'. This aimed to distinguish foster care from adoption (Ito, 2015; Shoji et al., 2010) and 'clarified that regular foster families are professional foster care providers who have gone through training programs' (Harada, 2013: 21). As such, 'regular' and 'kinship' foster carers were obliged to complete training from April 2009 (MHLW, 2016b: 13). This reform also allowed foster care services to be provided by organisations other than the CGC and increased foster parents' monthly payments, from 34,000 yen (£237) to 72,000 yen (£503) for regular foster carers, and from 90,200 yen (£630) to 123,000 yen (£859) for specialist foster carers (MHLW, 2011b: 14).[25]

The 2008 reform also formally introduced 'family-homes' (Aizawa, 2011; Yokobori and Yamamoto, 2013), though these already existed in some local authorities (Kashiwame, 2010). In a lecture to CGC staff, Miyajima

42 The context of alternative care

explained that the legal definition of family-homes[26] can be paraphrased as 'public care that is carried out in an individual's home' (2014).

The next significant change came in 2010 with the 'Vision for Children and Childrearing' (MHLW, 2010. See also Matsumoto and Takada, 2012; Miwa, 2011). This set targets for 2029[27] of having one-third of children in care in foster care or family-homes, one-third in small-scale 'group-home' CWIs housing around six children, and one-third in CWIs with 45 children or fewer in the main facility, organised into units of six to eight children (MHLW, 2010).[28] The Vision also tasked local authorities with creating five- and fifteen-year plans to achieve this.[29]

The wording of the 2010 Vision does not imply that the increase in foster care will be at the expense of institutions: 'in conjunction with working to reducing child abuse, to meet the needs of the increasing amount, and increasingly diverse needs of children who require out of home care, we will work to promote family style care' (MHLW, 2010). This is also clear in the call for an increase in the number of CWIs, from 567 in 2008 to 610 in 2014 (see also Harada, 2013).

The impact of the increasing number of children entering care on the increasing foster care rate should not be underestimated. Figure 2.1 shows both the increasing foster care rate from 2000, and the increase in children entering care from around 1995 until 2010. Miwa (2016) argues that the stability of the number of children in institutional care is the result of institutions acting to protect their interests.

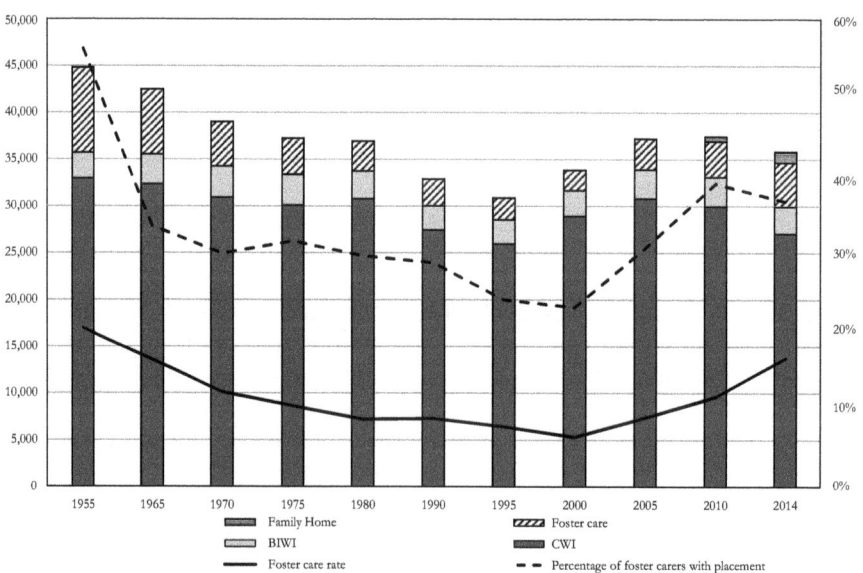

Figure 2.1 The foster care rate and the percentage of foster parents with a placement and the number of children in different care placements. 1955–2014.

Data Sources: 1955–1995: Goodman (2000: 137). 2000–2014: Calculated from MHLW Welfare Administration Reported Cases

The 2010 Vision speaks of 'Children first' and 'meeting the individual needs of children', which suggests a child-centred approach and ties into UN discourses on rights. Yet the emphasis is also on 'shifting the burden of raising a child from the family on to the whole of society' (MHLW, 2010, 2012b), a goal that ties into policy on increasing female participation in the labour force and the birth-rate (Matsumoto and Takada, 2012).[30] There is tension in this Vision, between children's needs and the need for more children.

Ito captures the central concern about the Vision, noting that 'the focus is promoting foster care but there is not enough discussion about how to do this safely and with support' (2015: 1). The 2011 'Foster care guidelines' (MHLW, 2011a) set out to address this.[31]

This guideline urged CGCs to consider foster care as the default placement. An MHLW letter to the local authorities gave three primary reasons for this: concerns over attachment, the family acting as a model, and for the child to learn how to behave in society (MHLW, 2011c). The letter also stated that the 'family is the basis of society, so it is natural for children to be raised in a family' (MHLW, 2011c: 2).

The letter also acknowledged the issue of parental consent and notes the change from the need for 'active' consent for foster care to an informed lack of opposition (MHLW, 2011c). The letter suggests that children who have been in a BIWI for six months or in a CWI for a year with no parental contact are moved to foster care (MHLW, 2011c), though no mechanisms are created to facilitate this. Finally, it calls for local authorities to have a 'coherent policy' on foster care (MHLW, 2011c).

Another change introduced in 2011 allowed aunts and uncles who are kinship foster parents to claim the foster parent allowance as well as the child-rearing allowance.[32] This change came in response to the March 2011 earthquake and tsunami (Tsuzaki, interview, 2012).[33] The year 2011 saw two further significant changes. The first, a revision to the Civil Code that allowed the suspension of all parental rights for up to two years. This change came in response to CGC reticence to apply for parental rights to be cut (Goldfarb, 2013). The second was the recognition of 'foster care service agencies' (Hirada, 2014). This stemmed from concerns over a lack of service providers (Japan Child and Family Research Institute, 1998; Kikuchi, 2007; MHLW, 2012a; Tsuzaki, 2009). Welfare institutions can also be foster care service providers. The two largest providers, Key Assets and SOS Children's Villages,[34] are building capacity, though currently have little market share.

In 2012, the MHLW created the 'specialist counsellor for foster care support' position within BIWIs and CWIs.[35] These counsellors are tasked with supporting foster carers, identifying children who can move from institutions to foster care, and promoting foster care to the public and within the institution. The number of welfare institutions with specialist counsellors rose from 115 in 2012 to 325 in 2014 (MHLW, 2016d: 33).

The outsourcing of foster care service provision to institutions has been met with scepticism. Hirada's (2014) survey of 589 CWI and 131 BIWI suggests this scepticism is valid. This survey, which allowed multiple responses, found that 16 per cent of counsellors were working in collaboration with a CGC or a foster care agency, 15 per cent had foster parent consultations, 14 per cent were promoting foster care for children in their institution, 13 per cent helped with foster care training, 12 per cent were helping prepare children to move to foster care, and 12 per cent were conducting home visits of children in foster care (Hirada, 2014; see also Ito et al., 2014; Yokobori and Yamamoto, 2013). It is perhaps unsurprising that this use of taxpayers' money is starting to be questioned by some within local authorities and the MHLW.[36]

Attending a conference (SBI, 2014) for specialist counsellors left the impression that most counsellors are left to create their own job roles, under constraints set by their institutions and often with scepticism from their institution and the local CGC. There are exceptions here: Yuno has worked closely with participating BIWIs and CWIs to create a job description and assessment mechanisms. Yuno has also introduced a lump sum payment for institutions that transfer at least one child to foster care, to counter fiscal incentives to 'keep' children in the institution, a measure MHLW bureaucrats have also contemplated on a national level.

The 2016 Child Welfare Act reform is the most significant to date.[37] The most critical amendment is the addition of Article 3.2, which lays out the principle of 'family-based care' (MHLW, 2016e, 2016f, 2016g). This argues that foster care, family-homes and adoption should be considered the default placements, particularly for pre-school children because of attachment issues. HRW, who advocated for this change, argue that 'if this revised Child Welfare Act is diligently observed, the alternative care system will drastically migrate from institutions to families' (Doi, 2016).

The reform also states that the 'special' adoption system will be reviewed and that local authorities must proactively promote foster care. The reform aims to strengthen the CGCs' specialist knowledge, with each CGC appointing a lawyer, creating a new role of 'supervisor' who must have at least five years' experience as a caseworker, and increasing the number of mental health professionals in CGCs.[38] This reform also introduces regulations for adoption and foster care agencies for the first time (MHLW, 2016e). The lack of regulation resulted in cases, including one I encountered during fieldwork, where the CGC suspects an organisation of child trafficking but feel they have no legal foundation with which to challenge it (see Bryant, 1990).

In August 2017, the MHLW 'Investigation committee on the new way of alternative care' published 'The New Vision of Alternative Care' (MHLW NWAC, 2017). This calls for 75 per cent of babies and infants under three years of age to be in foster care within five years and for 75 per cent of pre-school children to be in foster care within seven years. The vision calls for reform of the CGCs, temporary care, and welfare institutions.

The 'New Vision' also calls for national support instead of a reliance on local authorities to promote change, the strengthening of foster care service providers, and support for children ageing out of care, as well as the collection of more data at a national level. Finally, the vision calls for the promotion of adoption, with reference to the importance of permanency, for placement fees to be related to the complexity of need, and for measures to increase practitioners' expertise and role specialisation within CGCs.

So, what is the relationship between this policy change and the foster care rate? Miwa argues that 'national policy and systems have a large impact' (2014: 145) but qualifies this by noting that the increase in the foster care rate started before the 2002 Child Welfare Act reform. Sano, the Teru CGC head, notes that national policy change takes time to filter down to local practice change. Discussing the Child Abuse Prevention Act, Sano (2014, interview) stated that:

> This law has been in effect for about 14 years and finally the CGC are pretty equal now. This is in part as all local authorities basically started from zero knowledge on this. With foster care, each prefecture already has their own history, so this is not something that can change very easily... Unlike abuse, everyone is starting in different places.

Sano's second point, on the differences between local authorities in foster care, speaks to the heart of this book. The changes that are occurring in the foster care rate are not occurring uniformly across Japan. The MHLW highlights local authorities that have seen the largest increases in their foster care rate. Between 2004 and 2014, for example, Fukuoka city saw an increase of 25.5 per cent, Oita of 21.1 per cent, and Saitama city of 20.7 per cent (MHLW, 2016a).[39] Figure 2.2 maps this data out for all local authorities.[40] During this same period, four local authorities, Kawasaki City (−18.4 per cent), Akita (−6.0 per cent), Yokohama City (−4.8 per cent), and Chiba City (−2.3 per cent), saw decreases in their foster care rate.[41]

One of the reasons for this variation is that in alternative care the responsibility for determining local policy and practice lies with the local authorities, rather than the MHLW. This is made explicit in guidelines on the 2012 'Three Acts related to Children and Childrearing', which state that municipalities are to 'formulate implementation plans according to local needs' (MHLW, 2015b: 179).

Following the 2011 Foster Care Guidelines, each local authority was required to report plans to achieve these targets. Prior to the submission of these plans, one MHLW bureaucrat voiced their concerns to me that some local authorities were completing the exercise as *tatemae*, a façade. When the plans were received, it became clear that some local authorities did not even show *tatemae*. Thirty of the 50 local authorities that submitted plans on time were aiming for targets of under one-third and two local authorities, Iwate and Okinawa, were aiming to decrease their foster care rate (King, 2017).

There is a tension between the principle of equality (see the Basic Act on Education, Article 4.1; the Children's Charter, Article 2; the Vision for Children and Child Rearing, Section 3.2) and this delegation of power and responsibility to local authorities. There have been discussions within the MHLW on this. The tentative conclusion was that while there is no evidence

46 *The context of alternative care*

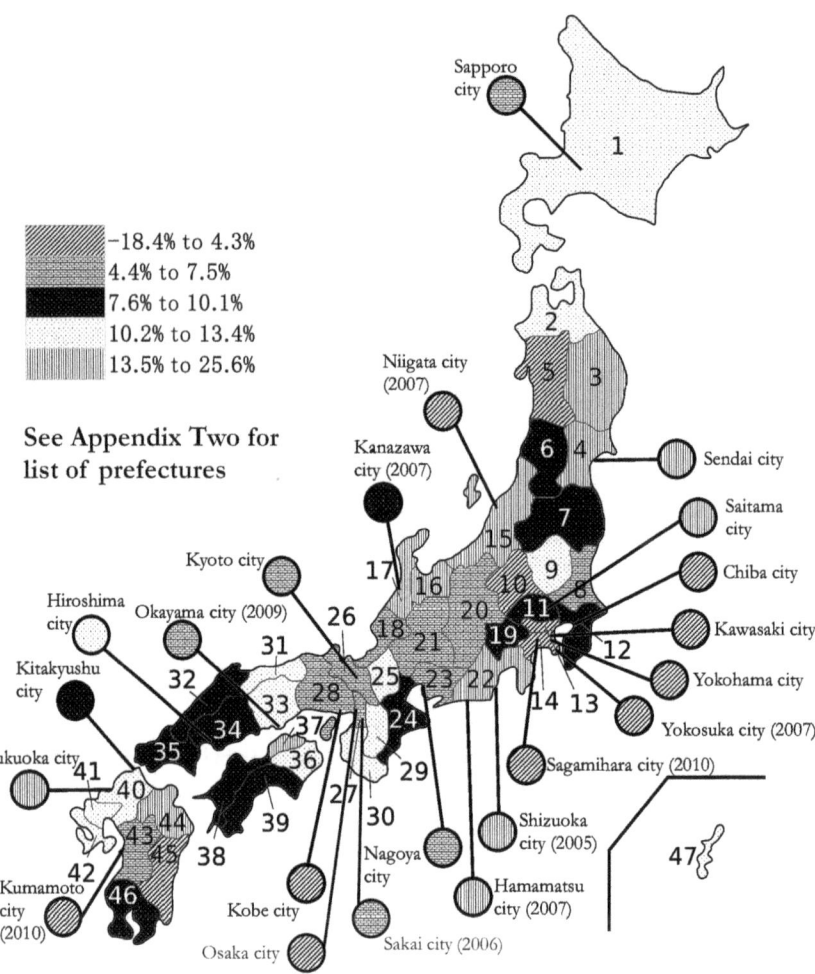

Figure 2.2 Mapping the change in the foster care rate. 2004–2014.

that there is a difference in outcomes between foster care and institutional care, regional variation is not a problem. Given the increased awareness within Japan of international discourse on the use of institutions, particularly for babies and infants, and the desire of two international NGOs to commission research on the impact of institutionalisation in Japan, it seems likely that this evidence may soon exist, which would lead to regional variation being problematized. Whether or not regional variation is problematized, attempts to promote foster care that do not account for the 'thick description' offered in this book will only achieve limited success.

3 Budget allocation and financial incentives

One of the contributing factors to the stability of the alternative care system is the structuring of budgets and the financial incentives that this creates. This is at first counterintuitive. Institutional care in Japan is more expensive than foster care, with some BIWI placements costing over seven and a half times of foster care (see Table 2.2). Given that cost has contributed to de-institutionalisation elsewhere (Browne, 2008; EuroChild, 2012; Tobis, 2000), it is strange that this seems to have had a limited affect in Japan. There are three reasons for this. The first is that the numbers in Table 2.2 do not reflect the full cost of foster care. While a placement into a welfare institution covers all the running costs, in foster care the CGC must also recruit, train, select, register, and support foster parents.

The second reason is that institutions in Japan are not as expensive as they are elsewhere. In 2003–2004 in New South Wales, Australia, each residential care placement cost the local authority up to AUS $346,000 per child per annum (Ainsworth and Hansen, 2009: 146).[42] Japanese welfare institutions achieve lower costs through economy of scale, by employing fewer staff, and by requesting that children with more complex needs be moved to specialist institutions or foster care. Staffing costs are further reduced by the high staff turnover, the result of long hours, low pay, and a glass ceiling on promotion (Goodman, 2000).

The final reason is that placement costs are split between the local authority and national authority, while the cost of any locally initiated reform is met locally. To understand this, we must first outline the funding structure for alternative care.

The local authority's alternative care budget is framed by an MHLW 'menu'. This has broad categories, such as 'foster care recruitment' and 'careleaver support'. The local authority hall allocates money to each category and the MHLW matches this up to a cap. Local authorities do not have to allocate a budget to every category: for example, Yuno does not allocate any money to the 'careleavers' support' as bureaucrats have been tackling the largest challenges sequentially, rather than in parallel.

In theory, the use of both MHLW and local funds can be audited. In reality there is no national accountability here as the sums involved are a fraction of those in areas such as construction. Nor does the MHLW menu define how goals, such as the 'support of careleavers', are to be achieved. A Yuno hall bureaucrat explained,

> There are so many ways you can do foster care promotion and recruitment, it could be giving out leaflets at shopping centres, asking foster carers to help with recruitment, there is no "correct" way to do this, so we are left to work it out on ourselves.
>
> (interview, 2015)

48 The context of alternative care

Table 2.2 Costs of alternative care

	Payment per month to care provider for first child	Payment per month for subsequent children
Foster care	72,000 (£493)	36,000 (£247)
Specialist foster care	123,000 (£843)	87,000 (£596)
Additional general allowance for foster parents[a]	Babies and Infants: 57,290 (£393)	Babies and Infants: 57,290 (£393)
	Children: 49,680 (£341)	Children: 49,680 (£341)
Approx: Foster care[b]	125,485 (£861)	89,485 (£614)
Approx: Specialist foster care[b]	176,485 (£1,210)	140,485 (£964)
CWI[c]	280,000 (£1,921)	As first
BIWI[d]	532,000 – 959,000 (£3,650 – £6,579)	As first

Data sources: Foster care, specialist foster care, CWI: MHLW. (2016b). *Shakaiteki yougo no genjyou ni tsuite (sankoushiryou)*. 2016, July: 7–13.

BIWI: Chiba. (2007). *Shakai-teki yōgo o hitsuyō to suru kodomo tachi no tame ni ~ Chiba ken ni okeru shakai-teki shigen no arikata ni tsuite tōshin ~*: 7. Azabu BIWI. (2015). *Zaimushohyō-tō*

[a] Foster parents are given further payment to cover the child's nursery, education, medical, commuting, or training costs
[b] Approximate payment to foster parent and specialist foster parent adds the basic payment to the average of the two different general allowances
[c] CWI payment depends on the size of the CWI and the age of the children there. The figure given is an approximate figure given by the MHLW based on a CWI having 45 children of school age. This figure includes the costs noted for foster carers by the *. The CWI receives additional funding for younger children to meet the higher staff to child ratio required here. The CWI also receives an additional 87,000 yen for each child cared for in group care. Given that every CWI I have seen has children younger than school age, the average payment per child will be higher than the number cited here. This also contributes to the fact that some CWI are reluctant to facilitate the transfer of younger children, who are seen as less demanding, to foster care. Public CWI are more expensive than private CWI, largely due to increased staff costs.
[d] BIWI payments vary significantly and are not normally made public. The range that I have found so far is given here. Private BIWI are significantly cheaper than public ones. The public figures cited here are from 2007 and are likely to have risen

Exchange rate of £1 = 145.87 yen (December 13th 2016).

The local authority, then, decides both the allocation of funds to menu categories and how this money is to be used. These decisions are often shaped by local events. Prior to the current focus on foster care, the death of two babies known to the Yuno CGC led to a focus on risk assessment. In many countries, including the UK, Ireland, and Australia, incidents such as this have prompted national policy and practice change. In Japan, with a notable exception in 2004,[43] investigations and subsequent practice changes occur at a local authority level. Political influence is an important factor in the allocation of resources. This is explored further in Chapter 5.

The fees paid to foster parents and institutions are also split equally between the MHLW and the local authority.[44] A placement into foster care, rather than a CWI, saves around 158,000 yen (£1,104) per month.[45] The local authority recoups half of this but must provide foster care services for this amount. While this difference is marginal for CWIs, the saving per child for BIWIs rise to as much as 830,000 yen (£5,799) per month. Even when halved, it seems that developing foster care services for babies and infants would save local authorities money. So, why has this not happened?

One reason is that the CGC holds greater moral responsibility for a child in foster care than it does for one in institutional care. A child being abused or dying in foster care, where the CGC is the service provider, has more of an impact than the same occurring in an institution, which is staffed by professionals and where the CGC is the service regulator (Goldfarb, 2013; Tsuzaki, 2009).

Practice change in Tokyo illuminates this. There have been deaths in Tokyo BIWIs over the last few decades, none of which resulted in major structural changes. Following the death from abuse of a baby in foster care in Suginami in 2010, the natal mother sued Tokyo metropolitan authority for placing her child in an unsafe environment (Yamamoto, 2014). Two senior Tokyo bureaucrats independently explained that this resulted in an increased caution over foster care. One of the bureaucrats explained that a decision was made to extend the *kouryuu*, acclimatisation, period to six months, 'to reduce risk for the institution', that is, the CGC. As temporary care placements are not supposed to last more than two months this led to an increase of placements in BIWIs.

The Tokyo bureaucrats also both noted a case where a baby had been found to have a disability, which led the foster parents to 'reject' the child. One bureaucrat noted, 'the mothers are weak, have not been very healthy when [they] give birth to the child... for these kind of children from weak births/mothers to go straight to foster care can be tough' (interview, 2015). The response to the Suginami incident meant that in 2013 only one infant under one year of age, out of 224, was placed into foster care in Tokyo (MHLW, 2015c: 85).

It is perhaps unsurprising, then, that BIWI pamphlets often highlight that they 'protect the lives' of babies and infants (Shion Gakuen, N.D.). Indeed, the MHLW 'Committee on the Issues relating to Alternative Care and Institutions' defines the role of the BIWI as being to 'protect the lives of babies and infants who need alternative care. That is, to guarantee the lives of babies and infants who cannot express their volition in words' (MHLW, 2011d: 14). This not only highlights the dangers of abusive households but also implicitly contrasts BIWIs with foster parents, very few of whom have professional experience with babies and infants.

Tversky and Kahneman argue that 'losses and disadvantages have greater impact on preferences than gains and advantages' (1991: 1039), a phenomenon they term 'loss aversion'. Any marginal gains that CGCs may see in placing a child into foster care are weighed against the potential impact of the placement going badly. This serves to minimise the impact of the cost difference between BIWIs and foster care.

The final issue related to finance is the fact that around 98 per cent of children in BIWIs or CWIs are cared for in private institutions (King, 2017: 160). It is harder for a CGC to close a private institution than a public institution, and the private institutions are active in lobbying at both the local and national levels. Goodman notes that

> there is no doubt that those who run the *yogoshisetsu* [CWIs] have vested interests in maintaining them as going concerns. There is no doubt also that this may not always be in the best interests of the children in care.
> (1999: 79; see also Tsuzaki, 2006, 2009)

The dominance of the private sector here leads to what Donahue and Zeckhauser (2008) term 'diminished capacity'. Donahue and Zeckhauser (2008: 508) argue that

> In some cases opting for indirect production may discourage or even preclude the maintenance of capacity for direct governmental action... To the extent that government becomes dependent on private capabilities, it puts itself in a disadvantaged position in future rounds of negotiation with its agents. Whether "path dependency" presents trivial or profound barriers to reverting to a direct delivery model, and whether reliance on external capacity entails minor or major future costs, will depend on the details of each case.

In the alternative care system, the sunk costs of the institutions represent a profound barrier to reverting to a direct delivery model. While the cost of service delivery is split between the MHLW and the local authority, the local authority has to meet the costs of transitioning from institutional care to foster care. This represents a significant investment (European Commission, 2013; Lumos, 2011; UNICEF and World Bank, 2003; World Health Organization, 2010) and a significant barrier to change. As yet, policy attempts to create external foster care service providers have not taken sufficient account of the additional costs associated with providing or developing this service.

Notes

1 A literal translation of this is – [child] rearing foster parents.
2 I have used the term 'foster parents' rather than 'foster carers' as this reflects more accurately the Japanese, *'sato-oya'*. *Sato* literally translates as natal village, *oya* as parents. Caseworkers often saw the word *oya* as exacerbating natal parents' fears of being replaced. A few local authorities use other terms, including Tokyo which uses *Yōiku katei*, [child] rearing home.
3 The status of family homes as foster care is discussed in Chapter 6.
4 *Kōryuu* can be translated as an exchange, relationship building, acclimatisation, or interaction. The process is discussed in greater depth in Chapter 4.

5 If a child does not progress to high school, they must leave the CWI at 15 years of age. In 2011 the MHLW permitted extensions from 18 until children are 20 years old. A placement can be extended to facilitate the child progressing to tertiary education, to support children in or seeking employment, and to support children with illness or disabilities (MHLW, 2011c). In practice, very few children stay in CWIs past the age of 18 (National Foster Care Association, 2015). In 2016 the Specialist Committee for Investigating a New Way for Child Welfare suggested that this be extended to 22 years old (MHLW, 2016c).
6 This MHLW dataset does not include the self-reliance assistance homes, which have a capacity of between five and 20, with the most common capacity being six (MHLW, 1998, 2015a).
7 Some CWIs do this by building temporary walls in corridors and labelling the resulting spaces as two distinct 'units', rather than by building self-contained detached units.
8 In child psychotherapy institutions and in Children's self-reliance support institutions there is one staff member for every 4.5 children (MHLW, 2016b: 11). For comparison, in the UK residential care system there is an average of three staff members for every one child (Berridge et al., 2012).
9 There are also tens of thousands of children in institutions for children with disabilities. These institutions are managed separately from alternative care, though CGC bureaucrats noted that some of these children had been placed primarily due to abuse or neglect. In 2005, 670,000 adults and children with physical, intellectual, or mental disabilities were institutionalised (MHLW, 2006). This represents nearly 10 per cent of 7,091,000 adults or children with disabilities (MHLW, 2006). The use of institutional rather than community-based care is also found in mental health practice (Taplin and Lawman, 2012). Oketani and Akiyama (2012) argue that this is the result of the Japanese Association of Psychiatric Hospitals lobbying against reforms that would impact upon their role and business.
10 In one case I saw, the mother, who had been in care from 7 until 13 years of age, gave birth at 14. The father was 30 years old. The police were not involved in this case.
11 The figures for parental nationality are likely to be slightly low, as non-Japanese parents are occasionally not registered by the other parent for fear of them removing the child from Japan.
12 Nagano and Arimura (2014) attribute the new focus on careleavers to Tsuzaki's (2006) translation of Goodman's (2000) work. Two earlier studies are Matsumoto's (1987) work on poverty and careleavers and Hayashi's (1992) survey of careleavers.
13 Japanese statistics do not take into account children in specialist institutions, including self-reliance support institutions or self-reliance assistance homes, very few of whom progress to tertiary education. Despite this, it seems likely that Japan has the highest progression to tertiary education from alternative care of any OECD country.
14 See, for example, Sweden (13 per cent), England (9 per cent), and Denmark (3 per cent) (Jackson, 2013). Kerr (N.D.) notes that many careleavers in the UK are missed from statistics as they enter tertiary education after a period of employment.
15 Kariya's work on education credential inflation demonstrates that the cost of not attending tertiary education in Japan has increased with the number of people attending tertiary education (2011a, 2011b).
16 This term can also be translated as protective custody.

17 Children aged under two years of age enter BIWIs on a temporary placement order. Children older than two can be placed into any institution or foster care for temporary care, though this is rare.
18 This study also found that 61.8 per cent of children in temporary care had previously been in contact with the CGC, and 25.2 per cent had previously been in alternative care.
19 See Takahashi et al. (2002, 2003) and Wada et al. (2013) for overviews of temporary care.
20 Where other countries record 'temporary' stays in alternative care statistics, the average stay will appear shorter.
21 Residential care in other countries is closest in form and function to the self-reliance assistance homes and child self-reliance support institutions. Despite this, I occasionally heard arguments for BIWIs and large CWIs based upon the existence of residential care abroad. A senior member of the International Association of Residential Care (FICE) expressed concern over this 'lost in translation' justification for institutionalising babies and infants (interview, 2014).
22 The official foster care rate is not problematized in Japan. Tsutsui and Otaga (2011) are a rare example of researchers who consider the specialist welfare institutions when discussing the foster care rate.
23 It is unclear what led to this change. There was external pressure from the UN (Goldfarb, 2013; Goodman, 2000), which was used by domestic advocates of change (Tsuzaki, 2006), but there is little evidence that this had an impact on the MHLW until the 2011 'Foster Care Guidelines', which Miwa (2012) argues were partly in response to the UN 'Guidelines for the Alternative Care of Children'.
24 In alternative care, the 20 designated cities, *seireishi*, and two additional cities, Kanazawa and Yokosuka, function as local authorities independently from the prefecture they are located in.
25 Currency conversion 30 December 2019. For any further children, regular foster carers now receive 36,000 yen and specialist foster carers receive 87,000 yen. A child allowance, calculated primarily by age, is paid on top of this.
26 Child Welfare Act Article 6-3-8.
27 The original wording, *jūsū,* means more than 10 and under 20 years. Later guidelines defined this as 19 years.
28 The move towards smaller CWIs predates the 2010 vision (Zenshakyō, 2007). Ogiso (2010) argues that this stems from changes led by innovative CWIs.
29 Some of these are publicly available (see Chiba Prefecture, 2015; Kanagawa Prefecture, 2015; Nagano Prefecture, 2013).
30 Policy documents on this vision emanated from the Supra-ministerial Organ on Population Decline and the Equal Employment, Children and Families Bureau within the MHLW.
31 Miwa argues that the MHLW made this guideline 'while strongly conscious of the 2009 UN guidelines for alternative care' (2012: 54). There is a need for further research on the mechanisms of UN influence on this policy change.
32 Grandparents still cannot claim this.
33 This policy had an immediate impact. Nine months after the disaster only two of the 1,580 children who lost one or both parents had been placed into institutional care, despite local unemployment rates of up to 90 per cent.
34 SOS Children's Villages are working in 135 countries (SOS Children's Village, N.D.). A senior manager of SOS in Japan noted that in every country, but Japan and Colombia, they are considered residential care not foster care.
35 This policy echoes the practice of a pioneering Tokyo CWI (see Goodman, 2000: 137).

36 One elite interviewee alluded to the possibility that this role may have been created in part to limit opposition from the National CWI association to the creation of the one-third foster care target and the Foster Care Guidelines.
37 I was fortunate to be asked to take part in an MHLW consultation on this legislative change, with a focus on the role of adoption and foster care agencies
38 See MHLW (2016g, 2016h) for more details.
39 This excludes Miyagi and Iwate because 'a lot of these are kinship foster parents resulting from the effects of the Tohoku earthquake and tsunami' (MHLW, 2016a: 16).
40 See King (2017: Appendix 1) for the foster care rates of all local authorities in 2004 and 2014.
41 Sagamihara City, which was granted designated city status in 2010, had a reduction of 17.9 per cent between 2010 and 2014, while Niigata City, granted designated city status in 2007, had a reduction of 4.6 per cent.
42 £141,810 per annum (1 October, 2003).
43 The Kishiwada incident of 2004, which led to a change in legislation from having to report known abuse to having to report suspected abuse, is a rare exception.
44 The local authority is responsible for meeting additional costs associated with education, training, or medical procedures.
45 Currency conversion 30 December 2019.

References

Abe, T., & Ogiso, K. (2011). Jidōsōdanjyo ichijihogō no gakushū ni kansuru shokuin no ishiki to gakushū no kōka – 'A' jidōsōdanjyo no shokuin ankēto chōsa kara [Thoughts of those educating children in temporary care in the CGCs and the results of this education: Results of a questionnaire of staff from 'A' CGC]. *Nihon Shakai Fukushi Gakkai.* (Poster presentation).

Ainsworth, F., & Hansen, P. (2009). Residential programs for children and young people: Their current status and use in Australia. In M. Courtney, & D. Iwaniec (Eds.), *Residential care of children: Comparative perspectives.* New York: Oxford University Press.

Aizawa, M. (2011). Shakai-teki yōgo no kadai to sono taisaku ni tsuite jidō jiritsu-shien shisetsu nado no jūjitsu ni mukete [Challenges in alternative care and countermeasures to these: Towards developing the self-reliance support institutions]. *Nihon Shakai Fukushi Gakkai,* 1–12.

Azabu Baby and Infant Welfare Institution. (2015). *Zaimushohyō-tō* [Financial statements]. Retrieved from URL: http://homepage3.nifty.com/keihuku/ (last accessed 2015, July).

Basic Act on Education. (2006). Act number 120 of 2006, December 22.

Berridge, D., Biehal, N., & Henry, L. (2012). *Living in children's residential homes.* Department for Education Research report DFE-RR201. n.p.: University of Bristol.

Bridge for Smile. (2005). *A survey of the child welfare institutions of the eight prefectures of Kyushu and Okinawa.* Retrieved from URL: http://www.canayell.com/about.html (last accessed 2015, November 15).

Browne, K. (2008). *The overuse of institutional care for young children in Europe.* (PowerPoint presentation). Second International Conference on Community Psychology. Lisbon. 2008, June 5.

Bryant, T.L. (1990). Sons and lovers: Adoption in Japan. *The American Journal of Comparative Law*, 38(2), 299–336.
Cabinet Office. (2009). *White paper on youth 2009 in Japan*. Retrieved from URL: http://www8.cao.go.jp/youth/english/whitepaper/2009/ (last accessed 2017, August 21).
Chiba Prefecture. (2007). *Shakai-teki yōgo wo hitsuyō to suru kodomo tachi no tame ni ~ Chiba ken ni okeru shakai-teki shigen no arikata ni tsuite tōshin ~* [For children who need alternative care: Report on how to use social resources in Chiba Prefecture]. Chiba Prefectural Government: Chiba. Retrieved from URL: https://www.pref.chiba.lg.jp/jika/kenriyougo/toushin/documents/arikata-tosin4gaiyoban.pdf (last accessed 2017, August 21).
Chiba Prefecture. (2015). *Chiba ken katei-teki yōgo suishin keikaku* [Chiba Prefecture home-like alternative care promotion plan]. 2015, November. Chiba Prefectural Government: Chiba.
Child Welfare Act. (1947). Act No. 164 of 1947, December 12.
Children's Charter. (1951). 1951, May 5.
Doi, K. (2016). *Revised Child Welfare Act: The principle of family-based care now guaranteed by the law*. 2016, May 7. Retrieved from URL: https://www.hrw.org/news/2016/05/27/revised-child-welfare-act-principle-family-based-care-now-guaranteed-law (last accessed 2017, August 28).
Donahue, J.D., & Zeckhauser, R.J. (2008). Public private collaboration. In M. Moran, M. Rein, & R.E. Goodin (Eds.), *The Oxford handbook of public policy*. Oxford: Oxford University Press.
Dower, J. (1999). *Embracing defeat: Japan in the aftermath of World War II*. London:Penguin.
EuroChild. (2012). De-institutionalisation and quality alterative care for children in Europe: Lessons learned and the way forward. *Eurochild Working Paper*. Brussels: EuroChild.
European Commission. (2013). *Investing in children: Breaking the cycle of disadvantage*. Commission recommendation of 20.2.2013, C(2013), 778 final.
Goldfarb, K. (2012). *Fragile kinships: Family ideologies and child welfare in Japan*. (Doctoral dissertation). The University of Chicago.
Goldfarb, K. (2013). Japan. In P. Welbourne, & J. Dixon (Eds.), *Child protection and child welfare: A global appraisal of cultures, policy, and practice*. London: Jessica Kingsley Publishers.
Goodman, R. (1999). The entrepreneurial children's home: Approaches to the study of the Japanese child welfare system. *IDS Bulletin*, 30(4), 71–81.
Goodman, R. (2000). *Children of the Japanese state: The changing role of child protection institutions in contemporary Japan*. Oxford: Oxford University Press.
Goodman, R. (2006). Thoughts on the relationship between anthropological theory, methods and the study of Japanese society. In J. Hendry, & D. Wong (Eds.), *Dismantling the East-West dichotomy: Views from Japanese anthropology*. London: Routledge.
Goodman, R. (2012). The 'Discovery' and 'Rediscovery' of child abuse (*jido gyakutai*) in Japan. In R. Goodman, Y. Imoto, & T. Toivonen (Eds.), *A sociology of Japanese youth: From returnees to NEETs*. London: Nissan Institute/Routledge Japanese Studies.
Harada, A. (2013). Children in need of permanent families: The current status of and future directions for the Japanese foster care system. *Illinois Child Welfare*, 6(1), 14–29.

Hayashi, H. (1992). Yōgonenreiji no jittai to jiritsu enjō no arikata [The situation of older children who have been through care and how their independence should be supported]. *Osaka-shi Shakai Fukushi Kenkyū*, 15, 25–35.
Hirada, M. (2014). Satooya shien senmon sōdan-in no yakuwari to kadai: zenkoku jidō yōgo shisetsu nyūji-in e no ankēto chōsa kara [The role and issues facing foster care specialist consultants: Based on a national survey of child welfare institutions and baby and infant welfare institutions]. *Nihon Shakai Fukushi Gakkai*, 62, 143–144.
Hoshi, T. (2012). Shūro ni muketa torikumi to shien — jiritsu enjo hōmu 'hoshinoka' no hibi [Helping to start employment: Daily life at the self-reliance assistance home 'Star home']. *Mother and Child Wellbeing around the World*, 72(4), 62–67.
Human Rights Watch (HRW). (2014). *Without dreams. Children in alternative care in Japan*. New York: Human Rights Watch.
Ito, K. (2015). Satooya no shien nīzu to shien kikan ni motomeru yakuwari [Foster care support needs and clarifying the role of the foster care support agencies]. *Nihon Shakai Fukushi Gakkai*, 231–232.
Ito, K., Takada, M., & Morito, K. (2014). Jidō fukushi shisetsu to satooya to no pātonāshippu kōchiku ni muketa no kadai — jidō yōgo shisetsu nyūji-in shokuin no intabyū chōsa kekka kara no kōsatsu [Task for going into good partnership with a child foster care institution and the foster parent: Consideration from the interview findings of the staff of child foster care institutions]. *Shakaimondai Kenkyū*, 63, 27–38.
Jackson, S. (2013). *Leaving care: Outcomes for fostered young people*. Presentation at the REES Centre, University of Oxford. Oxford. 2013, March 20.
Japan Child and Family Research Institute. (1998). *Nihon kodomo katei sōgōkenkyūsho kiyō dai 35-shū (Heisei 10-nendo)* [Japan child and family research institute bulletin No. 35 (1998)]. n.p.: Japan Child & Family Research Institute.
Kadonaga, T., & Fraser, M.W. (2015). Child maltreatment in Japan. *Journal of Social Work*, 15(3), 233–253.
Kanagawa Prefecture. (2015). *Kanagawa ken katei-teki yōgo suishin keikaku* [Kanagawa Prefecture home-like alternative care promotion plan]. 2015, April. Kanagawa: Kanagawa Prefectural Government.
Kariya, T. (2011a). Japanese solutions to the equity and efficiency dilemma? Secondary schools, inequity and the arrival of 'universal' higher education. *Oxford Review of Education*, 37(2), 241–266.
Kariya, T. (2011b). Credential inflation and employment in 'universal' higher education: Enrolment, expansion and (in)equity via privatisation in Japan. *Journal of Education and Work*, 24(1–2), 69–94.
Kashiwame, R. (2010). Kodomotachi ni atarimae no seikatsu wo [Towards a lifestyle that is obviously right for children]. *Shakai-teki yōgo to famirīhōmu*, 1, 6–9. 2010, June.
Kashiwame, R. (2011). Iken shakai-teki yōgo no kinmirai chūchōki taisaku no gurando dezain no hitsuyō-sei to kinmirai taisaku no jitsugen [The near future of alternative care: The need for a medium-term policy and grand design, and for realising policy in the short term]. *Jidō yōgo shisetsu-tō no shakai-teki yōgo no kadai ni kansuru kentō iinkai*.
Kerr, M. (N.D.). *Outcomes of care: A 4-year study investigating evidence base for LAC policy*. (Powerpoint presentation). Retrieved from URL: http://www.ncctc.co.uk/files/2813/7449/8661/Mark_Kerr_Critical_Appraisal_for_Outcomes.pdf (last accessed 2017, August 28).

Kikuchi, M. (2007). Nihon de satooya seido ga riyō sarenai riyū to wa? Kokusai hikaku kenkyū wo tōshite ieru koto [Why would not be the foster care system utilized well in Japan?: Through international comparison]. *Kodomo no gyakutai to negurekuto*, 9(2), 147–155.

King (nee Rivera King), M. (2017). *Child guidance centres in Japan: Regional variation in policy implementation and the family-bond*. (Doctoral dissertation). The University of Oxford.

Krogness, K.J. (2014). Jus Koseki: Household registration and Japanese citizenship. *The Asia-Pacific Journal, Japan Focus*, 12(35), 1–24.

Kumasaka, Y., & Aiba, H. (1968). Foster care in Japan: Past and present. *The Milbank Memorial Fund Quarterly*, 46(2), 253–265.

Lumos. (2011). *Lumos annual review, 2011*. London: Lumos.

Matsumoto, I. (1987). Yōgo shisetsu sotsuen-sha no 'seikatsu kōzō' 'hinkon' no kotei-teki seikaku ni kansuru kōsatsu ['"Labours and social networks" of young people who was left residential care for children – A study on persistence of 'poverty']. *Hokkaidō daigaku kyōiku gaku-bu kiyō*, 49, 43–119.

Matsumoto K., & Takada, H. (2012). 'Kodomo kosodate shin shisutemu' jidai no hoikujo keiei [Nursery management in the era of the 'New system of children and child rearing']. *Seikatsu fukushi kenkyū*, 80, 1–17.

Matsuura, N. (2011). Youth corrections in Japan: Family-like setting for delinquents with the experiences of child maltreatment. *Child & Youth Services*, 32(4), 281–285.

Mehrotra, V., Morck, R., Shim, J., & Wiwattanakantang, Y. (2013). Adoptive expectations: Rising sons in Japanese family firms. *Journal of Financial Economics*, 108, 840–854.

Ministry of Health, Labour, and Welfare. (MHLW). (1998). *Todōfuken chiji shitei toshi shichō Kōseishō jidō katei kyokuchō jidō jiritsu seikatsu enjo jigyō (jiritsu enjo hōmu) no jisshi ni tsuite, Ko-hatsu dai 344-gō Heisei 10-nen 4 tsuki 22-nichi* [Letter from MHLW children and family bureau director to all prefectural governors and designated city mayors. On the implementation of self-reliance support (self-reliance assistance homes). No 344, 1998, April 22].

MHLW. (2000–2001 to 2014–2015). *Fukushi gyousei houkoku rei* [Annual welfare administration reported cases]. Retrieved from URL: http://www.e-stat.go.jp/ (last accessed 2017, August 28).

- *Satooya-sou oyobi satooya ni itaku sareteiru jidou-sou, todōfuken – shitei toshi – chūkaku-shi betsu* [The number of foster carers, the number of children placed into foster care, by prefecture, designated city and core city].

- Shōkibo jūkyo-gata jidō yōiku jigyō (famirīhōmu) no jigyōshosū, teiin, nyūsho jin'in, taisho jin'in, nendomatsu zaiseki jin'in oyobi shōkibo jūkyo-gata jidō yōiku jigyō (famirīhōmu) ni itaku sareteiru jidō-sū, todōfuken – shitei toshi – chūkaku-shi betsu [The number of small scale residential type child rearing businesses (family homes), capacity, new staff, and staff leaving over the year, current number of staff, number of children in family homes by prefecture, designated city and core city].

- Shakai fukushi shisetsu-tō chōsa 8-hyō shakai fukushi shisetsu-tō no teiin zaisho-sha-sū, -koku — todōfuken — shitei toshi — chūkaku-shi, shisetsu no shurui keiei shutai no kōei — shiei betsu [Social welfare institutions survey, table 8, institution capacity, current number of children, nationwide, by prefecture, designated city, and core city, and by type of institution, and by management status, public and private]. NB. For 2014 onwards refer to: Fukushi gyōsei hōkoku rei etsuran jidō dai 11-hyō jidō fukushi shisetsu (josan shisetsu oyobi boshi seikatsu shien shisetsu wo nozoku) no shisetsu-sū, teiin oyobi zaiseki jin'in, todōfuken – shitei toshi – chūkaku-shi × shisetsu no shurui-betsu [MHLW, welfare administration reported cases, Table 11: Children's welfare institutions (excluding midwives facilities and mother and child living support institutions) – institution capacity, current number of children, nationwide, by prefecture, designated city, and core city, and by type of institution].

MHLW. (2002). *Ko-hatsu dai 0 905001-gō. Heisei 14-nen 9 tsuki 5-nichi: 'Satooya no nintei-tō ni kansuru shōrei' oyobi 'satooya ga okonau yōiku ni kansuru saitei kijun' ni tsuite* [Letter to all governors, and mayors of designated cities. From the MHLW equal employment and family bureau director: On 'Ministerial ordinance on the accreditation of foster parents' and 'The minimum standards for care with foster parents'. Correspondence No. 0905001]. 2002, September 5.

MHLW. (2006). *Services and supports for persons with disabilities in Japan*. 2006, January. Retrieved from URL: http://www.mhlw.go.jp/english/wp/policy/dl/02.pdf (last accessed 2017, July 1).

MHLW. (2010). *Kodomo ~ kosodate bijyōn ~ kodomo no egao ga afureru shakai no tame ni* [Vision for Children and Childrearing ~ in order to build a society overflowing with children's smiles].

MHLW. (2011a). *Sato-oya itaku gaidorainu* [Foster care guidelines].

MHLW. (2011b). *Shakai-teki yōgo no genjou ni tsuite (sanka shiryou)* [Current status of alternative care (reference)]. 2011, July.

MHLW. (2011c). *Sato-oya itaku gaidorainu ni tsuite* [Letter to all governors, mayors of designated cities, and cities with designated child guidance centres. From the MHLW Equal Employment and Family Bureau Director: On the foster care guidelines. Correspondence No. 0330–9]. 2011, March.

MHLW. (2011d). *Jidō yōgo shisetsu-tō no shakai-teki yōgo no kadai ni kansuru kentō iinkai dai 1 kaigi jijitsu dai* [Committee on the issues relating to alternative care and institutions. First proceedings]. 2011, January 28. Retrieved from URL: http://www.mhlw.go.jp/stf/shingi/2r98520000011cpd-att/2r98520000011cqu.pdf (last accessed 2016, July 1).

MHLW. (2012a). *Shakai-teki yōgo no genjou ni tsuite (sanka shiryou)*. [Current status of alternative care (reference)]. 2012, September.

MHLW. (2012b). *Jidō yōgo shisetsu-tō no shōkibo-ka oyobi katei-teki yōgo no suishin ni tsuite* [Letter to all governors, mayors of designated cities, and cities with designated child guidance centres. From the MHLW Equal Employment and Family Bureau Director: On promoting the implementation of a move towards smaller child welfare institutions and family like alternative care. Correspondence No. 1130–1133]. 2012, November 30.

MHLW. (2015a). *Jiritsu enjo hōmu un'ei shishin* [Self-reliance assistance home management guidelines]. 2015, April 17.

MHLW. (2015b). *Annual health, labour, and welfare report 2015, Equal Employment and Child Welfare*. Retrieved from URL: http://www.mhlw.go.jp/english/policy/children/children-childrearing/index.html (last accessed 2017, August 24).

MHLW. (2015c). *Shakai-teki yōgo no genjou ni tsuite (sanka shiryou))* [Current status of alternative care (reference)]. 2015, July.

MHLW. (2016a). *Shakai-teki yōgo no genjou ni tsuite (sanka shiryou)* [Current status of alternative care (reference)]. 2016, January.

MHLW. (2016b). *Shakai-teki yōgo no genjou ni tsuite (sanka shiryou)* [Current status of alternative care (reference)]. 2016, July.

MHLW. (2016c). *Shakai hoshō shingikai jidō bukai aratana kodomo katei fukushi no arikata ni kansuru senmon iinkai hōkoku (teigen)*. [Social security council, children's subcommittee. Report on new ways of carrying out child welfare technical committee report (recommendations). 2016, March 10.

MHLW. (2016d). *Shakai teki yōgo no kadai to shourai zou no jitsugen ni mukete* [On the challenges and realising the future form of alternative care]. 2016, January.

MHLW. (2016e). *Jidō fukushi-hō-tō no ichibu wo kaisei suru hōritsu-an shinkyū taishō jōbun* [Draft law amending part of the Child Welfare Act. Highlighting original and amended articles].

MHLW. (2016f). *Jidō fukushi-hō-tō no ichibu wo kaisei suru hōritsu no kōfu ni tsuite (tsūchi)* [Letter to all governors, mayors of designated cities, and cities with designated child guidance centres. From the MHLW Equal Employment and Family Bureau Director: On the promulgation of the law amending a section of the Child Welfare Act (notice). Correspondence No. 0603-1]. 2016, August 3.

MHLW. (2016g). *Jidōsōdanjyo un'ei shishin no kaisei ni tsuite* [Letter to all governors, mayors of designated cities, and cities with designated child guidance centres. From the MHLW Equal Employment and Family Bureau Director: On the amendment of guidelines for managing child guidance centres. Correspondence No. 0929-1]. 2016, September, 29.

MHLW. (2016h). *Jidōsōdanjyo un'ei shishin ni tsuite* [Letter to all governors, and mayors of designated cities. From the MHLW Children and Family Bureau Director: On child guidance centre guidelines. Correspondence No. 0929-1]. 2016, September 29.

MHLW. (2019). *Shakai-teki yōiku no suishin ni mukete* [On the promotion of alternative care]. 2019, April.

MHLW Investigation Committee on the New Way of Alternative Care (MHLW NWAC). (2017). *(Aratana shakai-teki yōiku no arikata ni kansuru kentōkai). Atarashī shakai-teki yōiku bijon* [The new vision of alternative care]. 2017, August.

Ministry of Internal Affairs and Communications. (2015). *Sōmu-shō dai 53-gō. Heisei 27-nen 3 tsuki 10-nichi sōmu-shō gyōsei hyōka kyokuchō kōsei rōdōshō koyō kintō jidō katei kyokuchō-dono ikuji kyūgyō-hō no taishō to naru ko no yōken no minaoshi (assen)* [Letter to the Director of Equal Employment, Children and Families, MHLW, from the Director of Administrative Evaluation, Ministry of Internal Affairs and Communications: Evaluation phase no. 53. 2015, March 10. Review of the requirements of children who are to be the subject of child care leave law (mediation)]. Retrieved from URL: http://www.soumu.go.jp/main_content/000345850.pdf (last accessed 2016, April 6).

Miwa, K. (2011). Satooya itaku to shisetsu itaku no kankei no chōki-teki dōtai 1953-nen –2008-nen no jikeiretsu dēta no bunseki kara [The longitudinal dynamics of the relationship between the foster care placement and the residential care: Time-series analyses of the macro data 1953–2008 Japan]. *Japanese Journal of Social Welfare*, 52(2), 43–53.

Miwa, K. (2012). 2000-Nen ikō no satooya itaku no zōka wo motarashita mono jidō gyakutai no zōka no chokusetsuteki kōka to kansetsu-teki kōka wo megutte [What has caused an increase of the placement in foster care after 2000: Direct and indirect effect of child abuse increase]. *Japanese Journal of Social Welfare*, 53(2), 45–56.

Miwa, K. (2014). *Satooya seido no chouki-teki doutai to tenbou* [The long-term dynamics and outlook of the foster care system]. (Doctoral dissertation). Tokyo Metropolitan University.

Miwa, K. (2016). Naze satooya itaku wa shinten shinai no ka? Satooya touroku-sha fusoku kasetsu to satooya itaku jidō gentei kasetsu [Why has family-based foster care not become more common in Japan? A lack of registered fostered carers and of children who are able to be fostered]. *Japanese Journal of Social Welfare*, 56(4), 1–13.

Miyajima, K. (2014). *Famirīhōmu un'ei no kihon: Kono kuni no shakai-teki yōgo no korekara no tame ni* [The foundations of running family homes: For the future of alternative care in our country]. Lecture to anonymised CGC, 2014.

Mulheir, G., & Browne, K. (2007). *Deinstitutionalising and transforming children's services: A guide to good practice*. European Commission Daphne programme in collaboration with WHO regional office for Europe and the University of Birmingham UK. Birmingham: University of Birmingham (WHO Collaborating Centre for Child Care and Protection).

Murata, K. (2006). *Why do not foster carers increase in Japan?* Paper presented at Ajia kodomo no kenri to satooya kaigi. 2006, September 23.

Nagano Prefecture. (2013). *Nagano ken shakai fukushi shingikai: Nagano ken ni okeru shakai-teki yōgo no arikata ni tsuite (tōshin)*. [Nagano Prefecture social welfare council: Report on alternative care in Nagano Prefecture]. 2013, February. Nagano Prefectural Government: Nagano.

Nagano, S., & Arimura, T. (2014). Shakai-teki yōgo sochi kaijo no seikatsu jittai to depuribēshon: Niji bunseki ni yoru kasetsu seisei to ichiji dēta kara no shisa [Deprivation of former youth in care: The hypothesis generated by secondary analysis and suggested from original dates]. *Shakai Fukushi-Gaku*, 54(4), 28–41.

Nakagawa, A. (2010). *Jidō yōgo shisetsu no kakaeru kyō-teki kadai no kenshō shokuin no rōdō kankyō ni shugan wo oita Gunma ken'nai shisetsu e jittai chōsa* [Investigation into contemporary challenges for child welfare institutions: A survey of the reality of staff in Gunma Prefecture]. Gunma: Gunmadaigaku shakai jōhō gakubu jōhō shakai kagakka.

National Child Guidance Centre Directors' Committee. (2011). Zenkoku jidōsōdanjyo-chō-kai jidōsōdanjyo ni okeru satooya itaku oyobi iki jidō ni kansuru chōsa [Survey on abandoned children and foster care placements at child guidance centres]. *Zaidanhōjin zenkoku satooya-kai*, 91. 2011, July.

National Child Welfare Administration Division Head Meeting. (2015). *Zenkoku jidō fukushi shukan kachō kaigi: katei fukushi-ka boshi katei-tō jiritsushien shisetsu kankei* [National Child Welfare Administration Division Head meeting: The relationship between household welfare division and mother and child self-reliance support room]. Retrieved from URL: http://www.mhlw.go.jp/file/05-Shingikai-11901000-Koyoukintoujidoukateikyoku-Soumuka/0000113639.pdf (last accessed 2017, July 15).

National Foster Care Association. (2015). *Sato oya dayori* [Foster care newsletter]. 104. 2015, August 20. Tokyo: National Foster Care Association.

Ogiso, H. (2010). Jidō yōgo shisetsu jidō jiritsushien ni nyūsho suru jidō no genjō to shien shisaku no kadai [The current status of children in child welfare institutions and self-reliance support institutions and the challenges in support measures]. *Kikan shakai hoshō kenkyū*, 45(4), 396–406.

Oketani, H., & Akiyama, H. (2012). National federation of families for the mentally ill in Japan: Historical and future perspectives. In R. Taplin, & S.J. Lawman (Eds.), *Mental health care in Japan*. Abingdon: Taylor and Francis.

Osaka. (2012). *Shisetsu taishosha jidoushien no tame no jittai chousa: houkokusho* [Osaka City Child Welfare Division Factual investigation in order to support the leavers of institutional care: Written report]. 2012, March 19.
SBI. (2014). *SBI burokku betsu kenshū kōryū-kai (Kyūshū Okinawa burokku)* [SBI block training and network event (Kyushu and Okinawa block)]. 2014, May 16.
Shion Gakuen. (N.D.). Website. Retrieved from URL: http://www.shiongakuen.or.jp/n.php (last accessed 2017, July 1).
Shoji, J., Arimura, T., Miyajima, K., Ito, Y., Watanabe, M., Thomson, S., ... Takahashi, T. (2010). Satooya no konpitensu keisei to hyōka ni kansuru chōsa kenkyū [Research on the formation and evaluation of competence in foster carers]. *Nihon Shakai Fukushi Gakkai*, 1–2.
SOS Children's Village. (N.D.). Website. Retrieved from URL: http://www.sos-childrensvillages.org/ (last accessed 2016, May 16).
Suzuki, T. (1999). Jidōsōdanjyo ichijihogō ni okeru jidō no gakushū-ken hoshō ni kansuru ichikōsatsu: itsutsu no jidōsōdanjyo no hikaku kentō kara [How do we guarantee the right of the child to education in the temporary shelter of the child welfare centre?: From a comparative study of the five child welfare centres in Japan]. *Meijigakuindaigaku daigakuin shakaigakukenkyūka shakai-gaku senkō shakai-gaku senkō kiyō*, 22, 13–30.
Takahashi, S., Shibuya, M., Saimura, J., Shoji, J., Nakatani, S., Kurihara, N., ... Sakamoto, M. (2002). Jidōsōdanjyo ichijihogō no genjo to kadai ni kansuru kenkyū [A study of current issues and situation of temporary shelters of child guidance centres]. *Nihon-kodomo katei sōgōkenkyūsho kiyō*, 39, 7–46.
Takahashi, S., Shibuya, M., Saimura, J., Shoji, J., Nakatani, S., Kurihara, N., ... Sakamoto, M. (2003). Jidōsōdanjyo ichijihogō no genjo to kadai ni kansuru kenkyū (2) [A study of current issues and situation of temporary shelters of child guidance centres (2)]. *Nihon-kodomo katei sōgōkenkyūsho kiyō*, 40, 7–46.
Taplin, R., & Lawman, S.J. (Eds.). (2012). *Mental health care in Japan*. Abingdon: Routledge.
Tobis, D. (2000). *Moving from residential institutions to community-based social services in Central and Eastern Europe and the former Soviet Union*. Washington: The World Bank.
Tokyo. (2011a). *Tōkyōto ni okeru jidō yōgo shisetsu-tō taishosha e no ankēto chōsa hōkoku-sho* [Tokyo Metropolitan government. Social welfare and public health bureau (supported by the Supra-Ministerial organ on population decline: A survey of Tokyo Metropolis care-leavers from institutional and foster care)].
Tokyo. (2011b). *Tokyoto no jidō yogo shisetsu jiritsushien hōmu ni okeru afutakea jittai chosa* [Tokyo council of social welfare, the research committee of childcare workers, factual investigation on the after-care provision of child welfare institutions and self-reliance support centres in Tokyo].
Tokyo. (2012). *Oitachi no seiri: Atarashī shuppatsu ni mukete* [Tokyo council on social welfare, child division, leaving care committee. Preparing for upbringing: Towards a new departure].
Tsutsui, T., & Otaga, M. (2011). Shakai-teki yōgo taisei no saihen ni muketa kenkyū no genjō to kadai — shakai-teki yōgo kanren shisetsu nyūsho jidō no henka, kore ni tomonau kea teikyō taisei no saikōchiku no tame no kenkyū no arikata — [The system of child protection in Japan: Shift in residential placements for children and the necessary conditions to restructure the care provision system]. *Hoken iryō kagaku*, 60(5), 401–410.

Tsuzaki, T. (2006). *The vested interests vs. children's rights: Children's rights and foster care in Japan.* Presentation at Asia conference on children's rights and foster care. Retrieved from URL: http://www.geocities.jp/hokukaido/satooya/seoul2006/article/12-japan-tsuzaki-e.htm (last accessed 2017, August 22). Seoul. 2006, September 16.

Tsuzaki, T. (2009). *Kono kuni no kodomotachi: Yōhogo jidō shakai-teki yōgo no Nihonteki kōchiku; otona no kitoku ken'eki to kodomo no fukushi* [This country's children: Constructing social care for children in need of care; The vested interests of adults and children's welfare]. Tokyo: Nihon Kajo Shuppan.

Tversky, A., & Kahneman, D. (1991). Loss aversion in riskless choice: A reference-dependent model. *The Quarterly Journal of Economics*, 106(4), November, 1039–1061.

United Nations Committee on the Rights of the Child (UN CRC). (1998). *Concluding observations of the committee on the rights of the child: Japan. Eighteenth session: Consideration of reports submitted by states parties under Article 44 of the convention.* CRC/C/15/Add.90 (June).

UN CRC. (2004). *Consideration of reports submitted by states parties under Article 44 of the convention: Concluding observations: Japan.* CRC/C/15/Add.231. 2004, February 26.

UN CRC. (2010). *Consideration of reports submitted by states parties under Article 44 of the convention: Convention on the Rights of the Child: Concluding observations: Japan.* CRC/C/JPN/CO/3. 2010, June 20.

United Nations General Assembly. (2010). *Guidelines for the alternative care of children. Resolution adopted by the General Assembly 64/142.* A/RES/64/142*, on the report of the Third committee A/64/434.

UNICEF & World Bank. (2003). *Changing minds, policies and lives: Improving protection of children in Eastern Europe and Central Asia: Gatekeeping services for vulnerable children and families.* Florence: UNICEF & World Bank.

Wada, I., Yamamoto, T., Tsutsumi, C., Ookubo, M., Tamai, N., Bando, M., ... Kawamatsu, R. (2013). Ichijihogō no gaiyō haaku to nyūsho jidō no jittai chōsa [For the better shelter care facility at the child guidance centre. The study of the shelter care facility and the actual condition of placed children]. *Nihon kodomo katei sōgōkenkyūsho*, 50, 1–73.

World Health Organization. (2010). *Better health, better lives: Children and young people with intellectual disabilities and their families: Transfer care from institutions to the community.* EUR/51298/17/PP/3. Bucharest, Romania.

Yamamoto, M. (2014, October 23). Satogo joji bōkō shi: Jitsubo ga miyako wo teiso 'tekisetsuna shidō kainyū okotatta' [Foster girl child beaten to death: Natal mother takes city to court 'They neglected to provide good guidance']. *The Mainichi Shinbun*.

Yamamoto, T., & Sato, K. (2008). Jidōsōdanjyo to keisatsu katei saibansho-tō no shihō kikan to no renkei ni tsuite [Research on the cooperation of the child guidance centre, police, and family court]. *Nihon kodomo katei sōgōkenkyūsho*, 45, 331–380.

Yamamoto, T., Shoji, J., Arimura, T., Shinto, N., Itakura, T., Nemoto, A., ... Miyaguchi, T. (2009). Jidōsōdanjyo-tō ni okeru hogo-sha enjo no arikata ni kansuru jisshō-teki kenkyū 3 hogo-sha enjo shuhō no kōka, datōsei, hyōka, tekiō ni kansuru jisshō-teki-ken [A study on the system for supporting family preservation in the child guidance centres 3: Efficiency, validity, evaluation, and discerning of parents' supporting methods]. *Nihon kodomo katei sōgōkenkyūsho*, 46, 177–230.

Yamamoto, T., Ookubo, M., Sato, T., Tsuroka, Y., Itakura, T., Nagano, S., ... Kawamatsu, R. (2013). Jidōsōdanjyo ni okeru hogo-sha shien no arikata ni kansuru jisshō-teki kenkyū [A study on the system for supporting family preservation in the child guidance centres]. *Nihon kodomo katei sōgōkenkyūsho*, 50, 1–24.

Yokobori, M., & Yamamoto, M. (2013). *Nihon ni okeru satooya katei no jisshi no keiken to kore kara no satooya katei shien ni mukete* [Experiences as a biological child in a foster family in Japan and how to support foster families in the future]. Presentation at International Foster Care Organisation (IFCO). Osaka. 2013, September 13.

Zenshakyō (Zenkoku shakai fukushi kyōgi kai). (2007). *Zenshakyō tsūshin* [National social welfare communication]. No. 185. 2007, November 27.

Note: Where the author(s) provided an English translation of their work I have given their translation rather than my translation.

3 Child guidance centres

1 Child guidance centres

1.1 Introduction

The CGCs are the gatekeepers of alternative care. Their staff implement national and local policy to determine whether a child is removed from the family and, if they are, what type of care they are placed into. CGCs are also responsible for a range of related services. Tsuzaki notes that in the US these are provided by eight different legal bodies: The Child Protection Service, Children's Advocacy Centre, Juvenile Court, children's hospitals, community health centres, the Board of Mental Retardation/Developmental Difficulties, the Board of Education, and child guidance clinics (2009: 169). The CGCs I visited worked with children with disabilities, supported school-refusers,[1] and in one case worked with 'women's issues', often related to domestic violence.

Despite these sweeping responsibilities, and in the absence of social work as a profession in Japan (Tsuzaki, 2006), the CGCs are largely staffed by local government bureaucrats, who are moved between different offices every one to five years.[2] These generalist staff often have no experience in child welfare. CGCs can also hire contract-staff on full or part-time annual contracts. This chapter explores the CGCs before homing into the decision-making process by which children enter care.

1.2 CGCs and the family

The family plays a central role in the Japanese welfare state (see Campbell, 2002; Estevez-Abe, 2008; Goldfarb, 2016a; Schoppa, 2006). This role has been justified as 'natural' (Goodman, 2000) and inhibits state intervention in the family. This reluctance may have served to reinforce, or may have been reinforced by, the widespread belief held as late as the 1990s that parental rights were 'virtually inviolable, and a child was seen by and large as the property of the parent' (Goodman, 2002a: 21).

Goldfarb notes that 'when CGCs were first established, there was no focus on intervening into or addressing child maltreatment, which was not yet recognized as a social problem' (2012: 34). The belief that the domestic sphere was beyond the acceptable boundary of state intervention was altered by the 'discovery of child abuse' in the 1990s (Goodman, 2000). Goodman tracks a paradigm shift from the late 1980s, when 'the majority of Japanese, including many professionals in child welfare, believed that there was no, or virtually no, child abuse in Japan' (2000: 160), to a few years later where child abuse 'took on the aura of a moral panic... that it was endemic' (2000: 171). In 2002, Goodman argued that 'the "discovery" of child abuse in Japan has already had profound effects for the relation between the state and families and for the development of Japanese social policy towards children' (2002b: 157). This manifested in some CGCs being willing to be more interventionist (Kashiwame et al., 2012).

Goldfarb argues that the discovery of abuse created a tension in the construction of the family, as 'simultaneously... "in crisis", and yet the family form itself is powerfully naturalized as supportive, nurturing, and requisite for the creation of healthy human relationships' (2012: 13). The justification of the family's role as 'traditional' and 'historical' meant that these challenges were 'often represented as a pathology of modernity' (Goldfarb, 2013: 145; see also Motomori, 2016), centred on fears around 'the family's imminent collapse, the loss of 'traditional' values, and the decline of Japanese society itself' (Goldfarb, 2012: 1).

These fears often touched on the nuclearisation of the family and the belief that families are now isolated from communities (see Bamba and Haight, 2007; Nakagawa, 2010; Sakakibara, interview, 2014).[3] It is possible that the speed of the nuclearisation of the family (Sugimoto, 2010) contributes to this focus. It is also possible that the reframing of the Japanese family, which came after a decade of recession, relates to a shift in discourse from looking to explain Japan's strength to looking to explain its decline (Goodman, 2002b).

It is hard to assess the extent of the change in the relationship between state and family. The fact that 'by the end of the decade [1990s], the idea of children being endowed with their own rights had gained enormous ground' (Goodman, 2002a: 21) does signify radical change, but the relatively recent nature of this change may mean that it has not permeated into the practice of the judiciary and CGCs. While abuse has been seen as endemic since the late 1990s, for example, it was only in 2012 that Tokyo opened a centre to record and review all deaths from abuse (Kato, 2014).

This may help explain the gap between predictions of the alternative care system being on the cusp of a change (see Bamba and Haight, 2009a, 2009b; Goodman, 1999, 2000, 2012)[4] and Goldfarb's observation that 'many people who had dedicated their lives to transforming or improving the child welfare system asserted over and again that the system would never dramatically change' (2012: 75; see also Kubo, 2014).

1.3 Child protection in local authorities

Figure 3.1 shows the standard structure of child protection within local authorities.[5] While this shows the organisations involved in child protection, there is a clear delineation of roles and responsibilities and in practice inter-agency cooperation is limited. Abe argues that

> multi-agency cooperation is indispensable in the response to child abuse, yet due to the small number of people, their caseload, and the weight of responsibility involved, the idea that a network should be involved in case meetings seems to be scarce.
>
> (2014: 2)

This is most starkly visible in the absence of children, parents, or care providers in the CGC meetings in which decisions are made about a child's future.[6]

Since the 2004 and 2008 revisions to the Child Welfare Act, municipal offices and CGCs have more overlapping responsibility for tackling abuse (MHLW, 2016b: 32; Japan Child Welfare Association, 2005). Indeed, municipal offices now encounter more, though less serious, cases of abuse than CGCs (MHLW, 2015a: 24). Abe (2014) clarifies that CGCs have more expertise and power but are unable to provide day-to-day ongoing support, whereas municipal offices have more regular contact with vulnerable families and access to benefits and support services that facilitate preventative work, but lack power and expertise (see also Tashiro and Yamamoto, 2011). As such, municipal offices refer serious cases to the CGCs.

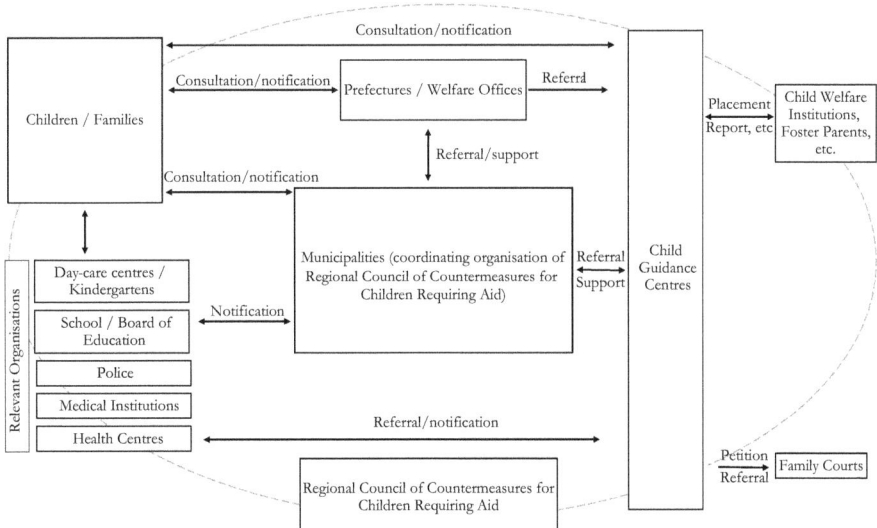

Figure 3.1 The organisation of child protection (MHLW 2011).
Source: Adapted from MHLW (2011e) Equal opportunities and child welfare (including current status of child welfare facilities, etc.): 186

66 *The context of alternative care*

CGCs have limited support from schools (Takahashi et al., 2010), police (Yamamoto and Niiro, 2009; Yamamoto and Sato, 2008), and medical institutions (Goodman, 2000). On schools, Sano, the Teru CGC head, explained that 'some traditional teachers see this role, of caring for the child's overall well-being, as primarily their responsibility rather than the CGC's, and are unwilling to act in a way that will compromise their relationship with the parents' (interview, 2014). On hospitals, Sano (2014, interview) noted that:

> Doctors in Japan still often don't contact CGCs when they find gonorrhoea or chlamydia in children as young as 5. They still believe that it can be passed through towels and sharing a bath as they still don't recognise that parents may be abusing their children. For example, if a teacher goes in with his five-year-old child and she has gonorrhoea they will just think, oh he's a teacher, he can't have abused her.

Sano argued that under-reporting is 'particularly acute with private hospitals, because the patients are customers, and will not come back to the hospital if they report them to the CGC' (interview, 2014).

The relationship between the CGCs and the police is improving, in part due to CGCs hiring police or ex-police officers (MHLW, 2015b: 317). There has been an increase in the number of cases reported by police to the CGCs, from 3,516 in 2007 to 37,020 in 2015,[7] an increase in the number of arrests due to abuse, from 300 in 2007 to 785 in 2015, and an increase in the number of children taken into protective custody by the police, from 1,611 in 2012 to 2,624 in 2015 (National Child Welfare Administration Division Head Meeting, 2016: 127–128). This increase is linked to the 2004 revision of the Child Welfare Act, which redefined witnessing domestic violence as child abuse: just over 40 per cent of police referrals relate to this (National Child Welfare Administration Division Head Meeting, 2016: 128).

1.4 The judiciary and parental consent

It is notable, if perhaps accidental, that in the MHLW organisational chart (Figure 3.1), family courts have been placed outside the circle of cooperation and responsibility. The judiciary very rarely plays a role in the decision-making process (Harada 2010; Kubo, 2012, 2014; Kurihara, 2011; Tsuzaki, 2008). CGCs can place a child into care where the parental rights holder has been informed and does not oppose the placement or by a court order. Courts can order a partial suspension of parental rights allowing a two-year placement into care, the suspension of all parental rights for two years, the cutting of the parental right to manage the child's assets, or the cutting of parental rights. CGCs 'can act without parental consent only in the case of temporary measures to safeguard a child.' (Goldfarb, 2012: 26).

The two-year partial and full suspension of parental rights can only be renewed when the CGC can demonstrate that the 'child will be abused, significantly neglected or extremely harmed by the parent unless the social care placement is continued' (Harada, 2010: 227).[8] Parental rights are rarely cut: Bamba and Haight note that in 2007, of 40,649 cases of reported abuse, CGCs appealed for forfeiture in four cases, of which one was successful (2011).[9] Further, even when cut parental rights can be restored (Harada, 2010).

The need for parental consent limits the CGCs' capacity to place children into care. Harada cites a 2005 study of Tokyo CGCs that found that 'parental consent was quickly or fairly easily obtained in 49.6% of cases… [and] after intensive efforts to convince parents in 31.0% of cases' (2010: 226). Harada continues:

> the plan of placement was abandoned because parental consent was not obtained or because the social workers could not even talk to the parents in 14.9% of the cases. The centres filed a petition for court approval of an involuntary placement in only 4.5% of the cases.
>
> (2010: 226–227)

Inaction sometimes results in death; the Japanese Federation of Bar Associations stated that in 2005 'CGCs were already involved in almost 20 per cent of known abuse cases that resulted in a child's death' (Goldfarb, 2013: 164). The voluntary nature of placements also limits the CGC's ability to prevent parents from removing their children from care. These issues led Kubo, the first full-time CGC lawyer, to conclude that 'the participation of the judiciary in child abuse in our country is equal to nothing' (2014: 242).

Harada (2010) argues that there are 'technical difficulties' and 'structural difficulties' in CGCs taking a legalistic approach. These include limited expertise on legal procedures and fear of damaging the relationship between the CGC and the family, which is central to facilitating family reintegration (Goldfarb, 2013; Harada, 2010; Kurihara, 2011).

Sato, a CGC caseworker, argues that the dual responsibility of investigating abuse and building a relationship with the parent to facilitate family support represents a fundamental tension for caseworkers (2009). Sato (2009) argues that for CGC staff to be able to do the 'social work' of their role, they need more support from the police (see also Kadonaga and Fraser, 2015; Yamamoto and Niiro, 2009; Yamamoto and Sato, 2008) and the judiciary (see also Kubo, 2012, 2014; Kurihara, 2011; Miyajima, 2001; Tsuzaki, 2008). The challenges this creates prompted Goldfarb to describe casework as an 'intensely emotional form of labour' (2016b; see also Kashiwame, 2011).

The need for parental consent strengthens the parents' ability to determine the placement type, with a parental preference for institutional care over foster care well documented (MHLW, 2012: 28; Tsuzaki, 2009). Fukaya et al. describe this limit on the caseworkers' discretion as 'the wall of parental rights' (2013: 33).

This 'wall' leads Saimura et al. (2002a) to argue for more involvement from the family courts in the decision-making process, though Harada notes that 'we will have to overcome many challenges, both technical and philosophical, since our child welfare system has been operating without court authority for many years' (2010: 233).[10]

The position of the courts is not unrelated to public opinion, public norms, or the beliefs of CGC caseworkers. Indeed, Goldfarb argues that there 'is a perception, among the public in general, child welfare practitioners, and family court officers, that biological parental rights to decide a child's living arrangement and eventually retain custody should guide child welfare placements' (2019: 157). While the positions of the court and the CGC are not unrelated, courts have a higher threshold for removing a child than do the CGCs (Kubo, 2012; Yoshiaki, 2000).

Ironically, judicial unwillingness to intervene in families may inhibit the capacity of CGCs to facilitate family reunification. Where the placement is voluntary the parental rights holder can remove the child at any time (Goldfarb, 2016b). This increases CGC caution over contacting the parent (Yamamoto et al., 2010) and the importance of the CGC's relationship with the parent. In Harada's words, 'if the child guidance centre's relationship with the parent is destroyed, reunification will be impossible, since there is no effective measure to encourage the parent to cooperate with the centre's services' (2010: 231).

Gilbert (2012) argues that the 'family service' orientation in alternative care is built upon a cooperative partnership.[11] In Japan, this partnership appears to be an unequal one, where the parent has the power and interventions are based upon what the parent will allow rather than what the caseworker deems necessary. The CGCs' awareness of their limited ability to facilitate family reunification serves to increase caution over removing the child and, as we shall see, apprehension about foster care.

The need for parental consent inhibits the CGCs' ability to use foster care in three ways. First, foster care can only be used where the guardian is informed and does not oppose the placement. Second, the need to gain parental consent for the placement into care makes securing this, rather than the preferred placement type, the caseworker's primary concern. Finally, the need for consent limits the number of children entering care, thus increasing competition between institutions and foster parents.

1.5 National authority and local authorities

Local policy implementation occurs within a broader context. At a national level, the key policy actors are the MHLW, the Liberal Democratic Party's (LDP) 'Committee on the future of alternative care', the National CWI Association, which has close links to the LDP committee, the National BIWI Association, and, to a lesser degree, the national associations of foster parents, family-homes, and specialist institutions.

Within the MHLW, welfare is understood as less powerful than health and labour, and within welfare, children are understood as the least powerful target group (Tsuzaki, interview, 2014). Within the MHLW, the 'Specialist Committee for the Promotion of Foster Care', established in 2012, has grown in influence and is conducting research aimed at establishing and sharing best practice on foster care (see MHLW SC 2013a, 2013b, 2014, 2015, 2016).

Changes of personnel within the MHLW, particularly the head of the MHLW Child and Family Welfare Division, impact upon policy change. Many elite interviewees pointed to the importance of two previous division heads, the first of whom introduced family-homes, a decision that one interviewee described as influenced by his 'personal views on the importance of fostering' (anonymised, 2015). The subsequent division head was also 'pro' foster care. His stewardship coincided with Ms Komiyama serving as Deputy Minister at the MHLW, who Sakakibara describes as having 'strongly supported the kicking-off of reforming children's social care' (interview, 2014).[12] This political support facilitated the MHLW Child and Family Welfare division head in passing the 2011 foster care guidelines. Similarly, Mr Shiozaki, the Minister of Health, Labour, and Welfare, is understood by advocates of change as having been central to the 2016 reforms (interviews, 2017). Change in Teru, where the CGC has strong allies within local government, suggests that support over 'two-tiers' of government is also important at a local level.

The relationship between national and local authority was succinctly explained to me by an MHLW bureaucrat, who stated that 'we don't want to be fascist, you know, or dictatorial, telling local government what they have to do' (interview, 2014), before adding that it was the responsibility of the Ministry to 'create the framework, the targets' and that it was for 'local government to address local issues using local resources' (interview, 2014).

This position is largely shared by local authorities. The head of a CGC that had seen a rapid rise in their foster care rate explained that 'the country is following a general mode of government of *chihou bunken* [decentralisation to local jurisdictions]. The way of thinking, generally speaking, is that the areas do their own planning for their own problems' (anonymised, interview, 2014). When I asked whether the MHLW should have a more direct role in local authorities that are not reforming, the CGC head responded, 'No. I just wish the local authorities would try a bit harder' (anonymised, interview, 2014). Goldfarb's account of the establishment of a 'baby-hatch' for parents to 'abandon' their children, which occurred 'in the face of then Prime Minister Abe Shinzo's emphatic disapproval' (2016b: 2), is a striking example of this local autonomy.

The MHLW does issue guidelines on the basic functions and organisation of the CGCs (see MHLW, 2016d) but these do not detail practice. Local policies are created by the local authority hall and senior CGC managers, with input from local care providers. There are echoes here of the 'collaborative policy formation' that Stoker (1991) outlines in the relationship between the US federal government and the states.

May and Winter note that 'given that municipalities are not direct arms of central government and that each is subject to a variety of political, economic, and labor market pressures, they cannot be expected to readily endorse the national goals' (2007: 462). The rejection of the one-third foster care target by local authorities, noted in Chapter 1, highlights this tension. In the words of one MHLW bureaucrat, some local authorities have submitted 'a piece of paper that they wrote because they have to, with no real meaning' (interview, 2014).[13] The gap between national policy and local practice can also be seen in the use of foster parents: 40 per cent of CGCs do not permit couples who both work to become foster parents, despite MHLW guidelines explicitly allowing this (Makimoto, 2015).

Despite the belief that local authorities should exercise discretion, several CGC staff complained that most of the directions from the MHLW come in the form of *gijutsu-teki-na jogen*, technical guidance. This is not legally binding and, in the words of one caseworker, usually contains no 'practical information on how to do these things' (interview, 2014). The caseworker gave an example of guidance on inspecting family-homes, which stated that this should occur every six months (MHLW, 2009) but included 'nothing at all about what the inspection has to be or include' (interview, 2014). When asked why this was so, the caseworker posited that the MHLW may be shirking legal responsibility of any negative outcomes of policy implementation.

Similarly, while the structure of the meetings in which the decision-making process occurs is established (MHLW, 2016d), there are no detailed national 'decision trees' to help determine when a child should be removed from the family or to help determine the placement type.[14] Some local authorities, including Yuno and Osaka, have created 'risk assessment tools' that aim to codify the decision-making process around removing a child in emergency situations, though these are only used at a local level.

This tension speaks to a broader debate on street-level bureaucrats. Where should the power to make decisions lie? Is it for the national government, local authorities, implementing organisations, or individual caseworkers to make these decisions? This debate has oscillated between seeing street-level bureaucrats as subverting the will of an elected national body, to seeing them as tailoring impersonal national policy to local issues (Hill, 2013).

The MHLW's 'technical guidance' echoes Torenvlied and Ackerman's concept of 'soft policy', which covers 'recommendations, information campaigns, and action plans rather than collectively binding decisions' (2004: 32). Hill and Hupe argue that this approach can result from 'complexity [or a] deliberate commitment to delegated discretion' (2014: 76), both of which are found here.

Where discretion is delegated, it is often counterbalanced by an independent assessment to ensure national standards. Hill, when looking at 'how guidelines affect occupational practice' (2013: 265), argues that 'there is… a need to give attention to the sanctions that follow from disregarding them' (2013: 265). Here Hill includes 'immediate reporting back to a superior…

regular collection of monitoring data... intermittent inspections... [and] attention to whether practice followed guidelines when something has gone wrong or complaints arise' (2013: 265). In the CGC there is no collection of monitoring data and no inspections. Decisions are run past superiors, who are also non-professionals, and only the most serious issues are investigated externally.[15] There is no independent national assessment body to ensure that CGCs, and indeed welfare providers, are carrying out their work to national standards.[16]

During my fieldwork, the tension between national and local authority was most visible when the CGCs felt unable to make the changes they deemed necessary to increase the use of foster care. Issues raised by CGCs included their inability to remove a child or determine placement type without parental consent, the lack of regulation for foster care and adoption agencies, and the funding structure for placements into different types of care. CGCs also raised challenges with funding de-institutionalisation, staff rotation, the lack of specialised training, and the limited involvement of courts, police, schools, and hospitals. Responding to these issues requires coordination across vertical as well as horizontal layers of government.

With some issues, including foster parent registration, local authorities can compensate for their limited authority. The national threshold for registration is low: a potential foster carer must have financial stability, be healthy enough to care for the child for the expected placement duration, complete local training, and not have been convicted of child pornography offences, child abuse, or other similar crimes.[17] This means that CGCs are obliged to register almost everyone who completes training. Here local authorities have low discretion. The caseworkers respond to this by exercising discretion in determining which of the registered foster parents have children placed with them. Staff acknowledge that this can cause heartache for foster parents left waiting for a child who will never come, but see this as a lesser evil than placing a child with unsuitable foster parents.[18] The local exercise of discretion leads to regional variation in the rate of registered foster parents who are used. In 2014, for example, Miyagi used 56.7 per cent of their 90 registered foster carers, whereas Fukui used only 19.4 per cent of their 72 registered foster parents (MHLW, 2016e).

Previous research has divided foster carers into two categories, those who can be used and those who cannot (see Miwa, 2014; Miyajima, 2001). My research resulted in three categories of registered foster carers. The first group are those considered obviously suitable. These include those with professional experience working with children and often those in 'traditional' families, with a male breadwinner and female housewife who have support from the community or extended family. These foster parents were often referred to as '*itaku dekiru sato-oya*', foster parents who you can place a child with.

The second group are those who are considered clearly unsuitable. One such foster parent had been discovered to be abusing her foster child, and a second was being investigated for fraudulently spending their foster children's inheritance. The abusive foster parent could not be de-registered as the abuse could not be proved,[19] though the couple suspected of fraud were de-registered as their acts were being investigated as a criminal matter.

I term the third group *giri giri* foster carers. The term *giri giri* is most commonly heard in baseball commentary when someone is 'just' safe or 'just' out. The ability of a CGC to use this group of foster carers is dependent on the CGC's ability to support them and on the CGC's confidence in their ability to provide this support. A confident CGC with good support systems can use more of these foster parents than one with limited capacity and confidence.

The tension between local and national authority on this issue was made explicit during a 2014 visit by an MHLW bureaucrat to the Teru CGC. During this visit a senior manager asked if Teru could register only foster parents who had the potential to be used. The MHLW bureaucrat initially replied in the affirmative. The senior manager then asked, 'But what would happen if we were sued by someone who met the national standards but who we refused to register?' The MHLW bureaucrat was reticent to respond and the matter was left unresolved.

Here the local authority can overcome its limited authority by exercising discretion elsewhere, by registering but not using foster parents. In other cases, such as obtaining parental consent, the limits on discretion are harder to challenge. Where discretion is exercised through alternate routes, the impact of the caseworker's values, norms, and the organisational culture in which they work upon policy implementation will be amplified, increasing regional variation in practice.

Sano, the Teru CGC head, argued that a language barrier had resulted in Japan's alternative care system developing in isolation, as a kind of 'Galapagos' (interview, 2014). Taking this metaphor further, local authorities appear to be developing in isolation from one another, much as biodiversity developed within the Galapagos archipelago. There is some peer-to-peer policy and practice learning, but this is undertaken only by proactive local authorities.[20]

Hayes' argument that 'the decentralized structure of Japan's adoption service has tended to limit reform efforts to a local level' (2008: 82) holds true for foster care. Despite the limitations of the local authority, for example, on parental consent, most actors are calling for increased devolution of power to facilitate the development of foster care (see Kashiwame, 2011) rather than an increased role of central government (Miyajima, 2014).

This section has outlined the *yoko-wari*, horizontal divisions, between national and local authorities. In addition to these divisions, Japanese bureaucracy has *tate-wari*, vertical divisions between siloed ministries. A third split, that is rarely discussed, is divisions over time, what I term *keiji-wari*, caused by staff rotation at all levels of government. These three divisions dissipate authority, increasing the likelihood of path-dependent change.

1.6 Organisation

A 2015 MHLW report gives a 'standard' CGC organisational structure, for a city of over 1.5 million people (2015a: 3). This distinguishes five divisions. The first is responsible for general affairs and administrative work. The second for receiving consultations and implementing the first stage of responses. The third for assessments required to begin the decision-making process, and the fourth for making and implementing the decision. The final arm is responsible for administering the temporary care facility. The CGC consultations themselves are organised into six categories: welfare, health, disability, delinquency, childrearing, and other.

The organisation of the Teru (Figure 3.2) and Irifune CGCs (Figure 3.3) differ from this model. Teru's CGC is organised into four divisions – the Children's Support, Children's Consultation, Children's Emergency Assistance, and Education Consultation divisions. The Children's Support division is split into five sections: planning, foster care promotion, and three child support sections divided by geographical area. A 'chief investigator', responsible for self-reliance plans and for liaison with welfare institutions, is also part of this division. The planning section is responsible for administration – from staff salaries to collecting money from guardians of children in care.[21] The foster care promotion section is responsible for foster care services, including support. The child support sections manage the bulk of casework within the CGC.

The Children's Consultation division is split into three sections. The first is responsible for 'general' consultations and includes a 'telephone consultation' team. The second is responsible for 'psychological consultations'.

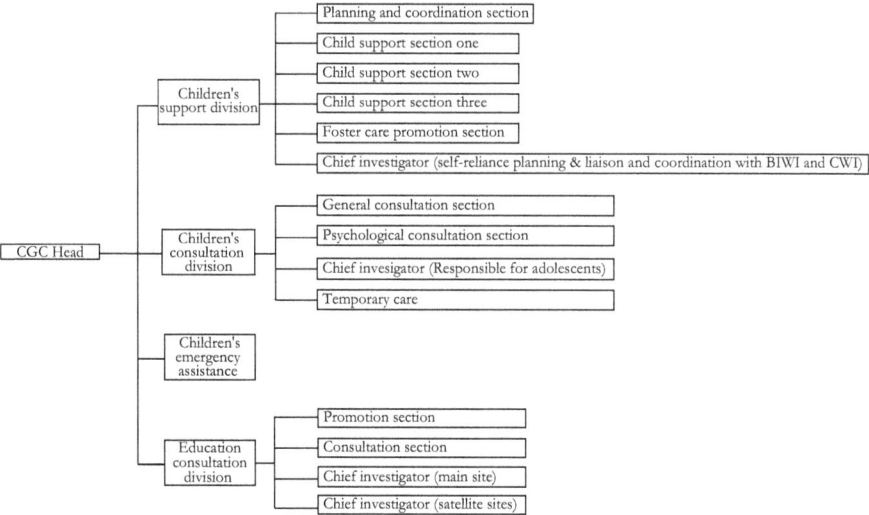

Figure 3.2 The organisation of the Teru child guidance centre.

74 *The context of alternative care*

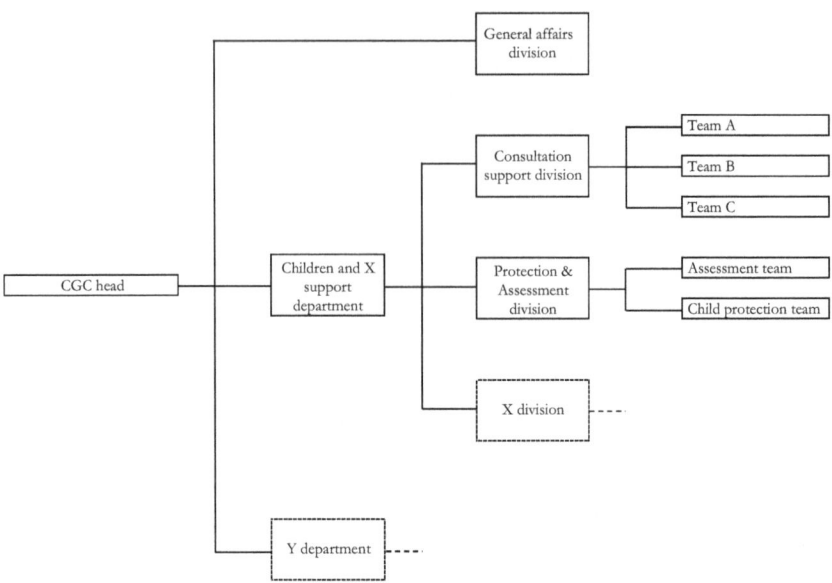

Figure 3.3 The organisation of the Irifune child guidance centre.

This includes mental health assessments for all children in temporary care, which inform the decision-making process. The third section manages the temporary care facility. This can house 40 children and is split over two floors, allowing children who need intensive support or who cannot be with the main group for other reasons to be cared for separately. Temporary care care-workers, who are on contracts, and the temporary care head are not part of the staff rotation system. The temporary care facility also employs a teacher. Finally, the 'chief investigator' responsible for adolescent issues also works in this division.

The Teru and Irifune CGCs respond differently to cases that require emergency intervention. In Teru, the Children's Emergency Assistance division manages these cases. All the caseworkers in this division are graded as section heads, reflecting the onerous nature of their work. Teru CGC is unusual in employing a full-time lawyer, who is graded as a division head and sits within the emergency assistance division. This division occasionally manages cases post-placement, though normally it transfers cases to the Children's Support division at this point. Irifune does not separate emergency interventions from 'regular' cases, with the Consultation Support division caseworkers responsible for both.

The Teru and Irifune CGCs also handle education consultations differently. In Teru, these cases are managed by the Education Consultation division. This division is split into two sections, with one managing consultations and one promoting educational support. This division employs a lot of school counsellors and 'school social workers'. In Irifune education cases are managed by the Consultation Support division caseworkers or referred to the Board of Education.

Most children entering care in Teru are processed by the Children's Consultation division and the Children's Support division. If necessary, the supervising caseworker can draw on support from staff members in any division who have relevant experience or knowledge, as well as requesting support from external actors, including the police, doctors, and municipal welfare offices.

The organisation of work in Irifune CGC is less sub-divided than it is in Teru. The Irifune CGC is part of a larger organisation that also provides support to adults. The CGC itself is divided into the Consultation Support division and the Protection and Assessment division, with administrative support from the General Affairs division.

The Consultation Support division is responsible for consultations and support, responding to child abuse, and placing children into alternative care. This division is split into three teams.[22] Within Team A and Team B, each caseworker is assigned a geographical area and one or two welfare institutions. Team C is responsible for coordinating with municipalities, supporting children in welfare institutions, and working with foster carers, family-homes, and specialist welfare institutions for children with disabilities. The Consultation Support division in Irifune undertakes the work that in Teru is carried out by the Children's Support division, the Children's Emergency Assistance division, and the Education Consultation division.

The Protection and Assessment division is split into two sections. The assessment team is responsible for assessing the psychological and physical health of children in contact with the CGC. The Child Protection team is responsible for temporary care and providing lifestyle guidance. There is also a telephone helpline for children within this division. This division is similar to Teru's Children's Consultation division. Having outlined the organisation of the Teru and Irifune CGCs, this section next discusses the people who staff them.

1.7 Staff

Within the CGCs there are senior managers,[23] supervisors,[24] caseworkers, and staff focusing on initial consultations. There are also 'specialist' staff, including child psychologists, psychiatrists, and paediatricians. Excluding temporary care staff, the two largest groups of staff are the caseworkers and the child psychologists. All CGC staff members I met worked extremely hard and for long hours, sometimes to the detriment of their own family (see Miyajima, 2001). This occasionally led to empathy for 'hard-working' single parents who were struggling to meet their children's needs.

CGC staff are predominantly local bureaucrats who move between government offices every one to five years. Staff rotation creates major challenges in developing professional expertise within CGCs (Imanishi et al., 2015; MHLW SC, 2016: 102; Miwa, 2014, 2016; Saimura et al., 2010, 2014; Takahashi et al., 2010) and weakens the potential voice of social workers for change (Tsuzaki, 2003). Despite calls to professionalise social work in the early 2000s (Goodman, 2002b), ongoing calls for increased staff training in CGCs (Fukaya et al., 2013; Kashiwame et al., 1996; Saimura et al., 2002b; Shibuya, 2005; Takahashi et al., 2010) and a 2007 MHLW report stating the need for 'well-qualified social workers' (Harada, 2013: 20), little has changed since CGCs were created (Tsuzaki, 2006).

The number of caseworkers has increased from 1,230 in 2000 to 2,924 in 2014. This increase, by a factor of 2.4, is significant but is less than the 7.6 times increase in the number of abuse cases reported to CGCs in this period (MHLW, 2016c: 4).

The Child Welfare Act establishes who is eligible to be a CGC caseworker.[25] This research classifies CGC caseworkers as street-level bureaucrats. There are two characteristics of policy implementation in the CGCs that distinguish this work from most street-level bureaucrat studies: the CGC staff's generalist status, and the power afforded to their 'clients'.

Literature on street-level bureaucrats often distinguishes 'professionals', such as doctors, from 'semi-professionals' such as social workers (DiMaggio and Powell, 1983; Evans, 2012; Freidson, 2001). While CGC caseworkers enjoy high status as government bureaucrats, they are neither professionals nor semi-professionals, but generalists. Kashiwame et al.'s (1995: 141) study on CGCs highlights the challenges this poses to the exercise of discretion:

> There is a need for appropriate procedures, and reference to these in order to comply with impartiality and fairness in government services. However, the CGC carries out the specific criteria and procedures of administration, which in reality gives them a significant amount of discretion... Under the premise that those in the CGCs were experts, we could say that this is being left to professional discretion. In order to term it professional discretion we have to be able to see a shared standard of expertise in the CGCs and it is a prerequisite that the management is standardised... This equality of expertise and service provision should occur with the CGC acting under the MHLW guidelines for how to act... However, this study has shown considerable variation in the quantity and quality of expertise in CGCs and in the way that CGCs are run.

Meyers and Vorsanger (2003), May and Winter (2007) and Hill (2013) all note the importance of 'professional norms'. Yet CGC caseworkers do not have 'professional norms' related to social work.[26] Given the lack of 'professional knowledge', it is necessary to start not with caseworkers' 'policy predispositions', as May and Winter (2007) do, but with their predispositions more generally. This approach is supported by Bradt et al.'s (2014) quantitative study on the impact of poverty on decision-making in alternative care.

Bradt et al. find that decision-making in Flanders is influenced by 'a rather dominant social, cultural and historically rooted construction of middle-class family life' (2014: 2161).

The distinction between policy predispositions and predispositions echoes Sabatier's distinction between 'deep core', 'policy core', and 'secondary beliefs' (see Sabatier and Weible, 2007), and Parsons' (1935, 1972) distinction between values and norms. Parsons (1972: 263, emphasis in original) defines norms as

> not a category of interests or desires, but a category of what in some sense is desirable. Unlike values, however, we conceive of norms as relatively specifically situation-linked... One way of putting the distinction is to say that values serve to legitimize modes of more concrete action, whereas norms serve to justify them.

Thus, in addition to exploring the context of organisational structures, in this chapter, this book also outlines the context of the caseworkers' values, in Chapter 4.

The second difference between CGC caseworkers and the typical constructions of street-level bureaucrats lies in the power relationship between the bureaucrat and the client. In Lipsky's (1980) classic study clients are understood as 'non-voluntary' and as 'only having limited resources inasmuch as the street-level bureaucrats need their compliance for effective action' (Hill, 2013: 252). Hasenfeld and Steinmetz also argue that 'the power advantage social services agencies have enables them to exercise considerable control over the lives of the recipients of their services' (1981: 85).

In almost all cases the CGCs require parental consent both to place the child into care and on the placement type. The minimal role of the judiciary means that the CGC has minimal formal power over their 'client'.

There are studies on street-level bureaucrats that operate under similar circumstances as CGC caseworkers. Mashaw's (1983) work proposes three models built upon different constructions of justice. The CGCs fit much of the 'moral judgement' model. This aims at conflict resolution, usually by independent organisations. Hill (2013: 266) notes that this model fits the work of police and other law enforcement agents, before arguing that

> The difficulties that beset the police are even more likely to apply in relation to the wide range of civil law regulatory tasks that concern officials like this – where the 'offenders' see themselves as engaged in carrying out their legitimate business, not as polluters or producers of impure food etc.

For the caseworkers, it seems likely that the parents that they see as 'offenders' may see themselves as legitimately disciplining their child or may believe that this is a domestic matter.

The 'moral judgement' model requires the enforcement of standards that are likely to be disputed, and is likely to involve 'conflicts of interest between those who are the source of the alleged problem and those who are affected by it' (Hill, 2013: 266). The fact that the child may not consider themselves to be neglected or abused, that they may rather stay with the abusive parent than enter care, or that they may have accepted their situation as normal, may cause further challenges for the caseworkers.

Mashaw (1983) argues that in these situations policy implementation could be controversial. This is more likely when there is 'an absence of unambiguous support for the enforcing agency' (Hill, 2013: 266). This leads Hill (2013: 267) to argue that

> What is often involved in these cases, given that officials need to work very closely with the objects of their regulatory activities, is a process of bargaining between regulator and regulatee... Such bargaining will not merely deal with costs and consequences, but will also be likely to take into account past behaviour... and the likely impact of any outcome on the behaviour of others. Hanf has described this process as one of 'co-production' in which the determinants of regulatory behaviour need to be seen as 'embedded in the social worlds within and outside the regulatory agency' (Hanf in Hill, 1993: 109...).

In the case of the CGCs, the voluntary nature of almost all placements is likely to result in this 'co-production' of policy. For the CGCs the 'joint-production' of policy occurs not at the regulatory level, as is often the case in Mashaw's moral judgement model, but, in a Lipskian sense, as the 'decisions of street-level bureaucrats, the routines they establish, and the devices they invent to cope with uncertainties and work pressures, effectively become the public policies they carry out' (Lipsky, 1980, pxii, emphasis in original). This approach considers the importance of the distribution of power in determining what is considered 'legitimate' or 'socially appropriate'.

In addition to their lack of 'professional' knowledge and the relative power of their clients, CGC caseworkers are also defined by their workload, the diversity of their work, and their short staff rotations.

Some CGCs seek to redress the challenges these characteristics cause. The Teru CGC tries to recruit local bureaucrats with a welfare background and is trying to improve working conditions to lengthen postings. The CGCs can also hire additional staff on rolling contracts. These are usually annual and can be renewed indefinitely. These staff sometimes support administrative work, though they are used by some CGCs to develop specialist knowledge; much of the pioneering work in Aichi prefecture, which is famous for placing new-born babies directly into adoption placements rather than into a BIWI first, has been done by a long-term contract worker. Similarly, Teru has long-term contract staff working on foster care. While these staff members are paid less than local bureaucrats, their expertise and experience are highly valued.

The most numerous of the 'specialist' staff are the child psychologists, who are also local bureaucrats. A time-study of these staff by Saimura et al. (2013) found an increasing role in responding to abuse (see also Imanishi et al., 2015). Some local authorities put child psychologists in rotation through offices that require their specialist knowledge, including public specialist welfare institutions and hospitals. Other local authorities do not make this distinction and child psychologists can be moved to any office. In Teru, the local authority hall accepted the CGC's request that child psychologists should not be moved so frequently, and placements of over ten years are not uncommon. This allows this division to acquire and retain specialist knowledge. The Teru CGC also employs a full-time lawyer, strengthening their position in relation to parents and the judiciary. Most CGCs currently consult with lawyers on a weekly, monthly, or ad-hoc basis.

Within all CGCs, there is at least one staff member responsible for foster care. In 2014 in the 207 CGCs, there were 335 foster care caseworkers, of whom 237 held a concurrent position, and 162 foster care promotion workers, of whom 37 were employed full time (MHLW, 2016a: 92). Foster care promotion workers can be employed within the CGC or in external foster care service agencies.

The lack of social work 'professional norms' increases the importance of the CGCs' training in shaping how policy is understood and implemented by staff. Formal training is conducted at the start of the fiscal year for new staff. I attended this training in the Teru CGC. This training, which in Teru lasted just over two weeks, provides an insight into the diverse work of CGCs. There were lectures on the organisational structure of alternative care, legal norms, removing a child, temporary care facilities, domestic violence, abuse, neglect, disabilities, juvenile delinquency, telephone support services, mental health support, children's rights, institutional care facilities, foster care, sex, drugs, school refusal, shut-ins, working with the police, working with schools, working with hospitals, developmental disorders, mother and child cases, BIWIs, CWIs, and the role of and relationship with municipal welfare offices. New staff also visited local BIWIs, CWIs, and specialist institutions.

Teru's training is longer than the average training. Saimura et al.'s (2000) survey, based on the responses of 42 CGCs, found that four CGCs had no training and that over half the CGCs had training that lasted half a day or one day. This work also highlights the lack of a training system tailored for different roles or experience and the absence of an evaluation of the training.

There is also informal training 'on the job'. In Teru this saw new staff auditing case meetings and being supported within their section. Informal training is integral to the transmission of office practices, norms, and culture over generations of staff. Both Teru and Irifune CGCs also had regular practical training sessions led by staff or external experts aimed at improving practice.[27]

There were many differences in the staffing of the Teru and Irifune CGCs. The most significant relates to senior management. Irifune mirrors national norms, with senior staff moved to new offices every one to three years, and had one senior manager with 15 years of accumulated CGC experience. In

80 *The context of alternative care*

the Teru CGC, the CGC head has been in this position for over a decade, the Children's Support division head has served in this CGC for over 30 years, and the Children's Emergency Assistance division head for nearly 20 years. This gives these senior managers a wealth of experience to draw on in the decision-making process, as well as time to have conceptualised and operationalised a vision of policy and practice. This experience also strengthens the CGC in relation to the welfare institutions which, in most local authorities, are understood as having more knowledge than the CGCs (Goodman, 2000).

2 The decision-making process

2.1 Overview

The decision-making process is best understood as layers of triaging, with more serious cases afforded more time at each progressive meeting. There are two main decisions made in this process: the decision to remove the child from the family, and the decision on the placement type. This section presents an overview, with differences between Teru and Irifune discussed in the later chapters.

The decision-making process begins with a *consultation*. The cases that the CGC takes on are presented at the weekly *acceptance meeting*, where the decision to place a child into temporary care is made. Once assessments have been carried out the *ruling meeting* is held to create a firmer care plan. In Teru, ongoing cases, including those of children in temporary care, are reviewed in this meeting. In Irifune these cases are reviewed in acceptance meetings. The final decision is made in the *aid objectives meeting*. The decisions are then presented at a monthly meeting of a subcommittee of the local authority's social welfare and public health committee. Representations of the Teru and Irifune CGCs' processes are shown in Figures 3.4 and 3.5, respectively.

Prior to this research, this decision-making process has remained closed, with Harada's (2010: 221) overview of the legal framework of this process the most detailed one available. Although dated, it is worth noting Ushijima and Yukawa's (1975) study, which found regional variation in the use of meetings and in how many people were involved in decisions.

2.2 Consultations

Consultations, *soudan,* are normally received by telephone and are recorded on a 'consultation summary form'. The telephone consultation team can offer words of guidance, introduce the person to another organisation, or pass the case on to the relevant CGC division. This team occasionally cannot pass on cases, for instance, when the caller does not identify themselves. Despite their exponential increase, abuse consultations accounted for just over 5 per cent of telephone consultations in Teru in 2012. In these cases, an 'abuse consultation form' is also completed.

Child guidance centres 81

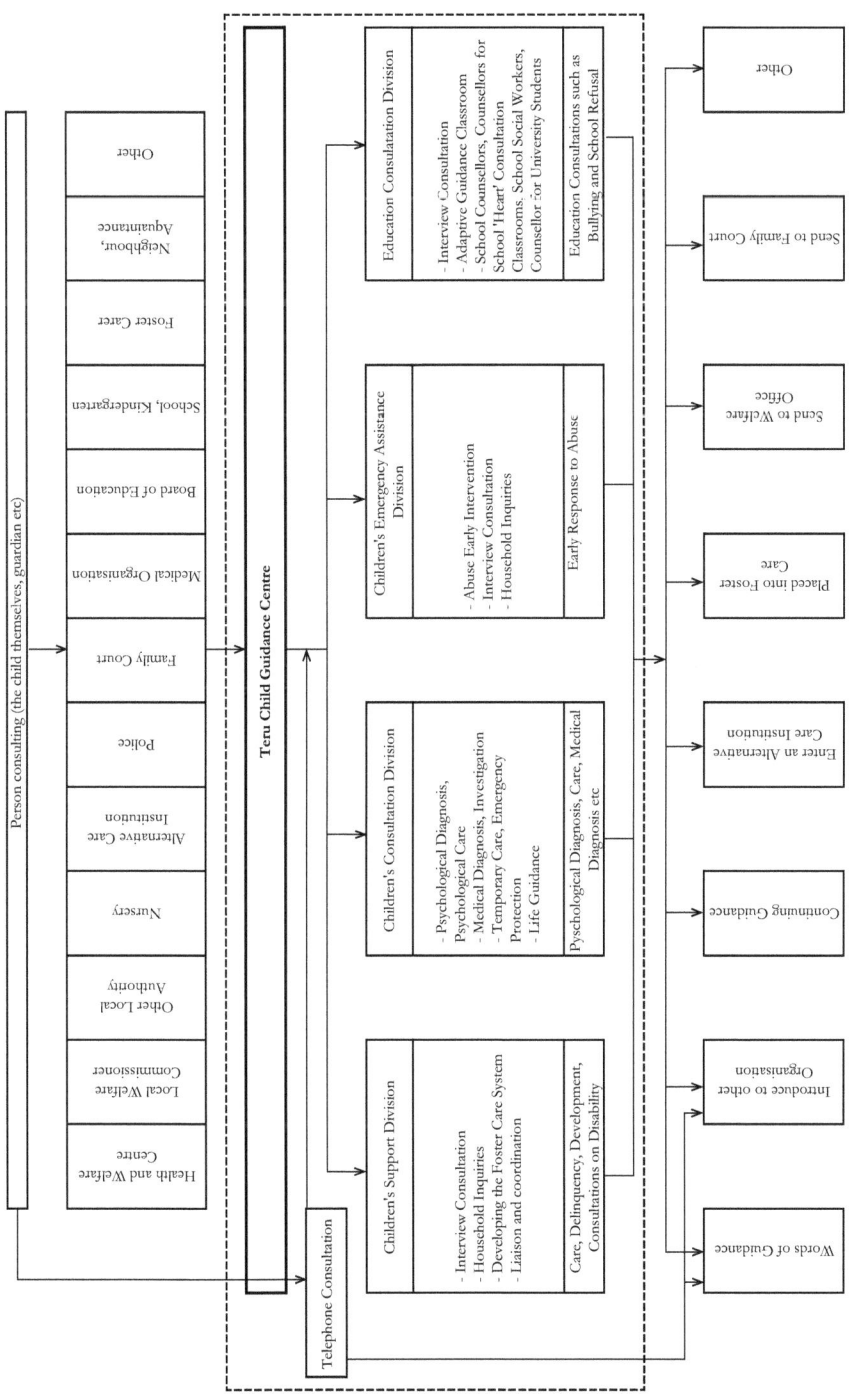

Figure 3.4 Teru child guidance centre consultation flow.

82 *The context of alternative care*

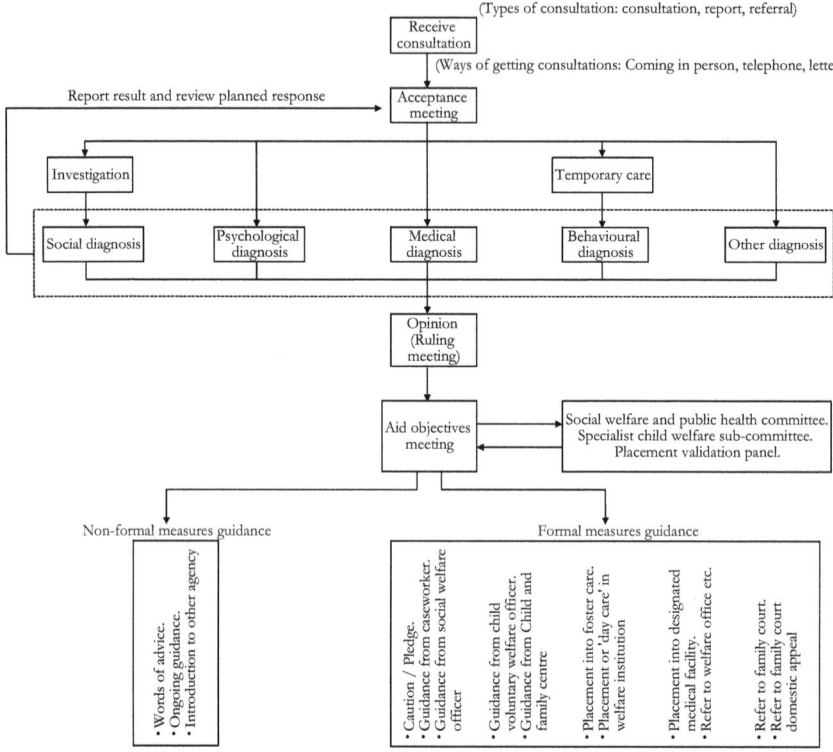

Figure 3.5 Irifune child guidance centre consultation flow.

2.3 Acceptance meeting

Cases the CGC takes on are presented at the weekly acceptance meeting, *juri-kaigi*, with immediate meetings held only for emergency cases. Emergency cases sometimes require caseworkers to enter a home, with consent, to remove a child.[28] Between 2008 and 2015, permission to forcibly enter a home had only been granted eight times nationwide (MHLW, 2015a: 33). Cases that are dealt with solely by the telephone consultation team are not presented at the acceptance meeting.

Prior to this meeting, the staff member usually discusses their anticipated response in their section or division. At the acceptance meeting the staff member outlines the case and their planned course of action, called the 'support policy'. The senior management can provide input. In Irifune all cases are managed by the Children's Consultation division. In Teru, all division heads attend this meeting to facilitate a coordinated response.

There are seven initial 'support policies' available to the Teru caseworkers. The process is similar in Irifune. The first response is to offer words of guidance to the family; where there will be no follow-up from the CGC the caseworker can ask the child's nursery, school, or hospital to report any further concerns. Caseworkers are anxious that the child should be able to send out an 'SOS' and are more cautious about children who do not leave the house regularly.

The second response is for the caseworker to continue working on the case on their own. This can involve interviews with the guardian or child and discussions with other actors. The third response is the same, but with cooperation from another division. The fourth option is to await a forthcoming assessment.

The fifth option is to place the child into temporary care. This is normally done to ensure the child's safety or allow further assessments. These assessments cover the family or care situation, the child's mental and physical health, their behaviour, and other relevant issues.[29] Temporary care is also used as 'respite care' or to 'reset' a child's relationship with their carers.

The decision to place a child into temporary care occurs without a court ruling, even if the parent is opposed to this decision. The 2007 revision of the Child Abuse Prevention Act allows CGC heads to 'restrict the guardian's visitation or communication with the child who is under temporary protection' (Harada, 2010: 225) for up to six months without court review. Harada (2010) argues that this poses a challenge to the due process of law and contravenes the UN CRC.

MHLW guidelines state that temporary care placements should last under two months. Two groups of children stay longer than this: those for whom the CGC carries out the acclimatisation period with foster parents from temporary care, rather than from a welfare institution, and those who are the most challenging to place.

The sixth 'support policy' option is to introduce the child or guardian to another welfare or support agency, such as municipal welfare offices and NPOs. The final option is 'other'. This covers cases referred to the police or family court. Most cases presented at the acceptance meeting do not enter temporary care. The ruling meeting and aid objectives meeting for these cases are usually brief.

The categorisation of the case into welfare, health, disability, delinquency, childrearing, and other (MHLW, 2015a: 1) is made during the acceptance meeting. Cases often fit multiple categories, leading to variation in classification. Cases are often assigned a secondary sub-category, with abuse recorded as an additional label.[30] These labels impact on the divisions involved with a case – a decision also made at this meeting.

2.4 Ruling meeting

Teru and Irifune use the ruling meeting, *hantei-kaigi*, differently. In Teru this meeting is used to review ongoing cases and, once assessments are complete, to propose an initial plan. In Irifune ongoing cases are reviewed in further acceptance meetings (see Figure 3.5), with the ruling meeting occurring when assessments are complete. There is no specific paperwork for the ruling meeting. The caseworker may use the 'consultation overview form' or the simpler 'progress notes form'. The supervising caseworker, CGC division heads, and the CGC head must attend this meeting, with other staff attending as required.

A second decision, called the 'processing decision', is made at the ruling meeting. This decision is provisional, with the final decision made in the aid objectives meeting. In Irifune there are 14 options (see Figure 3.5); in Teru there are 13 options, as presented below.

The first is to issue the guardian a caution, under Article 27.1.1 of the Child Welfare Act. The parent signs a 'contract' pledging to stop problematic behaviour (see Aichi Prefecture, 2011). This contract is unenforceable, and should be understood in a Foucauldian sense as a 'political technology', by which those with power try to solidify their authority by shifting discourse 'onto a sacred plain, where users are obliged to draw upon limited, and highly ritualized, sets of metaphors, references and images' (Shore and Wright, 1997: 12).

The second and fourth options are covered under Article 27.1.2 of the Child Welfare Act. The second option, used for children who have been 'badly behaved' (caseworker, interview, 2014), is for guidance from a caseworker. The fourth option is for guidance from a child welfare officer, a volunteer outside the CGC (see Goodman, 2000). Harada (2010) notes that parents are obliged, under Article 11-2 of the Child Abuse Prevention Act, to comply with this guidance. If they do not, the governor may recommend that they do, under Article 11-3 of the Child Abuse Prevention Act, but has no authority to check-up on this. If the parents still do not comply, the CGC can file for the forfeiture of parental rights under Article 11-5 of the Child Abuse Prevention Act, though this rarely happens (Harada, 2010).

The third option, for less serious cases such as those needing public benefits, is for the caseworker to transfer the case to or request support from a municipal welfare office. The fifth option is to start the process for placement with a foster parent. The sixth option is to start the process to place the child into a welfare institution. The seventh option is to start the process for a child to be an 'in-patient' at a specialist institution outside alternative care, including institutions for children with severe learning difficulties, serious mental health issues, or physical disabilities. These three options are covered under Article 27.1.3 of the Child Welfare Act.

The eighth option, for children who have committed serious offences, is to transfer the case to a family court under Article 27.1.4 of the Child Welfare Act. The court can rule that the child must enter a CWI,[31] a children's self-reliance support institution, or a juvenile detention centre, be observed at home, or that the CGC should determine the outcome. The age of responsibility, 14 years, normally determines whether a placement is made into a children's self-reliance support institution or a juvenile detention centre.[32]

The ninth option is to transfer the case to another agency or advise the person to use another agency. The tenth option is for continuing guidance from a caseworker, the eleventh is for one-off 'words of advice or guidance', and the twelfth is for the education division to start the process of admitting the child to facilities for school-refusers. These four options are non-compulsory and are termed 'non-formal' measures. The final option is simply called 'other' and includes cases referred to the police. This is distinct from option nine, as this referral is compulsory.

Cases where any placement in care is cancelled, suspended, or extended until the child is 20 years old are processed differently. Instead of a 'support policy', these cases have a simpler 'treatment policy'. There are four options here: give one-off guidance, ongoing guidance, cancellation or suspension of the placement, or 'other'.

Irifune differs slightly in that it does not have 'other' or 'education referral' categories. The Irifune CGC has an additional category for a referral to family court for appeals, and has two additional categories of guidance, from a social welfare officer, a junior CGC staff member, and from a Child and Family Centre, a municipal office that promotes family welfare.

2.5 Aid objectives meeting

The final decision is made in the aid objectives meeting, *enjo-houshin-kaigi*. These are called by the supervising caseworker. These meetings are also convened for children in care after serious incidents, such as when a child is caught shoplifting or starting fires, or when a child in care is abused or abuses others. There are two types of aid objectives meetings. The first, for more straightforward cases, are brief and process the earlier ruling meeting decision. Meetings for more complex cases can last over an hour and can involve any CGC staff with relevant experience or knowledge. Participants receive paperwork in advance.

This meeting follows a set format. The caseworker opens by stating the meeting's objectives and providing a case summary. Where present, the clinical psychologist then reports on the child, referencing paperwork that notes the IQ of the child, any recognised or suspected diagnoses, and any behavioural and emotional issues.

Additional reports, if any, are then presented. Where the child is in temporary care, the section head presents on the child's education level and their behaviour. Where a baby or infant has been placed into temporary care, in a BIWI, the caseworker presents the institution's summary of the child's behaviour and emotional state. Where relevant the caseworker will summarise the CWI's views, or the foster care caseworker will report the foster parents' position. Other staff members, including school social workers and the lawyer, can also give reports. The caseworker then presents their opinion on the outcome. Finally, the floor is opened for discussion, led by the senior management.

Any decision to take a case to court is made in this meeting. The first option is to appeal, under Article 28-1 of the Child Welfare Act, to suspend for two years the parental right to determine where the child resides.[33] Here parental consent is still required on other matters, including education and health.

For this to be granted the case must meet one of the three criteria: serious and significant abuse, serious and significant neglect, or that the removal is desirable for the child's welfare. The court is most likely to rule that removal is 'desirable' as this is less onerous than proving or stating that abuse or neglect has occurred. This echoes Hendry's finding that in Japan 'a judge seeks solutions to cases that satisfy both sides, and there is a reluctance to apply principles in which declarations are made about absolute right and wrong' (2003: 235; see also Ramseyer, 1998).

A CGC can use Article 28 to secure a foster care placement where the parent will only consent to an institution, though this is extremely rare, with the first case recorded in 2013. One CGC head stated that he believes most courts would respond 'but the parent is happy with an institution, so what's the problem with that?' (interview, 2014).

Since 2005 the CGC can apply for this partial suspension to be extended by two years, under Article 28-2 of the Child Welfare Act. Between 2005 and 2015, there were between 184 and 300 cases of Article 28-1 per year and 43 to 150 cases of Article 28-2 per year (see King, 2017: 195). Although only used in a fraction of cases, in 2015, 209 of 254 applications under Article 28-1 were approved.

Since 2012 the CGC can appeal under Civil Law Article 834-2 for the suspension of all parental rights for two years. This option is designed for when a guardian is obstructing the best interests of the child, including refusing consent for essential medical treatment (see Ministry of Justice, 2012, 2013). Of the 181 cases that were settled in 2015, 58 were successful, 26 were declined, and 94 were withdrawn (see King, 2017: 196). Since 2012 the CGC can also apply under Civil Law Article 835 to cut the parental right to manage a child's financial assets. Of the 39 cases settled since 2012, 10 cases have been successful (see King, 2017: 196).

Any actor can apply for the cutting of parental rights under Civil Law Article 834.[34] In 2015 most applications were withdrawn, with 21 of the 68 settled cases successful (see King, 2017: 196). CGC appeals are more likely to be successful than family appeals (Supreme Court 2013: 7, 2014: 7, 2015: 7). Even when cut, parental rights can be restored under Article 836 of the Civil Code.

A Tokyo family court (2012: 3, emphasis added) newsletter explained why the option to suspend all parental rights was created:

> Under the system to cut parental rights permanently, the requirements for this to be proved, and the outcome if this is proved, are very heavy. *In addition to this, after a pronouncement of parental rights being cut it*

becomes very likely that this will prove a hindrance to family reintegration. These reasons indicate that in cases of child abuse it is hard to apply for parental rights to be cut.

This highlights the courts' construction of the goal of care as family reintegration, even in the most serious abuse cases. Yoshiaki argues that this results in the courts having a higher threshold for removing children than CGCs (2000).[35]

There are several barriers to CGCs using the courts. The first is the workload and expertise required. The second is a fear of alienating the family, which could hinder the CGC's capacity to facilitate family reintegration (Harada, 2010; Kurihara, 2011). Some CGCs, including Teru, have responded to this by creating an emergency division, to separate the roles of investigation and support (see Sato, 2009).

The third barrier was expressed concisely by a senior manager in Teru, who, during a case meeting, noted that 'if we have to take it to court and they say no, then our options are very limited'. CGCs sometimes raise the possibility of court action to exert leverage over parents. The fear of the court saying 'no' stems from concerns over the family courts' limited specialist knowledge. A discussion in Teru,[36] on the potential adoption of an infant who is in foster care under Article 28-1, highlights this:

SM2: If went to court have no idea what would happen right?
CW: Yep. We have to just see and try. Any normal person would say that this kid should be adopted, but not sure what the court would say... The father just agreed with the mother... It is possible that the mother will agree for now, and then change her mind after
SM1: We need to be able to go to court for these things.
SM2: This child is going to be in foster care until 18 right, whatever happens.
CW: Yes.
SM2: In that case adoption is clearly best. If the courts were normal they should understand this, but...
CW: It is written in the UN guidelines.[37]
SM2: They don't know what foster care is, let alone the guidelines
...
SM1: We want to do adoption whilst in time [given the legal age limit of 6 on adoption].
SM2: We want to make it like "real" parents and child.

The decision by the Teru CGC to take this case to court, despite being unsure of the outcome, was made as part of a concerted effort by the Teru CGC to 'educate' the courts on the role the CGC felt they should be playing.

The final barrier to the CGCs using courts is capacity. The head of HRW in Japan, herself a noted lawyer, believes that there would need to be a manifold increase in the number of courts, judges, and lawyers, as well as specific training, for courts to be able to take on all disputed child welfare cases (interview, 2015; see also Harada, 2010; Saimura et al., 2002a). Kubo, the first full-time lawyer employed in a CGC, also calls for an increased role for the judiciary but concludes that 'given the current state of the courts, the situation of the CGC, the resources, and the legal system, what I say is no more than a dream' (2014: 249).

These barriers mean that many CGCs do not engage with the legal system at all. Kurihara (2011) found that 55.5 per cent of CGCs surveyed used Article 28-1, with 38.5 per cent using Article 28-2. Kurihara (2011) also found that under 30 per cent of CGCs or local authorities had a procedure for using Article 28.

These barriers also mean that the importance of parental consent cannot be overstated. While the parent does not attend the decision-making meetings, their opinion frames everything. The caseworker's primary concern is to secure consent for the child to enter care. The parents' ability to withhold consent for this increases the weight of their opinion on the placement type. With parental preference for institutional care well established (MHLW, 2012: 28; Tsuzaki, 2009), it is perhaps unsurprising that a 2011 survey of CGC found that the most common response to the question 'What challenges do you face to increasing the foster care rate?' was 'The natal parent or guardian does not want foster care for the child (includes refusing consent)' (78.4 per cent of CGCs) (National Child Guidance Centre Directors' Committee, 2011: 55; see also Harada, 2013; Ministry of Foreign Affairs, 1996; Miyajima, 2001).[38]

The lack of judicial involvement continues to impact cases post-placement. Discussing placements made under different labels, a caseworker (2015, interview) explained, in English, that:

> In both cases, under 'child-rearing' and under 'abuse' with agreement, a parent agrees with what he/she will do [in] a prior discussion with the CGC before returning home when the CGC places a child into care. The discussion has no legal force and a parent can remove a child even though he/she does not discuss…

The caseworker explained that the only option the CGC has here is to 'change the "formal placement" to a "temporary care placement" (…in foster care, BIWI, CWI, temporary care institution) and then apply for an approval of family court' (2015, interview), though noted that many CGCs do not do this.

The challenges faced by the CGCs in securing judicial support echo the work of Alexy, who, in relation to the legal framework that coerces people to choose 'mutual' divorces, argues that the legal structure 'does not diminish conflict in the process, but instead hides it from the court records, thereby feeding the myth that Japanese people are less litigious or conflictual' (2011: 260–261; see also Bryant, 1990).

This section has outlined the formal decision-making process. Running parallel to this is an informal system, where the caseworker seeks advice from colleagues or managers. The formal meetings represent points where discussions become decisions and allow senior management the opportunity to challenge and redirect care-plans. Regional variation here is discussed in Chapter 6.

3 Conclusions

There are two points to raise in concluding this chapter. The first is that the gap between entering care and not is, in the words of one CGC head, 'a cliff-edge' (interview, 2014). The limited support offered to children not taken into care, which a second CGC head described as 'in reality very limited' (interview, 2015), means that a decision not to place a child into care often sees them returned to abusive households (Yamamoto et al., 2009, 2013). This led two CGC heads to argue the need for a 'more graduated set of care support services' (interviews, 2014, 2015). The lack of 'middle-ground' placements contributes to the low rate of children entering care.

A further contributing factor here is the challenge of accessing children in need. Sano believed this to be particularly true for youths aged 15 to 17 and estimated that there are many thousands of youths in need who are not in contact with CGCs. This group is, Sano noted, vulnerable to sexual exploitation (see also Osaki, 2014).[39] This is supported by the 2016 MHLW report on the response of CGCs to child prostitution and pornography, which found that many children did not approach CGCs as they were apprehensive of their response (MHLW, 2016f).

The second point to raise in this conclusion is the absence of the child's voice in the decision-making process. Despite Japan's ratification of the UN CRC, a core principle of which is children's participation in decisions that affect their lives, there are only a few situations where the child's voice is given weight. The first of these is where the child is older and must decide whether they will stay in school or seek employment, which entails moving to a self-reliance assistance home.[40] The second is when the child has been in alternative care for a long time and is aware of the differences between welfare institutions, and of their capacity to disrupt placements to force a move. It is rare for a younger child's voice to be given serious consideration. It is possible that Nussbaum's description of how 'habit, fear, low expectations and unjust background conditions deform people's choices and even their wishes for their own lives' (2000: 114) partly informs why the lack of voice has not been problematized by children in care or by most care-leavers.[41] The absence of the child's voice may result from a limited awareness of or scepticism about the child's right to a voice (see Aspinall, 2016), or may relate to a lack of confidence in CGCs in their ability to deliver what the child wants.

Perversely, given the courts' prioritisation of family reintegration, the lack of judicial involvement actually weakens the CGCs' ability to involve the parent in the decision-making process and to facilitate family-reintegration. Without legal support, the caseworkers cannot engage the parents as part of a 'team'. This often results in children being left in placements for many years for fear of 'awakening' parents who they cannot control. This further steepens the 'cliff-edge' of a placement into care.

The alternative care system operates largely on the creation of expectations on role performance: from the MHLW to local authorities, in foster care targets and in 'technical guidance' rather than legally binding policy; from the CGCs to parents, who are 'are taught ways to behave' (Hill, 2013: 252, referencing Hasenfeld and Steinmetz, 1981), to consent to their child entering care, to consent to the desired placement, and to promise not to continue abusing their child; and from the CGCs to the welfare institutions, to reform and promote foster care.

The lack of legal recourse or support undermines the ability of the caseworkers to act in the best interest of the child. It also means that local authorities cannot effect policy change based on ideals such as rights, instead of remaining bound by realities such as parental consent. The lack of legal support appears to extend to the top, with one MHLW bureaucrat commenting that the Ministry of Justice 'do not want to touch this problem at all' (interview, 2015).

These factors combine to create a plasticity in the decision-making process, in which the caseworker's discretion is critical. This book next turns to investigate this discretion more closely, looking at the values that underpin it (Chapter 4), the resources that shape and confine it (Chapter 5), the norms of the caseworker that determine how it is used (Chapter 6) and the organisational culture that moulds it (Chapter 7). These factors are understood as interactive: resources impact upon beliefs and beliefs impact upon resources, with organisational culture mediating this interaction and influencing both resources and beliefs. Chapter 8, the concluding chapter, draws these threads together and considers the policy implications of this research.

Notes

1 One CGC I visited ran a 'classroom' for school refusers and an 'open-room' for youth refusing to attend university.
2 A 2017 MHLW committee white paper calls for the strengthening of expertise of practitioners and for more role specialisation within CGCs (MHLW NWAC, 2017). This could represent the first step in reforming 'social work' or, conversely, may represent a small refinement of the status quo. This will be an important area for future research.
3 Concerns over the family also relate to the increased number of women working, divorces and family disassociations, and single parents, as well as the falling total fertility rate. These societal level changes contribute to the ongoing re-evaluation of the family and the household.

4 These beliefs may partly stem from these researchers conducting the bulk of their fieldwork in more 'progressive' CWIs.
5 There are variations here: Yuno has an office between the CGCs and the local authority hall that does all the 'shared' work of the CGCs, including foster care recruitment and administration.
6 I saw two exceptions to this. In both instances, in Teru, the CGC invited a CWI head to discuss the CWI's desire to transfer a child to foster care.
7 In 2015, these cases are approximately 30 per cent of all CGC abuse cases.
8 Harada (2010) notes the paradox that while involuntary placements into care, which are often for serious abuse, have a two-year limit and require the CGC to pursue family reintegration, voluntary placements have no time-limit.
9 Academic literature suggests there are institutional factors that mean legal interventions are rare in Japan (see Ginsberg and Hoetker, 2006; Hill, 2003; Kanazawa and Miller, 2000; Mouer and Sugimoto, 2002; West, 2011).
10 Harada highlights that the lack of judicial oversight cuts both ways, with current procedures 'insufficient to provide due process of law for the guardian' (2010: 224).
11 This is discussed more fully in Chapter 6.
12 A position shared by Tsuzaki (interview, 2014).
13 I do not attach any normative evaluation to this. These local authorities may have decided to focus their limited resources on reforming practice in another area, such as abuse prevention. Equally, it is not clear that local authorities with a high foster care rate are 'good'. Several interviewees expressed concern over Niigata, which has the highest foster care rate, because at 7.6 children per 10,000, Niigata has the lowest rate of placing children into care.
14 There are two kinds of cases where more concrete decision trees exist: for moderate to severe disability, where thresholds in IQ determine access to services, and where the child is criminally culpable and the CGC must refer the case to a court. These cases fall outside the alternative care system.
15 This normally only occurs when a child known to the CGC dies.
16 Recent interest in the role of OFSTED in the UK suggests that this issue is under consideration.
17 Some local authorities do not run police checks.
18 This definitely is not to suggest that all foster parents without children are considered unsuitable.
19 The CGC head expressed concern that this foster parent, who was moving outside the local authority, was likely to register in their new local authority. Senior politicians are currently discussing the creation of a national child protection register to ensure that children who move local authorities are not lost to the system, though this would not cover foster parents such as this one.
20 There is a National Association of CGC heads, but this appears to have limited influence. There is also a smaller association for CGC heads in the designated cities, which one CGC head described to me as being more dynamic.
21 As this is based on income, most guardians have no liability or are supposed to pay a token contribution. In one local authority I visited, a local bureaucrat estimated that 20 per cent of parents, those protected under the public assistance act, had no financial contribution, 30 per cent of parents, those exempt from paying municipal tax, paid 2,200 yen per month, with a further 20 per cent paying 4,500 or 6,600 yen per month (see King, 2017: Appendix 5 for details). Parents have no financial liability for placements under Article 28 or when parental rights are suspended or cut, as they have not consented to the placement. The local bureaucrat explained that 'to a degree it saves... the local authority the money it costs to follow up the parents for money as unlikely to pay' (interview, 2015). The bureaucrat continued,

> Many people want their child back from CWI/BIWI as they lose their child allowance when in care and they would then stop having to pay fees for CWI. Caseworkers say, it will cost you the same right, if child comes back costs money, but they either don't think about that, is just about incoming money, or they don't use the money on the kids. Some refuse to give consent as they say they can't pay fees.
>
> (interview, 2015)

22 There is no difference between a section, *kakari*, in Teru and a team, *han*, in Irifune.
23 I use this term to refer to the CGC head and division heads.
24 I use this term to refer to section/team heads.
25 Articles 13-2-1 to 13-2-5. The term caseworker does not constitute a 'professional' qualification.
26 It is quite likely that caseworkers are affected by 'professional norms' of the Japanese bureaucracy.
27 These were more frequent and better attended in Teru than in Irifune.
28 There is usually no police support. For particularly severe cases four bureaucrats enter a home: one to protect the child, two to restrain the guardian, and one to prevent access to knives. The CGC is more likely to request police support if a guardian is a gang member or is violent. One example was of a father who had brandished a machine gun at police.
29 These assessments can also be carried out for children not in temporary care who require further meetings, for example, children returning home from care who were placed due to abuse.
30 Abuse is split into four categories – physical abuse, psychological abuse, neglect, and sexual abuse – listed here in order of prevalence.
31 Children who have committed serious offences being 'sentenced' to CWI may contribute to an image of children in alternative care as responsible for their present situation. Some interviewees noted the stigma this can cause and questioned putting children 'convicted' of serious offences into institutions with children who have suffered similar offences.
32 Juvenile detention centre placements are made under the Juvenile Act.
33 Parental rights are divided into two categories: the right to manage assets, and the right to personally supervise. The right to determine the child's residence falls under supervision.
34 CGC heads can also apply for this under Article 33-8 of the (1947) Child Welfare Act.
35 The need for a higher burden of proof also inhibits police involvement.
36 All quotations from meetings are taken from the simultaneous translation I made at the time. The syntax is not perfect. This reflects my translating/typing speed and the practice in spoken Japanese of omitting the sentence subject. Additional notes or clarifying words added post facto are enclosed in square brackets. SM stands for senior manager, CW for caseworker
37 This was one of only three cases where reference was made to international standards. It is possible the reference relates to the timing of this case, which came a few days after HRW's damning report on Japanese alternative care.
38 Parents occasionally go further than refusing consent: Saimura et al.'s (2001) study reported death threats and incidents in the homes of CGC staff members.
39 In a (2014) CGC lecture, Watanabe, a juvenile delinquent centre head, spoke in depth about this issue. Watanabe explained that girls, who make up around 10 per cent (292 of 2498 children) of the juvenile detention population, had a higher incidence of drug use, which Watanabe said is associated with sexual

exploitation, and were more likely to have been involved with gangs. Watanabe stated that:

> The girls said that the sex trade is best in junior high school as you make the most money. They can't work formally until 18 so end up getting associated with gangs... The girls know how much they would get paid for different things in different prefectures. Get a lot of information from internet and get connected to various people. They go on 'holiday' with people – do actually go on holiday but also obviously have sex with them.

Watanabe reported that of 26 girls in one detention centre, '15 had been the victim of violent attacks, 19 had been the victim of sexual attacks, 19 had sold themselves for sex, and 9 had introduced another girl to this kind of work.' Following this lecture, a senior CGC manager explained to me that:

> In Japan it is very common for high school, junior high school, and even elementary school girls to exchange sex for money, and to live on that money. It is often linked with the yakuza and the police response is always relatively gentle. It is very hard to prosecute, very hard for the girl to testify... When these cases come up they are not particularly newsworthy and the public reaction is not so big. Sadly, it seems to be relatively socially accepted. The girl we discussed the other day had been sexually exploited since at least sixth grade of elementary school and potentially even earlier.

Newspapers have covered issues such as mobile phone applications, including one of a CWI care-worker who had bought sex from a junior high school girl he met using an application (Yomiuri shinbun, 2015). There has also been a proliferation of services facilitating child sexual exploitation including paying to 'go for a walk' with a child, during which other 'services' can be negotiated. The companies that organise these services are publicly visible and are usually known to the police and CGCs.

Sexual exploitation is sometimes linked to the production of child pornography. Despite international concerns over the creation and distribution of child pornography in Japan (UN General Assembly, 2016) and a slight increase in political attention, visible in a cabinet office (2014) symposium, convictions for child pornography are extremely rare. Further, there remains a 'grey' area, of DVDs and books of young children scantily dressed, and legal explicit child abuse images in anime and manga. The first criminal case of human trafficking for the production of child pornography, under the 1999 anti-child pornography law, did not occur until May 7th, 2015 (Lighthouse Project, 2015).

40 Even here the child's preference is not always respected. An aid objectives meeting for one such case had to be rushed forwards as the child's high school was very strict on attendance and would not take into consideration the fact that the child was in temporary care. The child strongly expressed their desire to stay in school. The caseworker was apprehensive about this, as a placement in the self-reliance assistance home could more easily be extended until the child was 20 than a placement in the CWI, which would probably end when the child was 18 and finished high school. The caseworker feared that if the child did not complete high school they could end up with nowhere to live and no support, as a placement into the self-reliance assistance home can only be made before the child turns 18. The senior managers sided with the caseworker and the child was placed into a self-reliance assistance home, had to leave school, and commenced part-time work.

41 Midori Nakamura, founder of the care-leavers group CVV (Children's Views and Voices) and a member of an MHLW specialist committee on alternative care, is a notable exception here (see also Watai, 2010).

References

Abe, T. (2014). Shichōson jidōsōdanjyo no yakuwari. Kodomo-tachi no sodachi ni okeru shakai-teki kea to kazoku no yakuwari [The role of the municipality and the child guidance centre. Symposium: Social Care and the family's role in raising children]. *Nihon Shakai Fukushi Gakkai.*

Aichi Prefecture. (2011). *Aichi ken jidousoudansenta- dayori* [Aichi Prefecture child guidance centre newsletter] 55. 2011, July 25. Aichi: Aichi Prefectural Government.

Alexy, A. (2011). The door my wife closed: Houses, families, and divorce in contemporary Japan. In R. Ronald, & A. Alexy (Eds.), *Home and family in Japan: Continuity and transformation.* London: Routledge.

Aspinall, R.W. (2016). Children's rights in a risk society: The case of schooling in Japan. *Japan Forum,* 28(2), 135–154.

Bamba, S., & Haight, W. (2007). Helping maltreated children to find their ibasho: Japanese perspectives on supporting the well-being of children in state care. *Children and Youth Services Review,* 29, 405–427.

Bamba, S., & Haight, W. (2009a). The developmental–ecological approach of Japanese child welfare professionals to supporting children's social and emotional well-being: The practice of mimamori. *Children and Youth Services Review,* 31, 429–439.

Bamba, S., & Haight, W. (2009b). Maltreated children's emerging well-being in Japanese state care. *Children and Youth Services Review,* 31, 797–806.

Bamba, S., & Haight, W. (2011). *Child welfare and development: A Japanese case study.* Cambridge: Cambridge University Press.

Bradt, L., Roets, G., Roose, R., Rosseel, Y., & Bouverne-De Bie, M. (2014). Poverty and decision making in child welfare and protection: Deepening the bias–need debate. *The British Journal of Social Work,* 45(7), 2161–2175.

Bryant, T.L. (1990). Sons and lovers: Adoption in Japan. *The American Journal of Comparative Law,* 38(2), 299–336.

Cabinet office. (2014). *Jidō poruno haijo taisaku kōkai shinpojiumu* [Public symposium on child pornography elimination measures]. Retrieved from URL: http://www8.cao.go.jp/youth/cp-taisaku/bosyu/symposium5-entry.html (last accessed 2014, December 24).

Campbell, J.C. (2002). Japanese social policy in comparative perspective. *World Bank Institute working papers.* Washington: The International Bank for Reconstruction and Development/The World Bank.

Child Welfare Act. (1947). Act No. 164 of 1947, December 12.

DiMaggio, P., & Powell, W.W. (1983). The iron cage revisited: Collective rationality and institutional isomorphism in organizational fields. *American Sociological Review,* 48(2), 147–160.

Estevez-Abe, M. (2008). *Welfare and capitalism in postwar Japan.* Cambridge: Cambridge University Press.

Evans, T. (2012). Organisational rules and discretion in adult social work. *British Journal of Social Work,* 43(4), 739–758.

Freidson, E. (2001). *Professionalism: The third logic.* London: Polity Press.

Fukaya, F., Fukaya, M., & Aoba, A. (2013). *Shakai-teki yōgo ni okeru satooya mondai e no jisshō-teki kenkyū — yōiku satooya zenkoku ankēto chōsa wo moto ni* [Empirical study on issues on foster parents in alternative care: Based on a nationwide questionnaire survey of normal foster parents]. Tokyo: Fukumura Publishing.
Gilbert, N. (2012). A comparative study of child welfare systems: Abstract orientations and concrete results. *Child and Youth Services Review*, 34, 532–536.
Ginsberg, T., & Hoetker, G. (2006). 'The unreluctant litigant?' An empirical analysis of Japan's turn to litigation. *Journal of Legal Studies*, 35, 31–59.
Goldfarb, K. (2012). *Fragile kinships: Family ideologies and child welfare in Japan.* (Doctoral dissertation). The University of Chicago.
Goldfarb, K. (2013). Japan. In P. Welbourne, & J. Dixon (Eds.), *Child protection and child welfare: A global appraisal of cultures, policy, and practice*. London: Jessica Kingsley Publishers.
Goldfarb, K. (2016a). Family at the margins: State, welfare and well-being in Japan. *Japanese Studies*, 36(2), 151–154.
Goldfarb, K. (2016b). *Anonymity, ancestry, and family registry: Adoption debates in contemporary Japan*. Conference paper for 2016 Association for Asian Studies, Seattle.
Goldfarb, K. (2019). Embodied relationality beyond 'nature' vs 'nurture': Materializing absent kinships in Japanese child welfare. In S. Bamford (Ed.), *The Cambridge handbook for the anthropology of kinship*. Cambridge: Cambridge University Press.
Goodman, R. (1999). The entrepreneurial children's home: Approaches to the study of the Japanese child welfare system. *IDS Bulletin*, 30(4), 71–81.
Goodman, R. (2000). *Children of the Japanese state: The changing role of child protection institutions in contemporary Japan*. Oxford: Oxford University Press.
Goodman, R. (2002a). Anthropology, policy and the study of Japan. In R. Goodman (Ed.), *Family and social policy in Japan*. Cambridge: Cambridge University Press.
Goodman, R. (2002b). Child abuse in Japan: 'Discovery' and the development of policy. In R. Goodman (Ed.), *Family and social policy in Japan*. Cambridge: Cambridge University Press.
Goodman, R. (2012). The 'discovery' and 'rediscovery' of child abuse (*jido gyakutai*) in Japan. In R. Goodman, Y. Imoto, & T. Toivonen (Eds.), *A sociology of Japanese youth: From returnees to NEETs*. London: Nissan Institute/Routledge Japanese Studies.
Harada, A. (2010). The Japanese child protection system: Developments in the laws and the issues left unsolved. *International Survey of Family Law*, Vol. 2010, pp. 217–236.
Harada, A. (2013). Children in need of permanent families: The current status of and future directions for the Japanese foster care system. *Illinois Child Welfare*, 6(1), 14–29.
Hasenfeld, Y., & Steinmetz, D. (1981), Client-official encounters in social service agencies. In C.T. Goodsell (Ed.), *The public encounter*. Bloomington: Indiana University Press.
Hayes, P. (2008). Special adoption in Japan: Its problems and prospects. *Adoption Quarterly*, 11(2), 81–100.
Hendry, J. (2003). *Understanding Japanese society*. London: Routledge.
Hill, M. (2013). *The public policy process*. London: Routledge.

Hill, M., & Hupe, P. (2014). *Implementing public policy: An introduction to the study of operational governance.* London: Sage.

Hill, P. (2003). *The Japanese mafia: Yakuza, law, and the state.* Oxford: Oxford University Press.

Imanishi, R., Arimura, T., Kimura, Y., Kurihara, T., Nagano, S., Shimizu, F., ... Kataoka, S. (2015). Jidōsōdanjyo ni okeru jidō shinri tsukasa no senmon-sei ni kansuru kenkyū (sono 1) [Research on the specialist knowledge of caseworkers in the child guidance centres (1)]. *Nihon Shakai Fukushi Gakkai,* 73–74.

Japan Child Welfare Association. (2005). Nihon jidō fukushi kyōkai. Kodomo katei no sōdan enjo wo suru tame ni ~ shichōson jidō katei sōdan enjo shishin jidōsōdanjyo un'ei shishin ~ [To support consultations on children and family: Guidelines for municipal child and family consultation support and guidelines for child guidance centres]. Tokyo: Zaidanhōjin Nihon jidō fukushi kyōkai.

Kadonaga, T., & Fraser, M.W. (2015). Child maltreatment in Japan. *Journal of Social Work,* 15(3), 233–253.

Kanazawa, S., & Miller, A.S. (2000). *Order by accident: The origins and consequences of conformity in contemporary Japan.* Boulder: Westview.

Kashiwame, R. (2011). Iken shakai-teki yōgo no kinmirai chūchōki taisaku no gurando dezain no hitsuyō-sei to kinmirai taisaku no jitsugen [The near future of alternative care: The need for a medium-term policy and grand design, and for realising policy in the short term]. *Jidō yōgo shisetsu-tō no shakai-teki yōgo no kadai ni kansuru kentō iinkai.*

Kashiwame, R., Nakatani, S., Hayashi, S., & Amino, T. (1995). Jidōsōdanjyo no unnei bunseki [Analysis of child guidance centres' operations]. *Nihon sōgō aiiku kenkyū kiyō,* 32, 137–147.

Kashiwame, R., Nakatani, S., Amino, T., & Hayashi, S. (1996). Jidōsōdanjyo senmon shokuin no shitsumu bunseki [Analysis of the child guidance centres' office works]. *Nihon sōgō aiiku kenkyū kiyō,* 33, 173–194.

Kashiwame, R., Arimura, T., Nagano, S., Mayumi, S., Ogi, M., Shibuya, M., ... Kawamatsu, R. (2012). Kodomo katei fukushi gyōsei jisshi taisei no saikōchiku ni kansuru kenkyū — sai kōchiku ni kansuru kore made no kentō ikisatsu to shōrai hōkō — [A study on reconstruction centred municipalities child and family welfare administration systems: Consider the future direction of the system reconfiguration from the previous discussions]. *Nihon-kodomo katei sōgōkenkyūsho kiyō,* 49, 1–14.

Kato, Y. (2014). Jidōsōdanjyo ga kakaeru jidō gyakutai mondai wo motsu kazoku no tokuchō ni kansuru kenkyū - 2004-nen 2009-nen no jidō gyakutai jittai chōsa no ni-ji bunseki wo tōshite [A study on the characteristics of families with abuse working with the child guidance centres: Based on two surveys, in 2004 and 2009]. *Nihon Shakai Fukushi Gakkai,* 155–156.

King (nee Rivera King), M. (2017). *Child guidance centres in Japan: Rregional variation in policy implementation and the family-bond.* (Doctoral dissertation). The University of Oxford.

Kubo, K. (2012). Jidōsōdanjyo ni jōkin suru bengoshi no nichijō to bengoshi jōkin no yūyō-sei [Employment of full-time lawyer at child guidance centre: Daily job and its merit to child protection]. *Kodomo no gyakutai to negurekuto,* 14(3), 340–346.

Kubo, K. (2014). Gyakutai taiō ni okeru kadai to kon'nan: jidōsōdanjyo no bengoshi no tachiba kara [The difficulties and challenges in the corresponding abuse: From the standpoint of full-time lawyer of child guidance centre]. *Kodomo no gyakutai to negurekuto*, 16(3), 242–249.

Kurihara, N. (2011). Jidō fukushi-hō dai 28-jō tekiyō no genjō to kadai ni tsuite: jidōsōdanjyo no genjō to kadai [The current state and challenges around the use of Article 28 of The Child Welfare Act: The current state and challenges of the child guidance centres]. *Nihon Shakai Fukushi Gakkai*, 23–24.

Lighthouse Project. (2015). *Lighthouse Newsletter 19*. 2015, April 28.

Lipsky, M. (1980). *Street-level bureaucracy: The critical role of street-level bureaucrats*. New York: Russell Sage Foundation.

Makimoto, M. (2015). *Satooya seido fukyū habamu 'kabe'* [A 'wall' limiting the expansion of foster care]. [NHK News Report, 2015, July 07]. Retrieved from URL: http://www3.nhk.or.jp/news/web_tokushu/2015_0507.html (last accessed 2015, December 28).

Mashaw, J. (1983). *Bureaucratic justice: Managing social security disability claims*. New Haven: Yale University Press.

May, P.J., & Winter, S.C. (2007). Politicians, managers, and street-level bureaucrats: Influences on policy implementation. *Journal of Public Administration Research and Theory*, 19, 453–476.

Meyers, M.K., & Vorsanger, S. (2003). Street-level bureaucrats and the implementation of public policy. In B.G. Peters, & J. Pierre (Eds.), *Handbook of public administration*. Thousand Oaks: Sage.

MHLW. (2009). *Kōsei rōdōshō koyō kintō jidō katei kyokuchō tsūchi shōkibo jūkyogata jidō yōiku jigyō no un'ei ni tsuite* [MHLW Equal Employment Head and Director of Child and Family Bureau: Correspondence No. 0331011. On the management of small-scale residential-type child care businesses]. 2009, March 31.

MHLW. (2011). *Equal opportunities and child welfare (including current status of child welfare facilities, etc.)*. Retrieved from URL: http://www.mhlw.go.jp/english/wp/wp-hw9/dl/07e.pdf (last accessed 2017, August 25).

MHLW. (2012). *Shakai-teki yōgo no genjou ni tsuite (sanka shiryou)*. [Current status of alternative care (reference)]. 2012, September.

MHLW. (2015a). *Shakai hoshou shingikai jidō bukai dai 2-kai aratana kodomo katei fukushi no arikata ni kansuru senmon iinkai, jidōsōdanjyo kankei shiryou* [Specialist Committee on New Methods of Child and Family Welfare. 2015, November 11 meeting. Reference materials (5) related to child guidance centres. (Social security council children's sub-committee)].

MHLW. (2015b). *Heisei 27-nendo zenkoku jidō fukushi shukan kachō jidōsōdanjyo-chō kaigi shiryō (Heisei 27-nen 10 tsuki 8-nichi) sonota kanren shiryō 1. Jidōsōdanjyo kankei dēta* [Meeting materials for 2015 National Child Welfare Administration Division Head, Child Guidance Centre Head meeting. Other related documents. 1. Data related to child guidance centres]. 2015, October 8.

MHLW. (2016a). *Shakai-teki yōgo no genjou ni tsuite (sanka shiryou)* [Current status of alternative care (reference)]. 2016, January.

MHLW. (2016b). *Shakai-teki yōgo no genjou ni tsuite (sanka shiryou)* [Current status of alternative care (reference)]. 2016, July.

MHLW. (2016c). *Shakai teki yōgo no kadai to shourai zou no jitsugen ni mukete* [On the challenges and realising the future form of alternative care]. 2016, January.

MHLW. (2016d). *Jidōsōdanjyo un'ei shishin ni tsuite* [Letter to all governors, and mayors of designated cities. From the MHLW Children and Family Bureau

Director: On child guidance centre guidelines. Correspondence No. 0929-1]. 2016, September 29.
MHLW. (2016e) *Fukushi gyōsei hōkoku rei (etsuran jidō dai 13-hyō satooya-sū, todōfuken – shitei toshi – chūkaku-shi × shinki – torikeshi-betsu* [Welfare administration reported cases. Data sheet 13 – The number of foster carers, the number of children placed into foster care, by prefecture, designated city, and core city].
MHLW. (2016f). *Heisei 27-nendo kodomo kosodate shien suishin chōsa kenkyū jigyō 'jidōsōdanjyo ni okeru jidōkaishun, jidō poruno higai jidō e no taiō jōkyō ni kansuru kenkyū' hōkoku-sho* [2015 research project on children and childrearing promotion. Research on the response of child guidance centres to victims of child prostitution and child pornography]. 2016, March. Retrieved from URL: http://lhj.jp/wp-content/uploads/2016/06/jisorepo_web_20160531original.compressed.pdf (last accessed 2017, August 24).
MHLW Investigation Committee on the New Way of Alternative Care (MHLW NWAC). (2017). (*Aratana shakai-teki yōiku no arikata ni kansuru kentōkai*). *Atarashī shakai-teki yōiku bijon* [The new vision of alternative care]. 2017, August.
MHLW Specialist Committee for the Promotion of Placements into Foster Care (MHLW SC). (2013a). (*Zenkoku satooya itaku-tō suishin iinkai). Satooya-tō itaku-ritsu appu no torikumi hōkoku-sho ~ itaku-ritsu wo ōkiku zōka saseta Fukuoka-shi Ōita ken no torikumi yori ~* [Report on efforts to increase the foster care rate: The efforts of Fukuoka City and Oita Prefecture, which have greatly increased foster care placements]. 2015, February.
MHLW SC. (2013b). *Satooya famirīhōmu yōiku shishin handobukku* [Foster parent and family home child rearing pointers handbook]. 2015, March.
MHLW SC. (2014). *Satooya shien senmon sōdan-in oyobi satooya shien kikan no katsudō, satooya saron katsudō ni kansuru. Chōsa hōkoku.* [On specialist counsellor for foster care support [in Baby and Infant Welfare Institutions and Child Welfare Institutions], the activities of foster care service providers, and the activities of foster care 'salons'. Research report]. 2014, February.
MHLW SC. (2015). *Heisei 26-nendo chōsa hōkoku-sho. Satooya saron un'ei manyuaru, satooya kenkyū de gurūpu enshū wo okonau fashiritētā no tame ni, itaku suishin no tame no kiban-dzukuri no senshin-tekina torikumi, satooya rikurūto ni kansuru chōsa hōkoku-sho (chūkan hōkoku)* [2014 Survey report. Manual for running foster care salons, support for facilitators running group exercises in foster care training, advanced initiatives to establish a foundation to promote [foster care] placements, survey report on foster care recruitment (interim report)]. 2015, March.
MHLW SC. (2016). *Heisei 27-nendo chōsa hōkoku-sho. Satooya katei no zenkoku jittai chōsa hōkoku, itaku sareta kodomo no jōcho to kōdō no mondai ni kansuru chōsa hōkoku, satooya rikurūto chōsa hōkoku-sho* [2015 Survey report. Nationwide survey report on foster care households, survey report on the emotional and behavioural issues faced by children in [foster care] placements, and survey report on foster care recruitment]. 2016, March.
Ministry of Foreign Affairs. (1996). *The initial report of Japan under article 44, paragraph 1 of the convention on the rights of the child.* 1996, May 30. Retrieved from URL: http://www.mofa.go.jp/policy/human/child/initialreport/care.html (last accessed 2016, May 16).
Ministry of Justice. (2012). *Minpō-tō no ichibu kaisei to atarashī shinken seigen no seido — jidō gyakutai wo fusegu tame ni — Heisei 24-nen 1 tsuki kōhō tēma* [Partial

revision of the Civil code and introduction of new limits on custody: To prevent child abuse. Public information theme]. 2012, January.

Ministry of Justice. (2013). *Shinken seigen jiken no dōkō* [The trends in restricted custody cases].

Miwa, K. (2014). *Satooya seido no chouki-teki doutai to tenbou* [The long-term dynamics and outlook of the foster care system]. (Doctoral dissertation). Tokyo Metropolitan University.

Miwa, K. (2016). Naze satooya itaku wa shinten shinai no ka? Satooya touroku-sha fusoku kasetsu to satooya itaku jidō gentei kasetsu [Why has family-based foster care not become more common in Japan? A lack of registered fostered carers and of children who are able to be fostered]. *Japanese Journal of Social Welfare*, 56(4), 1–13.

Miyajima, K. (2001). *Jidō gyakutai bōshi-hō shikōgo no jidōsōdanjyo to satooya seido no kongo ni tsuite* [On the child guidance centres and foster care system after the enforcement of the Child abuse prevention act]. Preliminary paper for dai 75-kai yōshi to satooya wo kangaeru kai kōjutsu-roku.

Miyajima, K. (2014). *Famirīhōmu un'ei no kihon: Kono kuni no shakai-teki yōgo no korekara no tame ni* [The foundations of running family homes: For the future of alternative care in our country]. Lecture to anonymised CGC, 2014.

Motomori, E. (2016). *How did Japan forget diverse childhoods?* Presentation at Joint East Asian Studies Conference, SOAS. London. 2016, September 7.

Mouer, R.E., & Sugimoto, Y. (2002). *Images of Japanese society: A study in the social construction of reality*. London: Kegan Paul.

Nakagawa, A. (2010). *Jidō yōgo shisetsu no kakaeru kyō-teki kadai no kenshō shokuin no rōdō kankyō ni shugan wo oita Gunma ken'nai shisetsu e jittai chōsa* [Investigation into contemporary challenges for child welfare institutions: A survey of the reality of staff in Gunma Prefecture]. Gunma: Gunmadaigaku shakai jōhō gakubu jōhō shakai kagakka.

National Child Guidance Centre Directors' Committee. (2011). Zenkoku jidōsōdanjyo-chō-kai jidōsōdanjyo ni okeru satooya itaku oyobi iki jidō ni kansuru chōsa [Survey on abandoned children and foster care placements at child guidance centres]. *Zaidanhōjin zenkoku satooya-kai*, 91. 2011, July.

National Child Welfare Administration Division Head Meeting. (2016). *Heisei 28-nendo zenkoku jidō fukushi shukan kachō jidōsōdanjyo-chō kaigi shiryō. (Heisei 28-nen 8 tsuki 4-nichi): Keisatsu to jidōsōdanjyo to no renkei ni tsuite* [2016 National Child Welfare Administration Division Head, Child Guidance Centre Head meeting material: On collaboration between the police and child guidance centres]. 2016, August 4. Retrieved from URL: http://www.mhlw.go.jp/file/06-Seisakujouhou-11900000-Koyoukintoujidoukateikyoku/4_6.pdf (last accessed 2017, August 28).

Nussbaum, M.C. (2000). *Women and human development: The capabilities approach*. Cambridge: Cambridge University Press.

Osaki, T. (2014, August 7). Foster parent shortage takes growing toll on children: Close to 90% of abandoned children placed in institutions. *The Japan Times*.

Parsons, T. (1935). The place of ultimate values in sociological theory. *The International Journal of Ethics*, 45(3), 282–316.

Parsons, T. (1972). Culture and social system revisited. *Social Science Quarterly*, 53(2), 253–266.

Ramseyer, J.M. (1998). Reluctant litigant revisited: Rationality and disputes in Japan. *Journal of Japanese Studies*, 14(1), 111–123.

Sabatier, P.A., & Weible, C.M. (2007). The advocacy coalition framework: Innovations and clarifications. In P.A. Sabatier (Ed.), *Theories of the policy process*. Oxford: Westview Press.

Saimura, J., Takahashi, S., Shoji, J., Kashiwame, R., Oyama, O., Saito, S., & Kato, H. (2000). Jidōsōdanjyo shokuin no gen'nin kenshūnado no arikata ni kansuru kenkyū [A study of training and supervision systems for staff of child guidance centres]. *Nihon-kodomo katei sōgōkenkyūsho kiyō*, 37, 181–198.

Saimura, J., Ito, K., Isogae, H., Akai, K., Tsuzaki, T., Takahashi, S., ... Kashiwame, R. (2001). Jidō gyakutai taiō ni tomonau jidōsōdanjyo e no hogo-sha no riakushon-tō ni kansuru chōsa kenkyū [A study of parents' reactions to the child guidance centres caused by coping with the child abuse cases]. *Nihon-kodomo katei sōgōkenkyūsho kiyō*, 38, 253–295.

Saimura, J., Shibuya, M., Ito, K., Tsuzaki, T., & Isogae, H. (2002a). Jidōsōdanjyo ni okeru hōteki taiō no jittai-tō ni kansuru chōsa kenkyū [A study of the actual conditions of legal measures for the child abuse cases in child guidance centres]. *Nihon-kodomo katei sōgōkenkyūsho kiyō*, 39, 307–352.

Saimura, J., Ito, K., Shibuya, M., Maehashi, N., Miyajima, K., Hosono, T., ... Sakamoto, M. (2002b). Jidōsōdan no jisshi taisei ni kansuru shichōson chōsa [A study of new child guidance service systems based on municipalities research]. *Nihon-kodomo katei sōgōkenkyūsho kiyō*, 39, 215–236.

Saimura, J., Arimura, T., Kashiwame, R., Yamamoto, T., Nagano, S., Tsuruoka, H., ... Yokoyama, T. (2010). Jidōsōdanjyo no gyōmu bunseki ni kansuru kenkyū (1) [Time-studies and incident-studies about social work for child abuse cases in child guidance centres]. *Nihon-kodomo katei sōgōkenkyūsho kiyō*, 47, 181–191.

Saimura, J., Wada, I., Yamamoto, T., Ookubo, M., Nagano, S., Arimura, T., ... Kawamatsu, R. (2013). Jidōsōdanjyo jidō shinri tsukasa no gyōmu jittai haaku ni kansuru kenkyū [The analysis of actual quantity of works of clinical psychologist in child guidance centres]. *Nihon-kodomo katei sōgōkenkyūsho kiyō*, 50, 1–19.

Saimura, J., Arimura, T., Yamamoto, T., Kashiwame, R., Nagano, S., Kawamatsu, R., ... Yokoyama, T. (2014). Jidōsōdanjyo no jimu bunseki ni kansuru kenkyū (3) [The analysis of actual quantity of works in child guidance centres (3)]. *Nihon-kodomo katei sōgōkenkyūsho kiyō*, 49, 1–37.

Sato, T. (2009). Jidōsodanjyo no genjyō to kadai: Jidō gyakutai taiō to taisei seibi [The contemporary conditions and challenges at child guidance centers: Response to child abuse and organizational structure]. In Nihon Kodomo wo Mamoru Kai (Ed.), *Kodomo hakusho*. Tokyo: Sōdo bunka.

Schoppa, L. (2006). *Race for the exits: The unraveling of Japan's system of social protection*. London: Cornell University Press.

Shibuya, M. (2005). Jidōsōdanjyo ni yoru kazoku hoken no genjō to kadai [Current state and challenges of family preservation by child guidance centres]. *Nihon-kodomo katei sōgōkenkyūsho kiyō*, 42, 217–236.

Shore, C., & Wright, S. (1997). Policy: A new field of anthropology. In C. Shore, & S. Wright (Eds.), *Anthropology of policy*. New York: Routledge.

Stoker, R.P. (1991). *Reluctant partners: Implementing federal policy*. Pittsburgh: University of Pittsburgh Press.

Sugimoto, Y. (2010). *An introduction to Japanese society*. Cambridge: Cambridge University Press.

Supreme Court. (2013). *Shinken seigen jiken no dōkō to jiken shori no jitsujō. Heisei 24-nen 1 gatsu ~ 12 gatsu Saikōsaibansho jimu sōkyoku katei-kyoku* [Supreme Court, General Secretariat, Family Division. Report into the facts and trends for

incidents and the processing of incidents regarding the limits of parental rights, January to December 2012].
Supreme Court. (2014). *Shinken seigen jiken no dōkō to jiken shori no jitsujō. Heisei 25-nen 1 gatsu ~ 12 gatsu Saikōsaibansho jimu sōkyoku katei-kyoku* [Report into the facts and trends for incidents and the processing of incidents regarding the limits of parental rights, January to December 2013, Family Division, General secretariat, Supreme Court, 2014].
Supreme Court. (2015). *Shinken seigen jiken no dōkō to jiken shori no jitsujō. Heisei 26-nen 1 gatsu ~ 12 gatsu Saikōsaibansho jimu sōkyoku katei-kyoku* [Report into the facts and trends for incidents and the processing of incidents regarding the limits of parental rights, January to December 2014, Family Division, General secretariat, Supreme Court, 2015].
Takahashi, S., Saimura, J., Yamamoto, T., Arimura, T., Nagano, S., Tsuruoka, H., ... Sakai, T. (2010). Jidōsōdanjyo jidō fukushi tsukasa no senmon-sei ni kansuru kenkyū [A study of social workers' expertise in child guidance centres]. *Nihon-kodomo katei sōgōkenkyūsho kiyō*, 47, 3–61.
Tashiro, M., & Yamamoto, T. (2011). Gyakutai yobō ni kansuru jidōsōdanjyo to shichōson no renkei ni tsuite [The cooperation of child guidance centre and municipalities regarding the prevention of child maltreatment]. *Nihon kodomo katei sōgōkenkyūsho*, 48, 1–12.
Tokyo Family Court. (2012). *Tōkyō kasai dayori. kagayaku ashita wo katei to shōnen ni: tōkyō katei saibansho 13* [Tokyo family court newsletter. Towards a bright tomorrow for families and youths: Tokyo family court No. 13]. 2012, July.
Torenvlied, R., & Ackerman, A. (2004). Theory of "soft" policy implementation in multilevel systems with an application to social partnership in the Netherlands. *Acta Politica*, 39(1), 31–58.
Tsuzaki, T. (2003). *Sōshiruwāku to shakai fukushi – Igirisu chihō jichitai sōsharu wāku no seiritsu to tenkai* [Social work and social service: The establishment and evolution of British local authority social work]. Tokyo: Akashi Shoten.
Tsuzaki, T. (2006). *The vested interests vs. children's rights: children's rights and foster care in Japan*. Presentation at Asia conference on children's rights and foster care. Retrieved from URL: http://www.geocities.jp/hokukaido/satooya/seoul2006/article/12-japan-tsuzaki-e.htm (last accessed 2017, August 22). Seoul. 2006, September 16.
Tsuzaki, T. (2008). Jidō gyakutai ni taisuru enjo no shikumi to sono kadai [The system to provide support for child abuse cases and its problems to be solved]. In T. Tsuzaki, & K. Hashimoto (Eds.), *Jidō gyakutai wa ima – renkei shisutemu no kochiku ni mukete* [Current situation in child abuse – Toward the establishment of a collaborative system]. Kyoto: Minerva shobo.
Tsuzaki, T. (2009). *Kono kuni no kodomotachi: Yōhogo jidō shakai-teki yōgo no Nihonteki kōchiku; otona no kitoku ken'eki to kodomo no fukushi* [This country's children: Constructing social care for children in need of care; The vested interests of adults and children's welfare]. Tokyo: Nihon Kajo Shuppan.
United Nations General Assembly. (2016). *Report of the special rapporteur on the sale of children, child prostitution and child pornography on her visit to Japan*. A/HRC/C31/58/Add. 2016, March 13.
Ushijima, Y., & Yukawa, R. (1975). Jidōsōdanjyo ni okeru hantei no kinō oyobi kijun ni kansuru kenkyū [A study on the decision-making function and standards of the child guidance centres]. *Nihon sōgō aiiku kenkyū kiyō*, 11, 305–331.

Watai, S. (2010). *Daijōbu. Ganbatteiru dakara* [It's OK. You are doing your best]. Tokyo: Toku masho ten.

Watanabe, R. (2014). *Shishunki ni okeru sei no mondai ni tsuite: shōjo no seihikō to kousei* [On sexual issues in adolescence: Sexual delinquency and rehabilitation in girls]. Presentation to anonymised CGC, 2014.

West, M.D. (2011). *Lovesick Japan: Sex, marriage, romance, law*. Ithaca: Cornell University Press.

Yamamoto, T., & Niiro, T. (2009). DV mondai ni kanren suru jidō gyakutai sōdan oyobi sono tsūkoku ni kansuru chōsa kenkyū keisatsu fujinsōdanjyo to jidōsōdanjyo to no renkei ni okeru kadai ni tsuite [The research on the cooperation of the child guidance center and the police: Notification in case of children exposed to domestic violence as child maltreatment]. *Nihon-kodomo katei sōgōkenkyūsho kiyō*, 46, 265–288.

Yamamoto, T., & Sato, K. (2008). Jidōsōdanjyo to keisatsu katei saibansho-tō no shihō kikan to no renkei ni tsuite [Research on the cooperation of the child guidance centre, police, and family court]. *Nihon kodomo katei sōgōkenkyūsho*, 45, 331–380.

Yamamoto, T., Shoji, J., Arimura, T., Shinto, N., Itakura, T., Nemoto, A., … Miyaguchi, T. (2009). Jidōsōdanjyo-tō ni okeru hogo-sha enjo no arikata ni kansuru jisshō-teki kenkyū 3 hogo-sha enjo shuhō no kōka, datōsei, hyōka, tekiō ni kansuru jisshō-teki-ken [A study on the system for supporting family preservation in the child guidance centres 3: Efficiency, validity, evaluation, and discerning of parents' supporting methods]. *Nihon kodomo katei sōgōkenkyūsho*, 46, 177–230.

Yamamoto, T., Shoji, J., Arimura, T., Nagano, S., Tsuruoka, Y., Sato, K., … Maebashi, N. (2010). Hogo-sha enjo shuhō no kōka, datōsei, hyōka, tekiō ni kansuru jisshō-teki kenkyū 2 [A study on the system for supporting family preservation in the child guidance centers: Efficiency, validity, evaluation and discerning of the parents' supporting methods 2]. *Nihon kodomo katei sōgōkenkyūsho*, 47, 193–301.

Yamamoto, T., Ookubo, M., Sato, T., Tsuroka, Y., Itakura, T., Nagano, S., … Kawamatsu, R. (2013). Jidōsōdanjyo ni okeru hogo-sha shien no arikata ni kansuru jisshō-teki kenkyū [A study on the system for supporting family preservation in the child guidance centres]. *Nihon kodomo katei sōgōkenkyūsho*, 50, 1–24.

Yomiuri Shinbun. (2015, July 3). Jidō yōgo shisetsu shokuin, apuri de shiriai chūgakusei baishun [A child welfare institution staff member, prostitution with a junior high school student he met on a mobile phone app]. *Yomiuri Shinbun*.

Yoshiaki, J. (2000). Katei saibansho no shōnin to fukushi no sochi no kettei ichiji no kanten kara mita katei saibansho to jidōsōdanjyo no kinō buntan [Approval of family court and the determination of welfare measures: Functional division of family court and child guidance center from a temporary point of view]. *Hōgaku ronshū (Yamanashigakuindaigaku)*, 46, 83–104.

Note: Where the author(s) provided an English translation of their work I have given this translation, rather than my translation.

4 The family-bond

1 Introduction and theoretical challenges

This chapter outlines the subconscious and unspoken values that frame policy implementation in the CGCs. Discussing adoption in Japan, Bryant (1990: 335–336) argues:

> Mediation has played an important role in the maintenance of legitimacy because disputes can be resolved without resort to the formal legal rules. In fact, the contours of the disputes and their resolution are difficult to draw precisely due to the facts that mediation is used so frequently and that it is a process that is generally closed to the public and to researchers.

This book gives a window into this and similarly closed processes and, in doing so, allows us to explore the values on the family. Drawing on Parson's (1972) distinction between values and norms (see Chapter 3), the decision-making process in alternative care can be understood on two levels. The first is normative, with the decision acting as a form of social control delineating what an 'acceptable' family is. The second relates to values on the family: 'in all their apparently aberrant modes of behavior, individuals, who are "ill" are just transcribing a state of the group, and making one or another of its constants manifest' (Levi-Strauss, 1950: 17).

Analysis of the 210 aid objective meetings across the three fieldwork sites led to a focus on the construction of the family-bond, the relationship between child and family. While three key aspects of this construction were shared across my fieldwork sites, despite their different foster care rates, I do not understand this construction as immutable, static or ahistorical. Instead, drawing on Bourdieu (1996: 25), I understand the CGCs as engaged in a process of continual production, rather than simple replication:

> In a kind of circle, the native category [of family], having become a scientific category for demographers, sociologists and especially social workers who, like official statisticians, are invested with the capacity to work on reality, to make reality, helps give real existence to that category.

This book argues that 'not only do policies codify social norms and values, and articulate fundamental organizing principles of society, they also contain implicit (and sometimes explicit) models of society' (Shore and Wright, 1997: 7), and that the implementation of welfare is 'an active force in the ordering of social relations' (Esping-Andersen, 1990: 23). Within this, 'representations, linguistically and symbolically codified, are seen as creating social reality rather than just reflecting it' (Russell and Edgar, 1998: 5).

There are challenges with this approach. The first is the fact that 'to commit oneself to a semiotic concept of culture and an interpretive approach to the study of it is to commit oneself to a view of ethnographic assertion as, to borrow B. Gallie's by now famous phrase, "essentially contestable"' (Geertz, 1973: 29). I address this by testing the construction of the family-bond presented here against all 210 aid objective meetings across all fieldwork sites, looking for a 'black swan', and by conducting 'auxiliary outcome' tests (Mahoney, 2010), including on divorce legislation, adoption legislation, and visual representations of the family. Indeed, Hann argues that 'only through ethnographic research can we assess the extent to which a dominant discourse turns out to be a smokescreen, and the frequency with which moral norms are honoured in the breach' (1996: 21).

The second challenge presented by this approach is the definition of culture (see van Oorschot, 2007). I do not frame the dominant discourse on the family-bond as 'culture', but as a narrowly defined Parsonian 'value' that has a legible impact upon policy implementation. This approach draws on Small et al., who argue that 'the best approach is a pragmatic one... While the umbrella term "culture" might serve as useful shorthand... it ultimately masks more than it reveals, at least when the purpose is to understand a specific problem' (2010: 13–14).

The third challenge relates to causality. Baldcock avoids this by stating that his paper on culture is 'no more than an exploration of how far "culture" and "social policy" might be linked' (1999: 459). I am braver, or perhaps more foolish; drawing on Pfau-Effinger (2005), I suggest that policy implementation shapes the dominant discourse on the family-bond, and the dominant discourse on the family-bond shapes policy implementation.

The final challenge is that some 'cultural interpretation is merely post facto: that, like the peasant in the old story, we first shoot the holes in the fence and then paint the bull's-eyes around them' (Geertz, 1973). Many cultural explanations for Japan's limited use of foster care and adoption face this charge, attributing importance to 'blood' (Kadonaga and Fraser, 2015: 13) or 'traditional views of the family' (Kendrick et al., 2011: 6) without outlining mechanisms or evidencing these assertions.

Here I draw on Pfau-Effinger, who argues that 'welfare culture and welfare state policies are connected via the ideas of social actors' (2005: 6), and focus on the impact caseworkers' values on the family-bond have on policy implementation. Investigating this requires an understanding of the power relations between actors (see Pfau-Effinger, 1998; Reinhold, 1994; Thelen,

The family-bond 105

1999), in this case between parents and CGCs (Chapter 6) and between CGC staff (Chapter 7).

Finally, I do not prioritise the impact of the caseworkers' values and norms on policy implementation over other factors, also considering organisational context, resources, beliefs, and organisational cultures.

This chapter introduces the three key characteristics of the family-bond before deconstructing the family-bond. It then presents evidence for each of the characteristics before considering the impact of the construction of the family-bond on policy implementation.

2 Three characteristics of the dominant values on the family-bond

The family-bond has three key characteristics:

1 A child can only have one family-bond. Forming a new family-bond weakens the existing or potential family-bond, and the formation of a new family-bond cuts the existing family-bond.
2 Removing a child from the family risks destroying the existing or potential family-bond.
3 Children are unable to form a family-bond after a certain age.

The decision to remove a child from their family is made by evaluating the risk this poses to the family-bond against the risk that not doing so poses to the child. The decision is based upon the assessment of the strength of the family-bond and of the family's capacity to care for the child. The relative importance assigned to these two factors varies.

The construction of the family-bond as singular also affects the decision on the suitability of foster care: where care in foster care is constructed as being built upon a new family-bond, it is seen as unsuitable for children for whom the goal of care is family-reunification. Where foster care is constructed as semi-professional care in a home it is seen as less of a threat to the family-bond so can be used for a wider range of children. This is explored in Chapter 6.

CGC staff have two fundamental fears: the death of a child known to them, particularly where there are questions over the actions that the CGC has or has not taken; and the child becoming a *sutego*, an abandoned child. The act of removing a child from the family risks destroying the child's family-bond with their parents. This risk is exacerbated by the child starting to form a family-bond with someone else. If this second formation process is understood as impossible, or the process breaks down, the child risks becoming a *sutego*, a child with no family-bond. In extreme cases, the decision on whether to remove a child can be understood as the evaluation of the fear of 'social death' and 'biological death'. Surprisingly, the fear of 'social death' sometimes appears to override the fear of 'biological death'.

These three characteristics of the family-bond contribute to our understanding of puzzles tangential to this book: on children being returned to abusive households, the low rate of children entering care, and the low foster care rate. This construction of the family-bond leads these decisions to sometimes being understood as in the child's best interest, a position that nuances arguments focusing on parental rights being prioritised over children's rights (see Goldfarb, 2018; Tsuzaki, 2009).

The three characteristics of the family-bond build upon evidence and develop Goldfarb's finding of 'a perception that parent-child ties cannot be multiple: a child's relationship with a caregiver who acts like a parent threatens the child's tie to his or her *actual* parent' (2012: 9–10, emphasis in original). Goldfarb later clarifies that 'many people... perceive foster care as a threat to a birth parent's potential relationship with a child, but my interlocutors never made explicit the reasons why' (2012: 98). This chapter makes the reasons explicit.

These characteristics of the family-bond are relatively uniformly understood across my fieldwork sites. This assertion risks being charged with orientalising *a* Japanese culture. In my defence, I first note that the importance given to the different components of the family-bond, discussed below, varies by case, according to the CGC's understanding of the best interests of the child and of their role. Second, this construction of the family-bond is not necessarily unique to Japan and may provide a mechanism for the long-standing hypothesis that the construction of the family in Catholic, or 'Mediterranean' countries, including Italy and Portugal, contributes to their low foster care rate (see Goodman, 1999; Madge, 1994).[1]

3 The constituent parts of the family-bond

3.1 Introduction

In 2011 the Asahi Shimbun featured a 13-part series on foster care (Inoue, 2011a, 2011b, 2011c; Sugiyama, 2011a–2011j). The series, titled 'Become a parent, become a child', largely constructed foster care as a proxy for adoption and focused on the creation of a new family or a new family-bond: 'We became a family on the southern island' (Inoue, 2011c), 'I 'proposed' with a picture book that she become my daughter' (Sugiyama, 2011e), 'More of a mother than my real mother' (Sugiyama, 2011g).

This series opened with the article 'Even more than ties of blood' (Sugiyama, 2011a). The emphasis on 'blood' in the family-bond is also found in Murata's 'Making a family: The way of life of regular foster parents', which explains how a connection can be built 'even without blood ties' (2005: 71).

Goldfarb (2012) attempts to untangle what she calls 'the parent-child ties' by exploring the relationship between blood and legal ties, and argues that the term 'blood ties' often refers to *uchi/soto*, inside/outside, relationships that have grown more prominent with the nuclearisation of the ideal family (see Ochiai, 1997). Shirai also argues that 'reproductive technologies have reinforced social norms that dictate the importance of blood relationships within modern families' (2010: 18).

This book develops this, and argues that the family-bond is a contested composition of legal bonds (parental rights), blood ties, the embodied practice of giving care, a sense of belonging to a place (*ibasho*), and familial love, and that it is understood to be durable, with expectations, obligations, and responsibility around future support.

3.2 Legal, blood, and practice bonds

The three components of the family-bond given the most weight in decision-making are legal bonds, blood bonds, and bonds from the embodied practice of caring.

The tension between legal bonds and bonds from caring is explored in the Palme d'Or nominated film *Soshite chichi ni naru*, 'Like father like son' (Harada and Koreeda, 2013).[2] In this, two families whose babies were mixed up in hospital must decide whether to 'switch' back their six-year-old sons. Two cases from Teru demonstrate how these bonds, of law, blood, and care are afforded different importance depending on how the CGC understands the best interests of the child.

Sosuke[3] is a nine-year-old boy. Born to an 11-year-old mother and a 13-year-old father, he spent much of his childhood in a BIWI and a CWI and believes his grandmother, who has previously abused him and with whom he is currently living, to be his mother. His grandmother is known to police over drug use. Sosuke wishes to enter care but wishes to stay at the same school as he has a sense of belonging there.

Sosuke's grandmother has not adopted him so his mother retains legal bonds. Sosuke's grandmother has bonds built through care, though these may be seen as qualified by her having abused Sosuke. Both mother and grandmother also have blood ties to Sosuke.

During the aid objectives meeting the caseworker reported that the grandmother initially opposed the placement into care and is now conflicted, and that the 'the real mother seems to have drawn a line and distanced herself from a self-concept of herself as being the mother'. This prompted a discussion between senior managers:

SM1: We have to explain in detail to the real mother about this situation, and about getting parental consent from her. She will sign everything, so we can't just get her to sign the child away.
SM2: We don't have to get her sign anything. She is not opposed to it. We have to confirm with her is ok.
SM3: In my experience she will just say, do whatever you like.
SM2: We can do it purely as information – this is what is happening – and if she doesn't oppose...

Here legal bonds are prioritised over bonds of care. Rather than attempting to convince the grandmother, which the CGC saw as potentially risking the placement into care, the CGC prioritised the legal bond as the natal mother did not oppose the course of action that Sosuke and the CGC wanted.[4]

In the second case, weak bonds from care and the assumption of blood bonds were prioritised over legal bonds. Jinpei, a three-year-old boy placed into a BIWI at birth, is the second child of an affair between a married man, who has children in his marriage, and a divorced lady, who has one child from her marriage. The father acknowledged paternity of the first child born from the affair, which resulted in that child being referenced on his family register, but has refused to acknowledge paternity of Jinpei.

During the aid objectives meeting the caseworker explained: 'I think it's that his wife knows about the first child but not about the second. For him to be on the birth certificate the child needs to go on his family registration and his wife will find out'. The mother could have taken the father to court but did not want to alienate him, hoping he would leave his wife, an outcome the caseworker considered unlikely.

The caseworker wanted to keep the possibility of a relationship between Jinpei and his father alive. The father was praised for having regularly visited the child in the BIWI, even though he did 'not go every time the mother went'. The caseworker's section head stated that there 'seems to be an ok relationship with the father and child'. Here the active refusal to acknowledge legal bonds was seen as less significant than the assumption of a blood bond, tentative bonds from 'caring', and the potential family-bond.

The decision on whether Jinpei, who was ageing out of the BIWI, could return home hinged on the CGC's assessment of the strength of the family-bond and the capacity of the mother to provide care. The mother was seen as capable, as 'she has raised another child, so not so concerned about how she will do raising children' (senior manager), but as having a weak family-bond with Jinpei. A senior manager was concerned 'about the fact that the mother is not raising this child' and the caseworker reported that the BIWI staff 'wish the mother would be a bit pushier asking for him back'. This concern was tempered by the fact that the mother 'does go to visit the child a lot'.

The outcome here followed the supervising child psychologist's suggestion that the CGC 'rebuild the relationship a little before the child goes home'. A senior manager followed up, 'we should do this as we would a foster parent, start with gradual exchange, building the relationship, and then keep an eye on the family'. Goldfarb's argument that 'kinship emerges in embodied daily practice' (2012: 5) focuses on the potential for children to gain kinship-like bonds with foster parents. Jinpei's case demonstrates that the embodied practice of caring is also seen as important in developing the family-bond with natal parents.[5]

3.3 Ibasho

The case of Maiko, a five-year-old girl being adopted in Yuno, shows the importance of *ibasho*, a sense of belonging.[6] Reporting on the acclimatisation process, the caseworker noted, 'this is the fourteenth time of meeting. Tried overnight stay for the first time. Have done day trips twice… The foster parents are making a big fuss for her to feel like is her *ibasho*'.

In Maiko's case, *ibasho* is a foundation for the creation of a family-bond. Sosuke's case, where his school was his *ibasho*, shows that this can exist independent of the family-bond (see Serizawa, 2012). This distinction is important: I argue in Chapter 6 that while welfare institutions aim to create *ibasho* (see Bamba and Haight, 2007) they do so in a manner that is divorced from the creation of a family-bond. Indeed, this is understood as one of their 'strengths'.

A key distinction between *ibasho* and the family-bond is that *ibasho* is considered beneficial even when temporary. This can be seen in the case of Taisei, a ten-year-old boy entering a CWI in Yuno due to serious 'child-rearing issues'. The CGC believed that the mother was likely to remove Taisei from care before they considered this safe, and that the abuse was below the threshold a court would accept to partially suspend parental rights. Despite the fear of the placement being short, referring to 6 to 24 months here, two senior managers retained pragmatic hopes:

SM1: At this age may be good for him to have some time away from his mother.
SM2: Yes. Want him to have *ibasho* for a while.

The creation of a family-bond was never constructed as temporary or as beneficial, even if brief. Indeed, children with more problematic behaviour, who have a greater risk of placement breakdown, were often placed into CWIs rather than foster care explicitly due to concerns over partially creating and then breaking a new family-bond.

In a 2014 presentation to the Teru CGC, the head of a juvenile detention centre explained *ibasho*: 'The key first step is being in a safe place. Getting normal correct life rhythm, having a person who will listen to them talk and believe them… regular food and rhythms'.

These characteristics can also be seen in a case from Teru. Akemi, a 17-year-old girl, has been in a CWI for most of her life and wishes to go home to her mother, who has ongoing mental health issues. Akemi is one of 11 children, eight of whom are in care, and recently starting refusing school after a teacher bullied her. The mother also wants Akemi back home, though the CGC fears Akemi will then leave school.

During the aid objectives meeting a senior manager asked, 'There is no one in the CWI she can talk to? Staff wise?' The caseworker replied, 'No. Her supervisor recently changed and is new, so a veteran staff member helps with communication etc'. A second senior manager responded, 'She came from a neglectful home to a neglectful institution. I hope her next home gives her an *ibasho*'.

Ibasho, then, requires the presence of support, with the child having someone they can talk to. It is linked to a sense of safety and the child having 'normal' daily rhythms, and is something that is understood to be beneficial even when temporary. *Ibasho* is a foundation for the creation of a family-bond and is desirable, but not necessary, for an existing family-bond.

3.4 Familial love

An important but overlooked component of the family-bond is familial love. An aid objectives meeting in Teru for Jiro, aged three, and his five-year-old brother, Ichiro, highlights this. Their mother is divorced, is 'working nights'[7] to repay a debt, and is suspected of having severe long-term depression. The mother came to the CGC as she felt it would be better for Ichiro and Jiro to be in care for a while.

> SM: Seems realistically that we will end up with the children in care for a longer time.
> CW: Mum seems to think that she will cope when they are a little older. The mum certainly does love them.
> SM: Would be best if the mother could live with an adult who could help with the childcare. We can take them into care, but that would be best.
> CW: The mother has no desire right now to care for them.

Here the mother is seen as lacking the capacity and the desire to care. Her love is seen as genuine, manifest in her attempt to do what she believes is best for her children and her desire to care for her sons in the future. This also speaks to the final component of the family-bond, expectations of future support.

3.5 Expectations of future support

The family-bond is understood to be durable, with expectations of future support. Haruto's case, in Teru, highlights these expectations and the CGC's fear of a child being left with no family-bond.

Haruto is a 15-year-old boy. He has been in institutional care for 12 years following abuse from his mother and attends a special-needs school. Haruto's mother, who has had no contact with Haruto for years, told the CGC that while Haruto is on the family register of her ex-husband he was born from an affair and that 'the "dad" is not his dad'. Haruto's uncle used to visit him in care but this was stopped after suspicions of abuse. Haruto's elder sister lives alone and his younger sibling is in foster care.

Haruto sexually assaulted a girl in his CWI, resulting in a meeting between the girl's mother, Haruto's mother, and officials from the CGC, and local authority office to discuss compensation. The caseworker reported that Haruto's mother said, 'It's not my fault, it's the CWI's responsibility. He is in the CWI. They are responsible for his acts'. The mother expressed a desire to cut her parental rights, which may, depending on the court's interpretation, waive her liability for compensation.

In a later CGC meeting, the caseworker explained his fear that cutting parental rights would result in Haruto having no support when he ages out of care. A senior manager raised the possibility of parental rights being suspended.[8] A second agreed, though was concerned that even here 'the court will think someone should be there for the child. This child has no one there for him, except the elder sister perhaps'. The caseworker summarised his concerns, stating:

> [Haruto] has mental health issues. It seems will be ok in CWI until he is 18, but I really worry about what will happen at 18. This is a problem with many long-term cases in CWI with mental health issues. I want to think about what we can do to promote the relationship with natal parent, but this parent is not good at all. So, we have the option of suspending parental rights, but I am not sure what is best... I want the elder sister to help support, but minimal contact from her at present. And I worry about court involvement here, it may push her away.

Haruto's case represents a near worst-case scenario for a CGC. His mother's rejection of him risks social death, of him becoming an adult *sutego*, the consequences of which are amplified by his care needs. Haruto is understood as being too old to create a new family-bond and as having needs that are too complex for a foster care placement.

On this rare occasion, the CGC was absolved from making the final decision. The natal mother's refusal to pay compensation despite her legal bond meant that the case went to court. While the local authority office and court framed expectations here in terms of financial responsibility, the CGC was primarily concerned with future support.

3.6 Defining the family-bond

This section has examined the components of the family-bond. These are legal bonds, blood ties, bonds that emerge from the embodied practice of caring, familial love, and expectations of future support, with *ibasho*, a sense of belonging, important in the development of a family-bond.

The families that the CGC work with overwhelmingly do not fit the postwar nuclear family 'norm'. Single parents, sex workers, drug users, and gang members were not problematized based solely on these statuses; indeed, single mothers working in the sex trade were at times respected for doing whatever they could to provide for their child.⁹ Daily exposure to 'atypical' families, whose numbers are increasing with societal changes, means that the frame of reference for the family-bond is one of 'normal-enough'[10] rather than 'normal'.

Having looked at the constituent parts of the family-bond, this chapter next turns to examine more closely the three defining characteristics of the family-bond.

4 I: A child can only have one family-bond

4.1 Introduction

The most important characteristic of the family-bond is that a child is understood as only being able to have one at any point in time. The process of forming a new family-bond weakens the existing or potential family-bond, and the formation of a new family-bond entails the cutting of the existing family-bond. Where foster care is constructed as a replacement family-bond, it is thus seen as unsuitable for children for whom the goal of care is family reunification. This section evidences this and suggests a link to the family registration system.

4.2 A case study

Ren entered care aged two and was placed with foster parents who were registered for 'fostering with a view to adoption'. Prior to the adoption being finalised, the couple began divorce proceedings, resulting in the halting of the adoption process.[11] Ren was cautious of his foster mother but had formed a strong bond with his foster father. The case discussion highlights two key assumptions: that a child can only have one family-bond at a time, and that institutions are sometimes used because they do not create a family-bond.

> SM3: How to word it to a two-year-old?
> SM2: Tell him they will live in different houses.
> SM1: But normally when [your parents] divorce you go live with one of the parents, but the adoption system does not allow that. He may wonder why didn't I go to the father etc.
> SH1[12]: He thinks that they are his parents, do I say – I will find you new parents?
> SM1: We should explain when he is 18 at the latest, need to record this and what we say now for future workers...

After discussing this as a 'system type problem with adoption' the participants continued:

> CW: We will find you a new house with mum and dad living together.
> SH2: He will not understand. But can tell again when he is older.

The family-bond 113

CW: Do I take the toys, his [A] and [B][13] which he plays with his dad?

SM1: Want to make it easy for the next caseworker too. As simple and true as possible. [pause] We will have to find a new adopter who can do [B]! This is something we will have to do in life-story work, stress the value of his relationship with these people. Where best for temporary care? Family Home?

SH1: But if he goes to a family home then he will become a child of that home and have to move again.

TCW[14]: Can he still see his [foster] father? He gets on very well with him.

CW: But, it will make moving forwards harder.

SM1: Better if he goes to a BIWI, he won't think of them as new family, but as staff.

Two decisions are made here. The first is to place Ren into a BIWI rather than a family home for temporary care in order to prevent him from building a new family-bond as this placement would only be temporary. Here an institutional placement, with 'staff' not a 'new family', is seen as protecting the potential family-bond with the next adopting parents, with staff shift patterns[15] and the low staff-to-child ratio[16] preventing a family-bond being created. The second decision is to cut the family-bond with his foster father, as maintaining it 'will make moving forwards harder'. This decision, to wipe the slate clean, is also made to protect Ren's potential to form a new family-bond.

Underlying Ren's case is the assumption that a child cannot maintain two family-bonds simultaneously. The institution here is a constructed limbo, a holding space that protects the existing or potential family-bond, in Ren's case until suitable adoptive parents are found.

4.3 Genograms and meeting discussions

The assumption that a child can only 'belong' to one household is also found in the genograms on CGC paperwork.[17] In 153 of the 185 genograms I saw, the caseworker had drawn a circle around the child's 'family', with a solid-line representing a physical household and a dotted-line showing a potential household.

In these genograms, with one exception, children were only ever encompassed in one circle. Following a divorce, children were placed in one circle with a parent or another guardian, such as a grandparent. The one exception was an Irifune case shown in Figure 4.1.[18] The dotted line on the hand-annotated[19] version of the genogram shows a potential household for the boy in the bottom right. As these circles represent different points in time, this unique genogram does not contradict the idea that a child can only belong to one household.

Genograms were used differently across my fieldwork sites. In Yuno, only the abuse report form had a box for genograms, titled family composition.

114   *The context of alternative care*

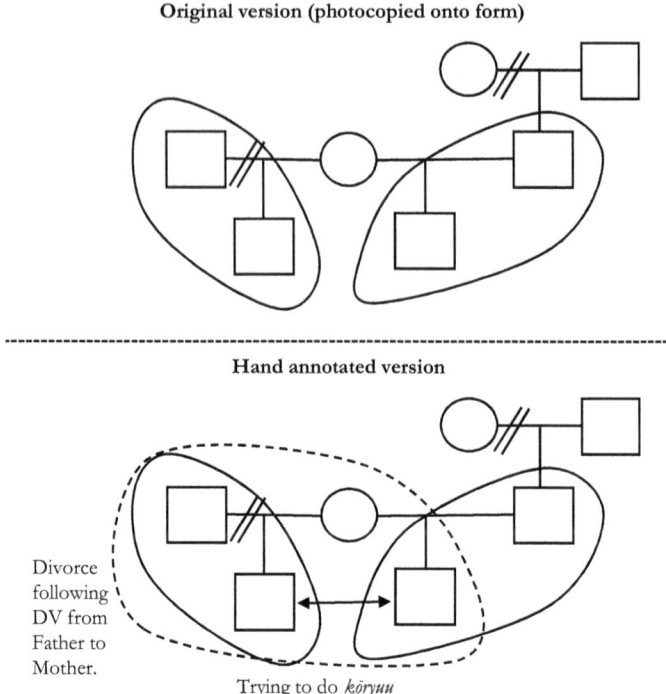

Figure 4.1 A unique genogram (Irifune).

This came pre-completed with a married father and mother. On other forms, a description of the family was written in text or tabular form.

The only other time genograms were routinely used in Yuno was in the monthly meeting of the subcommittee of the social welfare and public health committee. The genograms for these most complex cases were drawn using software. Figure 4.2 shows two examples.

In Irifune, hand-drawn genograms were included in the paperwork for aid objective meetings in a box titled family composition, with key ages listed separately. Most Irifune genograms showed few actors outside the immediate nuclear family. Two of the largest genograms, with hand annotations, are shown in Figure 4.3.

Solid circles in Irifune showed the child's 'home', in the sense of who they physically lived with. Where a child was in institutional care, the circle encompassed only the child (see genogram two), except where the child would shortly return home, where a dotted circle showed the future household.

In Teru, the consultation form, which is used to track information and in all meetings where a decision is taken, and the abuse consultation form have a hand-drawn genogram. These included more extended family than Yuno

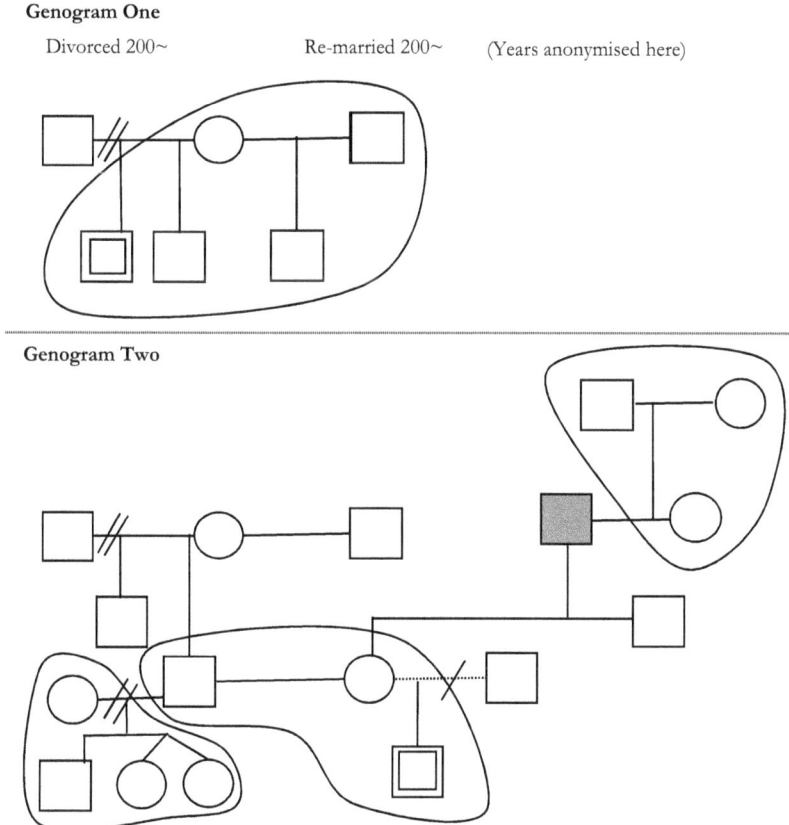

Figure 4.2 Two genograms: Yuno.

or Irifune genograms, though this does not correspond with a higher rate of kinship in foster care. The genograms were more heavily annotated than in Yuno or Irifune. The caseworker regularly updated the genograms, four of which are shown in Figure 4.4.

In Teru, where a child is in care or away at university they were usually left outside the circle, though in one case a runaway teenager was encompassed. The case of Jinpei, whose father was visiting the BIWI but did not recognise him legally, is shown in genogram three. Genograms without a circle in Teru were mostly from new caseworkers, suggesting oversight. On occasion, as in genogram two, this denotes the absence of a household.

Having found nothing to contradict the idea of a singular family-bond in the genograms, I turned to the transcripts to seek evidence of multiple family-bonds. To strengthen this test, I looked for multiple household

116 *The context of alternative care*

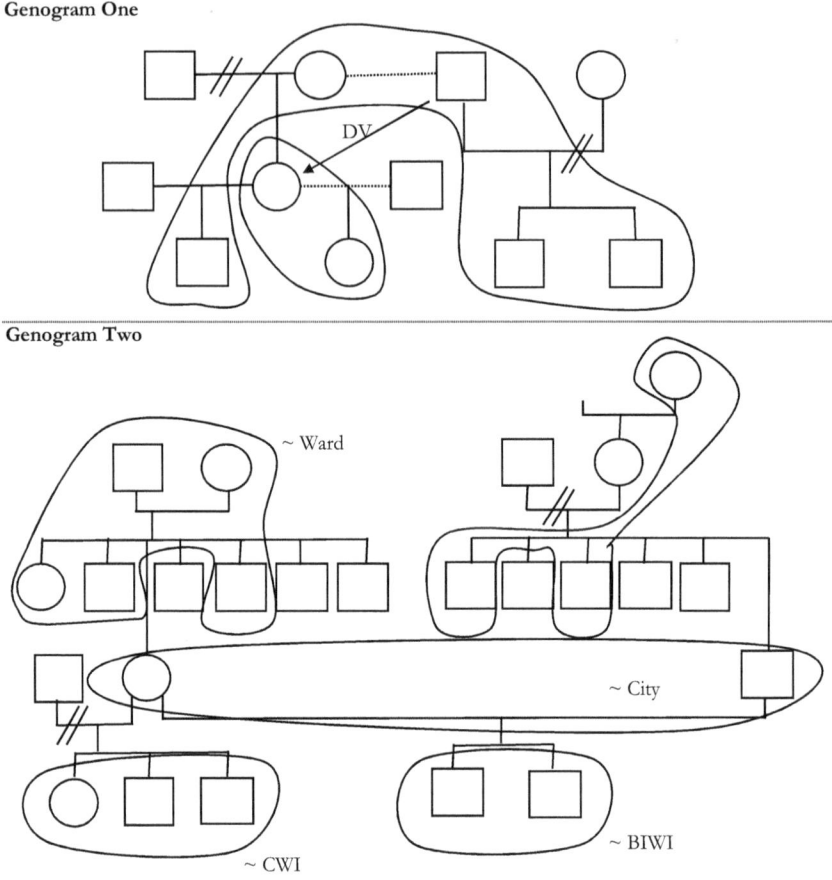

Figure 4.3 Two genograms: Irifune.

affiliation as well as multiple family-bonds. There were no suggestions of a child having two family-bonds, and only one case where there was a possibility of multiple households.

Yamato, a 13-year-old boy in Irifune, had recently returned home from a CWI. The police brought his case to the CGC as they suspected Yamato of theft and mentioned in passing that he had taken an 11-year-old girl to a love hotel. The aid objectives meeting focused on Yamato's approaching birthday as this would see him reach the age of criminal responsibility. Yamato's parents were divorced and lived in the same neighbourhood. During the meeting a senior manager queried the paperwork, asking, 'Two? He seems to have two addresses… Can he choose where to go?' to which the caseworker replied, 'Not sure, I didn't ask, sorry'.

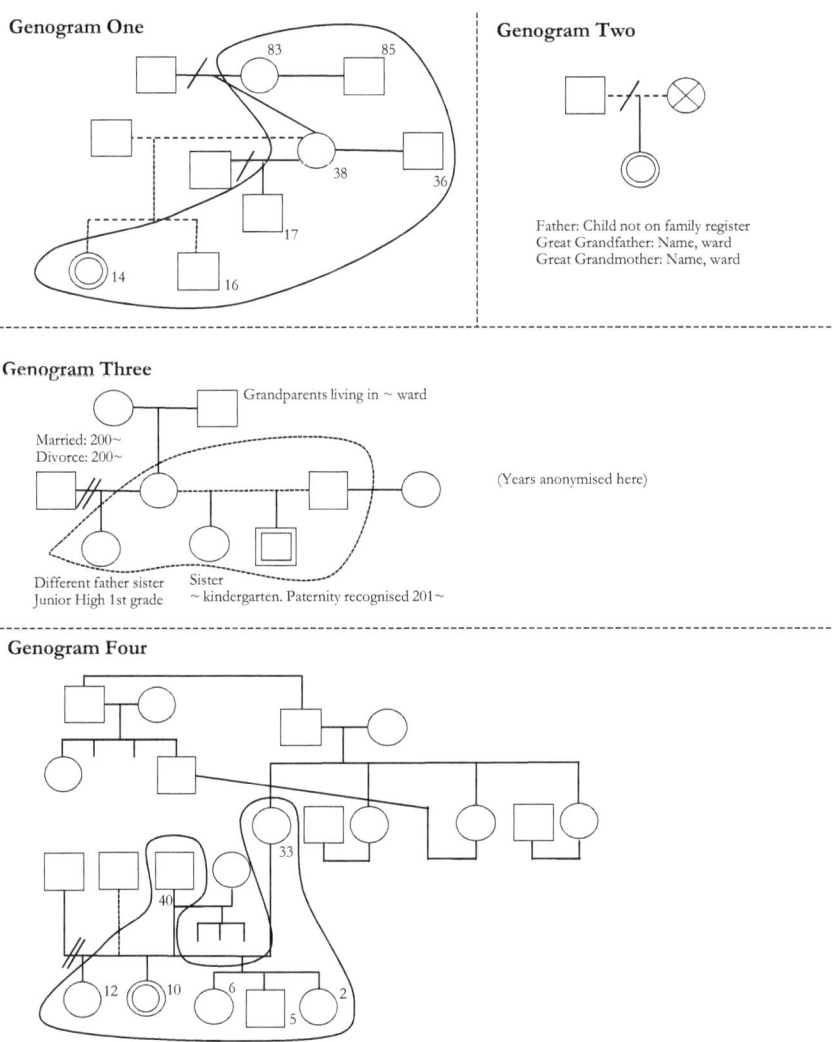

Figure 4.4 Four genograms: Teru.

The lack of clarity may have been the result of the caseworker, who was in their first year, not checking to which home Yamato had returned. Equally, it is possible that Yamato did flit between two households and that this was not considered worthy of further investigation.

This was the only case, of 210 transcripts over three research sites, in which 'atypical' family arrangements were the norm, where there was a possibility of a child belonging to two homes. In some cases, most commonly in Teru, a 'key person', often a grandparent, was identified outside the immediate family. This usually referred either to the possibility of future care or the ability to provide additional support. This relationship was always framed as complementing the child's existing or potential family-bond rather than threatening it.

4.4 The family registration system, divorce, and adoption

The construction of the family-bond as singular and discrete is likely to be related to the family registration system, the *koseki seido*. Krogness (2014: 4) explains:

> Any modern nation-state needs a civil registration system that collects, records and documents individual civil status and civil status changes, as well as family relations. Such systems in most developed states register by the unit of the individual, but Japan uses the unit of the administrative household, the 'ko' unit.

This system places every member of society into one discrete family unit: every child 'belongs' to one and only one family. This system anticipates that children will be born to a married couple. Where a child is born to a single mother they enter the mother's family register with the father noted, if the mother provides paternity information or the father successfully files for paternity with a court. Where paternity is acknowledged, a note linking to the mother's family register is made on the father's family register but the child is not entered onto the father's family register.

The modern *koseki* system, created with the 1871 New Household Registration Act, developed from the older *ie* system, which organised individuals into lineages or 'stem families' (see Hendry, 2003; Ochiai, 2008). The 1947 Family Registration Act limited family units to two generations and was amended in 1948 to remove the status of the *ie*, the home, as a legal entity. In structuring the relationship between individual and state, the *koseki* system 'developed into "an indispensable element in the formation of the underlying foundations of the civil law system" (Mukai and Toshitani, 1967: 48)' (Krogness, 2014: 3).

There are three characteristics of the family registration system that are relevant here. The first is that

> the ko unit principle makes the registrants perceive themselves as members of the larger ko unit, rather than as individuals. The ko unit is felt to represent family even though it is an administrative construct that often does not represent an actual cohabitating family unit.
> (Krogness, 2014: 7; see also Bryant, 1990)

This allows the family-bond to exist even where the child is raised entirely in welfare institutions. Goldfarb (2012: 113) argues that family court conservatism, allowing parents to hold rights even in cases of abuse or neglect, ensures continuity of the household over the long term, which itself can have affective value. By maintaining some aspects of shinken [parental rights], a natal parent is able to preserve a connection with a child that is neither about care nor practice nor performance, nor the emotional attachments that might emerge over time in intimate conditions.

The second characteristic is that the *koseki* records 'are in principle publicly accessible' (Krogness, 2014: 5). This creates what Krogness terms 'koseki consciousness', 'a concern with how one's family appears to the surrounding social world... on their koseki document' (2014: 7). Sugimoto argues that this 'works as a powerful deterrent to deviant behaviour as "stains" in *koseki* negatively affect the life-chances of all family members' (2010: 157; see also Krogness, 2014). These include divorce (Sugimoto, 2010) and childbirth outside wedlock (Hertog, 2008). Discussing a 'baby-hatch' facility, Goldfarb notes that 'the main reason people traveled all the way to Kumamoto to abandon a child was because they did not want to document the child in their family registry, as the child would in some way "dirty" or "taint" it' (2016a: 5).[20]

Despite arguments that changes in the way the *koseki* is recorded and accessed have decreased the importance of keeping the *koseki* 'clean' among younger generations (see Hertog, 2011), the *koseki* system still 'penetrates into the life of every Japanese and controls it in a fundamental way' (Sugimoto, 2010: 156). This is evident in the words of a care-leaver, who never imagined he would marry his girlfriend as 'marriage is between two households, and I have none' (Goldfarb, 2012: 161).

The final important characteristic of the *koseki* system is that 'it is the duty of the household to supply data on civil status, civil status changes and family relations' (Krogness, 2014: 5). Goldfarb argues that 'the act of family registration is a performative mode of social recognition' (2016a: 1) that entails rights and responsibilities and notes that 'by *not* registering a child, the child could be treated as though it had never been born' (2016a: 6, emphasis in original). This leads Goldfarb to argue, along 'with Elizabeth Povinelli... that in Japan, "the recognition of peoples' worth, of their human and civil rights, always seem[s] to be hanging on the more or less fragile branches of a family tree" (2002: 215)' (N.D.). The case of Jinpei, whose father refused to add Jinpei to his family register, adds weight to Krogness' (2014: 18) conviction that:

> The Japanese state's disinclination to interfere in koseki registration matters, and the koseki system's de facto reliance on trust in terms of birth notification submissions, can be interpreted as a remnant of the Meiji-era control of the population through the authority of the household head (whom koseki researchers in the 1950s likened to a family

level state bureaucrat). Registration within the koseki system documents fundamental individual rights, but given this system's laissez-faire character, the state appears to prioritize the household unit the koseki produces over securing the rights of its registered individuals.

The *koseki* system creates a boundary demarcating who is 'in' the family and, by extension, who is not.[21] As such, the registration of a child into the *koseki* should be understood as a component of the family-bond. This can be understood through what Stasch terms the 'contingency of attachment' (2009).

Goldfarb (2012: 9–10) states:

> We also see the sense of kinship relationships being singular, rather than diverse and multiple, in Japanese legal structures: the lack of dual custody systems, for example, requires a single entity as holder of each aspect of parental rights, so that the right to have custody and give care is that of one, rather than dual or multiple, individuals.

To add to this, where the parent with custody remarries it is common for the step-parent to 'adopt' the child, reshaping the family to fit the *koseki* structure.

Article 817–9 of the Civil Code on special adoption also makes this in/out demarcation clear, stating that the 'legal relationship between an adopted child and their natural parents and blood relatives shall be extinguished by special adoption'. The child is removed from the natal parents' *koseki* and placed onto the adoptive parents' *koseki*, with a discreet note acknowledging that the child is adopted.

Some countries have an 'open' adoption system, allowing the child to maintain a degree of contact with their natal parents.[22] Siegel explains this transition in America, from 'a world in which adoption agencies and the general public strongly believed that maintaining absolute secrecy and cutting off all connection with the child's birth family were essential for protecting the child's emotional well-being' (2012: 43) to a system where 'some agencies offer only open adoption, based on the view that secrecy and cut-offs in adoption are not in a child's best interests' (2012: 43). With one exception, discussed below, open adoption does not occur in Japan.

The construction of the family-bond as singular and discrete is not fixed or uncontested. Goldfarb documents one adoption organisation, Wa no Kai,[23] which 'maintains that the birth mother *must* remain in the child's life, because the *child* chose to be born to the birth mother' (2016b: 55, emphasis in original). Similarly, Arimura, a professor and MHLW advisor, noted in our correspondence on joint custody that 'with the increase in divorce, there is now debate around this' (personal correspondence, 2016, January 23).

It is possible that over time these debates and challenges to the boundaries of the 'norm' will lead to change in the construction of the family-bond. At present though, in relation to the family registration system, divorce, and adoption, a child can only belong to one family.

4.5 Foster care and the family-bond

The family-bond is constructed as discrete, singular, and exclusive, and there is little space for ambiguity here. Foster care exists in this ambiguous space and thus presents a challenge to those implementing policy. Whether constructed as a proxy for adoption, with care built upon a family-bond, or as semi-professional care in a home, foster parents provide care in a family environment and can thus be seen as a threat to the child's family-bond. Goldfarb (2012: 47, emphasis in original) argues:

> It is precisely the *contingent* and created forms of kinship between foster parents and children that seem to threaten natal parents with the permanent loss of their child. This tacit understanding of the performative power of caregiving motivates the tendency to place children in children's homes [CWI] if there is any possibility of that child's reunion with biological kin.

This thesis adds nuance to Goldfarb's account of foster care, which is shared by Omori (2016) and argues that foster care is not necessarily a threat to the family-bond. Chapter 6 explores how the function of foster care is constructed differently in the Teru and Irifune CGCs and the impact this has on policy implementation. Having established that a child can only have one family-bond, this chapter next addresses the CGC staff's fears of damaging this relationship.

5 II: Removing a child from the family risks destroying the existing or potential family-bond

With 19 children entering care per 10,000 (calculated from MHLW, 2016), Japan places the fewest children into care of any OECD nation (Ainsworth and Thoburn, 2014: 18). Bamba and Haight explain this with reference to *mimamori*, a concept they define as 'watching over children warmly as a protective figure with minimal adult interference' (2009: 797). Bamba and Haight (2009: 805) argue that:

> Although Japanese child welfare workers in our study recognized that keeping family contact can be problematic when parental maltreatment continued, they did not seek the involuntary severing of family ties. Instead, they watched over (mimamoru) both children and their families attempting to make adjustments to minimize the potential for maltreatment.

While I did find examples of a 'light-touch' approach to social work, Bamba and Haight's *mimamori* is descriptive rather than explanatory. This section uses case studies to argue that the decision to leave a child in an abusive household is sometimes due to the lack of judicial support and sometimes understood as being in the child's best interest.

One of the most challenging things during fieldwork was to sit silently in meetings where children were returned home despite significant risk of further abuse. In one case, Ayame, a 13-year-old girl, was returned to her mother, who claimed not to have known that she had been raped for years by her step-father, despite this resulting in a stillbirth. Ayame's IQ was low enough to entitle her to a disability handbook and reminded senior managers of a similar case where a girl had been returned home and then further sexually exploited, this time outside the home by a yakuza member.

In another case Hideo, a two-month-old boy, was returned to his mother who was 'on meth'. The CGC was wary of the mother as 'a child had died in a previous relationship' in unclear circumstances.

In a third case Chiyoko, a 15-year-old girl with an IQ of just over 60, was returned home following sexual abuse from her younger brother and in the belief 'that there may have been some issues with her stepfather'.

In a fourth case Kenji, a new-born, was returned to his mother, who had admitted the abuse that left him hospitalised with serious head injuries. The mother had mental health issues and was turning to alcohol over medication. My unspoken concerns were voiced by a clinical psychologist, who queried, 'If the head is hit, this is very serious child abuse. Are we ok just having support at home? Do we need to take the child into care?' The caseworker responded, 'For now, I think we need to investigate more and support'.

In Ayame's case the step-father had left and the mother's responsibility could not be categorically established. In Hideo's case his mother had voluntarily placed him into care, and a lack of evidence of abuse meant that the CGC had no legal grounds to prevent her from removing him. In these cases, in the words of one caseworker, there was 'basically no other choice'.

The CGCs did have a choice with Chiyoko and Kenji, yet did not pursue parental consent for a care placement. So why did the CGCs place these children back into potentially dangerous situations?

The case of Daiki, a two-year-old boy in Yuno, sheds light on this puzzle. Internal disagreement led the CGC to take the case to the monthly meeting of the subcommittee of the Yuno social welfare and public health committee.[24] The decision to return Daiki home, despite concerns over abuse, hinged on the fear that removing him could destroy his family-bond.

Daiki lived with his mother and her new husband, who had adopted him. Daiki had been hospitalised under a temporary care order following physical abuse, reported by his nursery. The adoptive father admitted the abuse but said it had not happened before. The mother told the caseworker that she had not seen the abuse happening.

The caseworker, who wanted to return Daiki home, had instructed the parents to complete a 'Common Sense Parenting' (CSP) course, and stated that the parents have 'started to show understanding that the way they had acted until now wasn't correct'. The caseworker requested guidance on 'if can return the child home as the parents are doing very well, but is a high-risk situation as is someone who didn't recognise what was abuse before [and the] adoptive father is a violent type'. The caseworker noted that parents want Daiki home, which was understood as being indicative of a strong family-bond, and that they were open to continuing CGC guidance, which was seen as positive for Daiki's safety.

The CGC nurse, who wanted Daiki to enter care, questioned the strength of the family-bond, stating that

> this child seems a bit like an accessory for couple, and now the child is not there it is affecting their relationship a bit, unbalancing them a bit, so is possible they are working very hard in CSP to get child back to be back to normal rather than [long pause].

The nurse also highlighted that Daiki had been hospitalised previously with head injuries, apparently sustained in a car crash where he had not been wearing a seat belt.

The CGC had run police checks on the adoptive father. This is unusual and had been done here as he had told the caseworker that his children from a previous relationship had been taken into care due to neglect. The caseworker noted that 'the dad is really shaken up by not being able to see his own children. He wants to raise [Daiki] as his own. They don't want their own children yet, they want to focus on [Daiki]'.

The committee initially focused on what concrete support the CGC would offer if Daiki was returned home. The caseworker responded:

> Support [pause]. They are really really doing their best in CSP, really reflecting on themselves, their own shortcomings and strengths. If [Daiki] goes home, we would do some support, such as trying to focus on rebuilding the parents' relationship with the nursery. Support [pause]. But in terms of practical hands on [pause]. In CSP, they have done three. Is a six-part course, we can make them finish the course even if we return the child home now. Think they would want to finish the course. We can also insist the child goes back to nursery.

The discussion next turned to the anticipated duration of a care placement. This makes explicit the fear that removing a child risks breaking the family-bond.

CM[25]: If you place in a child welfare institution, would be planning to go back home after right?
CW: Yes.
CM: What age would you want to place into child welfare institution until?
CW: I think now is the best chance for the child to go back home. There is real possibility that the parents may think the child is dead to them if the CGC takes him from them.
CM: They are young right, so could have own child right?
CW: Yes.

Here the staff must evaluate the risk of social death, of Daiki being 'dead' to the mother and adoptive father, a fear exacerbated by the parents' ability to have another child, against the risk of biological death, a fear exacerbated by the minimal support on offer.

A committee member, seeking compromise, argued the 'need to confirm the mother and child's relationship' as the child had been born into an abusive relationship, and suggested that 'if you place into a CWI for a year, could do group work etc'. The caseworker suggested that this work occurs from temporary care, rather than a CWI, though noted that this would require the breaching of the national guidelines of two months.[26] A committee member said 'one more month perhaps, but what will you actually do in this one month?' to which the caseworker responded, 'We can see how the parents develop in a month'. After collective giggles of embarrassment from the CGC staff, the committee chair responded, 'We want a clearer plan of care, but I think we can extend the temporary care here'. The caseworker concluded, 'If we do send the child home and it goes wrong again we will use Article 28 [to partially suspend parental rights for two years] and will make this clear to the parents'.

Despite grave concerns over abuse, the lack of concrete support for the family, and doubts over the strength of the family-bond, Daiki was returned home. Here the fear of cutting the family-bond outweighed the fear of death or further abuse.

Critically, in the position where 'the parents may think the child is dead to them if the CGC takes him from them', the risk is understood as being to the child, who could be abandoned, rather than to the parents, who could have another child. The decision to return Daiki is understood as being in his best interests as it reduces the risk of *his* family-bond being cut. This nuances arguments about the prioritisation of parental rights over children's rights (see Tsuzaki, 2009), and foster parents' concerns that CGCs prioritise parents' wishes over children's needs.

In other cases, such as Ayame's and Hideo's, the CGC does not feel that they have this choice. This is connected to the limited role of the judiciary and the weight assigned to protecting the family-bond by the courts (see Chapter 3). The case of Ryota, a three-year-old boy in Teru, highlights the discrepancy between the CGCs and the courts.

Ryota is in hospital on a temporary care order after his mother tried to kill him and commit suicide by jumping in front of a train while holding him. Both survived, though Ryota may lose a limb. The CGC also has reservations about Ryota's father, who suffers from depression and has a conviction for stabbing someone. An aid objectives meeting was convened to prepare for the different possible outcomes of the court hearing.

The CGC considered it likely that the judge would absolve the mother of responsibility due to her mental health issues and order her to return home after being discharged, either as an in-patient at a mental health clinic or after a period of hospitalisation. The CGC was concerned about both Ryota's safety and the impact of his mother returning home would have on him. One senior manager said, 'There is a gap between what the court thinks is OK and what we think is OK for the child'. At a minimum, the CGC wanted to help 'reacclimatise the child to the mother, rather than her just suddenly moving back in', a position shared by the father.

While extreme, Ryota's case is indicative of the challenge CGCs face in removing children or preventing them from being returned home. The absence of an interventionist judiciary forces CGCs to rely on parental consent. Even where the courts are involved, there is often a discrepancy between the court's and the CGC's evaluations of the importance to be assigned to the family-bond.

Goldfarb argues that 'for many in Japan, bonds between families—*ketsuen*, the ties of blood—*should* be seen as inviolable, the most obligatory of social bonds' (2016b: 58, emphasis in original). There are several possible explanations for the importance afforded to the family-bond by the CGCs. The first is that 'in contemporary Japan, exclusion from "normal" family forms often results in exclusion from caregiving relationships that last over time' (Goldfarb, 2012: iv). The second is that historically, CGCs are 'institutions that give advice about children but not to them' (Goodman, 2000: 36).

The third possible explanation relates to the *koseki* (family registration) system. This is built on the *ie* system of lineages. Despite legal changes, Hendry notes that 'the notion of the *ie* continues to be held... and... its underlying principles pervade the nuclear families which appear on the surface to be quite independent' (2003: 30–31; see also Bryant, 1990). Bamba and Haight argue that this results in a situation where the 'loss of family for maltreated children would represent not only the loss of specific relationships with parents, but would disrupt a culturally significant sense of continuity with previous and future generations' (2009: 798). Krogness (2014) also argues the perceived importance of the family register, citing respondents who describe their *koseki* as '*jibun no ibasho*', the place where they have a sense of belonging.

The *koseki* is also sometimes seen as essential for the person to be recognised by society; discussing children abandoned in the Kumamoto 'baby-hatch', Goldfarb acknowledges critics of the facility who felt that

> while the child would indeed be alive... a child lacking all knowledge of origin—concretely, a child existing outside of a normal family registry—would not be a socially recognized person in some of the ways that matter most in contemporary Japan.
>
> (2016a: 1)

The final explanation for the importance of the family-bond is that its singular nature increases its value: cutting *the* family-bond poses a greater threat than cutting one of multiple family-bonds would. The threat of a child being left with no family-bond is amplified by the belief that children are unable to form a new family-bond after a certain age. The next section discusses this threshold.

6 III: Children are unable to form a family-bond after a certain age

6.1 Children: infants, toddlers, and juveniles

Article 4 of the (1947) Child Welfare Act defines a child, *jidou*, as being under 18 years old.[27] Within this it distinguishes infants, *nyuuji*,[28] as being under one year old, young children, *youji*, as between one year old and the commencement of primary school, and juveniles, *shounen*, as between the commencement of primary school and 18 years old.

Children enter primary school when six years old, junior high school at 12 years of age, and high school, which is not compulsory, at 15 years old. These transitions closely mirror Stoetzel's (1955) work, which found the word *kodomo* used from birth to age 6 years of age, *shonen* from 6 to 15 years, and *seinen* from 15 to 20 years or marriage (Goodman, 2012).[29] The Child Welfare Act does not correspond to Article 4 of the (1896) Civil Code, which states: 'The age of majority is reached when a person has reached the age of 20'.[30]

6.2 Age and adoption[31]

The special adoption system (Civil Code Article 817 subsection 5) was implemented in 1988. The system is concisely explained in a Ministry of Internal Affairs and Communication memo:

> In principle, when custody of a child under six years old is extremely difficult or inappropriate, the special adoption system establishes a stable, legal, child parent relationship that conforms to a true child parent relationship for the welfare of the child.
>
> (2015: 2)

This age threshold is extended to eight years where a child has been cared for by the adopting parents prior to turning 6 years old (Article 817-5).

Tokunaga (2012) gives an overview of the reasons for this age threshold. These include that 'it corresponds with the age division in education legislation' (Tokunaga, 2012: 81), politicians' concerns that, 'to raise a child who has started primary school and entered into society as a new child of your own will normally cause problems' (Tokunaga, 2012: 81), and a policy-learning connection with Italy, where the threshold is eight years old.

Tokunaga (2012: 81) cites counsellor Hosokawa (1988: 83), a senior bureaucrat in the Ministry of Justice at this time, who stated:

> it is impossible for us to make a relationship like that of a real parent and child for elder children. Moreover, special adoption results in the natal parent child relationship ending. Simply put, this cuts[32] the legal relationship between the parent and child so for a small child you can understand this, but when a child enters school and starts to gain social discernment the question arises as to whether it is always appropriate to do such things. So, from that we determined that special adoption was suitable for a child prior to them entering school and we made these restrictions.

Despite these arguments, some politicians considered this threshold too low and, when debated, the possibility that it would be raised after legislation was passed was offered (Tokunaga, 2012). Tokunaga herself argues that this threshold should be raised so that adoption can play a greater role in alternative care (2012).[33]

The age threshold also matches the distinction between toddler and juvenile in the Child Welfare Act. The distinction made here and by Hosokawa has permeated practice. In the CGCs children are often labelled by school grade rather than age. The institutionalisation of this transition age into adoption legislation may have contributed to the age threshold until which children are understood as being able to make a family-bond. The possible impact of this on the use of foster care is explored in the following section, after a brief discussion on normal adoption and the adoption rate.

From the age of 15, a youth may be 'adopted' into a family without parental consent under the normal adoption system.[34] Normal adoption here is 'a contract between consenting adults… The adoptee, usually an adult male, agrees to carry forwards his new family's name in return for an inheritance' (Mehrotra et al., 2013: 842).

Where the adopter is the child's grandparent or step-parent 'normal adoption' can occur, under Civil Code 798, before the child turns 15 years old. In 2004 there were 83,505 adoptions, of which under 0.4 per cent were 'special adoptions', with a further 1.2 per cent by grandparents or step-parents under 'normal adoption' legislation (Mehrotra et al., 2013: 842).[35] The remaining 98.4 per cent of 'adoptions' were of adults.[36]

Special adoption extinguishes the existing family-bond (Civil Code Article 817–9). Upon completion of special adoption, a reference to the natal parents' family register is made on the adopting family register, though the details of the relationship are not listed. In normal adoption, the natal parent and child's relationship is listed on the family register of the adopting family. Mehrotra et al. (2013: 842) note:

> Ordinary adoption sanctifies the voluntary severing of most, but not all, ties to one's birth parents and their replacement with fealty to new

128 *The context of alternative care*

parents. The adoptee may contact his birth parents, and even inherit from them. If the adoptive relationship is disrupted, the adoptee may return to his biological parents.

There are two reasons why 'normal' adoption practice does not contradict the construction of the family-bond as singular and discrete. The first is its contractual nature (Bryant, 1990), which parallels marriage. Indeed, the term for breaking an adoption, *rien* (breaking of ties/connection), is also used for divorce. The second, related reason is that non-kin adoptees are understood as 'formed' adults exercising their volition.

Kinship normal adoption represents two scenarios. In the first, stepparents conform their legal relationships to the *koseki* family model. In the second, grandparents take formal control over a grandchild in their care. The limited evidence I have suggests that this is done to take on the role of a parent at the exclusion of, or to fill in for the absence of, the parents, rather than to create a second family-bond.

Goldfarb (2012) and Omori (2016) argue that some foster parents prefer normal adoption to special adoption as it lets the child decide whether to join the family and avoids imposing a sense of obligation towards the foster parents' future care needs.[37] While this may be true in some cases, the low number of children eligible for adoption means that this is not a choice most foster parents get to make.

The low numbers of adoption in Japan is an issue of 'supply' rather than 'demand'. As noted in Chapter 3, in 2015 parental rights were cut 21 times nationwide. This figure, which covers children of all ages, shows that the only children eligible for adoption are those whose parents have voluntarily ceded parental rights. This is rare, with natal parents preferring instead to leave the possibility of family reunification open.

The 'demand' for adoption can be seen in the 2008 survey on the motivation of foster parents, which found that '31.4% of foster family households answered that they "want to raise children" [and] 21.8% said that they "want to adopt children"' (Omori, 2016: 226). It can also be seen in the long waiting lists for adoption in the CGCs I visited. Cultural explanations for the low number of adoptions (see for example Hayes, 2008: 90) fail to explain this 'demand'.

6.3 Age and foster care

Where foster care acts as a proxy for adoption, we would anticipate a drop in the number of children placed into foster care around six to eight years old. Nationwide data (Figure 4.5) does reflect this. This data also shows a rise in the use of foster care for 15-to-18-year-olds. For this age-group, foster care is understood as a 'boarding house' (see Chapter 6). Family homes, which a prefectural hall bureaucrat described as having 'a scent of institution about them' (interview, 2012), make up a higher proportion of foster care placements for children over eight than they do for children under this age.

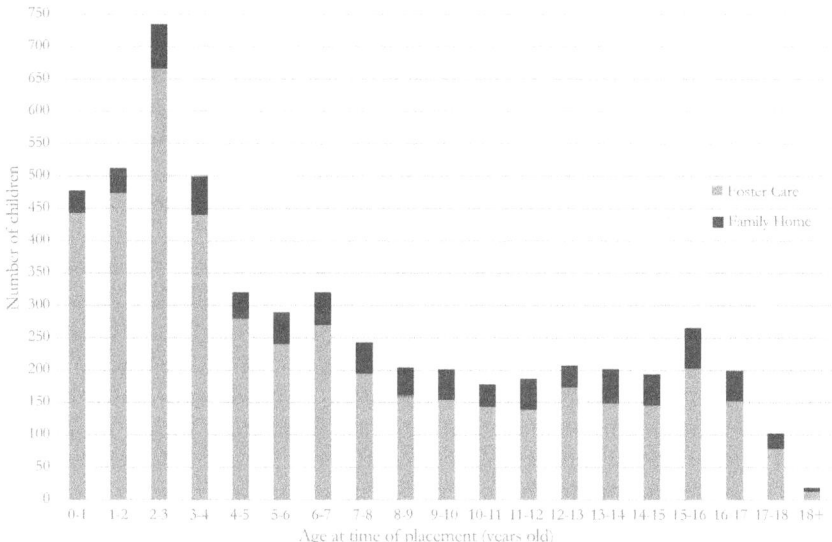

Figure 4.5 Age at time of placement into foster care or family home. Nationwide, in care on February 1st 2013.
Data Source: MHLW (2016a) *Shakai-teki yougo no genjou ni tsuite (sanka shiryou)*. 2016, January: 74

To find the threshold at which a child is no longer understood as being able to make a family-bond, I analysed cases where children over eight years old entered foster care. In these cases, foster care is not constructed as being based upon a family-bond, the child is understood as different in some way, or the CGC sees its role differently. The placement decision for Natsuko, a ten-year-old girl who entered foster care in Yuno, was shaped by all these factors.

Natsuko was seen as having a weak family-bond. She had been in a BIWI from two to three years of age and a CWI from five to eight years of age. At ten she wanted to re-enter the CWI after severe physical abuse. Recounting the case, the caseworker explained:

> Everyone thought CWI again. But, we started to think, she will become an adult and never know a normal household. So, we should try foster care, but we need a foster parent… with real power. It was her final chance to have a foster parent, experience of a household. The child actually wanted to go to a CWI as had spent half their life there but, we worried she wouldn't be able to do attachment, this could be the last age she gets to make trusting relationships with adults. As kids get older it is harder to do this.

The caseworker continued:

> She is doing really well at foster care now. The foster parent is *Tenri-kyō*.[38] Most foster parents would say no, no confidence and so on, but

this person said no problem at all, please let us care for her. The debate in the CGC was that the child had an image of the CWI. If the foster parent got sick tomorrow there would be no one who could care for her. If they have an argument in the house how will she do. Worried about her being in a personal space, rather than a CWI. If she ran away, if got involved with the police etc. If this foster parent hadn't been available would have been CWI. I don't know what will happen from now, may not go well, but even if doesn't then still have this experience.

The conclusion, on this being a beneficial experience even if the placement breaks down, contrasts sharply with CGC fears of foster care placement breakdown where care is built upon the family-bond. In all the CGCs I visited, a placement breakdown in foster care was normally constructed as far more damaging to the child than a placement breakdown in institutional care. Here, the gamble to place Natsuko into foster care was offset by the lack of a family-bond between Natsuko and her parents, by the responsibility the CGC felt for not having placed Natsuko into foster care earlier, and by the construction of this *Tenri* foster parent.[39]

Here the CGC hoped that Natsuko would be able to form *an* attachment to the foster parent,[40] to provide a template for relationships with adults, but did not construct this as being based upon a family-bond. Natsuko's caseworker alludes to this distinction, wanting Natsuko to 'know a normal household' and to have 'experience of a household', rather than to become a member of the family or household. This language is typical of cases of children aged over 6 to 8 entering foster care, with regional variation in this threshold discussed in Chapter 6.

7 Conclusions

This chapter has established that the family-bond is understood as a fluid, contested construction of legal bonds, blood bonds, bonds emerging from the embodied practice of care, facilitated at times by an acclimatisation process, a sense of belonging to a place, which may extend to belonging to a family register and perhaps even a lineage, familial love, and expectations around future support.

The construction of the family-bond as singular and discrete serves as a 'cognitive lock' (Beland and Cox, 2011: 14), setting the parameters within policy can be implemented. It is likely that the lack of professional training and the devolution of power to local authorities amplifies the impact of this 'value'.

This chapter also established the three key characteristics of the family-bond: that a child can only have one family-bond, that removing a child from the family risks the family bond, and that there is an age threshold above which the child cannot form a new family-bond. These characteristics contribute to our understanding of the low rate of children entering care and, when coupled with an understanding of some foster care serving as a proxy for adoption, the low foster care rate.

This construction also sheds light on a puzzle that one of my Doctorate supervisors, Roger Goodman, raised during my fieldwork: why are children returned to abusive families with the hope that things will get better, and not placed with foster carers in the fear that things may go wrong? Daiki's case showed us that the decision to return children to potentially abusive families is often constructed as being in the child's best interests – safeguarding their family-bond. The evaluation of the risk of 'social death' against the risk of 'biological death' varies across local authorities.

The singular nature of the family-bond helps us to understand the importance afforded to it. This can be seen in the greater fear of placement breakdown in foster care than in institutional care, as well as in the lengthy *kōryuu* process. This also helps us to understand the 'holding role' played by welfare institutions, in allowing the family-bond to exist in a suspended state.

Paradoxically, the importance given to the family-bond weakens the capacity of the CGCs to develop it. The lack of judicial support, in part related to the importance assigned to the family-bond by the courts, means that most placements are made with parental consent. This affords almost no control to CGC staff, who are thus wary of contacting the natal parents as this creates the risk of them removing the child from care before the CGC feels it to be safe. This explains the contradiction of welfare institutions being used as a holding space to allow family-bonds to develop, while little, if any, work is done with the parents to facilitate this.

In a position shared by Doi, the head of HRW in Tokyo, Bryant (1990: 328) highlights another effect of the reliance on parental consent:

> To the extent disputes are siphoned off through mediation, they do not become precedents that reflect alternative solutions to similar problems or changes in attitudes about appropriate solutions. Accordingly, there may well be considerable stunting of case law development.

Possible changes to joint custody and the recent focus on attachment in a clinical sense may eventually create a space in which a child is seen as being able to have two family-bonds. Similarly, the increased use of foster care itself may also contribute to this 'widening' of the construction of the family-bond, which could create a positive self-reinforcing feedback loop allowing more foster care to be used.

The importance of recognising underlying values to ensure that policy change leads to the desired results is both self-evident and well-evidenced (Pfau-Effinger, 2005; Small et al., 2010). The ongoing changes to legislation and guidelines aimed at developing the use of foster care do not take the construction of the family-bond laid out in this chapter into account. For these attempts to be successful, either the construction of foster care as based upon the family-bond, discussed further in Chapter 6, or the construction of the family-bond outlined here, must be addressed head-on.

Notes

1 I hypothesise that this factor is more important in Japan and the Mediterranean countries than in Eastern European countries, where the Soviet legacy is considered important (UNICEF, 2009). Further research into the family-bond in these countries is needed to test the international validity of this construction.
2 A literal translation is 'And so, I become a father'.
3 All names have been anonymised and identifying characteristics altered.
4 In this case, the mother was later fully consulted.
5 During the *kōryuu* process, the foster parent and child get to know each other and the caseworker assesses the suitability of the match. For adoption, and where the foster care is understood as long-term, the *kōryuu* process is best understood as a period aimed at facilitating the creation of a foundation, upon which, it is hoped, a family-bond will develop through the continued 'embodied practice' of care.

The *kōryuu* process is carried out from a BIWI or temporary care institution, or, less frequently, from a CWI or specialist welfare institution. Temporary care institutions inside the CGCs are seen as giving the CGC more control over the process but cannot care for children under two years old. This means that all *kōryuu* for babies and infants comes from a placement, or temporary placement, in a BIWI.

The process varies between welfare institutions but usually starts with a period where the prospective carers will visit the child, for example in a BIWI, on a weekly or fortnightly basis for one hour to play together. When the BIWI and CGC feel the child is comfortable with the carers these visits are lengthened or made more frequent. After another period of time has passed the child will go out on day trips with the carers and eventually stay overnight at the family's home. After a number of overnight stays the placement will be made. The CGC is responsible for assessing the suitability of the match, though the BIWI will give feedback to the CGC, for example on the baby crying during a visit or a behavioural change after a home visit. The weight that the CGC assigns these reports varies, though it can be hard for a CGC to place a child when the BIWI, which is providing the care to the child on a daily basis, states that the child is not ready. The shortest *kōryuu* I saw lasted three months and the longest two and a half years.

The 'Aichi method', where a baby is placed directly with foster parents who are registered to adopt rather than first into a BIWI, challenges the idea that an adoptive family will necessarily reject a child who is later found to have any special care needs, learning difficulties, or physical disabilities, and the idea that family-bonds developed through practice without blood require gradual development.
6 When I later asked about the adoption of five-year-olds, the caseworker responded: 'This is a very rare type of case'.
7 Caseworkers rarely used euphemisms, which suggests that this mother was working as a hostess or that the caseworker was unsure about the exact nature of the work.
8 Where parental rights are suspended the head of the CGC, or in specific cases the head of a welfare institution, takes on parental rights.
9 One mother working in the sex trade was praised in an aid objectives meeting for being *majime*, earnest, for self-studying customer service.
10 This echoes Winnicott's (1960) 'good-enough' mother.
11 Only married couples can adopt.
12 Section Head.
13 Toys anonymised.

14 Temporary Care Worker.
15 *Sumi-komi* institutions, where staff live in, are now rare, limited largely to self-reliance assistance homes. I would classify Japan's SOS children's villages as *sumi-komi* unit style CWIs, rather than as foster care.
16 Administrative commitments mean that there is one staff member for every four to five babies and infants during the day and, according to one ex-BIWI staff member, between 20 to 40 babies and infants at night (interview, 2015).
17 Squares represent males, circles represent females, and a cross through a person indicates that they are deceased. A solid horizontal line indicates marriage, a dotted horizontal line indicates a non-marital relationship and a diagonal line through these indicates divorce or the cessation of a relationship. In Teru and Yuno, a double square or circle was used to indicate the child to whom the form relates. In Yuno, the abuser was blocked in (see Figure 4.2).
18 DV stands for domestic violence.
19 Participants commonly annotated forms with comments, corrections, and questions.
20 The *koseki* system also prevents a married couple from having different surnames (Hendry, 2010; Sugimoto, 2010). In 2015, the high court ruled that this did not violate women's right to equality. McCurry, reporting in The Guardian, highlighted the comments of Masaomi Takanori, a constitutional scholar, who told NHK that 'names are the best way to bind families... Allowing different surnames risks destroying social stability, the maintenance of public order and the basis for social welfare' (2015). Others fiercely oppose this position (see Serizawa, 2012).
21 Ronald suggests that aversion to duality in Japan may be linked to the 'greater significance' accorded to the concepts of *uchi* and *soto* (2011: 176). Clear demarcations are found in the lack of dual nationality, and even in debates on the binary nature of death, prompted by medical advances related to brain death (see Lock, 2008: 489-496). Ronald (2011: 176) argues that:

> outside (soto) places and categories are [constructed as] dangerous and alien, and that individual security is accomplished through the integrity of the inside (uchi) community. This requires a strict regulation of inside and outside classifications and involves considerable identification with, and subjugation to, the interests and authority of members of one's *uchi*.

Hendry (2003) argues that the need to retain harmony within the *uchi* acts as a powerful agent of 'social control', that promotes conciliation over recourse to *soto* legal actions. These factors may impact the willingness of the state to intervene in the family and in the use of welfare institutions. I have not explored *uchi soto* further as these concepts did not arise in my analysis. They are acknowledged here as a potential analytical tool for other researchers.
22 The UK government (2017) explains this to natal parents: 'Depending on the child's situation, you may be able to stay in contact with them. This is often done using letters and photographs (and sometimes meetings)'
23 The Yomiuri Shinbun investigated Wa no Kai over their fees. The original article is no longer available online, but is discussed in a blog post on REFORM (2013).
24 Yuno used this committee in a more comprehensive manner than Irifune or Teru. The strategic advice given in this case, cut from the discussion below, focused on developing capacity to assess how risk has changed after an intervention.
25 Committee member.
26 Yuno assigned this guideline more weight than many other CGCs.
27 There is an array of transition ages in Japanese legislation. The voting age is 18 years, having been lowered from 20 years in 2016, compulsory education ends at

15 years, men can get married at age 18, women at age 16, criminal responsibility is 14 years, and the national holiday for the coming of age ceremony celebrates those who have turned 20 years old. Youth must leave care at 18 years, though this can be extended in specific circumstances until 20 years old.
28 A provisional government translation uses 'infants'. In BIWI, *nyuuji in*, I translate this as babies and infants.
29 Age 7 is also an important transition, with children seen as more fully formed at age. This is marked in traditional *shichi go san* ceremonies (see Seki, 1958; Sofue, 1965; Takeuchi, 1952).
30 This causes issues for care-leavers, who are unable to sign contracts for mobile phones or apartments (HRW, 2014; interviews with care-leavers, 2012).
31 Following the completion of this book, amendments to the Civil Code in 2019 increased the legal threshold for adoption to 15 years old. These amendments also split the decision to place a child for adoption from the decision to approve a specific adopting couple (see Tokunaga et al., forthcoming). The effects of this change are likely to be significant, particularly on the age threshold until which a child is understood as being able to make a family-bond and on the use of foster care. Further research is required on this change and its impact.
32 Here the word *kitte-shimau* is used. This means both completely cut and to cut with regret, an ambiguity that is hard to translate.
33 Only 31.5 per cent of the 3,000 respondents in a 2016 survey, who were told the current threshold, felt that adoption should be restricted to children under six years old (The Nippon Foundation, 2016).
34 Mehrotra et al. (2013) link this age to 'the age of consent'. This is not correct: the age of consent is 13 years old though it varies, above this threshold, by local authority (Penal Code (Act No. 45 of 1907), Article 176 (on Forced Indecency), Article 177 (on Rape). Confusingly, Article 177 only applies to females).
35 Moriguchi (2010) notes that about half the special adoption applications in the first two years were applications to convert normal adoptions to special adoptions.
36 Bryant argues that Civil Code Article 811, which is aimed at cancelling normal adoption of children, poses a 'danger for child adoptees… If agreement is reached between the adults involved, a child can be moved into and out of adoptive relationships without any judicial supervision of the adults' decisions' (1990: 333).
37 One caseworker noted that there is a spike in adoption enquiries every year following the national holiday where people go to visit their family graves. The caseworker 'joked' that these people are worrying about who will look after their graves when they die.
38 *Tenri kyō* is a Japanese new religion with around 1.2 million followers (Omori, 2016). It originates from the teachings of Nakayama Miki (1798–1887) and emphasises charitable acts. In explaining why so many followers of *Tenri* foster, Omori quotes foster parents who cited Nakayama Miki's words, 'There is no greater salvation that to care for and raise another person's child' (2016: 216).
39 The most concise explanation of Tenri foster parents' construction of their relationship with their foster children comes from Omori (2016: 214), who argues:

> while Tenri foster parents build and maintain fictive kinship with children in state care, these foster parents tend to use the framework of Tenri cosmology to conceive of their child as 'temporarily entrusted' to them. This contrasts starkly with non-Tenri foster parents, who often aspire to keep the child as their own.

40 The terms *aichaku*, attachment, and *aichaku shougai*, attachment disorder, are increasingly frequent in alternative care discourse, though one CGC head noted that 'in Japan biological attachment is prioritised over attachment as understood in a clinical sense' (interview, 2015). Mclean et al. (2013) document that the gap between the meaning assigned to 'attachment' between practitioners and academics is also found in Australia.

References

Ainsworth, F., & Thoburn, J. (2014). An exploration of the differential usage of residential childcare across national boundaries. *International Journal of Social Welfare*, 23, 16–24.
Baldcock, J. (1999). Culture: The missing variable in understanding social policy? *Social Policy and Administration*, 33(4), 458–473.
Bamba, S., & Haight, W. (2007). Helping maltreated children to find their ibasho: Japanese perspectives on supporting the well-being of children in state care. *Children and Youth Services Review*, 29, 405–427.
Bamba, S., & Haight, W. (2009). Maltreated children's emerging well-being in Japanese state care. *Children and Youth Services Review*, 31, 797–806.
Beland, D., & Cox, R.H. (2011). Introduction. In D. Beland, & R.H. Cox (Eds.), *Ideas and politics in social science research*. Oxford: Oxford University Press.
Bourdieu, P. (1996). On the family as a realized category. *Theory, Culture, and Society*, 13(3), 19–26.
Bryant, T.L. (1990). Sons and lovers: Adoption in Japan. *The American Journal of Comparative Law*, 38(2), 299–336.
Child Welfare Act. (1947). Act No. 164 of 1947, December 12.
Civil Code. (1896). Act No. 89 of 1896, April 27.
Esping-Andersen, G. (1990). *The three worlds of welfare capitalism*. Princeton: Princeton University Press.
Geertz, C. (1973). *The interpretation of cultures: Selected essays*. New York: Basic Books.
Goldfarb, K. (2012). *Fragile kinships: Family ideologies and child welfare in Japan*. (Doctoral dissertation). The University of Chicago.
Goldfarb, K. (2016a). *Anonymity, ancestry, and family registry: Adoption debates in contemporary Japan*. Conference paper for 2016 Association for Asian Studies, Seattle.
Goldfarb, K. (2016b). 'Coming to look alike': Materializing affinity in Japanese foster and adoptive care. *Social Analysis*, 60(2), 47–64.
Goldfarb, K. (2018). Beyond blood ties: Intimate kinships in Japanese foster and adoptive care. In A. Alexy, & E. Cook (Eds.), *Intimate Japan*. Honolulu: University of Hawaii Press.
Goldfarb, K. (N.D.). *Fragile kinships: Relational futures in Japanese state care*. Unpublished book manuscript.
Goodman, R. (1999). The entrepreneurial children's home: Approaches to the study of the Japanese child welfare system. *IDS Bulletin*, 30(4), 71–81.
Goodman, R. (2000). *Children of the Japanese state: The changing role of child protection institutions in contemporary Japan*. Oxford: Oxford University Press.
Goodman, R. (2012). The 'discovery' and 'rediscovery' of child abuse (*jido gyakutai*) in Japan. In R. Goodman, Y. Imoto, & T. Toivonen (Eds.), *A sociology of Japanese youth: From returnees to NEETs*. London: Nissan Institute/Routledge Japanese Studies.
Hann, C. (1996). Introduction: Political society and civil anthropology. In C. Hann, & E. Dunn (Eds.), *Civil society: Challenging Western models*. London: Routledge.
Harada, C., & Koreeda, H. (2013). *Soshite chichi ni naru* [Like father like son]. [Motion Picture]. Japan: Amuse.
Hayes, P. (2008). Special adoption in Japan: Its problems and prospects. *Adoption Quarterly*, 11(2), 81–100.
Hendry, J. (2003). *Understanding Japanese society*. London: Routledge.

Hendry, J. (2010). *Marriage in changing Japan: Community and society*. London: Taylor and Francis.
Hertog, E. (2008). The worst abuse against a child is absence of a parent: How unwed mothers evaluate their decision to have a child outside wedlock. *Japan Forum*, 20(2), 193–217.
Hertog, E. (2011). "I did not know how to tell my parents so I thought I would have to have an abortion": Experiences of unmarried women in Japan. In R. Ronald, & A. Alexy (Eds.), *Home and family in Japan: Continuity and transformation*. London: Routledge.
Hosokawa, K. (1988). Tokubetsu yōshi seido no haikei to seido no aramashi [A summary of the background of the special adoption system]. In A., Yonekura, & K. Hosokawa (Eds.), *Minpō-tō no kaisei to tokubetsu yōshi seido*. Tokyo: Nihon Kajo shuppan.
Human Rights Watch (HRW). (2014). *Without dreams. Children in alternative care in Japan*. New York: Human Rights Watch.
Inoue. (2011a, November 9). Mura de issho ni kurasu yorokobi [The joy of living together in the village]. In Sugiyama, & Inoue (Eds.), Oya ni naru, ko ni naru [Become a parent, become a child]. *Asahi Shinbun*.
Inoue. (2011b, November 15). Hōridasu no ga jiritsu ka ['Self-reliance' or being thrown out?]. In Sugiyama, & Inoue (Eds.), Oya ni naru, ko ni naru [Become a parent, become a child]. *Asahi Shinbun*.
Inoue. (2011c, November 18). Minami no shima de kazoku ni natta [We become a family on the southern island]. In Sugiyama, & Inoue (Eds.), Oya ni naru, ko ni naru [Become a parent, become a child]. *Asahi Shinbun*.
Kadonaga, T., & Fraser, M.W. (2015). Child maltreatment in Japan. *Journal of Social Work*, 15(3), 233–253.
Kendrick, A., Steckley, L., & McPheat, G.A. (2011). Residential child care: Learning from international comparisons. In R. Taylor, M. Hill, & F. McNeill (Eds.), *Early professional development for social workers*. Birmingham: The British Association of Social Workers.
Krogness, K.J. (2014). Jus Koseki: Household registration and Japanese citizenship. *The Asia-Pacific Journal, Japan Focus*, 12(35), 1–24.
Levi-Strauss, C. (1950). Introduction a l'oeuvre de Marcel Mauss. In M. Mauss (Ed.), *Sociologie et anthropologie*. Paris: Presses universitaires de France. (Available also as Lévi-Strauss, C. (1987). *Introduction to the work of Marcel Mauss*. London: Routledge and Kegan Paul.)
Lock, M. (2008). Preserving moral order: Responses to biomedical technologies. In J. Robertson (Ed.), *A companion to the anthropology of Japan*. Oxford: Blackwell.
Madge, N. (1994). *Children and residential care in Europe*. London: European Children's Centre and National Children's Bureau.
Mahoney, J. (2010). After KKC: The new methodology of qualitative research. *World Politics*, 62(1), 120–147.
McLean, M., Riggs, D., Kettler, L., & Delfabbro, P. (2013). Challenging behaviour in out-of-home care: Use of attachment ideas in practice. *Child and Family Social Work*, 18, 243–252.
Mehrotra, V., Morck, R., Shim, J., & Wiwattanakantang, Y. (2013). Adoptive expectations: Rising sons in Japanese family firms. *Journal of Financial Economics*, 108, 840–854.

MHLW. (2016a). *Shakai-teki yōgo no genjou ni tsuite (sanka shiryou)* [Current status of alternative care (reference)]. 2016, January.
Ministry of Internal Affairs and Communication. (2015b). *Ikuji kyūgyō-hō no taishō to naru ko no yōken no minaoshi (gaiyō): gyōsei hyōka kyokuchō gyōsei kujō kyūsai suishin kaigi no iken wo fumaeta assen* [Review of children who are eligible for the child-care leave act: A mediation based on opinions of the administrative complaint relief promotion council]. 2015, March 10. Retrieved from URL: http://www.soumu.go.jp/main_content/000345848.pdf (last accessed 2016, March 29).
Moriguchi, C. (2010). Child adoption in Japan, 1948–2008 – A comparative historical analysis. *Keizai kenkyū*, 61(4), 342–357.
Murata, K. (2005). *Kazoku wo tsukuru: yōiku satooya to iu ikikata* [Making a family: The way of life of regular foster parents]. Tokyo: Chuokoron-shinsha.
Ochiai, E. (1997). *The Japanese family system in transition: A sociological analysis of family change in postwar Japan.* Tokyo: LTCB International Library Foundation.
Ochiai, E. (2008). The *Ie* (family) in global perspective. In J. Robertson (Ed.), *A companion to the anthropology of Japan*. Oxford: Blackwell.
Omori, H. (2016). Creating families: Tenrikyō foster homes in Japan. *Japanese Studies*, 36(2), 213–229.
Parsons, T. (1972). Culture and social system revisited. *Social Science Quarterly*, 53(2), 253–266.
Penal Code. (1907). Act No. 45, Article 176 (on Forced Indecency), Article 177 (on Rape). Provisional English translation from the Cabinet Secretariat. Retrieved from URL: http://www.cas.go.jp/jp/seisaku/hourei/data/PC.pdf (last accessed 2016, April 5).
Pfau-Effinger, B. (1998). Gender cultures and the gender arrangement – A theoretical framework for cross-national gender research. *Innovation: The European Journal of Social Science Research*, 11(2), 147–166.
Pfau-Effinger, B. (2005). Culture and welfare state policies. Reflections on a complex interrelation. *Journal of Social Policy*, 34(1), 3–20.
Reform Ethics For Orphans and at-Risk Minors (REFORM). (2013). *Japanese Adoption Corruption*. Retrieved from URL: http://www.reformtalk.net/2013/07/12/japanese-adoption-corruption/ (last accessed 2016, December 27).
Reinhold, S. (1994). *Local conflict and ideological struggle: 'Positive images' and Section 28*. (Doctoral dissertation). University of Sussex.
Ronald, R. (2011). Homes and houses, senses and spaces. In R. Ronald, & A. Alexy (Eds.), *Home and family in Japan: Continuity and transformation*. London: Routledge.
Russell, I.R., & Edgar, A. (1998). Research and practice in the anthropology of welfare. In I.R. Edgar, & A. Russell (Eds.), *The anthropology of welfare*. London: Routledge.
Seki, K. (1958). Nihon no minzoku no rekishi [A history of Japanese folklore studies]. In T. Omachi (Ed.), *Nihon minzokugaku taikei* [An outline of Japanese folklore Vol. 2]. Tokyo: Heibonsha.
Serizawa, S. (2012). *Kazoku to iu ishi: Yorubenaki jidai wo ikiru* [The will of the family: Living in an age of isolation, with no-one to turn to]. Tokyo: Iwanami Shoten.
Shirai, C. (2010). Reproductive technologies and parent–Child relationships: Japan's past and present examined through the lens of donor insemination. *International Journal of Japanese Sociology*, 19(1), 18–34.

Shore, C., & Wright, S. (1997). Policy: A new field of anthropology. In C. Shore, & S. Wright (Eds.), *Anthropology of policy*. New York: Routledge.

Siegel, D.H. (2012). Open adoption: Adoptive parents' reactions two decades later. *Social Work,* 58(1), 43–52.

Small, M.L., Harding, D.J., & Lamont, M. (2010). Reconsidering culture and poverty. *The Annals of the American Academy*, 629, 6–27.

Sofue, T. (1965). Childhood ceremonies in Japan: Regional and local variations. *Ethnology*, 4(2), 148–164.

Stasch, R. (2009). *Society of others: Kinship and mourning in a West Papuan place.* Berkeley: University of California Press.

Stoetzel, J. (1955). *Without the chrysanthemum and the sword: A study of the attitudes of youth in post-war Japan.* New York: Columbia University Press.

Sugimoto, Y. (2010). *An introduction to Japanese society.* Cambridge: Cambridge University Press.

Sugiyama. (2011a, November 1). Chi wo tsunagari yori mo [Even more than blood ties]. In Sugiyama, & Inoue (Eds.), Oya ni naru, ko ni naru [Become a parent, become a child]. *Asahi Shinbun*.

Sugiyama. (2011b, November 2). Kono inochi min'na de sasaeru [We all support this life]. In Sugiyama, & Inoue (Eds.), Oya ni naru, ko ni naru [Become a parent, become a child]. *Asahi Shinbun*.

Sugiyama. (2011c, November 7). Anata wo motteita [I had you]. In Sugiyama, & Inoue (Eds.), Oya ni naru, ko ni naru [Become a parent, become a child]. *Asahi Shinbun*.

Sugiyama. (2011d, November 8). Funin datta kara aeta [Because we were infertile, we could meet you]. In Sugiyama, & Inoue (Eds.), Oya ni naru, ko ni naru [Become a parent, become a child]. *Asahi Shinbun*.

Sugiyama. (2011e, November 10). Ehon de musume ni puropōzu [I 'proposed' with a picture book that she become my daughter]. In Sugiyama, & Inoue (Eds.), Oya ni naru, ko ni naru [Become a parent, become a child]. *Asahi Shinbun*.

Sugiyama. (2011f, November 11). Mōmisutetari shinai [I will not abandon you]. In Sugiyama, & Inoue (Eds.), Oya ni naru, ko ni naru [Become a parent, become a child]. *Asahi Shinbun*.

Sugiyama. (2011g, November 16). Hontō no haha yori haha data [More of a mother than my real mother]. In Sugiyama, & Inoue (Eds.), Oya ni naru, ko ni naru [Become a parent, become a child]. *Asahi Shinbun*.

Sugiyama. (2011h, November 17). Jinsei no pazuru wo kansei shita [I have completed the puzzle of life]. In Sugiyama, & Inoue (Eds.), Oya ni naru, ko ni naru [Become a parent, become a child]. *Asahi Shinbun*.

Sugiyama. (2011i, November 21). 'Nihon no oba' ni mimamore [Watching over 'grandmothers of Japan']. In Sugiyama, & Inoue (Eds.), Oya ni naru, ko ni naru [Become a parent, become a child]. *Asahi Shinbun*.

Sugiyama. (2011j, November 22). 'Shakai no ko' tomo ni hagukumu [Growing up with a 'child of society']. In Sugiyama, & Inoue (Eds.), Oya ni naru, ko ni naru [Become a parent, become a child]. *Asahi Shinbun*.

Takeuchi, T. (1952). Kodomo-gumi [Children's group]. In Japan Society of Ethnology (Ed.), *Nihon shakai minzoku jiten* [Social and ethnographic dictionary of Japan]. Tokyo: Seibundo shinkosha.

The Nippon Foundation. (2016). *Tokubetsu yōshi engumi ni kansuru chōsa samarī* [Summary of survey on special adoption]. Retrieved from URL: http://www.

nippon-foundation.or.jp/news/articles/2016/img/14/1.pdf (last accessed 2017, August 22).
Thelen, K. (1999). Historical institutionalism in comparative politics. *Annual Review of Political Science,* 2, 369–404.
Tokunaga, S. (2012). The examination of the special adoption system: Focusing on the meaning, the characteristics, and the problems. *Kassui joshi daigaku katsu mizu ronbun-shū dai 55-shū kenkō seikatsu gakubu-hen Bessatsu,* 55. 2012, March 31.
Tokunaga, S., Fukui, M., Saigo, M., & Nagano, S. (Forthcoming). A new era for child protection in Japan. In J.D. Berrick, N. Gilbert, & M. Skivenes (Eds.), *The Oxford handbook of child protection systems.* New York: Oxford University Press.
Tsuzaki, T. (2009). *Kono kuni no kodomotachi: Yōhogo jidō shakai-teki yōgo no Nihonteki kōchiku; otona no kitoku ken'eki to kodomo no fukushi* [This country's children: Constructing social care for children in need of care; The vested interests of adults and children's welfare]. Tokyo: Nihon Kajo Shuppan.
UK Government. (2017). *Child adoption: 7. Birth parents: your rights.* Retrieved from URL: https://www.gov.uk/child-adoption/birth-parents-your-rights (last accessed 2017, August 20).
United Nations International Children's Emergency Fund (UNICEF). (2009). *Child well-being at a crossroads: Evolving challenges in Central and Eastern Europe and the Commonwealth of Independent States.* Florence: Innocenti Research Centre, Innocenti Social Monitor.
van Oorschot, W. (2007). Culture and social policy: A developing field of study. *International Journal of Social Policy,* 16, 129–139.
Winnicott, D.W. (1960). The theory of parent infant relationship. *The International Journal of Psychoanalysis,* 41, 585–595.

Note: Where the author(s) provided an English translation of their work I have given this translation, rather than my translation.

Part III
Regional variation of policy implementation

5 Regional variation of resources

1 Introduction

Having introduced alternative care and the CGCs and established the shared context of the family-bond, the next three chapters examine the factors that shape regional variation in how policy is implemented. This is structured to examine the impact of regional variation of resources, norms, and organisational cultures. These chapters consider *what* differs and *why* these differences occur, with the CGCs' organisational cultures, themselves shaped by beliefs and resources, understood as playing a critical mediating role between resources and norms.

Any examination of policy implementation must consider the resources available to the street-level bureaucrats (Brodkin, 1997). Meyers and Vorsanger (2003) note that 'front-line workers wield influence that goes well beyond their official positions in implementing systems; but they are also constrained in important respects by those systems' (251), and argue that

> if we fail to consider how the implementation context structures the job of front-line workers, we risk assigning them credit or blame for policy outcomes that are largely determined by features of the policy design, the organisational capacity or other implementation factors.
>
> (245–246)

This chapter looks at the impact of five different categories of resources on policy implementation: the physical geography of the CGC; the local political attention on alternative care; the capacity of care providers, divided into physical capacity, demand, and the perceived quality; the capacity of the CGCs, including the number of staff working on foster care and their level of expertise; the external actors, including NPOs and the foster care specialists within welfare institutions.

These chapters focus on two of my fieldwork sites: Teru, which has a high foster care rate, and Irifune, which has a low foster care rate. Data from Yuno and national data is used when it provides insight or perspective.

2 Physical geography and the CGCs

Physical geography is routinely overlooked in policy implementation studies. In one rare example of geography being considered in this research area, Kashiwame argues that there is an 'urban-rural divide in the foster care rate' (2010: 8), with rural areas having a higher relative CWI capacity due to post-war migration to cities. While this is not found in the mapping of foster care (see Chapter 1), every CGC must implement policy within the physical geography of its jurisdiction. This space is relatively static, though can change with the creation of a new local authority, such as Kanazawa City in 2007, or the establishment of a new CGC and the re-designation of jurisdictions within a local authority. To protect anonymity, physical geography is discussed in relative rather than absolute terms.

Teru is under one-tenth the size of Irifune. Despite this, the population of each is almost identical. There is more than one CGC in Irifune, though each CGC covers a much larger jurisdiction than the Teru CGC. Irifune also has many islands. The foster care caseworker noted that a visit to a foster parent can entail catching the 5 a.m. ferry and not returning until 11 p.m. This limits the caseworker's ability to support and the local authority's ability to recruit foster parents. Conversely, Teru's compact geography means that CGC staff can easily reach anywhere within its jurisdiction, increasing their capacity to provide foster care services.

On a national level, the relationships between the foster care rate and the total (land) area, the total population, the total population under 15 years of age, the total population density, and the density of the population of those under 15 years old are not statistically significant. Yet these figures do not account for the number of CGCs or the geographical jurisdiction of each CGC as the foster care rate is not available at CGC level.

While we cannot analyse the national level, physical geography was understood as important in all three of my fieldwork sites, in relation to how the CGC understands their capacity to provide foster care services and in relation to their strategies for developing these services. In Teru the local authority has invested within the CGC, while Irifune has outsourced foster care recruitment and training to a BIWI. In explaining this decision, discussed further below, Irifune CGC staff referenced the large geographical area that they cover.

The relative strength of each CGC to their local authority hall may also be affected by the population and the geography with which they work. A large CGC covering a large population may have more weight in local politics than a small CGC covering a small population in a large rural area. This is discussed further below.

3 Political attention

Miwa (2016) argues that the lack of political attention at the national level until 2000 resulted in national change being incremental in nature. The limited evidence I have from interviews suggests this is also true at the local authority level. Here we need to consider two factors: the nature and the strength of the attention. A governor may be pro-foster care, pro-institutional care, ambivalent, or unaware of this issue. The strength of this position will contribute to whether political attention results in concrete changes, for example, to the budget, in political signalling, or inaction.

There are differences in political attention between my fieldwork sites. Teru's vice-governor in the mid-2000s wanted to promote foster care. This led to the appointment of Sano, who was known for his reform work in mental health care, as CGC head.[1] These actors then successfully pressed for the CGC to secure part of a windfall from the privatisation of nurseries, which was largely allocated to developing foster care services.

The Teru CGC still enjoys political support, in part due to the perception that the CGC is 'doing a good job'. This increases the probability that the CGC's requests are received positively by the local authority hall. This has allowed the CGC to keep three senior managers in place for long postings, to increase the number of CGC staff working on foster care, and to appoint a full-time lawyer.

A similar process may be starting in Yuno. In April 2015, the Yuno governor allocated the largest increase within all budget sectors to alternative care, with a focus on increasing the quantity and quality of foster care. The importance of governors is highlighted by a local bureaucrat in an MHLW report: 'there has been a U-turn from what we did until last year. With one word from the governor we got a budget' (MHLW SC, 2016: 105).

A 2015 email from a senior Yuno bureaucrat explains their understanding of the 'default setting' for change, as well as the impact of political attention on the prioritisation of tasks:

> I don't think there is a strategic ranking of priorities in child welfare in Japan. If there are no particularly large problems, I think all areas are slowly improved at the same time. But, if there is a big problem, something that is big enough to make the newspapers or news, then there is a concentration of resources to make sure that the same thing does not happen again. I think you can probably say this for all Japan, but when there is an uproar all attention is put into resolving that problem, the result of this being that this issue rises up the ranking of priorities.
>
> On the risk assessment tool, I think the fact that two children died from abuse... was a big trigger. Both children's deaths occurred whilst the child was known to the CGCs, so this was a large shock for the local authority. There was a strong conviction that we could not let children die from abuse again, and the child guidance centres did their best. This resulted in the strengthening of the legal consultation section and the city, town, village support project team, in relation to dealing with abusive parents. This led to the strengthening of the city and town's abilities to deal with the first response to abuse fears. I think addressing this was a big thing.

146 *Variation of policy implementation*

> Just at the time when the abuse response had settled down, now, we started to put power into developing foster care but this was not something we had decided, to do foster care after responding to abuse. This was due to the strong convictions of Governor [name].

This echoes Meyers and Vorsanger, who argue that policies 'with strong political champions, are likely to command... appropriate resources for implementing agents' (2003: 253).

There is minimal political attention on the promotion of foster care in Irifune. The increase in the foster care rate of the last few years is understood within the CGC to be 'bottom-up', the result of the efforts of the previous and current foster care caseworker. The relatively limited nature of this change suggests that without political support, change is more likely to be incremental.

May and Winter state that 'street-level bureaucrats have a greater license to diverge from national goals when those local politicians who are closest to the street-level bureaucrats disagree with the national goals' (2007: 457). There were no national goals on promoting foster care until the early 2000s and no concrete goals until 2011. Thus, rather than framing divergence as divergence from 'national goals', it is more useful here to understand divergence as being from national or local 'practice norms'. Divergence from local path-dependent practice is easiest when, as in Teru, it is supported over the 'two-levels' of politics and bureaucracy.[2] The limited nature of change in Irifune and Yuno, with political attention in Yuno a recent development, suggest that reform efforts that do not occur at both levels will have less traction.

4 The capacity of care providers

4.1 The physical capacity of care providers

When explaining my interest in regional variation during fieldwork, I often highlighted Niigata and Sakai City, which had foster care rates of 39 per cent and 4.2 per cent, respectively, in 2011. Nearly everyone replied with a variant of, 'Well, Niigata has very few institutions'.

Japan's alternative care system grew exponentially in the aftermath of World War II. The number of BIWIs increased from 19 in 1945 to 131 in 1960, with 297 of the 520 CWIs (in 1998) founded between 1945 and 1955 (Goodman, 2000: 46–52). There was a concurrent increase in the use of foster care, though 'in almost all cases... the natal family and the fostering family knew each other' (Goodman, 2000: 141) and there was 'very little state support... and... no system to check on the well-being of the child' (Goodman, 2000: 141; see also Kumasaka and Aiba, 1968).

Following this surge there was a steady decline in the number of children entering care until around 1995. Goodman (2000: 51–52) notes that

In total in 1955 there were 528 *yogoshisetsu* [CWI] offering places to almost 33,000 children. In the following forty years the number of homes scarcely changed, so that in 1995 there was exactly the same number of homes, though with almost 7,000 fewer children. Over this forty-year period, however, the number of public homes more than halved (from 110 to fifty).

The decrease in the number of children entering care leads to an increase in competition between private and public CWIs, and between institutions and foster parents for placements. Discussing adoption, Moriguchi (2010) constructs this in terms of 'supply' and 'demand'. This section explores this relationship, framed here as 'capacity' and 'need', with the qualification that the rate of children entering care is not a perfect proxy for 'need'. There is regional variation in public willingness to report abuse, and in the assessment of these risks by the non-professional caseworkers. The response of Yuno to the deaths of the two babies suggests that the pendulum between authorities being interventionist and supporting the family (see Buchanan, 1996; Lepore, 2016) swings at the local rather than the national level in Japan.

In the decades after World War II the private CWIs were the most organised in protecting their interests (Hirada, 2014; Ito et al., 2014; Miwa, 2014), with the foster care rate increasing when the institutions were full and declining when the institutions were at a lower capacity (see Kashiwame, 2010; Miyajima, 2007; Tsuzaki, 2009; Yoshida, 2008). This leads Tsuzaki to argue that foster care has acted primarily as a 'safety valve' (2006), to absorb the overflow. Miwa's (2014) work supports this argument until around 2000, at which point the increasing number of children coming into care served to dampen this competition.

Teru and Irifune support the hypothesis of those I spoke to on fieldwork about Niigata and Sakai City: Teru has 11.8 places in CWIs for every 10,000 children aged under 18, almost exactly half of that of Irifune (see Table 5.1). As we would anticipate, there also appears to be a relationship between the number of registered foster carers, relative to the child population, and the foster care rate.

The capacity of care providers is not static. The CGC can recruit foster parents, and welfare institutions may close or change their capacity, for example, when restructuring from large dormitory-style into group homes. As a service provider for foster care, it is easier for the CGC to change the capacity of this than the capacity of welfare institutions. Nor is the need for alternative care static: for example, the 'discovery' of abuse led to more children entering care.

Figure 5.1 shows the relationship between the foster care rate and the capacity of BIWIs and CWIs, relative to the child population under 15 years of age, by a local authority in 2014.[3] At this fixed point in time, the relationship is strong ($r = 0.543$), negative, and statistically significant ($p = 0.000$). Local authorities with a higher relative institutional capacity are more likely to

148 *Variation of policy implementation*

Table 5.1 The capacity of care providers, relative to child population. Teru, Irifune, Japan

	Teru	Irifune	Japan (69 Local authorities)
Combined BIWI & CWI capacity per 10,000 children (Oct 2014)	14.7	25.4 (24.3)[a]	18.3
CWI capacity per 10,000 children (Oct 2014)	11.8	23.7 (22.7)[a]	16.4
BIWI capacity per 10,000 children (Oct 2014)	2.8	1.7 (1.6)[a]	1.9
Number of registered foster parents per 10,000 children (2013–2014)	5.5	4.5	4.9
Number of foster parents with placement per 10,000 children (2013–2014)	2.0	1.7	1.8

Data Sources: Population of children under 18 years of age. Calculated from: National population census. (2010). Note, this differs from MHLW figures which is based on the child population under 15 years of age.

Teru and Irifune CWI & BIWI capacity: Fieldwork.

Japan CWI and BIWI capacity: MHLW. (2016a). *Shakai-teki yougo no genjou ni tsuite (sanka shiryou)*. 2016, January: 92–93.

Japan Foster parents' capacity: MHLW. (2016d). *Fukushi gyōsei hōkoku rei (etsuran jidō dai 13-hyō satooya-sū, todōfuken – shitei toshi – chūkaku-shi × shinki – torikeshi-betsu)*.

[a] Figures in the brackets indicate a limit placed on capacity by the local authority below the total physical limit of the welfare institutions.

have a lower foster care rate than those with a lower relative institutional capacity.

Figure 5.2 shows the relationship between the number of registered foster carers, relative to the child population aged under 15, and the foster care rate by local authority in 2014.[4] At this fixed point in time the relationship is strong ($r = 0.688$), positive, and statistically significant ($p = 0.000$). Local authorities with a higher relative foster care capacity are more likely to have a higher foster care rate than those with a lower relative foster care capacity.

Miwa's (2011) analysis of the relationship between the occupancy rate of CWIs and the foster care rate from 1953 to 2008 finds competition between the two providers. Until 2003 there was a negative correlation between the combined BIWI and CWI occupancy rate and the foster care rate, as well as a negative correlation between the combined BIWI and CWI occupancy rate and the number of new placements into foster care (see also Kashiwame, 2010; Miyajima, 2007; Tsuzaki, 2009; Yoshida, 2008). This work also found that the increasing number of children entering care has reduced this competition from 2003.

Further, Miwa (2011) found that between 1994 and 2002 the foster care rate was lower than would be statistically predicted. Miwa argues that this indicates that the CWIs were particularly effective in protecting their interests during this period (see also Hirada, 2014; Ito et al., 2014). At a national

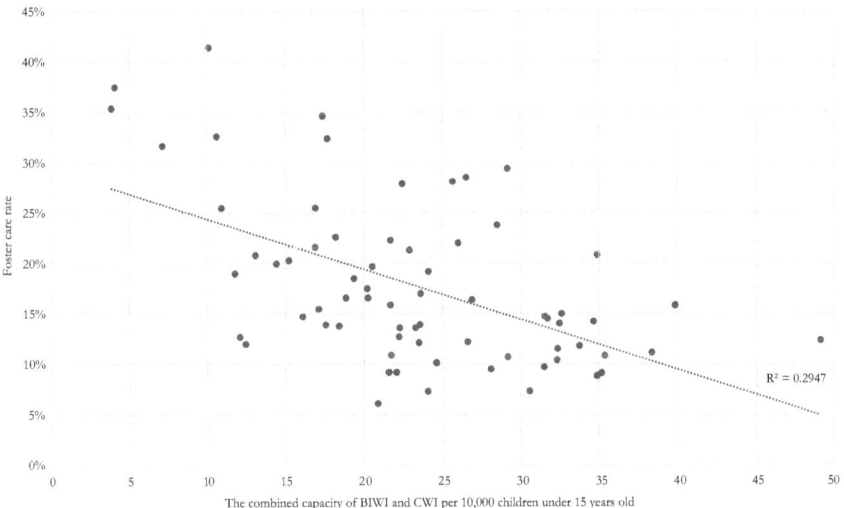

Figure 5.1 The capacity of BIWIs and CWIs, relative to child population, and the foster care rate. By local authority, 2014.

Data Sources: MHLW, Welfare administration reported cases, table 11: Child welfare institutions (excluding midwives facilities and Mother and Child living support institutions) -institution capacity, current number of children, nationwide, by prefecture, designated city, and core city, and by type of institution.
Child population: 2010 Census, children aged under 15 years old

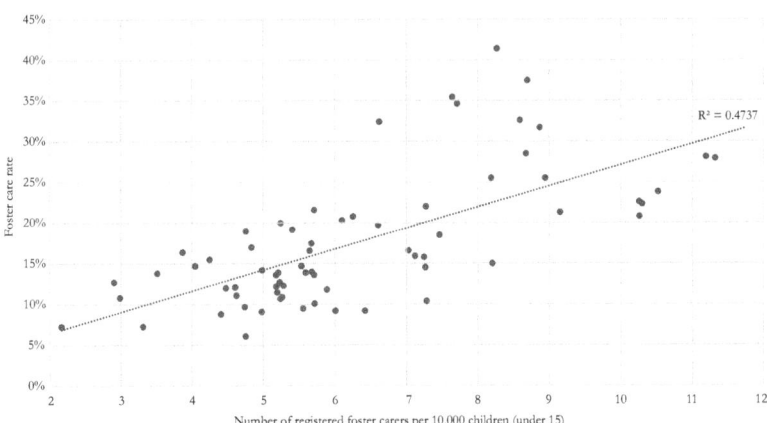

Figure 5.2 The number of registered foster parents, relative to child population, and the foster care rate. By local authority, 2014.

Data Sources: MHLW Welfare Administration Reported Casesreferencing data sheets:
1: The number of foster carers, the number of children placed into foster care, by prefecture, designated city, and core city
2: The number of small-scale residential-type child rearing businesses (family homes), capacity, new staff and staff leaving over the year, current number of staff, number of children in family homes by prefecture, designated city, and core city children, nationwide, by prefecture, designated
3: Ministry of Health, Labour and Welfare social welfare institutions survey, table 8, institution capacity, current number of city, and core city, and by type of institution, and by management status, public and private.
Child population: 2010 Census, children aged under 15 years old

level, lobbying is carried out by the National BIWI Association and the National CWI Association, which have a strong relationship with the Liberal Democratic Party's 'Committee on the future of alternative care'.

CWIs also attempt to influence policy implementation at a local level. In Irifune a caseworker recalled a CWI head who, after a sustained period where no children had been placed into his institution, began to regularly visit the CGC with bottles of sake to explain the danger of staff having to be laid off and the consequences this would have on the quality of care for the children already in the CWI. During a CWI visit in the Teru CGC staff training, a CWI manager expressed his concerns that as the foster care rate increases only children with more complex needs are placed into institutions, with 'easy' children entering foster care. He clarified this by saying that this would not be an issue if the staff-to-child ratio was better, but noted that this would not change any time soon.

In addition to lobbying their corner, CWI staff sometimes stray into criticising foster care. These critiques argue that foster parents are under-trained, under-supported and that they provide 'amateur' care behind closed doors, whereas the welfare institutions provide 'professional' care in a shared space with lots of eyes to catch abuse.

Turning to foster care, the relationship between the number of registered foster parents and the foster care rate at a fixed point in time should be interpreted with caution. Miwa's (2014, 2016) longitudinal analysis of the number of registered foster parents and the foster care rate leads her to argue that while the

> lack of foster parents[5] has been a focal point of research, there is limited empirical evidence for this and some data contradicts this hypothesis.
> (2016: 4)

Miwa argues that the number of registered but unused foster parents shows that 'the essence of the problem is not the lack of people wanting to become foster parents but rather the fact that we are in a situation where we cannot effectively use people who do want to be foster parents' (2016: 11; see also Suga, 2014).

The situation in Teru supports Miwa's position. Here, an increased capacity for supporting foster parents was coupled with an increased focus on foster parent recruitment. Caseworkers, prompted initially by senior management, slowly re-evaluated foster care in a more positive light as placements went better than expected (see Chapter 7). The impact of the increased number of foster parents was mediated by the combination of increased support for foster parents and increased caseworker trust of foster care. Before looking further at the impact of the evaluation of each care type, this chapter next explores the impact of changes in the level of need on the foster care rate.

4.2 The need for alternative care

In 2015 there were 602 CWIs, with a total capacity of 33,017 (MHLW, 2016b). This is almost unchanged from 1955, where there were almost 33,000 children in CWI, despite the child population having fallen from 29,786,000 to 15,887,000 in this period (Ministry of Internal Affairs and Communications, 2015).

The stability of the welfare institutions' capacity in the face of population decline is due to an increase in the rate of children entering care. This can largely be explained by the 'discovery' of child abuse in the 1990s (Goodman, 2000: 167–174), and its re-discovery in 2010 (Goodman, 2012: 99). As Harada (2010) notes, we cannot determine the degree to which the increase in reported abuse cases reflects an increased awareness of abuse, rather than an increase in abuse. The 'discovery' of abuse and the increased number of children entering care parallel a prolonged period of economic stagnation and recession that 'has resulted in rising poverty without a concomitant boost in social welfare provision' (Goldfarb, 2012: 30; see also Harada, 2010). There is a growing body of work in Japan that links poverty with abuse (see Kato, 2014; Matsumoto, 2010; Matsumoto, 2013; Mochizuki et al., 2014; Negishi, 2014)[6] and this, along with a sense that the welfare state is increasingly struggling to support the family (Aoyama et al., 2015; Rebbick and Takenaka, 2006; Ronald and Alexy, 2011), may have increased the amount of abuse as well as the validity of state intervention.[7]

Figure 5.3 maps the relationship between child poverty rates by a prefecture for 2012 (Mainichi Japan, 2016) and the foster care rate by a prefecture for 2011.[8] This relationship is statistically significant ($p = 0.004$), moderate ($r = 0.410$), and positive. Prefectures with a higher child poverty rate are more likely to take a higher rate of children into care than those with a lower child poverty rate. These findings were echoed in my fieldwork. One local authority created an internal report on the financial status of parents at the time of their child's placement into a CWI: only 12.6 per cent of households earned enough to pay income tax, with 31.4 per cent claiming social security and 38.3 per cent having no employed adults.

Miwa (2012), examining 2000 to 2009, argues that the increase in the number of children entering care has increased the foster care rate in two ways. The first is directly, by reducing competition between foster care and institutional care. The second, which Miwa (2012) argues is more significant, is that the discovery of abuse led to an increase in the number of caseworkers.[9] This reduced average caseload afforded caseworkers more time on each case.[10] Between 2000 and 2009, local authorities where caseworkers had a lower caseload were statistically more likely to have a higher foster care rate (Miwa, 2012).

These two factors may act in opposition: local authorities with a higher rate of children entering care may have less competition between care providers, increasing the foster care rate or, conversely, the higher rate of

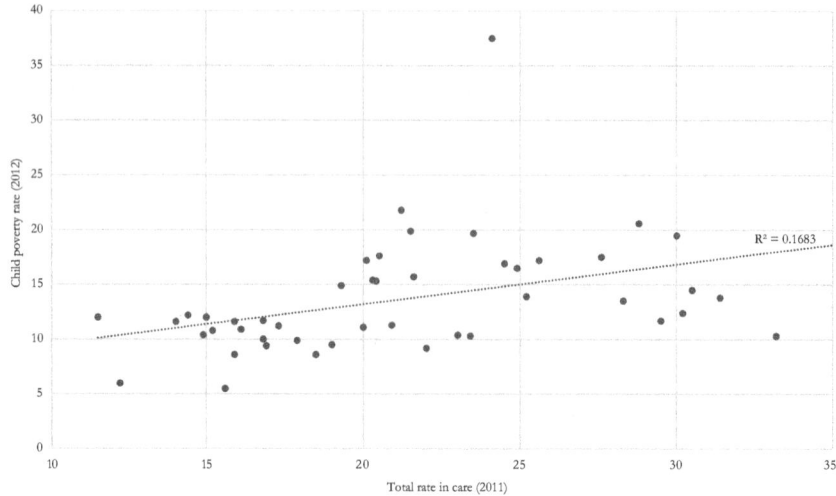

Figure 5.3 The child poverty rate (2012) and the total rate in care (2011). By prefecture.
Data sources: Child poverty by prefecture calculated by Tomuro, cited in: Mainichi Japan (2016). MHLW. (2012a). Shakaiteki yougo no genjou ni tsuite. 2012, September: 25
N.B. MHLW data on total rate in care for 2012 only available with prefecture, designated, and core cities separated so have just 2011 data (MHLW, 2012a) which shows total rate in foster care, family homes, BIWI & CWI by prefecture.

children entering care may lead to a higher caseload, reducing the foster care rate.

Figure 5.4 maps the relationship between the rate of children in care, per 10,000 children under 15 years of age, and the foster care rate in 2011–2012.[11] The relationship is moderate ($r = 0.340$), statistically significant ($p = 0.004$) and negative. Local authorities with a lower rate of children in care are more likely to place a higher rate of those children into foster care than those with a higher rate of children entering care.

Building on Miwa's findings on caseworker's workload and the foster care rate, it is worth noting that the caseworkers' average caseload has increased since 2009. Aoki reports that while the number of reported cases of suspected abuse increased over seven-fold between 1999 and 2014, 'the number of child welfare caseworkers increased only 2.3 fold… from 1,230 in 1999 to 2,289 in 2014' (2016). Saimura et al. express widely held concerns succinctly: 'in order to meet recent needs, it is indispensable to secure the apposite numbers of human resources in the CGC' (2010: 181; see also Takahashi et al., 2010).

In 2007, each CGC caseworker had an average of 107 active cases (Saimura, 2008). This, combined with the regular rotation of caseworkers, means that caseworkers cannot 'track any individual's progression or assess placement outcomes' (Goldfarb, 2012: 102) and cannot fully investigate some cases (Goodman, 2000; Miwa, 2012, 2016; Miyajima, 2001).[12] The consequences of this can be fatal. In 2013 there were 69 fatal cases of child abuse,[13] 36 of

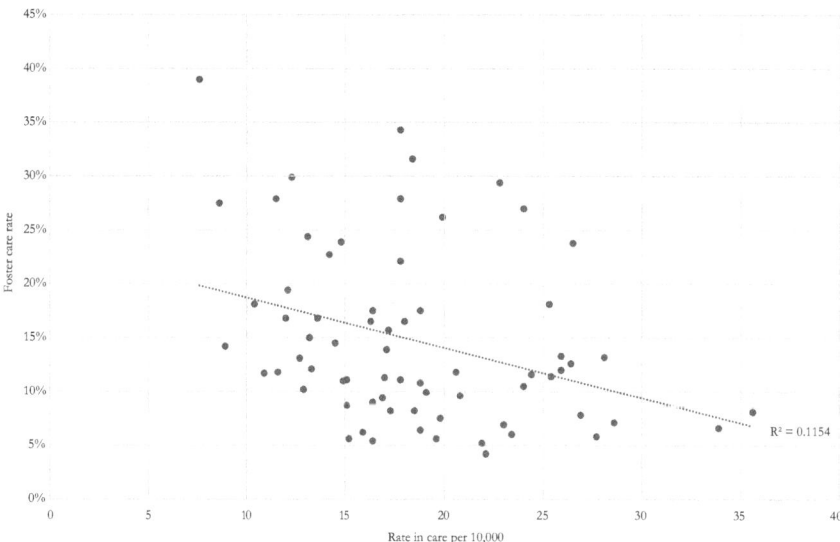

Figure 5.4 The rate of children in care, relative to child population, and the foster care rate. By local authority, 2011–2012.
Data Sources: MHLW. (2015f). Shakai-teki yougo no genjou ni tsuite (sanka shiryou). 2015, March: 12, 20.
Child population: National Population Census (2010). 2010, October 1.* Child population under 18 years old

whom were known to a CGC (Aoki, 2016). The supervising caseworkers in these cases had an average of 109 new cases in the past year, of which an average of 65 cases related to abuse (Aoki, 2016; The Japan Times 2016).

This caseload limits the caseworkers' ability to provide individualised care plans with comprehensive support in most cases (see Giller and Morris, 1981; Satyamurti, 1981; Weatherley and Lipsky, 1977). One CGC senior manager described his work as 'like playing whack-a-mole. An emergency arises, I deal with that. Another emergency arises, I deal with that'. In all my research sites caseworkers commonly described their work as 'firefighting'.

The relationship between the rate of children entering care and the foster care rate is known by senior foster carers. At the 2014 National Foster Care Association annual meeting, Niigata, which places the fewest children into care, was attacked for 'achieving' its high foster care rate by not taking enough children into care.

Having looked at the relationship between the 'need' for alternative care and the foster care rate at fixed points in time, this section closes by looking at the impact of the increasing number of children entering care on the foster care rate in Teru and Irifune, a relationship already demonstrated at the national level by Miwa (2012).

Interviewees in Teru explicitly referenced the impact that the increased need for alternative care had on the foster care rate. When asked what 'triggered' the increase in the foster care rate, senior managers all responded

154 *Variation of policy implementation*

that in 2002 the BIWIs and CWIs were 'full'. There are five responses that local authorities can use when the institutions in their jurisdiction are approaching capacity: develop capacity in the institutions; develop capacity in foster care; reduce the number of children entering care; use placements outside the local authority[14]; remove children from alternative care placements.

Teru increased the absolute capacity of the BIWI and CWI by 13 per cent between 2002 and 2006 while also investing in developing foster care services. Figure 5.5, which shows the combined occupancy rate of the BIWIs and CWIs, relative to child population, in Teru, Irifune, and Japan between 1997 and 2013, shows that the development of foster care services in Teru took about two years, with the foster care rate increasing from 2004 onwards.[15] A similar pattern can be seen in Irifune and nationwide, with the development of foster care services coming after a sustained increase in the occupancy rate of the BIWIs and CWIs.

The high occupancy rate of the welfare institutions in Teru may have reduced their opposition to the development of foster care services, which are more easily constructed as complementary in times of plenty. It is possible that the recent low occupancy rate of institutions in Irifune is inhibiting the continued expansion of foster care.

In Irifune, the issue of full occupancy arose during my fieldwork. Upon realising that the BIWIs were nearly full, emergency meetings were held.

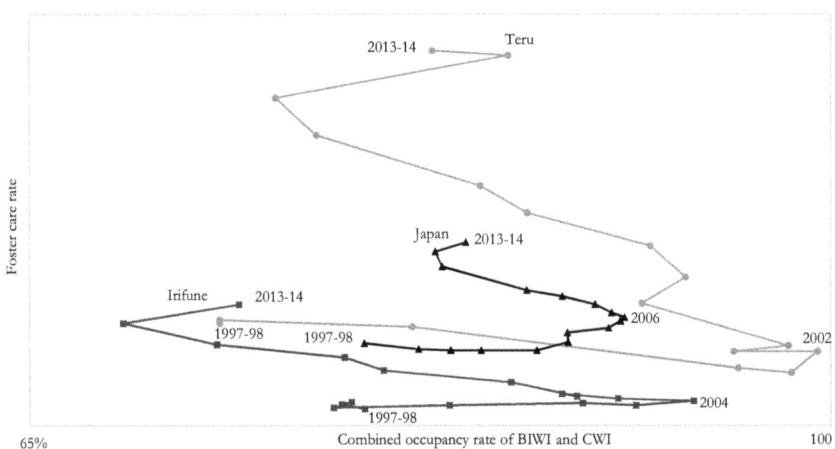

Figure 5.5 The occupancy rate of BIWIs and CWIs and the foster care rate. Teru, Irifune, Japan, 1997–2013.

Data Sources: MHLW: Welfare Administration Reported Cases. Referencing data sheets:
1: The number of foster carers, the number of children placed into foster care, by prefecture, designated city, and core city
2: The number of small-scale residential-type child rearing businesses (family homes), capacity, new staff and staff leaving over the year, current number of staff, number of children in family homes by prefecture, designated city, and core city
3: MHLW social welfare institutions survey, table 8, institution capacity, current number of children, nationwide, by prefecture, designated city, and core city, and by type of of institution, and by management status, public and private.
Child population: National census, 1995, 2000, 2005, 2010. Child population under 15 years old

Variation of resources 155

The oldest children were moved to CWIs with others returned to their parents. This was possible as the CWIs were not full. Had this occurred in a local authority with smaller relative institutional capacity it would have been more likely to have resulted in the development of capacity, in foster care or institutions, or in the outsourcing of care to other local authorities.

Street-level bureaucrats implement policy within the local resources at their disposal. The capacity of the care providers is not concrete: a CGC may develop capacity, or withhold or restrict placements, effectively limiting capacity. This often happens following an incident of abuse in care until the CGC is satisfied that the institution has sufficiently addressed the situation. Abuse in care can result in a change in the evaluation of one care provider or, as happened in Tokyo following the death of an infant in foster care (see Chapter 2), the type of care itself. This impacts upon the perceived capacity of available care. The following section explores this.

4.3 Evaluation of available care

Capacity of care is understood in terms of quantity and quality.[16] This is visible in the gap between the number of registered foster parents and the number that have placements (Miwa, 2016; Miyajima, 2001). This section addresses the CGC staff's perception of the quality of available care and the impact this has on the foster care rate.

When the decision to promote foster care was made in Teru, all the CWIs were large dormitory institutions. Sano explained that 'there is a much greater difference between large CWIs and foster care than small-style CWIs and foster care' (interview, 2014), before continuing:

> There were many children for whom the large child welfare institutions were not able to provide the right kind of care for, and there were several large abuse scandals [in CWIs]. This abuse, and the lack of appropriate care, were key factors. The choice was to build a new child welfare institution or promote foster care, as the existing institutions were full.

Here, the evaluation of available CWIs was shaped by the style of the CWI and by abuse scandals.[17] During a decade of volunteering, working with, and researching CWIs I have seen an array of institutions, from small six-child satellite community-based CWIs to an institution in an old hospital, one room of which saw eight boys aged 16 to 18 in a ward complete with curtains around their beds. BIWIs also vary, from around 15 babies and infants in a 'unit-style' institution to over 80 babies and infants in the largest Red Cross BIWI.

There are two hypotheses we can draw here. The first is that the 'type' of CWI may be important: a local authority with more 'group homes', which are more homelike, may feel less compelled to increase the foster care rate. The second hypothesis is that the average size of the CWI may be important. This factor may be important in two ways. If local authorities are aware of national norms, then local authorities with smaller CWIs may be less inclined to promote foster care, believing these CWIs to be providing higher quality care. The second possibility is that change within a local authority is important. A local authority where the CWIs are getting smaller may be less inclined to promote foster care, believing the relative quality of care to be improving.[18]

Despite the size and style of the CWI being significant in practice change in Teru, neither of these relationships are significant on a national level. The relationship between the percentage of children in group homes and the foster care rate by prefecture[19] for 1 April 2015, is not statistically significant ($p = 0.430$). Nor are the relationships between the foster care rate and the percentage of CWIs that are group homes ($p = 0.791$), the average size of CWIs ($p = 0.880$) or BIWIs ($p = 0.171$), statistically significant. Finally, the relationship between the change in the average size of the CWIs from 1997 to 2013 and the change in the foster care rate over this period is also not statistically significant ($p = 0.857$).

There are four reasons why these relationships are not significant at a national level. The first is that there is no uniform position on what a 'good' CWI looks like, with some CGCs favouring large-dormitory CWIs and others favouring small-unit-care CWIs. The second is that CGCs that have increased the foster care rate are more able to leverage CWIs to decrease in size or remodel into group-homes. In Teru, the increased foster care rate has empowered the CGC in relation to CWIs, as caseworkers now have more alternative placements available. This has resulted in over half the Teru CWIs physically reforming their institutions along CGC expectations. This negates the anticipated negative relationship between the size and style of the institutions and the foster care rate. Here the foster care rate itself acts as a resource for the CGC.

The third reason why these relationships may not be significant is the anticipation of change. At the turn of the millennium, Goodman (1999, 2000, 2002) argued that competition for children was likely to result in improvements in the quality of care, highlighting as an example the new role of psychotherapists in the CWI. Goldfarb's observation, a decade later, that 'in the majority of children's homes in Japan, psychotherapy is rarely used' (2012: 56) suggests that this competition has had limited effect on practice. Despite this, the perception of imminent reform may have limited CGC concerns about institutional care.

Finally, the CWIs actively promote their image, for instance, by highlighting their reforms. There are also cultural justifications offered for the use of CWIs. For example, Bamba and Haight argue the importance of the 'cultural context [for] everyday socialization beliefs and practices' (Bamba and Haight, 2009a: 429) and highlight the CWIs' role in cultural socialisation. CWIs often draw on their extensive histories and 'Japaneseness' to legitimise current practice.[20] This argument may also shape the CGCs' perception of the quality of the welfare institutions.

Academically, these cultural explanations are unsatisfying. First, it is unclear why children in institutions should be subjected to a different 'cultural context' from children in families. Second, arguments based on the CWIs meeting culturally required needs, such as Bamba and Haight's argument that CWIs provide *'Ibasho* (a place necessary to psychological well-being where one feels peace, security, acceptance and belonging*), anshin-kan* (a sense of security), and *mimamori* (the practice of watching over others carefully as a protective figure)' (2009a: 429), do not consider whether foster care could provide these. Third, the limitations in CWIs in providing these is rarely explored; Bamba and Haight argue, for example, both that welfare institutions can promote a child's sense of *ibasho*, a sense of belonging (2007), and that extended institutionalisation can impede the creation of *ibasho* (2009b), without attempting to disentangle this.

Another driver of the change of perceptions of welfare institutions worldwide has been the voice of careleavers, which until recently has been largely silent in Japan (see Goldfarb, 2016; Paige and Clark, 2010; Stein, 2014; Tsuzaki, 2009, 2011). A 'National Children's Voice Conference' was shut down by the National CWI Association when stories of abuse leaked to the press (Tsuzaki, 2006).

There has been a gradual increase in academic attention on careleavers since the 2006 publication of Tsuzaki's translation of Goodman's (2000) work on CWIs. This includes work addressing careleavers and social exclusion (Nishida et al., 2011; Taniguchi, 2011), poverty (Matsumoto, 1987), life chances (Nagano, 2008), employment (Arimura, 2012), and education (Nabekura, 2004; Nagano, 2008, 2012). There are also works addressing the challenges faced by those leaving care at 15 years of age (Tsuboi, 2011) and the challenge of leaving care at 18 years of age, since legal adulthood is 20 years (Hanada et al., 2015;[21] HRW, 2014). The most comprehensive study on careleavers, by Nagano and Arimura (2014), found that careleavers fare significantly worse than the general population.

These works are contributing to increased concerns about welfare institutions. There is a growing awareness of the damage that institutionalising babies and infants can do. These concerns draw on the literature on attachment (Fox, 2014; Fujibayashi, 2014; Kamikado, 2014, 2015; Nelson et al., 2013; Yamazaki et al., 2009), and the UN Guidelines on the Alternative Care of Children (Goldfarb, 2018). Yamazaki et al.'s research, based on self-reporting from BIWIs, found that 41.4 per cent of BIWIs said that babies and infants in their care had attachment issues, a figure that rose to 47.3 per cent for babies and infants in their care for over 24 months (2009: 15; see also Goldfarb, 2012).[22]

There are also concerns about the CWIs: Nakagawa, highlighting the low staff-to-child ratio in CWIs, argues that the current state of CWIs 'could do serious damage to the future of this country' (2010: 45). The most impactful work here is the 2014 HRW report 'Without Dreams'. Over time, this gradual increase in academic, advocacy, and public awareness of the issues faced by and within welfare institutions may impact on the CGCs evaluation of their quality.

Sano's observations on the impact of abuse in CWIs in Teru are also relevant to foster care. Indeed, where a child is abused or dies in foster care, the CGC, which is normally responsible for the recruitment, assessment, training, registration, and support of the foster parents, is considered more accountable than when a child is abused or dies in institutional care, where abuse is normally blamed on 'bad apples' in the system rather than the system itself. By placing a child into institutional care the CGC is outsourcing moral responsibility as well as responsibility for care (see also Goldfarb, 2013; Kikuchi, 2007; Miwa, 2016; Tsuzaki, 2009). This serves to inhibit the impact of abuse scandals in institutions, a factor that has contributed to de-institutionalisation in other countries (see Bullock and McSherry, 2009; Gilligan, 2009; Stein, 2006, 2014). The fact that policy and practice learning following abuse in care occurs at a local, rather than national, level, also inhibits this as a driver of change.

Miyajima (2001) lays out some of the CGCs' concerns about foster care, highlighting the lack of support facilitating self-reliance for children leaving care, the lack of peer support, and the limited numbers of foster parents who can provide temporary care, as well as noting concerns over divorce or the death of a carer (2001). Goldfarb notes that CGCs also have concerns about the impact of placement breakdown on foster parents (2012).

The evaluation of the quality of foster care is affected by regional variation in the registration (Hayashi et al., 2013; Sakai, 2005), training (Shoji et al., 2010), and support of foster parents (Miwa, 2016). A lack of confidence in national processes here impacts on the CGCs' overall confidence in foster care. This begins with registration: Miyajima states that 'there is a delicate aspect to registration. Registration does not equal can use this foster parent' (2001: 40; see also Miwa, 2016). The national standards for foster parent registration were eased in 1987 to facilitate recruitment (Goodman, 2000). Sakai's (2005) study on 15 local authorities, of which 12 registered all applicants and only one registered under 90 per cent of applicants, suggests that standards may have been lowered too far. Hayashi et al. (2013) found that only 15 of 54 CGCs had guidance for registering foster parents, while 12 of 56 CGCs did not have standardised application forms.

The challenges in assessing foster parents are exacerbated by the limited opportunities CGC staff have to get to know the foster parents (Miyajima, 2001), and by knowledge loss from staff rotation. Tanaka (2008) argues that this increases pressure in matching children to foster parents, which increases risk avoidance and placements into welfare institutions (see also Miwa, 2016). The CGC must also support foster parents. Miwa argues that 'the lack of support for foster parents led to caution in the use of foster care more generally' (2016: 7).

The evaluation of foster care sits within a broader discourse on childrearing. In the 1990s childrearing came to be seen as inherently challenging (Miwa, 2016). There have been attempts to alleviate this, in part motivated by a concern over the declining birth rate and a desire to get more women into work. These include the 1994 'Angel Plan' and the 2010 'Child and Childrearing Vision'. These use the rhetoric of moving the 'burden of childrearing off the family' to 'all society supporting child rearing'. Despite these attempts, childrearing is still often framed as a burden rather than a joy (Holloway, 2010).

Miwa (2016, referencing Shoji et al., 1998 and Sakurai, 1999) argues that this discourse led to the idea of a threshold of the complexity of needs, above which children are seen as 'unsuitable' for foster care (Chapter 4). This was the case in all my research sites and is discussed further in Chapter 6.

The construction of childrearing as a burden also leads foster parents to be 'seen as exceptional, "self-sacrificing" people (*tokushika*), definitely unusual and perhaps even a little strange' (Goodman, 2000: 142). The Ministry of Foreign Affairs also notes the common belief in the 'general public… that one must be an extraordinary philanthropist to become a foster parent' (1996).

The Teru CGC has a more in-depth registration process, which involves the CGC head interviewing every potential foster parent, more training, and significantly more support for foster parents than the Irifune CGC. This gives the Teru CGC more confidence in their ability to support foster parents than the Irifune CGC has, which in turn impacts upon the 'threshold' up to which children are seen as suitable for foster care.

The evaluation of foster care is also affected by the demographic of the children entering foster care. A placement breakdown or a case of abuse in foster care can lead CGC staff to become more risk-averse and to return to default practices. Here the response of senior managers is critical. The first attempts to increase the foster care rate in Teru saw children of all ages being placed into foster care. The lack of support for foster parents meant that many of the older children's placements broke down. Rather than abandon reform, senior managers decided to focus on placing younger children into foster care and on developing support capacity. This was coupled with a team approach to placement decisions, which meant that the blame for placement breakdowns was shared across the staff. This, along with a clear and consistent vision from senior management, allowed failures to be framed as lessons to learn from rather than a reason to abandon reform. This has created a positive feedback loop, with caseworkers, who saw better than expected results in the stable foster care placements, increasingly willing to use foster care.

In Irifune successful foster care placements were often described as 'lucky'. In one case, of a child who would normally have entered an institution, the foster care caseworker observed that 'if the child had gone to a different foster parent they may have been abused by them'. The fact that the senior management in Teru has been in post for over a decade is critical in understanding why this positive feedback loop, which is easily disrupted, exists in Teru but not in Irifune. The impact of organisational culture is examined in Chapter 7.

Negative feedback is amplified by the belief that harm done in foster care causes more damage to a child than harm done in an institution simply by the virtue of it occurring within a family. At times this is related to the construction of the family-bond, though CGC staff in each of my fieldwork sites explained that harm in foster care further damages the child's construction of what a family *should* be.

The CGC's decision to place a child into a specific institution or foster parent is not based solely upon the evaluation of the quality of care provided; it must also be approved by the care provider. The CWIs attempt to keep a balance based on the age and sex of the children and will sometimes refuse a child to keep this balance.[23] Similarly, the CGCs try to avoid placing children with a foster parent who has a natal or foster child of a similar age and sex, believing that this hinders the child's ability to find their own space within the family. These factors act as additional variables in the placement decision.

The capacity of available care is thus based on the absolute capacity, the CGC staff's evaluation of the 'type' of different placements, the evaluation of the quality of the specific placements available, and the compatibility of specific placements to a child's level of need, age, and sex. It is also based on the construction of the function of each different care placement (see Chapter 6). This chapter next examines the impact of the CGC's capacity on the foster care rate.

5 The capacity of the CGCs

Capacity consists of not just the care providers but also the CGCs. These too must be considered in terms of both quantity and quality. Miwa (2012) establishes a relationship between the foster care rate and average caseload. This book broadens the consideration of CGC capacity to include the number of staff working on foster care, the experience of senior managers, and the presence of specialist staff. It also examines the division of labour and the degree of role specialisation each staff member can attain, as well as the ability to acquire parental consent and the role of external supporting actors.

CGC caseworkers are generalists and, as such, normally have limited expertise (Imanishi et al., 2015; Ushijima and Yukawa, 1975; Yamamoto et al., 2008). This is compounded by the fact that CGCs 'don't have a sufficient system to develop specialist knowledge' (Miwa, 2016: 8). There are two reasons for this. The first is because 'Japan has no equivalent of British/North American state social work system' (Tsuzaki, 2006), a reality that Tsuzaki calls 'the most fundamental failure in the system of social work/services in Japan over the last half century' (2006).[24] The second reason is the limited capacity of the CGC to acquire and retain knowledge, and the capacity to change practice based upon that knowledge. Staff rotation (Miwa, 2014, 2016) and limited training (Saimura et al., 2000) mean that CGCs are continually having to fight knowledge loss.

Saimura et al. (2014: 190), discussing CGC attempts to facilitate family reintegration, argue that the lack of systems for sharing knowledge and practice across local authorities inhibits reform:

> Amid calls emphasising the importance of supporting abusive guardians, many organisations, starting with the child guidance centres but also including child welfare institutions and NPOs, are trying various practices. However, for the majority of these information and knowledge are not shared and these attempts are carried out separately and individually. This means we are losing time in establishing effective methods for supporting these guardians.

This evolution in isolation (see also Harada, 2013; Saimura et al., 2007) contributes to the 'considerable variation in the quantity and quality of expertise in child guidance centres and in the way that child guidance centres are run' (Kashiwame et al., 1995: 141).

One of the key components of CGCs' 'specific capacity' (May and Winter, 2007) is their expertise on foster care. The lack of specialist knowledge on foster care has a direct impact on its use (Fukaya et al., 2013; Matsumoto, 1991; Miwa, 2012; Nishizawa, 1987; Takahashi et al., 2010). Studies on this almost invariably conclude by calling for CGCs' specialist knowledge to be strengthened (see Kashiwame et al., 1995; Saimura et al., 2004; Ushijima and Yukawa, 1975).

There has been an increase in the number of caseworkers tasked with supporting foster parents. Miwa (2016) tracks the transition from 1991, where few CGC had staff dedicated to foster care support, through 2003, where 35 of 153 CGCs had a foster care caseworker, to 2014 where only 4.9 per cent of CGCs had no foster care caseworker. Miwa argues that it is likely that the increase in foster care caseworkers has a positive impact on the foster care rate (2016), though qualifies this by noting that in 2011 only 22 of the caseworkers worked exclusively on foster care (Miwa, 2012). Indeed Murata (2011) found that in Aichi Prefecture foster care caseworkers only spent 10 per cent of their time on foster care. Miwa also cites a 2014 national survey of CGCs that found that 75.5 per cent of foster care caseworkers had served for under three years, noting that this 'would seem this would place a limit on how much specialist knowledge can be developed' (2016: 8).

The CGCs also face challenges in retaining knowledge. In 2014, 55.4 per cent of CGCs had one staff member working on foster care, leaving them vulnerable to knowledge loss due to staff rotation (Miwa, 2014). Sadaka (2007) argues that staff rotation also limits the ability of the CGC to build supportive relationships with foster parents (see also Goldfarb, 2012). Ito's (2015) survey of five local authorities, which found that 26 per cent of foster parents found it hard to talk to their CGC, supports this argument.

Further, the default position in local authorities is for the CGC to be the service provider for foster care. As such, the CGC is responsible for recruiting, assessing, training, registering, and supporting foster parents.[25] In contrast, the CGC normally acts as a service regulator for welfare institutions, which are responsible for their staff recruitment and training and 'take on the burden completely' (Suga, 2014: 149; Tsuzaki, 2009: 157) following a placement.

The placement process itself also requires more work for foster care than institutional care: the caseworker must first gain parental consent before working with the foster care caseworker to match the child with a foster parent. There is then an 'acclimatisation' process, wherein the relationship is developed over a period of months or years, and ongoing support after a placement (Miyajima, 2001). In short, a placement into foster care requires more resources within the CGC than a placement into institutional care.

Over the last decade the Teru CGC has addressed this issue by focusing resources on developing the CGC's capacity to provide foster care services, including increasing the foster care team from one caseworker to a whole section. The CGC has also invested in developing the capacity of an NPO network and the local foster care association.

NPOs play two main roles in Teru. The CGC outsources the initial investigations in cases of suspected 'light' abuse to an NPO, training their staff and taking over cases when necessary. This allows more of the CGC's limited resources to be focused on foster care work. The second is by working with a local network of NPOs and the local foster care association to raise awareness of foster care and recruit foster parents. The local foster care association holds monthly meetings and provides peer support. The CGC hosts these meetings, for which they provide childcare, with the staff attending alternate months. CGC participation provides a regular channel of communication and allows the staff to get to know the registered foster parents.[26]

The relationship between the CGC and local foster care association is an important one. The low national threshold for registering foster parents requires CGCs to register almost all applicants who complete the process. Foster parents who are registered but deemed unsuitable are sometimes active in the foster care association. As time passes the foster care association will often relay the stresses of these foster parents to the CGC. The relationship between the association and the CGC can be affected if the association believes the CGC to be unfair in not using a registered foster parent. This is particularly problematic if the CGC is seeking the association's support in recruiting foster parents. CGCs often attempt to resolve this by saying that they need two or three times more registered foster parents than those with placements in order to effectively 'match' children and foster parents.[27]

The continuity of key staff in the Teru CGC mitigates this tension. Within the foster care section there are contract staff members who have served for longer than the foster care caseworkers. This provides continuity for the foster parents. The experience of these staff also helps the CGC improve foster care recruitment, assessment, and training (see Sakai, 2005), as well as the matching process. This dedicated foster care section and the supporting network of actors allows the Teru CGC to provide more individualised support.

Irifune does not use contract staff in this manner and struggles to deal with knowledge loss from staff rotation. The Irifune CGC has fewer staff working on foster care than Teru.[28] The Irifune foster care caseworkers more commonly hold this post concurrently with another role, while all staff working on foster care in Teru work solely on this.

The Irifune CGC is supported by one proactive CWI 'specialist counsellor for foster care support' who has started a small foster care group. The official local foster care association, headed by retired foster parents and adoptive parents, is divorced from those currently fostering and has even prohibited foster care 'salons', where foster parents met for peer support, as these sometimes resulted in disagreements.

Faced by a lack of internal capacity, the Irifune CGC decided to outsource foster care recruitment and training to a BIWI. One caseworker explained, 'in the CGC we have to do other work too, so we cannot focus just on foster care, so we have requested someone else helps us'. The caseworker expressed two reservations here. The first was that this reduced the time that the CGC staff spent with foster parents, meaning that it will be 'even harder for us to do the matching. It is tricky even now'. The second was that 'there is definitely the possibility that they are aware that if they place lots of kids into foster care they will lose money. There definitely is some conflict of interest here' (interview, 2015).

Puzzled, I asked whether a Child and Family Support Centre,[29] or an NPO could have taken on this role. The caseworker replied:

> Hmm, what do they do? [giggle] They do some lighter cases and the foster carers can go to them for consultation on issues. But they don't have ability to do this stuff yet. There is no NPO with the capacity to do this work here yet. The foster carer association are registered as an NPO but can only provide a very basic level of services.

Irifune is not unique in outsourcing foster care services to institutions; indeed, the MHLW explicitly calls for an increased role for welfare institutions here. It is unclear if this reflects a desire to utilise existing resources to promote foster care or an ambivalence towards the desirability of de-institutionalisation. Similarly, at a local level it is unclear whether Irifune's outsourcing of foster care services to a BIWI reflects the CGC's doubts over the validity of increasing foster care, or the CGC's lack of confidence in their own ability and their desire to draw on the experience of others in alternative care.

There are external foster care service providers, but these currently have a limited role. The first foster parent support agencies came in 2008 and were classified as 'foster care service agencies' in 2011 (Hirada, 2014). Hirada notes that because 'this is a business run on national subsidies there are difficulties in providing sufficient care' (2014: 143).

Hirada (2014) argues that these fiscal difficulties were anticipated, which contributed to the creation of the 'specialist counsellor for foster care support' in BIWIs and CWIs in 2012. These counsellors have three roles: to promote placement changes from their institutions to foster care, to support these children before and after the placement change, and to support local foster parents (Hirada, 2014). Hirada's (2014) survey of these counsellors suggests serious issues: 94 per cent of counsellors felt that they needed training, and comments included: 'a need for clarification of their role', and 'Why are welfare institutions providing foster care support?'

The limited role and expertise of the specialists mean that the relationship between the number of foster care specialists, per 10,000 children, and the foster care rate is not statistically significant ($p = 0.086$).[30] Despite concerns from local audit offices, the number of specialists has increased, from 115 in 2012 to 325 in 2014 (MHLW, 2016c: 33).

The different methods used by Teru and Irifune to develop foster care services may reflect different levels of political support, as increasing staff numbers requires political backing. The different approach may also relate to their physical geographies. Yet Irifune has outsourced foster care recruitment and training, which can be centralised, rather than foster care support, which cannot. Yuno, which is larger still than Irifune, has centralised recruitment and training into one local authority office and is starting to use institution foster care specialists to provide foster care support.[31]

Despite their importance in Teru and Irifune, the relationship between the foster care rate and the number of foster care caseworkers ($p = 0.80$), the number of dedicated foster care caseworkers ($p = 0.11$), the number of foster care promotion workers ($p = 0.50$), and the number of full-time foster care promotion workers ($p = 0.78$) are not statistically significant at a national level. Nor are these relationships statistically significant when considered relative to the child population under 15 years of age.

To understand this, we must consider the relative experience and expertise of staff in different local authorities (Matsumoto, 1991; Takahashi et al., 2010). The Teru team has several decades of experience between them and is working within a CGC where their role is considered central to change. The Irifune team had under four years' total experience and is concurrently responsible for mental health support for all children in care.

The higher level of expertise and experience in Teru allows staff to develop and pilot new practice in foster care. One example of this was a 'treatment foster care' pilot, with additional support and a family reintegration program (see Chapter 6).

A second example of innovative practice is a partnership with a media professor and a professional media team to develop promotional materials. This included a DVD that tells the story of three Teru foster care families, focusing on their decision to register and their lives as foster parents. This is used at events for potential foster parents and in meetings with Teru bureaucrats involved with welfare. The CGC hopes that by educating these bureaucrats, who are often the point of first contact for families in need, they can start to shift understandings of foster care.

The specialisation of staff in Teru, both with the caseworkers working solely on foster care and the long-term contract foster care promotion staff, is mirrored in how Teru responds to emergency cases. In Teru, cases that may require an emergency intervention are investigated by the Children's Emergency Assistance division, with other cases and the majority of emergency cases after the course of action has been determined managed by the Children's Support division. This attempts to diffuse the tension between investigation and support (Sato, 2009) and allows a greater degree of role specialisation, particularly on risk assessment. In Irifune, as in Yuno, these tasks are both carried out by caseworkers, with the local bureaucrats' 'generalist' skills given more importance than 'specialist' skills acquired by having a narrower role.[32]

The Teru CGC believes that they are approaching their capacity to provide safe foster care placements under their current structure, seen in the plateauing of the foster care rate in the last few years. This has led senior managers to start working with Key Assets, a non-profit foster care service provider.[33]

Teru and Irifune also differ regarding the experience of their senior managers. In Teru, the CGC head, the Children's Support division head, and the Children's Emergency Assistance division head have worked in the CGC for over a decade, over three decades, and approaching two decades, respectively.[34] This is connected to the CGC's political weight and in turn increases this political weight. This also increases the strength of the Teru CGC in negotiations with the welfare institutions, which has resulted in over half the CWIs restructuring from large dormitories to unit-style CWIs. The relative strength of the Teru CGC in relation to the welfare institutions was also visible in interactions between senior CGC staff and welfare institutions: while still polite, the Teru CGC staff spoke with more authority and conviction to CWI staff than the Irifune or Yuno CGC staff did.

In one case in Teru, of Izumi, a 17-year-old who had been in the CWI since she was four and who the CWI now wanted to be placed into foster care due to school-refusal, a senior manager reprimanded the CWI head, saying:

> This is about the ability of the CWI to provide care. You are not placing the needs of this child first. There will need to be a proper review as there are going to be more and more cases like this, high school kids in care refusing to go to school. We need to have more small specialist units and more local area small-scale homes run by the staff.

While Izumi was moved to foster care, after the meeting a senior manager noted to CGC staff: 'So, even if we didn't get this case, at least we said that in the future it will have to change. This was my target for today's meeting'.

166 *Variation of policy implementation*

I did not see this level of engagement with CWIs in Irifune. This strategic approach, setting precedents and building up expectations based on a coherent and constant vision, is made possible in Teru by the expertise and experience of the senior management and their ability to act consistently over a prolonged period with precise knowledge of what has come before.

The Irifune CGC is more standard in this regard, with one senior manager having accumulated approximately 15 years in CGCs over his career, and other senior managers having between one and six years of accumulated experience (see Goodman, 2002; Imanishi et al., 2015; Tsuzaki, 2006). In addition to the relative lack of experience, the lack of continuity in Irifune inhibits the CGC's ability to develop and implement policy and practice changes.

The Teru CGC also employs a full-time lawyer. This strengthens their negotiating position with parents and the courts and gives the CGC immediate access to technical and legal advice. The lawyer sometimes supports attempts to gain parental consent for foster care, though the increased foster care rate largely predates his appointment, relating instead to internal staff training and discussions on best practice for gaining parental consent. The Irifune CGC does not have a full-time lawyer, and attempts to develop best practice on gaining parental consent focus more on entrance into care than on placement type.

The ability of the CGC to gain consent for a foster care placement is particularly important in understanding regional variation in policy implementation. Following Miwa's (2016) argument that the critical factor in the low foster care rate is the lack of children eligible to be fostered and her (2016) argument that the approach of the CGC has a large impact on whether parental consent is gained, it seems likely that national dissemination of best practice would lead to an increase in the use of foster care.[35] The challenge then, which Teru and Irifune are both engaging with, becomes how to provide support for these additional foster parents, as well as establishing systems to prevent the loss of specialist knowledge due to staff rotation. Having examined the capacity of the CGCs, this chapter closes with some conclusions.

6 Conclusions

Regional variation of the resources available to the CGCs impacts upon the implementation of policy. This chapter opened the exploration of this with a consideration of the impact of physical geography on foster care services, arguing that geography may have contributed to Teru's decision to invest in the CGC and to Irifune and Yuno's decisions to develop the capacity of external actors.

The chapter next argued that local political support was critical in the development of foster care resources in Teru, and posited that change is more likely where it has 'two layers' of support, politicians and bureaucrats.

Political support also seems to play an indirect role in policy implementation by determining staff rotations and the longevity of posting.

Finally, this chapter considered the capacity of the care providers and the CGCs, with capacity understood in terms of both quantity and quality. We established that local authorities with a smaller relative capacity in BIWIs and CWIs are more likely to have a higher foster care rate, and that local authorities with a lower rate of children entering care are more likely to have a higher foster care rate. We also found a statistically significant relationship between the rate of children entering care and the child poverty rate of prefectures.

This chapter also argued that while the relationship between the occupancy rate of BIWIs and CWIs and the foster care rate is not statistically significant at a fixed point in time, a high occupancy rate in the institutions can act as a trigger for the development of foster care services. Teru's case suggests that the increased foster care rate, which reduces the CGC's reliance on welfare institutions, increases the CGC's power in relation to welfare institutions, effectively becoming a resource for the CGC.

This chapter also found that the relationship between the number of registered foster carers and the foster care rate is statistically significant. As with welfare institutions, the local authority's foster care capacity is determined by both the number of foster parents and the perceived quality of these carers. The number of registered foster parents who can be used is shaped by how many the CGC deems are able to care for children with minimal support, how many can care for children with more comprehensive support, and by the CGC's belief in their ability to provide or outsource this support. Despite their role in providing foster care services, there is no statistically significant relationship between the number of foster care specialists in BIWIs and CWIs in a local authority and the foster care rate.

The perceived quality of the types of care can change rapidly, as shown in Tokyo's response to the death of an infant in foster care. This 'negative feedback loop' occurs more easily in foster care than institutional care, due to the CGC retaining more responsibility for children in foster care placements and the belief that abuse in foster care is more damaging to the child than abuse in institutions. The practice learning that does occur following abuse occurs at a local rather than national level, which inhibits the impact of abuse in care as a national trigger for change.

Individual staff members with expertise and experience are a crucial resource for the CGCs (Miwa, 2014; Yamamoto et al., 2008). The CGCs that have developed effective models to facilitate the acquisition and retention of knowledge, and systems that facilitate practice change from this knowledge, are more able to change policy implementation than those which have not. This is discussed further in Chapter 7, on organisational culture.

The findings of this chapter suggest some policy and practice changes that would increase the likelihood that plans to increase the foster care rate are successful. The two most important of these are the development of a foster care provider system, and the development of a system that allows the CGC to acquire, retain, and build upon expertise and experience specific to foster care service provision. The foster care provider system could be within the CGCs, as in Teru, or using external actors, in the same way that welfare institutions provide alternative care services. The system to cultivate knowledge could involve the hiring of long-term contract staff to support local bureaucrats, as occurs with clinical psychologists in Teru, or the creation of a 'specialist' social worker position that means that local authority bureaucrats are only moved through posts that use these skills, in a similar way to the way that public teachers are only moved through education posts. This would require the development of a comprehensive social work training programme and accreditation or licensing system.

An easier first step would be to develop a system of sharing best practice across local authorities. The MHLW has attempted to do this before, most notably in its 2013 report outlining the development of foster services in Oita and Fukuoka City (MHLW SC, 2013), yet most peer-to-peer policy and practice learning still occurs through personal networks. An increase in the number of foster parents would also lead to an increase in the foster care rate, though in order for this to be done safely there is a need to ensure the simultaneous development of foster care services.

Finally, all major guidelines on de-institutionalisation speak of the importance of transferring funding from institutional care to family-based care services and actively closing down institutions (European Commission, 2013; European Expert Group on the Transition from Institutional to Community-Based Care, 2009; Fox and Gotestam, 2003; Mulheir and Browne, 2007; Tobis, 2000; UNICEF, 2012; UNICEF and World Bank, 2003; UN Office of the High Commissioner for Human Rights, 2011; World Health Organization, 2010). The promotion of foster care requires dedicated resources at a national level in addition to those provided by local authorities.

Even if all these suggestions were to be implemented, change that does not consider the normative beliefs of those implementing policy is likely to fall short. The book next turns to these beliefs.

Notes

1 The mechanisms by which staff rotation occurs and key posts are filled is a critical and understudied research area at both local and national level.
2 The role of Ms Komiyama and two senior MHLW bureaucrats in the 2011 Foster Care Guidelines suggests that this 'two-tier' model of change may also apply at a national policymaking level.
3 See King (2017) for data table.
4 See King (2017: Appendix 8) for data.
5 This is one of the arguments that a small section of the LGBT community has used to promote a potential role for LGBT fostering (see Fuji, 2013).

6 The issue of child poverty has grown in the public consciousness in the last decade, in part because Japan now ranks 34th out of 41 developed nations in the UNICEF child poverty index (UNICEF, 2016).
7 The relationship between poverty and alternative care is not unique to Japan (see Bradt et al., 2014; McConnell et al., 2006; Roose et al., 2014).
8 After 2011, the total rate in care was only released by a local authority, not by prefecture.
9 Revision of Article 2 of the Child Welfare Act Enforcement Order in 2005 changed the threshold of one caseworker per 100,000 to 130,000 people to one for every 50,000 to 80,000 people (Miwa, 2012).
10 One limitation of Miwa's studies is that they do not consider the increased proportion of cases involving abuse, which Saimura et al.'s (2004) work demonstrates take up more time than 'non-abuse' cases. Saimura et al.'s (2004) replication of Kashiwame et al.'s (1995) time-study of caseworkers found that caseworkers were busier in 2004 than in 1995.
11 A change in the way that data was reported meant that this was the most recent data available at the time of writing.
12 CGCs only investigate cases reported to them. Kashiwame (2010, 2011), Kashiwame et al. (2012) and Saimura et al. (2000, 2010, 2014) argue that CGCs need to work more closely with local municipal offices, in part to identify children at risk (see Abe, 2014; Tashiro and Yamamoto, 2011). There have been calls for a greater role for NPOs, including in reporting and investigating suspected abuse (see Mother and Child Wellbeing around the World, 2014).
13 In 33 of these, the parent killed themselves after killing their child or children. See Goodman (2000, 2002) for a discussion of this issue.
14 The local CGC must consent to the placement, with the placing local authority retaining responsibility for the child.
15 The foster care rate axis is intentionally left blank, to protect the anonymity of the research sites.
16 Concerns over the quality of care have led to the creation of a new publishing sub-genre on how to care, often penned by practitioners for practitioners (see Doi, 2009; Kanai, 2015).
17 Abuse within welfare institutions in Japan rarely has a significant impact on practice (Goodman, 2000; Tajima, 2014). Goodman argues that this is because cases are framed as 'the problematic behaviour of an individual member or small group of staff' (2000: 122) rather than as a systemic problem. Murata (2006) argues that the low public consciousness of welfare institutions, and of alternative care more broadly (see also Nakagawa, 2010), also limits the reaction to abuse scandals.
18 There is no data available to track changes in 'type' of CWI at a local authority level, so change over time here cannot be evaluated.
19 Data is unavailable at local authority level.
20 See Kojima (2013), who argues that his CWI is continuing the 'original spirit' of Dr Barnardo. This contrasts with Hosoi (2012), who argues that de-institutionalisation in Japan could learn from the changing mission of Barnardo's in the UK.
21 This work has many factual errors.
22 It is possible that the common use of the term '*shisetsu no ko*', children of the institution, by practitioners (Goldfarb, 2012: 58) reflects an awareness of the impact institutionalisation can have.
23 CWIs also occasionally reject based on the level of need. 'Better' CWI are more willing to reject children, knowing that the CGC will still use them. This can

create cases where the most challenging children to place end up in the CWIs that are least willing to reject placements.
24 The absence of a body of social workers, who can be an important force for policy and practice change (see Gal and Weiss-Gal, 2013), removes another potential driver for reform.
25 Non-CGC foster care service providers are discussed in Chapter 2.
26 There are also more formal meetings where local authority hall officials answer queries on financial or other legal matters.
27 Saitama has taken the novel approach of involving the foster care association in the matching process.
28 Teru has 0.26 foster care caseworkers and promotion workers per 10,000 children, of whom 0.13 are dedicated foster care workers and 0.13 are part-time promotion workers. Irifune has 0.21 foster care caseworkers and promotion workers per 10,000 children, of whom 0.04 are dedicated caseworkers, 0.08 are concurrent caseworkers, and 0.08 are part-time promotion workers (King, 2017: 272). For reference, the 69 local authorities in Japan have an average of 0.24 foster care caseworkers and promotion workers per 10,000 children, of whom 0.05 are dedicated caseworkers, 0.12 are concurrent caseworkers, 0.02 are full-time promotion workers, and 0.06 are part-time promotion workers (King, 2017: 272).
29 This is a government organisation that provides lower-level support to families.
30 Surprisingly, this relationship is negative in direction.
31 Senior Yuno bureaucrats and BIWI and CWI heads together created a job role with clear responsibilities and accountability procedures. The foster care specialists report monthly and bi-annually on how many phone consultations and home visits they have done and how many placement moves from their institution to foster care have occurred. The specialists also attend visits by the CGC to foster parents, with a view to being able to do this independently in the future. Despite this organisation there is still variation within Yuno, with one specialist logging over 70 calls and visits in six months and another only one.
32 Yuno has developed an innovative 'risk assessment tool' to aid their staff here.
33 This marks a break from foster care service providers being used by local authorities with low foster care rates. The general model of bureaucrats as service regulators rather than service providers suggests that a market will emerge for foster care service providers (see Kikuchi, 2007; Miwa, 2016).
34 Goodman argues that local authorities with a higher proportion of staff with specialist social welfare qualifications have 'often been at the forefront of social work practice' (2000: 37).
35 Saimura et al. (2014) call for a similar approach to develop best practice for supporting family reintegration.

References

Abe, T. (2014). Shichōson jidōsōdanjyo no yakuwari. Kodomo-tachi no sodachi ni okeru shakai-teki kea to kazoku no yakuwari [The role of the municipality and the child guidance centre. Symposium: Social Care and the family's role in raising children]. *Nihon Shakai Fukushi Gakkai*.

Aoki, M. (2016, April 18). Child welfare centres overworked but efforts afoot to ease the strain. *The Japan Times*.

Aoyama, T., Dales, L., & Dasgupta, R. (2015). *Configurations of family in contemporary Japan*. London: Routledge.

Arimura, T. (2012). Jidō fukushi shisetsu no taisho-ji wa ima — taishogo chōsa kara mita genjō to bunseki no kadai [An analysis of the circumstances and challenges facing care-leavers of welfare institutions]. *Mother and Child Wellbeing around the World*, 72(4), 52–56.

Bamba, S., & Haight, W. (2007). Helping maltreated children to find their ibasho: Japanese perspectives on supporting the well-being of children in state care. *Children and Youth Services Review*, 29, 405–427.

Bamba, S., & Haight, W. (2009a). The developmental–Ecological approach of Japanese child welfare professionals to supporting children's social and emotional well-being: The practice of mimamori. *Children and Youth Services Review*, 31, 429–439.

Bamba, S., & Haight, W. (2009b). Maltreated children's emerging well-being in Japanese state care. *Children and Youth Services Review*, 31, 797–806.

Bradt, L., Roets, G., Roose, R., Rosseel, Y., & Bouverne-De Bie, M. (2014). Poverty and decision making in child welfare and protection: Deepening the bias–need debate. *The British Journal of Social Work*, 45(7), 2161–2175.

Brodkin, E.Z. (1997). Inside the welfare contract: Discretion and accountability in state welfare administration. *Social Service Review*, 71(1), 1–33.

Buchanan, A. (1996). *Cycles of child maltreatment: Facts, fallacies, and interventions*. London: Wiley-Blackwell.

Bullock, R., & McSherry, D. (2009). Residential care in Great Britain and Northern Ireland. In M. Courtney, & D. Iwaniec (Eds.), *Residential care of children: Comparative perspectives*. New York: Oxford University Press.

Doi, T. (2009). *Seishōnen no chiryō kyōiku-teki enjo to jiritsushien – gyakutai hattatsu shōgai hikō nado shinkokuna mondai wo kakaeru seishōnen no chiryō kyōiku moderu to jissen kōzō* [Treatment, support, and preparation for independence for adolescents: A treatment and education model and practice structure for adolescents facing serious problems due to abuse, developmental disorders, and delinquency]. Tokyo: Fukumura Publishing.

European Commission. (2013). *Investing in children: Breaking the cycle of disadvantage*. Commission recommendation of 20.2.2013, C(2013), 778 final.

European Expert Group on the Transition from Institutional to Community-Based Care. (2009). *Report of the ad hoc expert group on the transition from institutional to community-based care*. Directorate-General for Employment, Social Affairs and Equal Opportunities.

Fox, L., & Gotestam R. (2003). Redirecting resources to community based services: A concept paper. *Social protection Discussion Paper No. 0311*. Washington: The World Bank.

Fox, N. (2014). *Timing Matters: How to think about the effects of early experience on brain and behavioral development*. Presentation at International Society for the Prevention of Child Abuse and Neglect Conference (ISPCAN). Nagoya. 2014, September 14–17.

Fuji, M. (2013). LGBT to shakai-teki yōgo katei wo hitsuyou to shite iru kodomotachi no tame ni [LGBT and social style welfare: For the children who need a home]. *Synodos Journals*. 2013, December 13.

Fujibayashi, T. (2014). *What can we learn from the BEIP in relation to infants in alternative care in Japan?* Presentation at International Society for the Prevention of Child Abuse and Neglect Conference (ISPCAN). Nagoya. 2014, September 14–17.

172 *Variation of policy implementation*

Fukaya, F., Fukaya, M., & Aoba, A. (2013). *Shakai-teki yōgo ni okeru satooya mondai e no jisshō-teki kenkyū — yōiku satooya zenkoku ankēto chōsa wo moto ni* [Empirical study on issues on foster parents in alternative care: Based on a nationwide questionnaire survey of normal foster parents]. Tokyo: Fukumura Publishing.

Gal, J., & Weiss-Gal, I. (Eds.). (2013). *Social workers affecting social policy: An international perspective on policy practice*. Bristol: Policy Press.

Giller, H., & Morris, A. (1981). 'What type of case is this?' Social workers' decisions about children who offend. In M. Adler, & S. Asquith (Eds.), *Discretion and welfare*. London: Heinemann.

Gilligan, R. (2009). Residential care in Ireland. In M. Courtney, & D. Iwaniec (Eds.), *Residential care of children: Comparative perspectives*. New York: Oxford University Press.

Goldfarb, K. (2012). *Fragile kinships: Family ideologies and child welfare in Japan*. (Doctoral dissertation). The University of Chicago.

Goldfarb, K. (2013). Japan. In P. Welbourne, & J. Dixon (Eds.), *Child protection and child welfare: A global appraisal of cultures, policy, and practice*. London: Jessica Kingsley Publishers.

Goldfarb, K. (2016). 'Self-responsibility' and the politics of chance: Theorizing the experience of Japanese child welfare. *Japanese Studies*, 36(2), 173–189.

Goldfarb, K. (2018). Beyond blood ties: Intimate kinships in Japanese foster and adoptive care. In A. Alexy, & E. Cook (Eds.), *Intimate Japan*. Honolulu: University of Hawaii Press.

Goodman, R. (1999). The entrepreneurial children's home: Approaches to the study of the Japanese child welfare system. *IDS Bulletin*, 30(4), 71–81.

Goodman, R. (2000). *Children of the Japanese state: The changing role of child protection institutions in contemporary Japan*. Oxford: Oxford University Press.

Goodman, R. (2002). Child abuse in Japan: 'Discovery' and the development of policy. In R. Goodman (Ed.), *Family and social policy in Japan*. Cambridge: Cambridge University Press.

Goodman, R. (2012). The 'discovery' and 'rediscovery' of child abuse (*jido gyakutai*) in Japan. In R. Goodman, Y. Imoto, & T. Toivonen (Eds.), *A sociology of Japanese youth: From returnees to NEETs*. London: Nissan Institute/Routledge Japanese Studies.

Hanada, H., Nagae, M., Matsuo, A., & Saunders, T. (2015). Current state and issues surrounding construction of an independent support network for child abuse victims over 18 years old in Japan. *Children & Society*, 29(1), 26–37.

Harada, A. (2010). The Japanese child protection system: Developments in the laws and the issues left unsolved. *International Survey of Family Law*, Vol. 2010, pp. 217–236.

Harada, A. (2013). Children in need of permanent families: The current status of and future directions for the Japanese foster care system. *Illinois Child Welfare*, 6(1), 14–29.

Hayashi, H., Yamamoto, T., Ookubo, M., Sato, T., Niiro, T., Kurihara, A., ... Tanaka, H. (2013). Jidōsōdanjyo ni okeru satooya nintei ni kansuru chousa kenkyuu [A study on the approval process as foster parents in the child guidance centres]. *Nihon kodomo katei sōgōkenkyūsho*, 50, 1–29.

Hirada, M. (2014). Satooya shien senmon sōdan-in no yakuwari to kadai: zenkoku jidō yōgo shisetsu nyūji-in e no ankēto chōsa kara [The role and issues facing foster care specialist consultants: Based on a national survey of child welfare

institutions and baby and infant welfare institutions]. *Nihon Shakai Fukushi Gakkai*, 62, 143–144.
Holloway, S.D. (2010). *Women and family in contemporary Japan*. Cambridge: Cambridge University Press.
Hosoi, I. (2012). Nichiei no jidō hogo no hikaku kenkyū: Bānādohōmu to Okuyama minashigo-in no jissen-shi no hikaku wo tsūjite [Comparative research on the UK and Japan: A comparison of the practical history of the Barnardo's home and the Okayama orphanage]. *Nihon Shakai Fukushi Gakkai*.
Human Rights Watch (HRW). (2014). *Without dreams. Children in alternative care in Japan*. New York: Human Rights Watch.
Imanishi, R., Arimura, T., Kimura, Y., Kurihara, T., Nagano, S., Shimizu, F., ... Kataoka, S. (2015). Jidōsōdanjyo ni okeru jidō shinri tsukasa no senmon-sei ni kansuru kenkyū (sono 1) [Research on the specialist knowledge of caseworkers in the child guidance centres (1)]. *Nihon Shakai Fukushi Gakkai*.
Ito, K. (2015). Satooya no shien nīzu to shien kikan ni motomeru yakuwari [Foster care support needs and clarifying the role of the foster care support agencies]. *Nihon Shakai Fukushi Gakkai*.
Ito, K., Takada, M., & Morito, K. (2014). Jidō fukushi shisetsu to satooya to no pātonāshippu kōchiku ni mukete no kadai — jidō yōgo shisetsu nyūji-in shokuin no intabyū chōsa kekka kara no kōsatsu [Task for going into good partnership with a child foster care institution and the foster parent: Consideration from the interview findings of the staff of child foster care institutions]. *Shakaimondai Kenkyū*, 63, 27–38.
Kamikado, K. (2014). *Shakai-teki yōgo ni tsuite no jisshō kenkyū oyobi datsushisetsuka no ugoki ni tsuite ~ shisetsu yōgo ga kodomo no hattatsu ni ataeru eikyō ni furenagara ~* [Empirical research on alternative care and the de-institutionalisation movement. Touching on the influence of institutionalisation on the development of children]. Presentation at Human Rights Watch and The Nippon Foundation Subete no akachan ga 'katei' de sodatsu shakai wo mezashite 'sekai kodomonohi' Kokuren kodomonokenrijōyaku saitaku 25 shūnenkinen shinpojiumu. Tokyo. 2014, November 20.
Kamikado, K. (2015). *Shakai-teki yōgo ni okeru kenkyū jissen shisaku no kyōdō no jūyō-sei ni tsuite ~ imawoikiru kodomo no kaizen no rieki kara kangaeru ~* [The importance of the collaboration of research, practice, and policies in alternative care: Improving the situation of children currently in care]. Presentation at Nihon fosutākea kenkyūkai. Tokyo. 2015, February 14.
Kanai, T. (2015). *Kodomo to oya no seishinka* [Children and parents' psychiatry]. Tokyo: Akashi Shoten.
Kashiwame, R. (2010). Kodomotachi ni atarimae no seikatsu wo [Towards a lifestyle that is obviously right for children]. *Shakai-teki yōgo to famirīhōmu*, 1, 6–9. 2010, June.
Kashiwame, R. (2011). Iken shakai-teki yōgo no kinmirai chūchōki taisaku no gurando dezain no hitsuyō-sei to kinmirai taisaku no jitsugen [The near future of alternative care: The need for a medium-term policy and grand design, and for realising policy in the short term]. *Jidō yōgo shisetsu-tō no shakai-teki yōgo no kadai ni kansuru kentō iinkai*.
Kashiwame, R., Nakatani, S., Hayashi, S., & Amino, T. (1995). Jidōsōdanjyo no unnei bunseki [Analysis of child guidance centres' operations]. *Nihon sōgō aiiku kenkyū kiyō*, 32, 137–147.

Kashiwame, R., Arimura, T., Nagano, S., Mayumi, S., Ogi, M., Shibuya, M., ... Kawamatsu, R. (2012). Kodomo katei fukushi gyōsei jisshi taisei no saikōchiku ni kansuru kenkyū — sai kōchiku ni kansuru kore made no kentō ikisatsu to shōrai hōkō — [A study on reconstruction centred municipalities child and family welfare administration systems: Consider the future direction of the system reconfiguration from the previous discussions]. *Nihon-kodomo katei sōgōkenkyūsho kiyō*, 49, 1–14.

Kato, Y. (2014). Jidōsōdanjyo ga kakaeru jidō gyakutai mondai wo motsu kazoku no tokuchō ni kansuru kenkyū – 2004-nen 2009-nen no jidō gyakutai jittai chōsa no ni-ji bunseki wo tōshite [A study on the characteristics of families with abuse working with the child guidance centres: Based on two surveys, in 2004 and 2009]. *Nihon Shakai Fukushi Gakkai*.

Kikuchi, M. (2007). Nihon de satooya seido ga riyō sarenai riyū to wa? Kokusai hikaku kenkyū wo tōshite ieru koto [Why would not be the foster care system utilized well in Japan?: Through international comparison]. *Kodomo no gyakutai to negurekuto*, 9(2), 147–155.

King (nee Rivera King), M. (2017). *Child guidance centres in Japan: Regional variation in policy implementation and the family-bond.* (Doctoral dissertation). The University of Oxford.

Kojima, K. (2013). Bānādohōmu to no saikai [Meeting Barnardo's home again]. *Ishii kinen yūai-en yuai dayori*, 258.

Kumasaka, Y., & Aiba, H. (1968). Foster care in Japan: Past and present. *The Milbank Memorial Fund Quarterly*, 46(2), 253–265.

Lepore, J. (2016, February 1). Baby Doe: A political history of tragedy. *The New Yorker*.

Mainichi Japan. (2016, February 18). Number of child-rearing households below poverty line doubled over 20 years: survey. *The Mainichi Shinbun*. (English ed.)

Matsumoto, I. (1987). Yōgo shisetsu sotsuen-sha no 'seikatsu kōzō' 'hinkon' no kotei-teki seikaku ni kansuru kōsatsu ['Labours and social networks' of young people who was left residential care for children – A study on persistence of 'poverty']. *Hokkaidō daigaku kyōiku gaku-bu kiyō*, 49, 43–119.

Matsumoto, I. (Ed.). (2010). *Kodomo gyakutai to hinkon — 'wasurerareta kodomo' no inai shakai wo mezashite* [Child abuse and poverty: Toward a society with no forgotten children]. Tokyo: Akashi Shoten.

Matsumoto, I. (Ed.). (2013). *Kodomo gyakutai to kazoku – 'kasanariau furi' to shakai-teki shien* [Child abuse and the family: Overlapping disadvantages and social support]. Tokyo: Akashi Shoten.

Matsumoto, T. (1991). *Satooya seido no jisshō-teki kenkyū* [Empirical study of the foster care system]. Tokyo: Kogyo.

May, P.J., & Winter, S.C. (2007). Politicians, managers, and street-level bureaucrats: Influences on policy implementation. *Journal of Public Administration Research and Theory*, 19, 453–476.

McConnell, D., Llewellyn, G., & Ferronato, L. (2006). Context-contingent decision-making in child protection practice. *International Journal of Social Welfare*, 15(3), 230–239.

Meyers, M.K., & Vorsanger, S. (2003). Street-level bureaucrats and the implementation of public policy. In B.G. Peters, & J. Pierre (Eds.), *Handbook of public administration*. Thousand Oaks: Sage.

Variation of resources 175

MHLW. (2000–2001 to 2014–2015). *Fukushi gyousei houkoku rei* [Annual welfare administration reported cases]. Retrieved from URL: http://www.e-stat.go.jp/ (last accessed 2017, August 28).
- *Satooya-sou oyobi satooya ni itaku sareteiru jidou-sou, todōfuken – shitei toshi – chūkaku-shi betsu* [The number of foster carers, the number of children placed into foster care, by prefecture, designated city and core city].
- Shōkibo jūkyo-gata jidō yōiku jigyō (famirīhōmu) no jigyōshosū, teiin, nyūsho jin'in, taisho jin'in, nendomatsu zaiseki jin'in oyobi shōkibo jūkyo-gata jidō yōiku jigyō (famirīhōmu) ni itaku sareteiru jidō-sū, todōfuken – shitei toshi – chūkaku-shi betsu [The number of small scale residential type child rearing businesses (family homes), capacity, new staff, and staff leaving over the year, current number of staff, number of children in family homes by prefecture, designated city and core city].
- Shakai fukushi shisetsu-tō chōsa 8-hyō shakai fukushi shisetsu-tō no teiin zaishosha-sū, -koku — todōfuken — shitei toshi — chūkaku-shi, shisetsu no shurui keiei shutai no kōei — shiei betsu [Social welfare institutions survey, table 8, institution capacity, current number of children, nationwide, by prefecture, designated city, and core city, and by type of institution, and by management status, public and private]. NB. For 2014 onwards refer to: Fukushi gyōsei hōkoku rei etsuran jidō dai 11-hyō jidō fukushi shisetsu (josan shisetsu oyobi boshi seikatsu shien shisetsu wo nozoku) no shisetsu-sū, teiin oyobi zaiseki jin'in, todōfuken – shitei toshi – chūkaku-shi × shisetsu no shurui-betsu [MHLW, welfare administration reported cases, Table 11: Children's welfare institutions (excluding midwives facilities and mother and child living support institutions) – institution capacity, current number of children, nationwide, by prefecture, designated city, and core city, and by type of institution].

MHLW. (2012). *Shakai-teki yōgo no genjou ni tsuite (sanka shiryou).* [Current status of alternative care (reference)]. 2012, September.

MHLW. (2015). *Shakai-teki yōgo no genjou ni tsuite (sanka shiryou)* [Current status of alternative care (reference)]. 2015, March.

MHLW. (2016a). *Shakai-teki yōgo no genjou ni tsuite (sanka shiryou)* [Current status of alternative care (reference)]. 2016, January.

MHLW. (2016b). *Shakai-teki yōgo no genjou ni tsuite (sanka shiryou)* [Current status of alternative care (reference)]. 2016, July.

MHLW. (2016c). *Shakai teki yōgo no kadai to shourai zou no jitsugen ni mukete* [On the challenges and realising the future form of alternative care]. 2016, January.

MHLW. (2016d) *Fukushi gyōsei hōkoku rei (etsuran jidō dai 13-hyō satooya-sū, todōfuken – shitei toshi – chūkaku-shi × shinki – torikeshi-betsu* [Welfare administration reported cases. Data sheet 13 – The number of foster carers, the number of children placed into foster care, by prefecture, designated city, and core city].

MHLW Specialist Committee for the Promotion of Placements into Foster Care (MHLW SC). (2013). (*Zenkoku satooya itaku-tō suishin iinkai). Satooya-tō itaku-ritsu appu no torikumi hōkoku-sho ~ itaku-ritsu wo ōkiku zōka saseta Fukuoka-shi Ōita ken no torikumi yori ~* [Report on efforts to increase the foster care rate: The efforts of Fukuoka City and Oita Prefecture, which have greatly increased foster care placements]. 2015, February.

MHLW SC. (2016). *Heisei 27-nendo chōsa hōkoku-sho. Satooya katei no zenkoku jittai chōsa hōkoku, itaku sareta kodomo no jōcho to kōdō no mondai ni kansuru* chōsa hōkoku, satooya rikurūto chōsa hōkoku-sho [2015 Survey report. Nationwide survey report on foster care households, survey report on the emotional and behavioural issues faced by children in [foster care] placements, and survey report on foster care recruitment]. 2016, March.

Ministry of Foreign Affairs. (1996). *The initial report of Japan under article 44, paragraph 1 of the convention on the rights of the child.* 1996, May 30. Retrieved from URL: http://www.mofa.go.jp/policy/human/child/initialreport/care.html (last accessed 2016, May 16).

Ministry of Internal Affairs and Communications. (2015). *Heisei 27-nen kokuseichōsa jinkō-tō kihon shūkei kekka kekka no gaiyō* [2015 National census. Population. Basic summary results, outline of results].

Miwa, K. (2011). Satooya itaku to shisetsu itaku no kankei no chōki-teki dōtai 1953-nen -2008-nen no jikeiretsu dēta no bunseki kara [The longitudinal dynamics of the relationship between the foster care placement and the residential care: Time-series analyses of the macro data 1953–2008 Japan]. *Japanese Journal of Social Welfare*, 52(2), 43–53.

Miwa, K. (2012). 2000-Nen ikō no satooya itaku no zōka wo motarashita mono jidō gyakutai no zōka no chokusetsuteki kōka to kansetsu-teki kōka wo megutte [What has caused an increase of the placement in foster care after 2000: Direct and indirect effect of child abuse increase]. *Japanese Journal of Social Welfare*, 53(2), 45–56.

Miwa, K. (2014). *Satooya seido no chouki-teki doutai to tenbou* [The long-term dynamics and outlook of the foster care system]. (Doctoral dissertation). Tokyo Metropolitan University.

Miwa, K. (2016). Naze satooya itaku wa shinten shinai no ka? Satooya touroku-sha fusoku kasetsu to satooya itaku jidō gentei kasetsu [Why has family-based foster care not become more common in Japan? A lack of registered fostered carers and of children who are able to be fostered]. *Japanese Journal of Social Welfare*, 56(4), 1–13.

Miyajima, K. (2001). *Jidō gyakutai bōshi-hō shikōgo no jidōsōdanjyo to satooya seido no kongo ni tsuite* [On the child guidance centres and foster care system after the enforcement of the Child abuse prevention act]. Preliminary paper for dai 75-kai yōshi to satooya wo kangaeru kai kōjutsu-roku.

Miyajima, K. (2007). Kodomo gyakutai no hontō no sugata to kazoku shien no arikata wo kangaeru sōsharuwāku no tachiba kara [The true form of child abuse and thinking about methods of family support. From the viewpoint of social work]. *Nihon shakai jigyō daigaku kenkyū kiyō*, 54, 219–242.

Mochizuki, Y. Tanaka, E., Shinohara, R., Sugisawa, Y., Tomisaki, E., Watanabe, T., ... Anme, T. (2014). Yōiku-sha no ikuji fuan wo yobiikuji kankyō to gyakutai to no kanren: Hoikuen ni okeru kenkyū [The influence of caregivers' anxiety and the home environment on child abuse: A study of children attending child-care centres [nurseries]]. *Nihon Kō Mamoru-shi*, 61(6), 263–274.

Moriguchi, C. (2010). Child adoption in Japan, 1948–2008 – A comparative historical analysis. *Keizai kenkyū*, 61(4), 342–357.

Mother and Child Wellbeing around the World. (2014). Sekai no jidō to bosei [*Mother and Child Wellbeing around the World].Tokushū: Chiiki ni hiraku shakai-tekiyōgo no kore kara [Special edition: 'Opening up alternative care in communities']* 76 2014-4.

Mulheir, G., & Browne, K. (2007). *Deinstitutionalising and transforming children's services: A guide to good practice*. European Commission Daphne programme in collaboration with WHO regional office for Europe and the University of Birmingham UK. Birmingham: University of Birmingham (WHO Collaborating Centre for Child Care and Protection).

Murata, K. (2006). *Why do not foster carers increase in Japan?* Paper presented at Ajia kodomo no kenri to satooya kaigi. 2006, September 23.

Murata, K. (2011). Jidōsōdanjyo ga shinseiji satooya itaku wo okonau igi Yorozuya Ikuko-san (zen Kariya jidōsōdansentā-chō) ni kiku [The significance of child guidance centres entrusting newborn babies to foster parents: Asking Ms Eriko Manya (Former head of Kariya child consultation centre)]. In National Foster Care Association. (2011). *Sato oya dayori*, 89, 6–9. 2011, August 19.

Nabekura, S. (2004). Jidō yōgo shisetsu ni okeru hi gyakutai jidō no kyōiku wo ukeru kenri no shomondai mensetsu chōsa oyobi san'yo kansatsu wo chūshin to shite [The problems of the right to education for the ill-treatment child in the child welfare institutions: Based on the interview investigation and the participatory observation]. *Bungaku kenkyū-ka kyōiku senkō hakushikōkikatei zaigaku*, 26, 261–276.

Nagano, S. (2008). *Jidō yōgo shisetsu ni okeru raifu chansu hoshō no hitsuyō-sei — jidō yōgo shisetsu seikatsu keiken-sha e no intabyū chōsa kara* [The necessity of guaranteeing life chances in child welfare institutions – Research based upon interviewing people with experience of living in child welfare institutions]. (Doctoral dissertation). Toyo University.

Nagano, S. (2012). Jidō yōgo shisetsu de seikatsu suru kodomo no daigakunado shingaku ni kansuru kenkyū: Jidō yōgo shisetsu seikatsu keiken-sha e no intabyū chōsa kara [A study on university attendance of child foster care [alternative care] leavers: Through an interview analysis]. *Nihon Shakai Fukushi Gakkai*, 52(4), 28–40.

Nagano, S., & Arimura, T. (2014). Shakai-teki yōgo sochi kaijo no seikatsu jittai to depuribēshon: Niji bunseki ni yoru kasetsu seisei to ichiji dēta kara no shisa [Deprivation of former youth in care: The hypothesis generated by secondary analysis and suggested from original dates]. *Shakai Fukushi-Gaku*, 54(4), 28–41.

Nakagawa, A. (2010). *Jidō yōgo shisetsu no kakaeru kyō-teki kadai no kenshō shokuin no rōdō kankyō ni shugan wo oita Gunma ken'nai shisetsu e jittai chōsa* [Investigation into contemporary challenges for child welfare institutions: A survey of the reality of staff in Gunma Prefecture]. Gunma: Gunmadaigaku shakai jōhō gakubu jōhō shakai kagakka.

National Population Census. (1995). *Heisei 7-nen kokuseichōsa* [National population census 1995].

National Population Census. (2000). *Heisei 12-nen kokuseichōsa* [National population census 2000].

National Population Census. (2005). *Heisei 17-nen kokuseichōsa* [National population census 2005].

National Population Census. (2010). *Heisei 22-nen kokuseichōsa* [National population census 2010].

Negishi, Y. (2014). Jidō gyakutai taiō seido no kihon kōzō to sono imi: Oya to ko no shutai-ka wo kijun to suru bunseki moderu no teishō [The basic policy structures of the prevention of child abuse and neglect and its meaning: introduction to the

analytical model based on autonomy of parents and children]. *Shakai Fukushi-Gaku*, 54(2), 32–43.
Nelson III, C.A., Fox, N.A., & Zeanah Jr., C.H. (2013). Chaushesuku no kodomo-tachi ikuji kankyō to hattatsu shōgai [Ceausescu's children: Child-care environment and developmental disorders]. *Nikkei Science*, 193, 114–119. 2013, August 22.
Nishida, Y., Tsumaki, S., Nagase, M., & Uchida, R. (2011). *Jidō yōgo shisetsu to shakai-teki haijo: kazoku izon shakai no rinkai* [Social exclusion and child welfare institutions: Criticality of family dependent society]. Tokyo: Kaihō shubbansha.
Nishizawa, E. (1987). Wa ga kuni ni okeru satooya seido no genjō to kadai-ten [Current status and problems of foster care system in Japan]. *Tōyōdaigaku shakaiga-kubu kiyō*, 24(2), 157–193.
Paige, L., & Clark, G.A. (2010). *Yōgo jidō no koe: Shakai-teki yōgo to enpawamento* [Voices of children in care: Alternative care and empowerment]. (Tsuzaki, T. Trans.). Tokyo: Fukumura Publishing.
Rebbick, M., & Takenaka, A. (2006). *The changing Japanese family*. London: Routledge.
Ronald, R., & Alexy, A. (2011). *Home and family in Japan: Continuity and transformation*. London: Routledge.
Roose, R., Roets, G., & Schiettecat, T. (2014). Implementing a strengths perspective in child welfare and protection: A challenge not to be taken lightly. *European Journal of Social Work*, 17(1), 3–17.
Sadaka, J. (2007). Jidōsōdanjyo ni okeru satooya seido un'ei ni kansuru kōsatsu zenkoku to Gifu ken no satooya itaku shien jōkyō ni chakumoku shite [Thoughts on the operation of the foster care system in the child guidance centres. Focusing on Gifu Prefecture and the nationwide picture of foster care placements and support]. *Nagoya-shi daigaku daigakuin bunka kenkyū-ka ningen bunka kenkyū*, 7, 93–109.
Saimura, J. (2008). Kore kara nihon ga susumibeki hōkō to wa [The directions the Japanese child abuse system should proceed toward]. In Tsuzaki, T., & Hashimoto, K. (Eds.), *Jidō gyakutai wa ima – Renkei shisutemu no kochiku ni mukete* [Current situation in child abuse – Toward the establishment of a collaborative system]. Kyoto: Minerva Shobo.
Saimura, J., Takahashi, S., Shoji, J., Kashiwame, R., Oyama, O., Saito, S., & Kato, H. (2000). Jidōsōdanjyo shokuin no gen'nin kenshūnado no arikata ni kansuru kenkyū [A study of training and supervision systems for staff of child guidance centres]. *Nihon-kodomo katei sōgōkenkyūsho kiyō*, 37, 181–198.
Saimura, J., Shibuya, M., Kashiwame, R., Shoji, J., Arimura, T., Aizawa, H., ... Yamamoto, T. (2004). Gyakutai taiō-tō ni kakaru jidōsōdanjyo no gyōmu bunseki ni kansuru chōsa kenkyū (2) [The analysis of actual quantity of works in child guidance centres (2)]. *Nihon-kodomo katei sōgōkenkyūsho kiyō*, 41, 129–174.
Saimura, J., Shoji, J., Arimura, T., Itakura, T., Nemoto, A., Abe, K., ... Honma, H. (2007). Jidōsōdanjyo ni okeru kazoku sai tōgō enjo no arikata ni kansuru kenkyū ~ jissen jirei no shūshū, bunseki [A study on the system for supporting family reintegration in child guidance centers: Gathering and analysis of pioneering practices]. *Nihon-kodomo katei sōgōkenkyūsho kiyō*, 44, 187–256.
Saimura, J., Arimura, T., Kashiwame, R., Yamamoto, T., Nagano, S., Tsuruoka, H., ... Yokoyama, T. (2010). Jidōsōdanjyo no gyōmu bunseki ni kansuru kenkyū (1) [Time-studies and incident-studies about social work for child abuse cases in child guidance centres]. *Nihon-kodomo katei sōgōkenkyūsho kiyō*, 47, 181–191.

Saimura, J., Arimura, T., Yamamoto, T., Kashiwame, R., Nagano, S., Kawamatsu, R., ... Yokoyama, T. (2014). Jidōsōdanjyo no jimu bunseki ni kansuru kenkyū (3) [The analysis of actual quantity of works in child guidance centres (3)]. *Nihon-kodomo katei sōgōkenkyūsho kiyō*, 49, 1–37.
Sakai, R. (2005). Yōiku satooya nintei asesumento ni kansuru ichikōsatsu [On the current assessment system to accredit foster carer]. *Shakai Fukushi Kenkyū*, 6, 61–73.
Sakurai, N. (1999). Satooya yōiku no shien no arikata ni kansuru kenkyū—satooya seido no kassei-ka o motomete [A study on the ways to support foster parents—Seeking to activate the foster care system]. *Aichi tankidaigaku kenkyū kiyō*, 21, 11–20.
Sato, T. (2009). Jidōsodanjyo no genjyō to kadai: Jidō gyakutai taiō to taisei seibi [The contemporary conditions and challenges at child guidance centers: Response to child abuse and organizational structure]. In Nihon Kodomo wo Mamoru Kai (Ed.), *Kodomo hakusho*. Tokyo: Sōdo bunka.
Satyamurti, C. (1981). *Occupational survival: The case of the local authority social worker*. Oxford: Blackwell.
Shoji, J., Taniguchi, W., Andoh, A., Oyama, O., Takahashi, S., Suzuki, Y., ... Masuda, S. (1998). Satooya e no shien no arikata ni kansuru kenkyū [A study on the training of foster parents]. *Nihon kodomo katei sōgō kenkyū kiyō*, 35, 33–39.
Shoji, J., Arimura, T., Miyajima, K., Ito, Y., Watanabe, M., Thomson, S., ... Takahashi, T. (2010). Satooya no konpitensu keisei to hyōka ni kansuru chōsa kenkyū [Research on the formation and evaluation of competence in foster carers]. *Nihon Shakai Fukushi Gakkai*, 58.
Stein, M. (2006). Missing years of abuse in children's homes. *Child and Family Social Work*, 11, 11–21.
Stein, M. (2014). *Igirisu no shakai-teki yōgo tōjisha no jinken yōgo undō-shi* [Care less lives: The story of the rights movement of young people in care]. (Tsuzaki, T. Trans.). Tokyo: Akashi Shoten.
Suga, M. (2014). Satooya shien no saikentō: satooya yōiku shisutemu no kōchiku no hitsuyō-sei [Reviewing foster care support: The need for a foster care support system]. *Nihon Shakai Fukushi Gakkai*, 62, 149–150.
Tajima, M. (2014). Jidō fukushi-hō kaisei to shisetsu-nai gyakutai no yukue — kono mama de wa ōi kakusa rete shimau kigu wo mekutte [The revision of the Child Welfare Act and abuse within child welfare institutions. The fears that this will lead in the ongoing obscuring over abuse]. *Shakai-teki yōgo to famirīhōmu*, 5, 12–24.
Takahashi, S., Saimura, J., Yamamoto, T., Arimura, T., Nagano, S., Tsuruoka, H., ... Sakai, T. (2010). Jidōsōdanjyo jidō fukushi tsukasa no senmon-sei ni kansuru kenkyū [A study of social workers' expertise in child guidance centres]. *Nihon-kodomo katei sōgōkenkyūsho kiyō*, 47, 3–61.
Tanaka, H. (2008). Tokutei kadai no chōsa kenkyū shakai-teki yōgo to shite no satooya seido no yakuwari to genkai – satooya seido to yōshi engumi seido no hikaku wo tsūjite [Research on specific subjects. The role and limitations of the foster care system in alternative care: Through comparison of foster care and adoption]. *Dokkyō rō jānaru*, 3, 89–124.
Taniguchi, Y. (2011). *Jidō yōgo shisetsu no kodomo-tachi no seikatsu katei ~ kodomo-tachi ha naze haijo jōtai kara datsu ke dasenai no ka* [The life process of the children of the Child Welfare Institutions: Why can they not escape social exclusion?] Tokyo: Akashishoten nishiami.

Tashiro, M., & Yamamoto, T. (2011). Gyakutai yobō ni kansuru jidōsōdanjyo to shichōson no renkei ni tsuite [The cooperation of child guidance centre and municipalities regarding the prevention of child maltreatment]. *Nihon kodomo katei sōgōkenkyūsho*, 48, 1–12.
The Japan Times. (2016, August 13). Editorial. Targeting scourge of child abuse. *The Japan Times*.
Tobis, D. (2000). *Moving from residential institutions to community-based social services in Central and Eastern Europe and the former Soviet Union*. Washington: The World Bank.
Tsuboi, H. (2011). Jidō yōgo shisetsu no kodomo no kōkō shingaku mondai: hi shingaku-sha no dōkō ni chakumoku shite [The problem of children in child welfare institutions progressing to high school: Focusing on the trend of non-progression]. *Ōtsumajoshidaigaku kasei-kei kenkyū kiyō*, 47, 71–77.
Tsuzaki, T. (2006). *The vested interests vs. children's rights: children's rights and foster care in Japan*. Presentation at Asia conference on children's rights and foster care. Retrieved from URL: http://www.geocities.jp/hokukaido/satooya/seoul2006/article/12-japan-tsuzaki-e.htm (last accessed 2017, August 22). Seoul. 2006, September 16.
Tsuzaki, T. (2009). *Kono kuni no kodomotachi: Yōhogo jidō shakai-teki yōgo no Nihonteki kōchiku; otona no kitoku ken'eki to kodomo no fukushi* [This country's children: Constructing social care for children in need of care; The vested interests of adults and children's welfare]. Tokyo: Nihon Kajo Shuppan.
Tsuzaki, T. (2011). Minpō kaisei to higyakutaiji no shyakaiteki yōgo: Jidō fukushi no shiten kara (Revisions to the civil code and social care for abused children: From a child welfare perspective). *Hōritsu Jihō*, 83(7), 72–77.
UNICEF. (2012). *Children under the age of three in formal care in Eastern Europe and Central Asia: A rights-based regional situation analysis*. (Amended 2013, January). Geneva: UNICEF.
UNICEF. (2016). *Fairness for children: A league table of inequality in child well-being in rich countries*. Florence: UNICEF.
UNICEF & World Bank. (2003). *Changing minds, policies and lives: Improving protection of children in Eastern Europe and Central Asia: Gatekeeping services for vulnerable children and families*. Florence: UNICEF & World Bank.
United Nations Office of the High Commissioner for Human Rights. (2011). *The rights of children under the age of three, ending their placement in institutional care*. n.p.: Regional Office for Europe of the Office of the United Nations High Commissioner for Human Rights.
Ushijima, Y., & Yukawa, R. (1975). Jidōsōdanjyo ni okeru hantei no kinō oyobi kijun ni kansuru kenkyū [A study on the decision making function and standards of the child guidance centres]. *Nihon sōgō aiiku kenkyū kiyō*, 11, 305–331.
Weatherley, R., & Lipsky, M. (1977). Street-level bureaucrats and institutional innovation. *Harvard Educational Review*, 47(2), 171–197.
World Health Organization. (2010). *Better health, better lives: Children and young people with intellectual disabilities and their families: Transfer care from institutions to the community*. EUR/51298/17/PP/3. Bucharest, Romania.
Yamamoto, T., Shoji, J., Arimura, T., Itakura, T., Sato, T., Ohta, K., ... Miyaguchi, T. (2008). Jidōsōdanjyo-tō ni okeru hogo-sha enjo no arikata ni kansuru jisshō-teki kenkyū 2 hogo-sha enjo shuhō no kōka, datōsei, hyōka, tekiō ni kansuru jisshō-teki kenkyū [A study on the system for supporting family preservation in

the child guidance centres 2: Efficiency, validity, evaluation and discerning of the parents' supporting methods]. *Nihon kodomo katei sōgōkenkyūsho*, 45, 235–283.

Yamazaki, T., Nagai, A., Masuma, K., Saito, S., Naito, Y., Kakiyama, A., ... Shoji, J. (2009). *Nyūji-in ni okeru aichaku jōtai no hyōka to aichaku keisei ni kansuru chōsa kenkyū* [Research into the assessment and development of attachment in baby and welfare institutions]. n.p.: Zaidanhōjin kodomo mirai zaidan.

Yoshida, Y. (2008). Shakai-teki yōgo no dōkō to kadai ni kansuru kenkyū: 2000-Nen kara 2007-nen made wo chūshin ni [On trends and issues in alternative care: Focusing on 2000 to 2007]. *Nagoyashiritsudaigaku daigakuin ningen bunka kenkyū-ka ningen bunka kenkyū*, 10, 61–76.

Note: Where the author(s) provided an English translation of their work I have given this translation, rather than my translation.

6 Regional variation of norms

1 Introduction

The actions of those implementing policy in the CGCs are framed by their values on the family-bond and informed by the resources available to them. They are also shaped by the staff members' beliefs on alternative care. Indeed Maynard-Moody and Musheno argue that 'street level decisions and actions are guided less by rules, training, or procedures and more by beliefs and norms, especially beliefs and norms about what is fair' (2003: 6; see also Sandfort, 2000; Winter, 2000). Meyers and Vorsanger identify two main categories here: 'socialisation into professional norms' (2003: 248) and 'personal beliefs about policy instrumentation and targets' (2003: 248).

The importance of norms in the CGCs is amplified by the absence of 'professional norms' related to social work, the devolution of power to local authorities, and the limited nature of MHLW guidelines. There are no inspections on the decision-making process, limited reporting of data, and no consequences if national guidelines are not followed.

This chapter focuses on the decision-making process by which a child is removed from the family and placed into care. The decision on the placement type centres on three norms: the goals of care, the functions of different care placements, and the threshold above which a child is seen as unsuitable for foster care.

The most important of these is the function of foster care. The construction of foster care exists on a spectrum between a proxy for adoption to specialist 'semi-professional' care in a family setting. Where foster care is understood as a replacement family it can only be used for children for whom the goal of care is not family reunification. This is tied to the construction of the family-bond as singular and discrete, which can lead foster care to be constructed as a threat. This chapter details the regional variation in these norms, focusing on Teru, which has a high foster care rate, and Irifune, which has a low foster care rate.

2 Goals of care: placing Japan into international context

In recent years academics have attempted to establish an international comparative framework for alternative care systems (Courtney and

Hughes-Heuring, 2009; Ezell et al., 2011; Knorth, et al., 2008; Negishi, 2014). These often take the 'goals' of alternative care as a key variable. Gilbert's (2012) model is the most nuanced of these and is used here.

Gilbert's 1997 work classified alternative care systems as being orientated towards child protection or family service. Gilbert's 2012 work (see Table 6.1) argues that a third orientation has emerged, that of child development. These orientations can be understood as the primary 'goal' of each care system.

Gilbert argues that different conceptualisations of abuse lead to different modes of intervention and a different relationship between the state and the parent. 'Child protection', which characterizes the problem of abuse as deviant behaviour of dysfunctional parents, sees the government responding in a legalistic manner, with an adversarial state-parent relationship and high rates of involuntary out-of-home placement. 'Family service', which characterizes abuse as arising from social or psychological stress and family issues, aims to strengthen family relationships with therapeutic needs-based intervention, based upon a cooperative state-parent relationship. 'Child development orientation', which aims at a constructive balance between child protection and family service, builds on the state's role in promoting child development that largely stemmed from the UN Convention on the Rights of the Child (UN General Assembly, 1989). Gilbert argues that countries most commonly now operate hybrid systems.

In 2013 Kawamatsu, the MHLW bureaucrat responsible for the CGCs, wrote an article that suggests that the MHLW is aiming at a hybrid approach. This defined 'the best interests of the child' in the short term as involving accurate risk assessment to ensure safety, and in the long term as

Table 6.1 Gilbert's orientations of alternative care systems.

Three orientations to child maltreatment: child development, family service, and child protection

	Child protection	*Family service*	*Child development*
Problem frame	Deviant behaviour and dysfunctional parenting	Social/ psychological stress, and family issues	Child's developmental needs and unequal outcomes for children
Mode of intervention	Legalistic/ investigative	Therapeutic/needs assessment	Early intervention and regulatory/ need assessment
State-parent relationship	Adversarial – state sanctioning parental misbehaviour and using coercive powers for involuntary out of home placement	Partnership, with state seeking to strengthen family relations and – voluntary out of home placement	Substitutive/ paternalistic – with state assuming family responsibility for support and care

Source: Gilbert, 2012: 533.

focusing on the child's healthy growth and development, their capacity to become a self-actualised adult, and the existence of family, or family-like, relationships and connections.

However, other literature suggests a gap between these aims and practice. Harada's (2010) estimate that only 4 per cent of placements due to abuse in 2006 were involuntary suggests that Japan does not fit the 'child protection' orientation (see also Zenshakyō, 2008).

The lengthy stays in care suggest a 'substitutive/paternalistic' state-parent relationship, found in the 'child development' orientation. Yet the mode of intervention cannot be described as 'early intervention', and children's developmental needs are only prioritised for children entering specialist institutions due to mental health issues or disabilities, or where the goal of care is the cultivation of self-reliance.

Abe's construction of abuse suggests a 'family service' orientation:

> the guardian abusing the child will be wrapped up in various problems and without resolving the problems facing the family they will not be able to stop child abuse. Because of that, the CGC and local authority need the cooperation of the family.
>
> (2014: 2)

Goodman's observation that abusive parents at times receive sympathy from the public for the circumstances that contributed to their behaviour (2002), and the voluntary nature of most placements, add weight to this categorisation.

Yet Japan does not fit the therapeutic mode of intervention of the 'family service' orientation. Therapeutic interventions in other OECD countries normally aim at short, intensive stays in care, coupled with work to prepare the family for the child to return home (see Mulheir and Browne, 2007). Alternative care in Japan is rarely framed as therapeutic,[1] and despite studies on the role welfare institutions can play in facilitating family reintegration (see Aizawa, 2011; Toma, 2014), and studies showing the abuse risk for children returned home without support (Yamamoto et al., 2010, 2011, 2013),[2] only 52 per cent of children returning home from CWIs and 40.5 per cent of those from temporary care had a 'step by step approach to rebuilding contact with parent and child' (Yamamoto et al., 2013: 143; see also Saimura et al., 2007).

Furthermore, placements in Japan are lengthier than in many other countries: Tsutsui and Otaga contrast Japan, where 49 per cent of children are in care for over five years, with America, where only 11.3 per cent of children are in care for over five years (2011: 406).[3]

Academics have suggested different responses to the lack of therapeutic support here. Yamamoto et al. (2008) argue that as each parent requires individualised support, developing CGC caseworkers' experience is critical. Similar findings led Saimura et al. (2005) to argue for more training for CGC caseworkers and clinical psychologists, as well as to investigate what approach worked for different types of parents (Saimura et al., 2006). In contrast, Ogiso argues for strengthening welfare institutions, rather than CGCs, as 'it has been pointed out since long ago that there are many legal limits on the amount of guidance that can be given in Japan' (2010: 405).

This presents a puzzle. Japan appears to be taking a 'hybrid' approach yet the mode of intervention is not therapeutic, early intervention, or legalistic. So how do the CGCs intervene, how do they attempt to achieve the goal of care placements, and what functions do different care placements play in achieving these goals?

3 Goals of care: regional variation in norms

There are three goals of care in Japan: family reunification, the cultivation of self-reliance (Harada, 2013),[4] or the provision of a new family, either through adoption or long-term fostering (Kawamatsu, 2013).

The most important factor in a CGC's determination of the goal of care is the feasibility of the child returning home. There is a national checklist to help with this decision (Kawamatsu, 2013), but this does not provide clear guidance. In reality the CGC makes this decision by assessing the strength of the family-bond and the family's present and future capacity to care. Where family reunification is considered impossible, the goal of care becomes cultivating self-reliance or finding a replacement family. This decision centres on the child's age and the complexity of their needs.

The CGC does not determine the goal of care on its own. The lack of judicial support strengthens the legal guardian's voice. Where it is involved, the court's default position is that family reunification is the goal of care. This is framed by the Child Welfare Act, Article 4, on the responsibilities of the nation and the public, and Article 11, on how to provide guidance to the guardian who abused the child, which assumes the goal of family reunification. This, in turn, connects with the political priority given to maintaining the family. Takeda, referencing Prime Minister Abe's (2006) book, argues that this discourse on the family is in turn linked to 'building a "beautiful" Japan' (2011: 59).

The lack of a judicial role means that this decision is a 'joint production process' (Meyers and Vorsanger, 2003: 246) between the CGC and the parent. Parental preference for welfare institutions (Kawamatsu, 2013; MHLW, 2012; Miyajima, 2001; Tsuzaki, 2009), based on the belief that they pose less of a threat to their family-bond than foster care, often prevents the CGC from using foster care whatever the goal of care.

While the parent must be listened to, the child's voice is usually absent from the decision-making process. Indeed, the decision is often not even explained to the child, leading Kawamatsu to outline the importance of 'explaining politely to the child what will happen so that the child is not anxious over what is going to happen to them' (2013: 41). Nakamura (2013), herself a careleaver, is one of the rare voices who problematises this.

The caseworkers' construction of the goal of care is also shaped by the available resources and the construction of the function of these resources, discussed in the following section. This book extends Brodkin's argument that 'caseworkers… do not do just what they want or just what they are told to want. They do what they can' (1997: 24), to acknowledge that what caseworkers 'want' is also shaped by the resources available to them.

Whether the goal of care is a new family, family reunification, or the development of self-reliance, placement stability is understood as critical. In each CGC I visited, I asked whether it would be preferable for a child in care from 2 to 18 years of age to be in one CWI placement or a few foster care placements. All staff stated a preference for the single placement, though Teru staff were the least confident with their position.[5]

This aversion to placement change was evident in the decision-making process in both CGCs. In one case in Irifune, the caseworker noted that they 'worry a little as this child has had one foster care placement breakdown and want to place with a foster carer who won't have a placement breakdown again'. In a case in Teru, one section head noted that

> if he goes to a home and it breaks down could be more damaging than a placement that is more secure. If it goes well it would be best in a house, but if it fails, having already had one foster care placement breakdown, he will feel a failure if another placement breaks down.

My fieldwork notes referred on several occasions to a 'pathological aversion to placement breakdown'.

Despite their concerns, Teru staff were more willing to accept the risk to placement stability than Irifune staff were. This is because of differences in the constructions of the functions and merit of foster care placements, and differences in the way that risk is shared across staff.

In Teru, placement decisions occur within formal meetings. In these, senior managers take an active role in reshaping the caseworker's proposed plan of action. The consensus decision, once made, is written by all participants on their copy of the form. In Irifune, the placement decision is 'provisionally' made prior to the formal meeting. Where a caseworker is considering foster care, for example, they ask the foster care supervisor prior to the meeting if a suitable foster parent is available. A negative response results in foster care not being raised as a possible placement in the formal meeting. The caseworker types the provisional decision onto the forms prior to the meeting and this is rarely changed, with senior managers limiting themselves to clarifying reasoning or noting additional steps to be taken. This results in the caseworker, rather than the managers, determining the goal of care and shouldering responsibility for this decision.

There is also a difference between Teru and Irifune in the staff's willingness to challenge the parents' goal of care. Caseworkers have a high degree of discretion in determining when to do this. This leads Miyajima (2001: 35) to argue that:

> parents always say they want their child back at some point in the future. If say, the child goes to foster care or adoption the parents feel

their 'sins' more than if the child goes into an institution. So, the caseworker has to say—but it will be difficult for you to actually have the child back in the future right.

Kawamatsu also argues that a placement into foster care 'from the perspective of the guardian, ... makes them feel that this is a denial of their way of child rearing' (2013: 42). A placement into a professional welfare institution with specialist staff lessens the parents' sense of responsibility for the child entering care.

Teru staff are more willing to broach this and challenge the parent's goals of care than Irifune staff. Teru's increased foster care rate has come with a concerted effort to gain parental consent, with the recent appointment of a lawyer further strengthening the CGC. This includes developing materials for natal parents explaining what foster care is and why it is more suitable for some children's development, as well as training sessions on how to get parental consent. The Irifune CGC also recently created a pamphlet distinguishing foster care from adoption, though this is rarely used. In many cases it is assumed that the parent will not consent to foster care and the possibility is not even raised.

Teru staff's greater willingness to accept 'positive risk' and to challenge the parents' construction of the goals of care is shaped by the attitude of senior management and caseworkers towards foster care and the construction of its function, as discussed below. The differences between Teru and Irifune also reflect the different weight afforded to the family-bond. Where the family-bond is considered the most important factor for a child's development there are cases where it is protected even where there is no possibility of family reunification, with the child's image of their family-bond prioritised over the possibility of a new family being created. This can lead to an institutional placement, in the belief that a foster care placement may lead the child to feel that they have 'been abandoned by their family' (Kawamatsu, 2013: 42). This occurs more frequently in Irifune than Teru.

The decision on the goal of care is based upon limited information, confined by parental preferences, and shaped within a legal and judicial system that prioritises family reunification. Any attempt to challenge these parameters, as Teru has done, requires a concerted and consistent effort.

4 Regional variation in norms on the functions of different types of care

4.1 Existing literature

With around 300 adoptions each year (Mehrotra et al., 2013: 842), adoption plays a minimal role in alternative care. While some argue for a greater role for adoption (Tokotani, 2009; Tokunaga, 2012), systemic issues (Bryant, 1990; Goldfarb, 2016; Hayes and Habu, 2006; Hideki, 2013; Moriguchi, 2010; Ochi, 2008; Shirai, 2010, 2014; Tokunaga, 2012), most notably the absence of judicial involvement, means that CGCs effectively 'provide adoption services only when the parents express a wish to place their child for adoption' (Harada, 2010: 231).

This means that long-term foster care is sometimes used as 'quasi-adoption'. Harada argues that this has 'obscured the basic characteristic of foster parents' rights and responsibilities' (2014: 1) and created a distinction in the function of foster care and welfare institutions that does not exist in the legal framework of care (2013). Miyajima (2001: 34) provides evidence of this:

> When a child goes to a child welfare institution the child guidance centre fills out a form with the details on the child and this is basis for how to care for them. It is unclear whether we should fill in the same form when a child goes to foster care, unclear in legal terms and seems to depend on whether foster parent is someone you can trust with this kind of information.

Paradoxically, the use of some foster care as quasi-adoption makes caseworkers apprehensive that some registered foster parents want to adopt (Fukaya et al., 2013; Miyajima, 2001; Omori, 2016). A National Foster Care Association newsletter addressed this; in the 'Foster Care Q&A for Beginners' section, one foster parent writes that 'I have no natal child and want to adopt. When I went to the CGC they recommended that I register as a 'regular foster carer'. The editor's response highlighted both the 'large numbers of foster carers who secretly want to adopt', and the fact that 'this can cause problems in the future for the system as foster care is different' (2012: 17; see also Goldfarb, 2015). Yamamoto's (1952) work demonstrates that these are longstanding concerns.

Kikuchi (2007) argues that this confusion stems from the wording of the Child Welfare Act, which describes foster care as being for 'children with no guardians or for children who it is not suitable for their parents to raise them' (Article 6-3). Kikuchi (2007) argues that this wording, unchanged even with the introduction of specialist foster parents in 2002, was written for post-war orphans, and that it frames foster care as a replacement family.[6]

Miyajima argues that some within CGCs fear that placing a child in 'foster care could cut the relationship with the natal parent' (2001: 35). Goldfarb develops this (2012: 9–10, emphasis added), arguing that:

> although both institutional and foster caregivers might be engaging in similar practices, the embodied intimacies, reiterated over time, between children and foster parents have the capacity to engender new kinship ties that are seen to threaten the bonds between a natal parent and child... *Implied within this logic is a perception that parent-child ties cannot be multiple*: a child's relationship with a caregiver who acts like a parent threatens the child's tie to his or her actual parent.

Goldfarb adds: 'just like adoption, many people—caseworkers, institutional caregivers, and perhaps even foster parents themselves—perceive foster care as a threat to a birth parent's potential relationship with a child, *but my interlocutors never made explicit the reasons why*' (2012: 98, emphasis added). The development of this concept, see Chapter 3, is one of the major contributions of this book.

Goldfarb argues that this construction of foster care results in caseworkers using welfare institutions 'if there is any possibility of that child's reunion with biological kin' (2012: 47; see also Kikuchi, 2007; Miyajima, 2001). Goldfarb states: 'if placement in an institution does not "cut the parent-child bond," it is precisely because parents may figure the institution as an open-ended space for waiting' (2012: 103). Here Goldfarb references a CWI staff member, who stated: 'we are not raising these children. We are temporality entrusted with their care (*azukatteimasu*)' (2012: 103; see also Ochi, 2008; Yamanta, 1995).

The conclusion to Ren's case, discussed in Chapter 3, that it was 'better if he goes to a baby institution, [as he] won't think of them as new family, but as staff' neatly encapsulates a distinction between the functions of welfare institutions and foster care and how they are understood as impacting upon the family-bond. Yet the function of different placements is not uniformly understood across local authorities or within local authorities for children of different ages. The following sections outline my findings on the functions of different types of care and discuss how these impact upon regional variation of policy implementation.

4.2 National overview

There is limited national data relating to the function of different placements. Some data that is instructive is the age at the time of placement into foster care (see Figure 4.5), and the percentage of children placed into each type of care by age group (Figure 6.1).[7]

In both figures there are two peaks of children entering foster care. For absolute numbers, these come at two years old and, in a smaller peak, at 15 years of age. In terms of the percentage of children of each age group entering each care placement, foster care peaks at 1 and 17 years of age.

Compulsory education, which lasts from 6 to 15 years of age, maps neatly onto both charts, with children older than 6 and younger than 15 years less likely to go into foster care. These are close to historical transition ages: Hara and Minagawa argue that in the Tokugawa era (1603–1868) 'one was considered to be an adult at about 15... Japanese since the late 12th century have generally considered the first seven years of life as the first half of childhood' (1996: 16). This second transition also corresponds to the age at which children can undertake 'normal' adoption without parental consent, that is, 15 years, and is close to the age of criminal responsibility, which is 14 years.

190 *Variation of policy implementation*

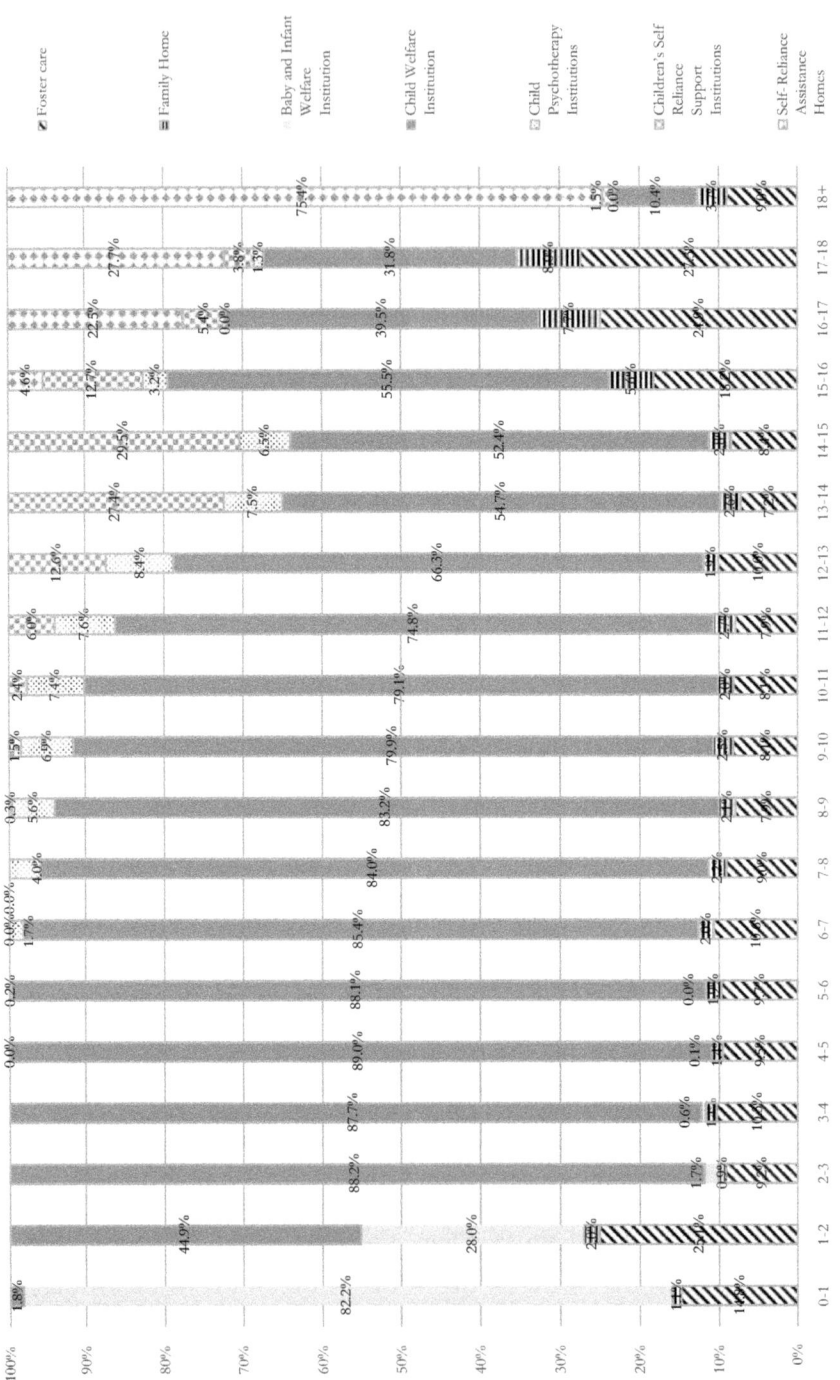

Figure 6.1 Percentage of children of each age group, at time of placement, by care placement. Nationwide, in care February 1st 2013. Excludes mother and child supported living institutions.

Data Source: MHLW (2016a) *Shakai-teki yougo no genjou ni tsuite (sanka shiryou)*. 2016, January: 74

Foster care for children after this second transition is not based on the premise of building a new family-bond. A discussion in Yuno, between a senior administrator, a foster care caseworker, and a caseworker illustrates the function of foster care for elder children:

SA: So, foster care for junior high school students is hard?
FC CW: For older kids can think of it like a boarding house [*geshuku*], a safe space to live.
CW: The... case is like that. Both parents died, two children, aged 23 and second grade of high school [16–17]. Elder child had been in a CWI. Tried to live together but the relationship... got very bad, had no money for food etc.... The younger child had an image of the CWI as the older brother had been there, but the older brother said it won't be good for you.[8] There was a new foster parent right by his school. Hadn't ever had a child with them. Is a very earnest person, maybe too earnest foster care family. We started with a short term-ish, one school term to see. The mother wanted to have a very deep relationship with the child, had an image of being like her own child. The foster parents wanted to give love and emotion but child was just wanting to get on without love. The foster parents said to us, we are not wanting to be a guest house. We can't.

Here the CGC staff and the child saw the function of foster care as 'a boarding house. A safe space to live'. This conflicted with the foster parents' construction of foster care as a proxy for adoption, resulting in placement breakdown.

There is also tension between different constructions of the function of foster care in Teru. At a monthly meeting, a foster parent explained how they had supported one foster child, who had been placed with them at 15 years of age, through university, noting cautiously that she hadn't minded doing this, but that it had been expensive and that she was not sure she would be able to do it again. Here the foster parent was expected to perform the function of a natal parent, a function the foster parent implied the local authority should have performed, without having a family-bond with this child.

CGCs also use foster care for older children when the CWI is unwilling to care for them. In Teru and Irifune the CWIs' requests to move 'disruptive' children to foster care were always framed by the CWI as being in the best interest of the child, though the child had rarely been consulted. Cases where the child's volition is given weight are those where the decision is finely balanced, where the placement change involves leaving school, where the child repeatedly and forcefully expresses a preference, or where the child has been in care for a long period and is aware of their ability to disrupt placements.

National data (calculated from MHLW, 2016a: 89) on parental contact by placement type sheds light on the functions of different care placements: 72.4 per cent of children in foster care have no contact with their parents, considerably more than the 18 per cent of children in CWIs and 19.4 per cent of children in BIWIs. Family homes sit between foster care and welfare institutions, with 40.5 per cent of children having no parental contact.

National data (calculated from MHLW, 2016a: 84) on the presence of parents by placement type is also illustrative: only 14.9 per cent of children in foster care and family homes have both parents present, a figure that rises to 32.5 per cent in CWI and 52.6 per cent in BIWI. Conversely, 42.4 per cent of children in foster care have neither parent, a figure that falls to 16 per cent in CWI and 2.8 per cent in BIWI. Further, national data (MHLW, 2016a: 84) shows that only 5.6 per cent of children from two-parent households enter foster care or family homes. This is considerably less than the 28.3 per cent of children from households where both parents are not present and 25.5 per cent of children from households where both parents' location is unknown. Finally, only 23.5 per cent of children leaving foster care in 2013 returned home, less than half the percentage of children leaving CWIs (calculated from MHLW, 2016a: 81–83). Having reviewed the national picture, the next section examines the function of foster care and institutional care more closely.

4.3 Foster care

The function of foster care has been contested since its creation (Kumasaka and Aiba, 1968). Two ongoing debates, on the introduction of maternity and paternity leave for foster parents and the classification of family homes, illustrate the current state of this contest.

Since 2014, some within the National Foster Care Association have advocated for child-rearing leave for foster parents, in the belief that the lack of leave acts as a barrier to potential foster parents (NHK, 2015). Such is the strength of conviction here that this was the discussion topic the first time a foster parent spoke at the Liberal Democratic Party's 'Committee on the future of alternative care', in 2015. Other foster parents and activists oppose this, concerned that introducing leave would further equate foster care with adoption, leaving CGCs less willing to use non-long-term foster care.

Statistics defining the foster care rate consider family homes as foster care, yet family-homes are distinguished from foster care in all other reporting.[9] The liminal status of family homes, as private and public, familial and professional, begins in their legal status. The Child Welfare Act distinguishes family homes, which it defines as 'small-scale home-type child-rearing businesses' (Article 6-3-8), from other foster care. Kashiwame outlines how this ambiguity led to debate at the fourth annual National Family Home Association meeting on the tension between being a business and providing 'homely warmth' (2010). By the ninth annual meeting, in 2014, the focus of the family home foster parents was more pragmatic, with the dominant concern being that local authorities were encouraging them to leave employment and to see their family home as their job, but then not placing enough children to ensure financial sustainability.

Variation of norms 193

Some foster parents running family homes have reacted to this ambiguity by emphasising what I called in my fieldwork notes 'an idealised Ghibli-esque[10] Japanese childhood – Japanese traditional values and countryside ideals'. During a visit to a Teru family home, run by experienced foster parents, the foster father gave me a small talk with slides. He noted that the strengths of his home were that

> it is a countryside place, in nature. Of course that is a very important thing for children, to play in nature and realise the importance of life. In the winter they play in the snow and cook on a wood burning stove.

The foster father continued, explaining that his relative 'has a temple and they have a dog and a cat. The animals are very important staff for the children!' The slideshow concluded with letters that children had written to the foster parents when they left, highlighting their continued connection.

At the other end of the spectrum exist family homes that are run by ex-CWI staff. Some CWIs offer an accounting and budgeting package to family homes, and in some cases children in the family home follow CWI rules, on the basis that it would be 'unfair' for these children to be allowed to do things that those in the institution are not. One example from my fieldwork saw children forbidden to play in a local park on certain days. These family homes would not be classified as foster care under the UN Guidelines for the Alternative Care of Children, which states that fostering occurs 'in the domestic environment of a family' (2010, Article 29-c-iii).

In an attempt to clarify the difference between family-homes and small community-based CWIs, in 2012 the MHLW issued the 'Clarification of the requirements of family homes' (2016b: 44–45). Ongoing debates on this issue focus on the carers' past and the atmosphere and care style of the home (Goldfarb, 2012; National Family Home Association, 2012).

National debates on the function of foster care are echoed within local authorities. Challenges with adoption mean that all local authorities construct some foster care as a proxy for adoption. Similarly, almost all local authorities use some foster care as a 'boarding house' for older children. This section focuses on the differences between Teru and Irifune in the function of 'non-adoption' foster care for children under 15 years of age.

Marketing material aimed at raising awareness of foster care and recruiting foster parents makes explicit the differences in how the function of foster care is constructed. Figure 6.2, given for context, shows two images (redrawn from the original promotional material by Sarah Garmston) used in a national MHLW foster care campaign. These images, both of which feature one child with a young couple, evoke family activities and suggest the filling of an 'empty nest'.

In their marketing, Irifune constructs foster care as a replacement family. Figure 6.3 (redrawn from the original promotional material by Sarah Garmston) shows four images from Irifune recruitment materials. The first

Figure 6.2 Marketing foster care. MHLW.

shows a new-born baby entering a family, surrounded by a giant heart, to the delight of grandparents. Everyone's gaze is turned to the contented baby, suggesting that the older child sat on the grandfathers' knee is a natal child rather than a foster child of the older couple. The other three images also call to mind a foster carer, cited by Kikuchi, who was told by a CGC 'we have no children who don't have parents so we don't have any children eligible for foster care' (2007: 150).

The Irifune CGC has outsourced the recruitment and training of foster parents to a BIWI. This BIWI's construction of foster care corresponds with

Variation of norms 195

Figure 6.3 Marketing foster care. Irifune.

the marketing material. At a recruitment event for people with an interest in foster care, the BIWI head explained that

> There are around … children [in Irifune] who cannot be cared for by their parents. One third of these have no way of going home to their natal parents. The foster care system is for these children… If you know that there is a foster parent or child around you, I would like you to know that they are normal kids in a normal house and please treat them warmly.

Figure 6.4 Marketing foster care. Teru.

The BIWI foster care counsellor did later explain the legal difference between adoption and foster care, but the session was concluded by the BIWI head stating,

> On ... there was a lecture at ... We had talks about foster care and abuse and explained the difference between adoption and fostering. I asked many children about their situation. They didn't distinguish between adoption and foster care, they just said I am happy with Mr/Ms X, and that they are happy to be living there. It is like the old days.

Variation of norms 197

The images used in Teru suggest a more diverse construction of foster care. The first difference is that Teru's promotional material (redrawn from the original promotional material by Sarah Garmston) distinguishes three types of foster care: regular foster care, foster care with a view to adopt, and family homes (Figure 6.4).

These images are simpler, less emotive, and not set in the context of a family activity. The age of the children differs, with foster care with a view to adoption showing an older child rather than a baby. The family home image is the first shown in promotional material. The age difference here means that the children cannot be mistaken as natal children. It is possible that the image of older foster parents aims to suggest experience or encourage potential older foster parents.

The diverse representations of foster care reflect the Teru CGC's construction of foster care, which senior managers are actively trying to broaden. The most obvious example of this during my fieldwork was a 'treatment foster care' pilot, distinct from the 'specialist foster carers' designation. A discussion in a Teru case meeting speaks to why the 'treatment foster care' pilot was created:

> SM1: At the moment it is still too easy to become a specialist foster parent. If you have the experience and do the course you will become a specialist foster parent. Just because they are classed as a specialist doesn't mean they are.
> SM2: There are more people with specialist status, but they are mostly family homes...
> SM1: I haven't yet placed a child into specialist foster care just because of the abuse history of a child.
> ...
> FCSH[11]: Why aren't tough kids in specialist foster care?
> SM1: At the moment they go to CWIs.

This pilot scheme saw Hinata, an eight-year-old boy with complex care needs that would normally have seen him placed into a CWI, enter foster care. This pilot had more caseworker support and a structured individual care plan aiming at family reintegration. The caseworker explained he was 'now doing interviews every two weeks and phone support, this is like American treatment foster care. However, there are still limits to how well we are doing this'. This pilot represents a conscious attempt in Teru to push the boundaries of both the 'type' of child that can enter foster care and what foster care is.

There were also occasional attempts in Irifune to place a child who would normally enter institutional care into foster care. The critical difference between the two CGCs is that in Teru these attempts were part of sustained efforts to expand the function of foster care, while in Irifune these were understood as 'one-offs'. A discussion with a section head in Irifune demonstrates this.

198 *Variation of policy implementation*

In two separate cases in Irifune, a child had been locked in a room with no stimulus for several years. Both children were diagnosed with attachment disorder and received hospital treatment before entering care. One child, whose sibling had been starved to death by their parents,[12] was placed into a specialist welfare institution; the other entered foster care.

Both children were described as 'robot-like' when they entered care. The section head explained that the child in the specialist welfare institution was now 'more human-like',[13] and that the child in foster care 'is now so "normal" that many people would have no idea he had a difficult past, he passes as a child. Perhaps child specialists would notice some small things different about him, but neighbourhood people wouldn't notice at all'.

The decision to place this child into foster care had been made because a caseworker at the time posited that if a lack of attachment had been the cause of the child's issues, a new attachment may resolve them. This decision was possible as the CGC had one particularly experienced foster carer. The section head explained,

> The strength of this foster carer is that they live way out in the countryside and had the support of the whole community. Is the kind of traditional little town where if the kid is being naughty in town other people will tell him off.

While the child in foster care was understood to have made considerably more progress than the child in institutional care, the section head felt that 'there was also some luck in how the child and the foster parents clicked... if [the child] had been placed with another foster parent could have ended up being abused'.

Explaining the increased foster care rate in Teru, Sano explained that one of the most important factors was a sea-change in the caseworkers' attitude towards foster care. Sano explained that this change stemmed from caseworkers seeing placements in foster care going better than they had expected, and better than they would have expected in institutional care. Unlike in Irifune, where success in placements was linked to luck, in Teru this created a positive feedback loop. Other staff in the Teru CGC explained that this was the result of strong clear leadership that supported caseworkers in taking positive risks, in trying foster care placements for children who would previously have gone to institutional care.

The sustained and consistent approach of senior managers towards expanding the function of foster care means that in Teru placement breakdowns are cases to learn from, rather than a reason to abandon change, and placement successes are evidence that the direction of change is a positive one, rather than a stroke of luck. The broader construction of foster care in Teru means that it is seen as suitable for a broader range of children than in Irifune, including for children for whom the goal of care is family reunification.

While there is regional variation, at a national level the construction of the function of foster care is considerably narrower than in many other OECD countries. There is, for example, very little LGBT fostering in Japan, despite recent attempts from NPOs such as Rainbow Foster Care to promote this. One case in Teru, which had the broadest construction of the function of foster care of any CGC I conducted research in, highlights the limited breadth of this construction.

Following the divorce of an experienced foster parent couple, the father, who was a 'great foster parent', continued fostering the two children. The foster carer lived simply on the allowance he was paid for caring for the two children and showed 'no signs' of getting a job.[14] The foster care section head reported an 'unsettled atmosphere amongst the foster carers', who were 'asking if this was ok'. One caseworker joked that 'he would be a good househusband, if he had a wife!', to which a senior manager smiled and responded:

> The model is about showing kids a working employed family. This is very important for the kids to see. This is the line we can press him on, can be farming, whatever, just show them you are working and earning money. Is a normal family model which foster care is based on.

It is possible that the increased use of family homes, *Tenrikyo* foster parents, and semi-professional foster *carers*, along with rising divorce rates, will eventually start to challenge the idea of a child as only being able to have one family-bond. Until then, attempts to increase the foster care rate must focus on expanding the function of foster care, as Teru has done.

Having considered the impact of the different constructions of the function of foster care in Irifune and Teru on how policy is implemented, this chapter next turns to the function of welfare institutions.

4.4 Welfare institutions

The continued use of large-scale welfare institutions is gradually being problematized within Japan. The 2010 Vision for Children and Childrearing called for CWIs to become smaller, setting a target of having no more than 45 children in the main building, organised into units of six to eight. The Vision is less explicit about BIWIs, though later MHLW plans (2016c: 19, 24) call for BIWIs to be reduced in size and converted from dormitory-style into unit-style institutions.

There are two international NGOs currently considering funding research into the effect of institutionalising babies and infants in Japan. When I asked an MHLW bureaucrat about this, they replied:

> I think the BIWIs should do research to show that their care does not affect the children's development, but, the problem with that is, if it does

show that children leaving the BIWIs have lower IQs... or that they have attachment disorders... then I fear people will give up on children and adults who were previously in BIWI, they will think – Oh, this child was in BIWI so I can't do anything to help them – and the children who were in BIWIs will be stigmatised.

Were this research to occur and produce similar findings to work elsewhere (see Nelson et al., 2007) it could have a large impact on the construction of the function of BIWIs.

The Teru CGC is already concerned about the impact that BIWIs can have upon a child's development, concerns not found in most local authorities. A discussion during a decision-meeting in Teru illustrates these concerns:

SM1: BIWI kids are always slow with development. They need experience, they don't have much experience of these things. This kid is about normal for having been in a BIWI, as there are many things that they don't do with the kids in the BIWI.
SM2: What does this development thing mean – food, toilet etc.?
SM3: This BWI doesn't do toilet training... Wear nappies until 3.
SM1: That is crazy.
SM3: The BIWI thought it was normal... said they are too busy.
CP[15]: The staff said it isn't us, it's the system we work in.
SM3: Can't dress themselves etc. Will be some problems moving to the different care placement. Maybe a problem with this BIWI rather than all BIWI.
SM1: Yeah, compared to [X] BIWI this one is worse.
SM4: Not [Y] BIWI's problem, is our problem. For leaving kids in these facilities for so long.
SM1: But need parental consent right?
SM4: Yeah.
CW: In this case the mother suddenly changed her mind and said yes.
SM4: Ideally we want to be aiming for specialist foster carers rather than BIWIs.

Similar concerns were raised in a second case in Teru, where a baby had been placed into a BIWI in the expectation that they would return home within six months but had eventually stayed for several years.

SM1: So, has been in BIWI since basically birth... We need to focus not just on child developmental issues when we go to the BIWI, we should also consider the parent-child relationship a little more.
...
SM2: Here seems to have not had a terrible effect, however we really don't want these cases where a child ends up staying 2–3 years *zuruzuru*, should be looking at foster care, adoption. We need to explain to the parents BIWIs are bad for children.

The term *zuruzuru*, to slide or drift, was often used in Teru to describe cases where the child had remained longer than anticipated in institutional care. Concerns over long-term institutionalisation led Teru to establish a new section in 2015 to review cases of children who had been in institutional care for five or more years, to determine whether they could return home or move to foster care.

Despite their concerns, staff in the Teru CGC are not opposed to institutional care, and in both Teru and Irifune welfare institutions are sometimes considered the most suitable placement. The first reason for this is that welfare institutions are seen protecting an existing or potential family-bond. In one case, of an infant who was moving from a BIWI to a foster parent to be adopted, a senior manager said, 'it is good that it is [A] BIWI, not [B] BIWI. Seems to be that is not particularly attached to any staff member in particular'.

The second reason is that welfare institutions are sometimes seen as the best environment for a child's development. An example of this in Teru saw a caseworker argue,

> I don't think it is a good thing for her to go home. I think for her development would be better for her to be in a CWI. When she was in [X] CWI she really grew and developed, and had good relationships with adults.

The third reason is that welfare institutions are sometimes seen as more capable of dealing with complex needs. At times this seemed logical, for older children with challenging profiles; in other instances, I felt instinctively less comfortable, such as when a baby entered a BIWI as 'this child cries a lot, so will be difficult for foster carers, perhaps'. Finally, welfare institutions are sometimes preferred as they allow siblings to stay together.

Family homes are normally understood as being in-between institutions and foster parents in terms of the complexity of needs that they can cater for, though some family homes and foster parents are seen as providing an exceptional level of care. A discussion in Teru illustrates the in-between role of family homes:

SM1: So, needs to be a CWI that is far away and with no stress.
SM2: A CWI with no stress??
　　　[All giggled]
SM1: Well, low stress! Seems hard for foster care.
FCSH: Hmm... [tone implied yes]
SM2: Minimum would have to be family home.
FCSH: At moment only two have space.
SM1: His age would clash with the kids there right?
FCSH: There are younger kids in the family home but not the same age.
TCW[16]: He is aggressive to younger kids.

202   *Variation of policy implementation*

This child was placed into a CWI, in part due to the impact he would have had on the children in the available family homes. This decision was also based on the temporary care worker's assessment that the child needed 'thoughtful guidance and rules', that he 'listens carefully to staff when told off' and that the 're-establishment of a good life rhythm' had been very important in his development in temporary care.

In Irifune, the use of welfare institutions is not problematized. As in Teru, BIWIs were often used in Irifune to facilitate the possibility of family reunification. In one case, the caseworker explained:

> I am worried about long-term ability to care for this child, and think the baby should enter BIWI on permanent not temporary basis. I want the mother to start seeing the baby regularly. If it seems that the mother will not be able to care for the child long-term and they will be long-term in care I want to look at foster care.

A second case in Irifune highlights how BIWIs are understood as the most suitable placement for children who have particular care needs. This case also highlights how the Irifune CGC actively pursues foster care placements for babies and infants for whom the goal of care is not family reunification.

SM1: The mother wants to care and tries best but not connected to ability in reality to care for the child.
...
SM2: I think if goes to foster care could well become adoption so need to start moving faster and start relationship with foster parent earlier. Need to clarify more clearly if this is going to be long-term and if it isn't then look at foster care and adoption earlier.
SH: What does she think about foster care?
CW: She hasn't said no to foster care but wants the child back.
SM1: There is no reason on the kid's side why the kid has to be in BIWI not foster?
CW: No.
SM3: If the BIWI can care for now normally, and no special needs.
CW: The carer there said is normal.
SM1: So, we need to clarify this foster care situation based on whether the mother isn't going to get married, and when know what is happening place in foster care, don't want to start thinking about CWI. Need to speed up this process.
SH: Need to write clearly – This is a three-month placement in BIWI then will find foster care, something like that. Don't want to let this slip [*zuruzuru*].

Variation of norms 203

Irifune's concern over 'slipping' mirrors Teru's. In a separate case in Irifune, the caseworker used the stronger term *sutego*, abandoned child: 'There is a possibility they may end up being a *sutego* in a CWI. We should look at foster care... Don't want the child to end up in an institution until 18'.

As in Teru, in Irifune welfare institutions were seen as the most suitable placement for children with more complex needs. In one case, when questioned on whether a ten-year-old boy could enter foster care, the caseworker responded,

> I think he struggles to express his opinion, so is possible could get stressed and internalise it and then explode, and would be very tough for foster carers. Has also smashed windows, set small fires with loo paper, so perhaps a bit problematic for a foster parent.

In another case, of a child who had closed himself off from the world, the supervising clinical psychologist noted that it 'would be good for him to be around other children. At the moment... he can only communicate on the internet or with violence'.

Care placements can be placed onto a spectrum, from care being based upon the family-bond to it being understood as professional. Figure 6.5 represents the CGCs' baseline understanding of this spectrum of alternative care. Specific care providers can occupy a different place on this spectrum: in one local authority, for example, all children who returned from the two national self-reliance support institutions, which care for children with the most challenging backgrounds, were placed into a specific family home.

The construction of the function of welfare institutions can change, including following abuse scandals. There were cases of abuse within welfare institutions during my fieldwork in both Teru and Irifune. These provoked a stronger reaction in Teru than they did in Irifune. In one case in Irifune a CWI staff member used excessive physical force on a child, who then complained to the CWI and the CGC. One caseworker noted, 'We keep having reports about this staff member, came up in the [X] case too... whenever we have reports from this CWI it is often this person'. A senior manager responded, 'I think the CWI needs to think about this person, it is a risk to keep employing them. People's character doesn't change'. One senior manager noted that they would

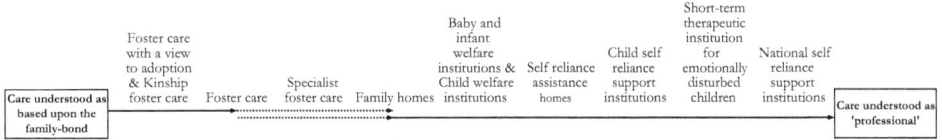

Figure 6.5 An overview of the spectrum of alternative care.

need to say to the CWI that they need to consider kids' concerns more seriously. May have to say to them, there are now some things you have to do, may have been ok in the past not to do so.

The meeting closed as follows:

SM1: There is another case of abuse happening in CWI we will have to discuss soon
CW: Same institution?
SM1: No, this time is [Y] CWI
SM2: [Y] CWI again?!

In addition to speaking with welfare institution staff, CGCs can limit or withhold further placements into an institution until they believe that an issue has been sufficiently addressed. The Teru CGC has used this tool effectively: following one abuse case in a CWI the Teru CGC stopped all placements for a full year, which one senior manager stated had led to 'a big change in how the CWI listened to the CGC'. This decision also contributed to further investment into foster care, as, unlike in Irifune, the remaining welfare institutions could not meet the required placements. Paradoxically, Irifune's greater institutional capacity has limited abuse in institutions acting as a trigger for change. In Teru, the expansion of capacity in foster care has further strengthened the CGC's ability to pressure the CWIs, visible in the reform of the majority of the Teru CWIs, into unit-style.

Both Teru and Irifune use welfare institutions as a constructed limbo space to protect the family-bond of children for whom the goal of care is family reunification. Both also use institutions for children with complex needs, for children whose profile suggests that they will develop more in institutional care, and to keep sibling groups together.

Both Teru and Irifune also have concerns over specific institutions. Where the CGCs differ is that Teru considers these issues to be systemic rather than the fault of individuals, leading to the re-evaluation of the function of institutional care, rather than just the quality of specific institutions. The connection of these concerns to practice and policy change in Teru, including the development of alternate capacity in foster care, is facilitated by the long placements of senior managers in Teru and prompted by the limited capacity of the welfare institutions. Teru's response to stop placements for a year contrasts with Irifune's decisions to temporarily limit capacity, or to have a quiet word with CWI managers and hope that they discipline the staff member. The longevity of the staff placements in the Teru CGC also allows them to act with more confidence in discussions with welfare institutions than the Irifune CGC does. Having considered regional variation in the function of different types of care, this chapter next turns to the threshold until which a child is seen as suitable for foster care.

5 Regional variation in norms on the threshold until which a child can enter foster care

So far, this chapter has established that placements are influenced by the constructions of the goals of care and of the function of different placements. The third norm that affects the decision-making process is the threshold above which a child is seen as unsuitable for foster care. This threshold largely depends on the child's age and the complexity of their needs.

The construction of the goals of care and the function of different placements impact upon this threshold: where foster care is understood to be semi-professional, it is seen as better able to cope with children with complex needs and children for whom the goal of care is family reunification than foster care that is understood as based upon the family-bond.

The age of a child is not only understood in terms of a threshold. In Teru, Yuno, and Irifune there was an aversion to placing a child into a foster care placement where there was another child of the same age, which was linked to concerns over the child having their own place in the family. CGC staff also consider how the child interacts with children of other ages, as in the case discussed earlier, where a child who is aggressive to younger children was not placed into a family home with younger children in it.

In addition to the age and complexity of needs, other variables were on occasion important in defining this threshold. These included the construction of the child's vulnerability, the danger they posed to others, the danger they posed to themselves, their strength of character, intelligence, social class, and ability to function in society, for which school attendance was often used as an equivalent, their sense of belonging, their ability to understand what is happening to them, their ability to send out an SOS, their ability to function in a group, their specific care needs, often linked to abuse history, and even, in one case, their allergies.

In a manner similar to the British social workers in Giller and Morris' (1981) 'What type of case is this?', CGC staff often compared children to previous cases. This was more prevalent in Teru than Irifune, in part as the staff there had more experience to draw upon. These comparisons attempted to project a child's trajectory in different care placements. Different constructions of the child saw the same care placement being constructed as safe or dangerous, as being in a state of limbo in a negative or a positive way, as aiming at correcting the behaviour of one child or as facilitating the continued good behaviour of another. At times a change of environment was seen as beneficial, while in other, less frequent, cases a similar environment was seen as serving the child's best interests.

Returning to the age threshold, there is a sharp drop in the number of children entering foster care in Irifune at seven years of age, and in Teru at nine years of age. This is connected to the fact that Teru has more 'semi-professional' foster care, more capacity to support foster care, and more experience with school-aged children in foster care to draw on.

206 *Variation of policy implementation*

Even though foster care is not aiming for the creation of a new family-bond for children above this local age threshold, it can still be seen as problematic for older children. Discussing the case of a nine-year-old boy, Sano explained that it 'is hard for this age of kids to go to foster care right… It becomes a small trauma for them'. This idea was found in other cases in both the other fieldwork sites and relates to the desire to protect the child's image of their natal family by not exposing it to unfavourable comparisons. Older children are understood as more able to compare and contrast, and to realise the extent of the challenges they have faced in their family, which is sometimes seen as damaging their family-bond and reducing the chance of family reintegration.

As these children are seen as too old to create a new family-bond, welfare institutions are sometimes used to protect the image of the natal family in school-aged children even where family reunification is considered unlikely. The connection to the *idea* of a family is understood as being important in facilitating the child's development and sense of self. Where the creation or maintenance of a family-bond is seen as impossible, discussions often turn to creating a place where the child feels a sense of belonging, *ibasho*.

6 Conclusions

CGC staff make two decisions for each child that enters care. The first is whether to remove the child from their family. This is made by evaluating the risk this poses to the family-bond against the risk that leaving the child in the family poses to the child. The second decision is on the placement type. This centres on the CGC staff's constructions of the goals of care, which are shaped by the assessment of the strength of the family-bond and the parents' present and future capacity to provide care, the functions of different care placements, and the threshold above which a child is seen as unsuitable for foster care.

The most important of these three norms in explaining regional variation in policy implementation is variation in the construction of the function of foster care. Where foster care is constructed as a replacement family, with care built upon a new family-bond, it is seen as unsuitable for children for whom the goal of care is family reunification. While foster care for children over 15 years of age is understood as being like a guest house, it is understood as potentially traumatic for school-aged children under 15 years. Foster care is used for school-aged children who are entering care for more 'innocent' reasons, such as the temporary hospitalisation of a parent. In these cases, the family-bond is understood as being strong, and thus less at risk from foster care placements, and the child is normally understood as having less complex needs than a child who has suffered abuse or neglect.

Teru and Irifune differ in each of these norms. Teru is more willing than Irifune to challenge the natal parents in shaping the goals of care. Teru CGC staff also give slightly less weight to the family-bond in relation to other factors considered important for the child's well-being and development. Finally, there is a subtle but important difference in the assessment of risk in the Teru and Irifune CGCs. While both CGCs value placement stability, Teru CGC staff are more willing to accept positive risk here than Irifune CGC staff. This is partly because the decision in Teru is understood as more collective than it is in Irifune, and partly because the Teru CGC staff are starting to frame institutional placements as carrying risk, a belief that is not found in Irifune.

The function of foster care is broader in Teru than in Irifune. In both, some foster care is used as a proxy for adoption. In Teru, more foster care is constructed as semi-professional care in a family setting than is the case in Irifune. This allows some children in Teru for whom the goal of care is family reunification to be placed into foster care. In Teru, children are placed in foster care until about nine years of age, two years later than the drop-off in placements occurs in Irifune. The greater number of children entering foster care in Teru indicates that children with more complex needs are placed into foster care here than in Irifune. This is due to Teru's greater support capacity and the CGC's concerted efforts to expand the function of foster care.

All of these norms are underpinned by the foundational belief, what Parsons terms a 'value', that the family-bond is discrete and exclusive, and that the creation of a new family-bond necessitates the destruction of the existing family-bond. This leads welfare institutions to be used precisely *because* they do not create attachments that threaten the family-bond.

The policy advice that follows these findings is simple: any attempt to increase the use of foster care in Japan must involve the semi-professionalization of foster carers. Recent attempts to lower the hurdles to registering as a foster parent, including arguments on extending childcare leave (NHK, 2015), are well-intentioned but risk limiting the function of foster care. Instead, it is necessary to raise the registration threshold so that CGCs only register foster parents who they can use, to increase the quality and quantity of training and support offered to foster parents, and to transition from foster 'parents' to foster 'carers'.

This is not to say that there is no place for long-term fostering in Japan. The most efficient way to introduce these changes would be to create a new category of foster parents called 'long-term foster parents', for children who are expected to spend over two or three years in care, and to introduce training for 'regular' foster parents to facilitate family reunification and increase specialist skills. Similarly, the introduction of a 'baby and infants foster carer' category with specialist training would be a major step towards practice change.

These proposals are of limited value without investment in developing the infrastructure of foster care services. The CGC still acts as a service provider of foster care in most local authorities, and as service regulator for institutional care. The caution over non-profit foster care service providers seems strange, given the predominance of non-profit service providers in welfare institutions. The primary bottleneck here is that foster care service providers appear more expensive than 'in-house' foster care, as in-house foster care costs do not reflect the true staffing costs involved. The much higher relative cost of BIWIs to foster care, not to mention the global consensus on best practice around not institutionalising infants under three years of age, make these the most logical place to start this de-institutionalisation process.

Having considered the impact on policy implementation of resources (Chapter 5) and norms, this book next addresses why these differences exist. It does this by looking at the organisational cultures of the CGCs.

Notes

1 Child self-reliance support institutions, for children with behavioural issues bordering on criminal, and the specialist institutions serving children with serious disabilities, IQs under 70, or very complex behavioural issues could be considered therapeutic. 'Child psychotherapy institutions' explicitly aim at a therapeutic intervention and family reintegration. These institutions have a suggested placement length of up to two years, though, as noted in Chapter 1, 42.2 per cent of children currently in these institutions have been there for over two years (MHLW, 2016a: 78). Matsuura argues that the child self-reliance support institutions are 'correctional educational facilities' (2011: 281) where, within 12 to 18 months, which is the normal placement length, 'most admitted juveniles who have reactive attachment disorder... come to show stable attachment behaviours' (2011: 283).
2 Yamamoto et al. (2013) found that 44.2 per cent of those returning home from CWI and 68.3 per cent of those returning home from temporary care were considered at risk of further abuse.
3 The average placement length in the current CWI is 4.6 years (Goldfarb, 2012: 27). As children sometimes move to a second institution, the average total time in care for some is longer than this. A 2011 survey of Tokyo careleavers showed that 20 per cent of careleavers surveyed had been in care for five to ten years, 19 per cent had been in care for 10 to 15 years, and 17 per cent had spent over 15 years in care (Tokyo, 2011a, 2011b).
4 One care-leaver expressed her disappointment that 'they speak about self-reliance, but it seems like they have no idea what self-reliance is. Self-reliance shouldn't be about being able to prepare food or do your own washing. It is more about mental self–reliance' (interview, 2012). Both foster care and CWI attempt to create an environment where 'particular skills... cultural norms, values and beliefs and rules for interacting with others' (Pelissier, 1991: 82) can be acquired. This can be seen in the emphasis on children using chopsticks correctly (Goldfarb, 2019) and using daily greetings, such as 'good morning'. This closely matches Allison's definition of self-reliance, as not 'the ability of the inclination to chart one's own course in life and act in isolation from others, but the aptitude to internalize certain habits of self-maintenance that are expected' (2000: 109).
5 While placement stability is understood as critical, there is almost no discourse on 'permanency' in alternative care (see Harada, 2013; Kikuchi, 2007).
6 Confusion between foster care and adoption is common: A 2016 survey of 3,000 people by the Nippon Foundation found that only 19.7 per cent knew the difference between the two. Unfortunately, some of those highlighting this confusion may have inadvertently contributed to it. Murata's (2006) work highlights this as

contributing to the low foster care rate, yet her (2005) book on foster care is titled 'Making a family: The way of life of regular foster parents'.
7 This graph excludes mother and child supported living institutions on the basis that the child is still living with a family member.
8 I saw several cases where the guardian had been in a CWI and preferred foster care. Conversely, one prefectural bureaucrat noted that about 40 per cent of children in that prefecture's CWI came from families where at least one parent had been in a CWI (interview, 2012). Inter-generational cycles of care suggest serious issues in care systems.
9 Tsuzaki posits that Japan may have classified family homes as foster care to inflate numbers for UN reporting (Goldfarb, 2012: 125).
10 Studio Ghibli is a Japanese animation company whose films often reflect on the beauty, simplicity, and purity of a rural Japanese way of life.
11 Foster care section head.
12 In the case where one sibling had been starved to death neither parent was charged by the police. The CGC staff believed that this was because the police were unclear which parent held responsibility. The lack of a charge inhibited the CGC taking the case to court and meant that the placement was made with parental consent. During my fieldwork the mother contacted the CGC, asking them to return the child. The staff member was mortified, explaining that the CGC could delay this with bureaucratic measures but had no legal power to prevent this.
13 *'motto ningen-rashiku natte'*.
14 Foster parents who are seen to be motivated by money are often considered unsuitable (Goldfarb, 2018; Goodman, 2000; Kashiwame, 2010). This may explain why registered foster carers have an average income above the national average (MHLW, 2009: 15).
15 Clinical psychologist.
16 Temporary care worker.

References

Abe, T. (2014). Shichōson jidōsōdanjyo no yakuwari. Kodomo-tachi no sodachi ni okeru shakai-teki kea to kazoku no yakuwari [The role of the municipality and the child guidance centre. Symposium: Social Care and the family's role in raising children]. *Nihon Shakai Fukushi Gakkai*.

Aizawa, M. (2011). Shakai-teki yōgo no kadai to sono taisaku ni tsuite jidō jiritsu-shien shisetsu nado no jūjitsu ni mukete [Challenges in alternative care and countermeasures to these: Towards developing the self-reliance support institutions]. *Nihon Shakai Fukushi Gakkai*, 1–12.

Allison, A. (2000). *Permitted and prohibited desires: Mothers, comics, and censorship in Japan*. London: University of California Press.

Brodkin, E.Z. (1997). Inside the welfare contract: Discretion and accountability in state welfare administration. *Social Service Review*, 71(1), 1–33.

Bryant, T.L. (1990). Sons and lovers: Adoption in Japan. *The American Journal of Comparative Law*, 38(2), 299–336.

Child Welfare Act. (1947). Act No. 164 of 1947, December 12.

Courtney, M., & Hughes-Heuring, D. (2009). Residential care in the United States of America: Past, present, and future. In M. Courtney, & D. Iwaniec (Eds.), *Residential care of children: Comparative perspectives*. New York: Oxford University Press.

Ezell, M., Spath, R., Zeira, A., Canali, C., Fernandez, E., Thoburn, J., & Vecchiato, T. (2011). An international classification system for child welfare programs. *Child and Youth Services Review*, 33, 1847–1854.
Fukaya, F., Fukaya, M., & Aoba, A. (2013). *Shakai-teki yōgo ni okeru satooya mondai e no jisshō-teki kenkyū — yōiku satooya zenkoku ankēto chōsa wo moto ni* [Empirical study on issues on foster parents in alternative care: Based on a nationwide questionnaire survey of normal foster parents]. Tokyo: Fukumura Publishing.
Gilbert, N. (1997). *Combatting child abuse: International perspectives and trends*. New York: Oxford University Press.
Gilbert, N. (2012). A comparative study of child welfare systems: Abstract orientations and concrete results. *Child and Youth Services Review*, 34, 532–536.
Giller, H., & Morris, A. (1981). 'What type of case is this?' Social workers' decisions about children who offend. In M. Adler, & S. Asquith (Eds.), *Discretion and welfare*. London: Heinemann.
Goldfarb, K. (2012). *Fragile kinships: Family ideologies and child welfare in Japan*. (Doctoral dissertation). The University of Chicago.
Goldfarb, K. (2015). *Beyond blood ties: Intimate kinships in Japanese foster and adoptive care*. Presentation at Foster care and adoption: Japan in the world. Japan Women's University. Tokyo. 2015, March 8.
Goldfarb, K. (2016). *Anonymity, ancestry, and family registry: Adoption debates in contemporary Japan*. Conference paper for 2016 Association for Asian Studies, Seattle.
Goldfarb, K. (2018). Beyond blood ties: Intimate kinships in Japanese foster and adoptive care. In A. Alexy, & E. Cook (Eds.), *Intimate Japan*. Honolulu: University of Hawaii Press.
Goldfarb, K. (2019). Embodied relationality beyond 'nature' vs 'nurture': Materializing absent kinships in Japanese child welfare. In S. Bamford (Ed.), *The Cambridge handbook for the anthropology of kinship*. Cambridge: Cambridge University Press.
Goodman, R. (2000). *Children of the Japanese state: The changing role of child protection institutions in contemporary Japan*. Oxford: Oxford University Press.
Goodman, R. (2002). Child abuse in Japan: 'Discovery' and the development of policy. In R. Goodman (Ed.), *Family and social policy in Japan*. Cambridge: Cambridge University Press.
Hara, H., & Minagawa, M. (1996). From productive dependents to precious guests: Historical changes in Japanese children. In D.W. Shwalb, & B.J. Shwalb (Eds.), *Japanese childrearing: Two generations of scholarship*. New York: The Guildford Press.
Harada, A. (2010). The Japanese child protection system: Developments in the laws and the issues left unsolved. *International Survey of Family Law*, Vol. 2010, pp. 217–236.
Harada, A. (2013). Children in need of permanent families: The current status of and future directions for the Japanese foster care system. *Illinois Child Welfare*, 6(1), 14–29.
Harada, A. (2014). *Satooya no kenri gimu: Jidō fukushi-hō to minpō no kakyō* [Rights and responsibilities of foster parents: Bridging public and private law perspectives]. Kakenhi grant project report 22730094. n.p.: Kakenhi.
Hayes, P., & Habu, T. (2006). *Adoption in Japan: Comparing policies for children in need*. New York: Routledge.

Hideki, Y. (2013). *Funin chiryō wo hete tokubetsu yōshi engumi wo sentaku shita kanja no keiken: tokubetsu yōshi engumi seiritsu made no purosesu ni chakumoku shite.* [The experiences of patients who selected special adoption after they stopped infertility treatments: The process until special adoption is permitted]. *Hoken iryō shakai-gaku ronshū*, 23(2), 49–58.

Kashiwame, R. (2010). Kodomotachi ni atarimae no seikatsu wo [Towards a lifestyle that is obviously right for children]. *Shakai-teki yōgo to famirīhōmu*, 1, 6–9. 2010, June.

Kawamatsu, R. (2013). Jidōsōdanjyo ni okeru kodomo no saizen no rieki no hoshō [Guaranteeing the best interest of the child at the child guidance centres]. *Mother and Child Wellbeing around the World*, 75, 40–44.

Kikuchi, M. (2007). Nihon de satooya seido ga riyō sarenai riyū to wa? Kokusai hikaku kenkyū wo tōshite ieru koto [Why would not be the foster care system utilized well in Japan?: Through international comparison]. *Kodomo no gyakutai to negurekuto*, 9(2), 147–155.

Knorth, E.J., Harder, A.T., Zandberg, T., & Kendrick, A. (2008). Under one roof: A review and selective meta-analysis on the outcomes of residential child and youth care. *Children and Youth Services Review*, 30, 123–140.

Kumasaka, Y., & Aiba, H. (1968). Foster care in Japan: Past and present. *The Milbank Memorial Fund Quarterly*, 46(2), 253–265.

Matsuura, N. (2011). Youth corrections in Japan: Family-like setting for delinquents with the experiences of child maltreatment. *Child & Youth Services*, 32(4), 281–285.

Maynard-Moody, S.W., & Musheno, M.C. (2003). *Cops, teachers, counselors: Stories from the front lines of public service.* Michigan: University of Michigan Press.

Mehrotra, V., Morck, R., Shim, J., & Wiwattanakantang, Y. (2013). Adoptive expectations: Rising sons in Japanese family firms. *Journal of Financial Economics*, 108, 840–854.

Meyers, M.K., & Vorsanger, S. (2003). Street-level bureaucrats and the implementation of public policy. In B.G. Peters, & J. Pierre (Eds.), *Handbook of public administration.* Thousand Oaks: Sage.

MHLW. (2009). *Jidō yōgo shisetsu nyūsho jidō-tō chōsa kekka no gaiyō* [Survey results on children entering child welfare institutions]. 2009, July. Retrieved from URL: https://www.mhlw.go.jp/toukei/saikin/hw/jidouyougo/19/ (last accessed 2017, August 22).

MHLW. (2012). *Shakai-teki yōgo no genjou ni tsuite (sanka shiryou).* [Current status of alternative care (reference)]. 2012, September.

MHLW. (2016a). *Shakai-teki yōgo no genjou ni tsuite (sanka shiryou)* [Current status of alternative care (reference)]. 2016, January.

MHLW. (2016b). *Shakai-teki yōgo no genjou ni tsuite (sanka shiryou)* [Current status of alternative care (reference)]. 2016, July.

MHLW. (2016c). *Shakai teki yōgo no kadai to shourai zou no jitsugen ni mukete* [On the challenges and realising the future form of alternative care]. 2016, January.

Miyajima, K. (2001). *Jidō gyakutai bōshi-hō shikōgo no jidōsōdanjyo to satooya seido no kongo ni tsuite* [On the child guidance centres and foster care system after the enforcement of the Child abuse prevention act]. Preliminary paper for dai 75-kai yōshi to satooya wo kangaeru kai kōjutsu-roku.

Moriguchi, C. (2010). Child adoption in Japan, 1948–2008 – A comparative historical analysis. *Keizai kenkyū*, 61(4), 342–357.

Mulheir, G., & Browne, K. (2007). *Deinstitutionalising and transforming children's services: A guide to good practice.* European Commission Daphne programme in collaboration with WHO regional office for Europe and the University of Birmingham UK. Birmingham: University of Birmingham (WHO Collaborating Centre for Child Care and Protection).

Murata, K. (2005). *Kazoku wo tsukuru: yōiku satooya to iu ikikata* [Making a family: The way of life of regular foster parents]. Tokyo: Chuokoron-shinsha.

Murata, K. (2006). *Why do not foster carers increase in Japan?* Paper presented at Ajia kodomo no kenri to satooya kaigi. 2006, September 23.

Nakamura, M. (2013). Kodomo no saizenn no rieki no tame ni — tōjisha dantai no yakuwari to tenbō [For the best interests of the child – The role and outlook of a careleavers organisation]. *Mother and Child Wellbeing around the World,* 75, 26–30.

National Family Home Association. (2012). *Famirīhōmu jittai chōsa hōkoku-sho* [Report on a survey on the actual state of family homes]. 2012, August. n.p.: National Family Home Association.

National Foster Care Association. (2012). *Sato oya dayori* [Foster care newsletter]. 93. 2012, August 15. Tokyo: National Foster Care Association.

Negishi, Y. (2014). Jidō gyakutai taiō seido no kihon kōzō to sono imi: Oya to ko no shutai-ka wo kijun to suru bunseki moderu no teishō [The basic policy structures of the prevention of child abuse and neglect and its meaning: introduction to the analytical model based on autonomy of parents and children]. *Shakai Fukushi-Gaku,* 54(2), 32–43.

Nelson III, C.A., Zeanah, C.H., Fox, N., Marshall, P.J., Smyke, A.T., & Guthrie, D. (2007). Cognitive recovery in socially deprived young children: The Bucharest early intervention project. *Science,* 318, 1937–1940.

NHK. (2015). *Shigoto motsu satooya ni ikuji kyūgyō wo atsu rōshō ni yōbō* [Request to the Ministry of Health, Labour and Welfare for child care leave for working foster parents]. 2015, July 24. Retrieved from URL: http://www3.nhk.or.jp/news/html/20150724/k10010165151000.html (last accessed 2015, August 05).

Ochi, M. (2008). Kodomo no shōrai kara miru 'akachan posuto': Doitsu no genjō to hikaku shite ['Baby-Post' from the perspective of children's futures: A comparison with the current situation in Germany]. *Reference,* 58(6), 53–72.

Ogiso, H. (2010). Jidō yōgo shisetsu jidō jiritsushien ni nyūsho suru jidō no genjō to shien shisaku no kadai [The current status of children in child welfare institutions and self-reliance support institutions and the challenges in support measures]. *Kikan shakai hoshō kenkyū,* 45(4), 396–406.

Omori, H. (2016). Creating families: Tenrikyō foster homes in Japan. *Japanese Studies,* 36(2), 213–229.

Pelissier, C. (1991). The anthropology of teaching and learning. *Annual Review of Anthropology,* 20(1), 75–95.

Saimura, J., Shibuya, M., Arimura, T., Kashiwame, R., Shoji, J., Sakuma, T., ... Yoshida, T. (2005). Jidōsōdanjyo ni okeru kazoku sai tōgō enjo jisshi taisei no arikata ni kansuru kenkyū [A study on service systems for family re-integration in child guidance centres]. *Nihon-kodomo katei sōgōkenkyūsho kiyō,* 42, 147–175.

Saimura, J., Shibuya, M., Kashiwame, R., Shoji, J., Arimura, T., Seno, H., ... Miyaguchi, T. (2006). Jidōsōdanjyo ni okeru kazoku sai tōgō enjo no jisshi taisei no arikata ni kansuru kenkyū – gyakutai-sha no zokusei to kōka-teki na enjo ni shisuru yōin to no sōkan kankei-tō ni kansuru jisshō kenkyū – [A study on the system

implementation for supporting family reintegration in child guidance centres]. *Nihon-kodomo katei sōgōkenkyūsho kiyō*, 43, 181–202.
Saimura, J., Shoji, J., Arimura, T., Itakura, T., Nemoto, A., Abe, K., ... Honma, H. (2007). Jidōsōdanjyo ni okeru kazoku sai tōgō enjo no arikata ni kansuru kenkyū ~ jissen jirei no shūshū, bunseki [A study on the system for supporting family reintegration in child guidance centers: Gathering and analysis of pioneering practices]. *Nihon-kodomo katei sōgōkenkyūsho kiyō*, 44, 187–256.
Sandfort, J.R. (2000). Moving beyond discretion and outcomes: Examining public management from the front lines of the welfare system. *Journal of Public Administration Research and Theory*, 10, 729–756.
Shirai, C. (2010). Reproductive technologies and parent–child relationships: Japan's past and present examined through the lens of donor insemination. *International Journal of Japanese Sociology*, 19(1), 18–34.
Shirai, C. (2014). Ninshin kattō-ko no yōiku kon'nan ni aru josei no yōshi ni dasu ishi kettei purosesu to kōteki fukushi: Tokubetsu yōshi engumi de ko wo takusu josei no katari kara [The decision making process in public welfare of conflicted pregnancies and women facing challenges in child rearing regarding giving the child up for adoption: From the narratives of women who gave their child up for adoption]. *Wakōdaigaku gendai ningen gakubu kiyō*, 7, 55–75.
Takeda, H. (2011). Reforming families in Japan: Family policy in the era of structural reform. In R. Ronald, & A. Alexy (Eds.), *Home and family in Japan: Continuity and transformation*. New York: Routledge.
Tokotani, F. (2009). Teigen (hōkoku no matome wo kanete) (Nihon kazoku <shakai to hō> gakkai) dai 25-kai gakujutsu taikai shinpojiumu tokubetsu yōshi seido 20-nen – kodomo no shiawase wo motomete [Recommendations (For summary of reports). Japanese family <Society and Law> society 25th academic conference. 20 years of adoption: seeking child's happiness symposium]. *Kazoku < shakai to hō >*, 25, 104–114.
Tokunaga, S. (2012). The examination of the special adoption system: Focusing on the meaning, the characteristics, and the problems. *Kassui joshi daigaku katsu mizu ronbun-shū dai 55-shū kenkō seikatsu gakubu-hen Bessatsu*, 55. 2012, March 31.
Tokyo. (2011a). *Tōkyōto ni okeru jidō yōgo shisetsu-tō taishosha e no ankēto chōsa hōkoku-sho* [Tokyo Metropolitan government. Social welfare and public health bureau (supported by the Supra-Ministerial organ on population decline: A survey of Tokyo Metropolis care-leavers from institutional and foster care)].
Tokyo. (2011b). *Tokyoto no jidō yogo shisetsu jiritsushien hōmu ni okeru afutakea jittai chosa* [Tokyo council of social welfare, the research committee of childcare workers, factual investigation on the after-care provision of child welfare institutions and self-reliance support centres in Tokyo].
Toma, K. (2014). Kazoku sai tōgō no shosō: Aru jidō jiritsushien shisetsu no jissen kara [Various phases of family reunification: from qualitative research at a children's self-reliance support facility]. *Japanese Journal of Family Sociology*, 26(2), 127–138.
Tsutsui, T., & Otaga, M. (2011). Shakai-teki yōgo taisei no saihen ni muketa kenkyū no genjō to kadai — shakai-teki yōgo kanren shisetsu nyūsho jidō no henka, kore ni tomonau kea teikyō taisei no saikōchiku no tame no kenkyū no arikata — [The system of child protection in Japan: Shift in residential placements for children and the necessary conditions to restructure the care provision system]. *Hoken iryō kagaku*, 60(5), 401–410.

Tsuzaki, T. (2009). *Kono kuni no kodomotachi: Yōhogo jidō shakai-teki yōgo no Nihonteki kōchiku; otona no kitoku ken'eki to kodomo no fukushi* [This country's children: Constructing social care for children in need of care; The vested interests of adults and children's welfare]. Tokyo: Nihon Kajo Shuppan.

United Nations General Assembly. (1989). *Convention on the rights of the child*. Document A/RES/44/25. 1989, December 12.

United Nations General Assembly. (2010). *Guidelines for the alternative care of children. Resolution adopted by the General Assembly 64/142*. A/RES/64/142*, on the report of the Third committee A/64/434.

Winter, S.C. (2000). *Information asymmetry and political control of street-level bureaucrats: Danish agro-environmental regulation*. Paper prepared for the annual research meeting of the Association for Public Policy Analysis and Management. Seattle, 2000.

Yamamoto, M. (1952). Yōshi to satogo—minpō to jidōfukushihō to no kōsaku [Adopted children and fostered children: The intersection of civil law and the child welfare law]. *Kōbe hōgaku zasshi*, 2(1), 52–86.

Yamamoto, T., Shoji, J., Arimura, T., Itakura, T., Sato, T., Ohta, K., ... Miyaguchi, T. (2008). Jidōsōdanjyo-tō ni okeru hogo-sha enjo no arikata ni kansuru jisshō-teki kenkyū 2 hogo-sha enjo shuhō no kōka, datōsei, hyōka, tekiō ni kansuru jisshō-teki kenkyū [A study on the system for supporting family preservation in the child guidance centres 2: Efficiency, validity, evaluation and discerning of the parents' supporting methods]. *Nihon kodomo katei sōgōkenkyūsho*, 45, 235–283.

Yamamoto, T., Shoji, J., Arimura, T., Nagano, S., Tsuruoka, Y., Sato, K., ... Maebashi, N. (2010). Hogo-sha enjo shuhō no kōka, datōsei, hyōka, tekiō ni kansuru jisshō-teki kenkyū 2 [A study on the system for supporting family preservation in the child guidance centers: Efficiency, validity, evaluation and discerning of the parents' supporting methods 2]. *Nihon kodomo katei sōgōkenkyūsho*, 47, 193–301.

Yamamoto, T., Arimura, T., Nagano, S., Tashiro, M., Ito, K., Hachinohe, H., ... Itakura, T. (2011). Jidōsōdanjyo-tō ni okeru hogo-sha enjo no arikata ni kansuru: jisshō-teki kenkyū hogo-sha enjo shuhō no kōka, datōsei, hyōka, tekiō ni kansuru jisshō-teki kenkyū [A study on the system for supporting family preservation in the child guidance centers: Efficiency, validity, evaluation and discerning of the parents' supporting methods]. *Nihon kodomo katei sōgōkenkyūsho*, 48, 1–49.

Yamamoto, T., Ookubo, M., Sato, T., Tsuroka, Y., Itakura, T., Nagano, S., ... Kawamatsu, R. (2013). Jidōsōdanjyo ni okeru hogo-sha shien no arikata ni kansuru jisshō-teki kenkyū [A study on the system for supporting family preservation in the child guidance centres]. *Nihon kodomo katei sōgōkenkyūsho*, 50, 1–24.

Yamanta, T. (1995). Okizarinisareta katei yoikusei kyuken: kokusai kazoku nen ni idaita kitai to shitubou [The forgotten right to family life: Expectations and disappointments in the international year of the family]. *Atarashii Kazoku*, 27, 66–80.

Zenshakyō. (2008). *Kodomo katei fukushi shakai-teki yōgo ni kansuru seido no arikata kentō tokubetsu iinkai hōkoku-sho* [On child and family welfare and alternative care. Report of the special committee for examination of the system]. 2008, May 8.

Note: Where the author(s) provided an English translation of their work I have given this translation, rather than my translation.

7 Regional variation of organisational cultures

1 Introduction

During my fieldwork, a fellow researcher asked for an introduction to the Teru CGC. I attended the resulting interview in which Sano, the CGC head, gave three reasons for how Teru had increased their foster care rate. The first was that the CGC had 'earnestly' started recruiting foster parents. Sano explained that this had been facilitated by a CGC staff member starting an NPO to recruit foster parents after seeing a bumper sticker recruiting foster carers while visiting Canada. Sano stated that this international inspiration was atypical, noting that 'Japan is outside the circle of sharing data about foster care, or practice and policy development on children in care'. A few days later Sano expanded on this, describing Japan's alternative care system as having evolved as a kind of 'Galapagos'.

The second reason Sano gave was a 'sea change' in the attitude of caseworkers towards foster care. Sano related this to the third reason he gave, the increased experience level of CGC staff. Sano explained how this increased the CGC's capacity to successfully 'match' foster parent and child and then support them post-placement. This increased experience was linked to longer postings in the CGC and a policy of requesting bureaucrats with welfare experience. At the end of the interview I 'joked' that Sano had missed an important factor, namely leadership. Sano chuckled and noted that this was not something that he could possibly say himself.

Chapters 5 and 6 focused on *what* differences exist between local authorities and the impact these have on policy implementation. This chapter addresses *why* these differences exist, with the differing organisational culture of the CGCs assigned central importance. The importance of organisational cultures is amplified by the absence of a social work profession. In Collier's terms, this chapter proposes an 'explanatory model' (2011: 824) for the regional variation in norms and resources.

This approach allows us to understand why there has been a 'sea change' in the caseworkers' beliefs on foster care, why Teru moved away from 'the consciousness that foster care is a special, or exceptional thing' (Miyajima, 2001: 34). It also allows us to understand why there is regional variation in how policy is implemented.

There are two key differences in the organisational cultures of Teru and Irifune: the decision process, and the ways in which knowledge is acquired, retained, and used in informing change.

This chapter draws on earlier chapters, with organisational culture understood as both shaping and being shaped by resources and norms. The relationship with values is less iterative, with CGC staff's values on the family-bond framing organisational cultures. This chapter first introduces the relevant theory before introducing a day in each CGC to give the reader a feel of them. It then turns to an in-depth analysis of the decision process.

2 Organisations and organisational culture

The organisational cultures of the CGCs both structure the decisions made, as policy instruments, and mediate the interaction between beliefs and resources. The importance of organisational culture is addressed in street-level bureaucrat literature: Preston-Shoot et al. argue that policy implementation is 'influenced by local management agendas and group professional cultures... the way things are done here' (2001: 9); Bloom et al. (2001) argue that caseworkers' understanding of their office's service approach is important; and May and Winter highlight the importance of 'signals from political and administrative superiors about the content and the importance of the policy' (2007: 454). May and Winter summarise the important factors here, noting the importance of 'organizational arrangements... administrative emphasis of policy goals... and managerial supervision' (2007: 454).

Murray's (2006) work on child protection in Scotland develops the idea of managerial expectations. Hill notes Murray's argument that caseworkers' actions 'that might be seen as disregarding policy... derive from assumptions of social workers about appropriate action which are shared by their immediate managers who tacitly condone this action' (2013: 260). Work such as this leads Evans to question the assumption 'that managers and workers are separate and fundamentally antagonistic categories' (2011: 380–381).

In a similar vein to Murray, Lin (2000: 162, emphasis added) argues that

> When policies are bent to purposes other than those that policymakers anticipated... it is not because staff do not understand their work. Instead, it is precisely because they try to make sense of their work, and thus to understand their jobs as a series of related tasks all bent towards the same purpose. This naturally leads them to refer each new policy *to the values that are most salient in their organisation.*

Similarly, Sandfort (2000) argues that in understanding policy, street-level bureaucrats are 'guided largely by the shared knowledge and collective beliefs that staff developed to make sense of their day to day work' (Meyers and Vorsanger, 2003: 248).

This chapter explores the organisational cultures of the CGCs, focusing on the role managers play in the decision-making process: in how they structure the decision-making process, in the organisation of staff training, in the emphasis they give to policy goals, which may reflect their own 'values' and 'norms', and in how they supervise and monitor performance. The chapter also considers the role of management in determining the CGCs' ability to acquire, retain, and use knowledge to change policy and practice.

May and Winter (2007: 470) caution against overstating the importance of managers, arguing that

> The signalling of policy goals by municipal elected officials and managerial actions of employment services managers are relevant, but these factors seem to have a limited influence. More important are the understanding of the national policy by street-level bureaucrats and their knowledge of the rules under the reform. These likely come from other sources than political signalling and managerial actions. As aptly put by Brehm and Gates (1997: 202), substantial numbers of caseworkers seem to be "principled agents" in fulfilling their professional roles in implementing the national reforms.

The absence of a social work 'professional role' in Japan, coupled with the absence of political and media attention, means that the CGC is the key mediator of information on policy goals. Indeed, May and Winter find that 'increased municipal emphasis... has the strongest effects on policy actions when caseworker knowledge is weak' (2007: 468).

The term 'organisational culture' here draws on Weber's ideal types, many of which 'refer to collectivities rather than to the social actions of individuals, but social relationships within collectivities are always built upon the probability that component actors will engage in expected social actions' (Coser, 1977: 223–224). I share Dubois' construction of the relationship between the caseworker and the organisation as characterised by 'both a "social-bond" and coercion' (2010: 16), and recognise that the degree of cohesion of organisational cultures in different CGCs will vary, with senior management likely to play a critical role in determining both the nature and the strength of the organisational culture.

One theoretical contribution this book makes is to develop the construction of organisational cultures by drawing on Holliday's (1999) work on 'small cultures'. Holliday states that this refers to 'the composite of cohesive behaviour within any social grouping, and not to the differentiating features of prescribed ethnic, national and international entities' (1999: 247).

Holliday's model has been used in a Japanese context, in Aspinall's (2006) explanation of policy failure in foreign language education. Aspinall (2006: 262, emphasis added) argues that this approach allows researchers to examine a given group of Japanese people without having to assume that the fact of their 'Japaneseness' alone determines or restricts their behaviour. We can acknowledge, however, that the culture of the community they have grown up in as well as the culture of *the particular institution or institutions where they spend the majority of their time* will have an influence on the make-up of their 'small culture'.

Aspinall (2006: 271) continues

> Ethnographic research can examine what is going on in a small number of selected groups, but the only way to make sense of the picture as a whole is to discuss these interactions at the level of national norms and values that relate to teaching and learning. Political scientists are often unwilling to bring these factors into the explanatory picture because of concerns that they may be too vague or all-encompassing... one solution to this problem can be found in the paradigm of the 'small culture'. This is because this paradigm explores the ways in which national and other norms of behaviour are reproduced, put into effect and, on occasion, undermined in the day-to-day interactions of small groups

The work on decision-making in the CGCs provides a unique insight into national values on the construction of the family-bond and allows us to examine how it is reproduced and challenged. Incorporating Holliday's theory of 'small cultures' allows us to incorporate caseworkers' values, as well as their norms, without falling into national-cultural determinism.

3 The start of a day in Teru and Irifune

Teru's formal working hours are from 9.15 a.m. until 5.45 p.m., though most staff arrive before 9 a.m. to check emails, voice messages, and order their day's bento. Sano emphasises working hard over working long hours, and it is rare for staff to stay after 8 p.m.

Each of the four divisions holds a morning briefing at 9.15 a.m. Within each division, each section head reports on their staff's plans for the day. The division head then updates everyone on their schedule and the CGC head's schedule. The division head then gives reminders and notifications for the day and upcoming week. The temporary care institution also holds a morning meeting, to handover from night to day staff. The children's support division briefing closes with all staff repeating an oath:

> I will defend the Japanese constitution and laws that were enacted at the will of the Japanese people. I solemnly swear that I will respect the orders, guidance, and rules of this office. As a servant of the whole body of citizens, I am deeply aware that I should do my public duty democratically and efficiently and I solemnly swear that I will execute my duties sincerely and fairly.

Irifune's normal working hours are also from 9.15 a.m. to 5.45 p.m., and as in Teru, the staff normally arrive before 9 a.m. to check their emails and listen to voicemails. It is more common for staff to stay late in Irifune than in Teru, though Yuno had the longest working hours of the three CGCs. In Irifune the morning bell is the cue for staff who have time, normally about half the caseworkers and managers, to go outside to a small garden to do morning stretches with the children in temporary care. This gives the staff a chance for an informal chat with the children.

Instead of a division meeting, each section head usually briefly checks with their staff on their plans for the day. There is less of an understanding across the division as to the activities of the other staff.

The Irifune CGC is quieter than the Teru CGC, both in terms of the number of phone calls and the number of discussions between staff. There is less discussion about cases between the caseworker and the section head, between section heads, and between section head and division head. The differences in communication between Teru and Irifune also extend to the decision process. This chapter next turns to this process, looking at differences in the use of meetings, the organisation of work processes, and the construction of the CGC's role.

4 The decision process

Ushijima and Yukawa's (1975) survey was the first to study decision-making in CGCs. This found that in 33 CGCs, of the 96 that responded, the placement decision was made by one or two people, in 37 CGCs it was made by three or four people, and in 26 CGCs by more than five people. This study also found variation in the input of the clinical team. These findings were later mirrored by Kashiwame et al., who found 'considerable variation... in the way that child guidance centres are run' (1995: 144) and Saimura et al. (2004, 2010, 2013).

These studies highlight differences in procedures, but do not explore why these exist or how they impact policy implementation. For example, more people being involved in the decision process may mitigate the caseworker's sense of individual responsibility, which could decrease risk aversion, or, conversely, may add cautious voices to the process.

Discussing the challenges of preventing placement breakdown in foster care, Miwa states that 'most child guidance centres do not have a standardised way of assessing or a systematic way of making decisions' (2014: 147–148). Miwa argues that a caseworker's willingness to use foster care is 'greatly dependent on the individual qualities and experience of the caseworkers' (2014: 148).[1]

There are also differences in how CGCs use the legal system that is there to support them. Kurihara's (2011) study found regional variation in the use of Article 28 of the Child Welfare Act to partially suspend parental rights for two years. This was based on a 2010 national survey of CGCs, which found that 55.5 per cent of responding CGCs had applied to use Article 28 in the last two years, and 38.4 per cent had applied for a renewal of Article 28 (Kurihara, 2011). Only 12.7 per cent of responding CGCs had a protocol for applying for Article 28, with a further 16.9 per cent of CGCs stating that their local authority had a protocol for this (Kurihara, 2011). Kurihara (2011) found that CGCs feared using Article 28 may hinder their capacity to facilitate family reintegration, and highlighted challenges CGCs faced in working with external organisations.

Despite differences such as these between the CGCs, the decision process by which a child enters care occurs over the acceptance, ruling, and aid objectives meetings (see Chapter 3). While the framework of the meeting process is uniform, the way these meetings are used varies across CGCs. Variations in the meeting process in Teru and Irifune reflect and contribute to distinct organisational cultures. These differences are shaped by the role of the senior management, by those who attend meetings, and by those who make the decision, as well as by the purpose of discussion, the use of paperwork, and the tone of the meeting.

In Teru all non-emergency meetings are held on Wednesdays. Paperwork for the aid objectives meetings is placed on the participants' desks the previous day, with paperwork for the acceptance meeting and ruling meeting distributed to all staff on Wednesday morning. The day commences with the morning briefing, which is followed by the ruling meetings, the acceptance meeting and, after lunch, the aid objectives meetings. The majority of CGC staff attend the ruling meetings and the acceptance meeting, with only the staff directly involved in a case attending the aid objectives meeting.

The ruling meetings in Teru, which update all the staff on the progression of all ongoing cases, last between an hour and an hour and a half. This covers around 30 to 40 cases, with more time afforded to new or complex cases. The meeting opens with the temporary care section head giving a summary of the children in temporary care, with a few cases highlighted. There is also a brief written report on each child in temporary care. Each caseworker in the emergency division and children's support division then briefly presents the current situation of each of their cases. This updates senior managers and temporary care staff on new information and the caseworker's plans. Senior managers give suggestions on the response or planned support policy. Some of the children in temporary care are likely to enter care. This meeting updates everyone on this process, with the final decision made in the aid objectives meeting.

The acceptance meeting, which briefly reviews all new cases, follows the ruling meetings. This normally lasts for one and a half to two hours, with each case normally lasting about five minutes. In one randomly selected week in Teru there were two emergency cases, 19 cases in the children's support division, 31 through the children's consultation division, and 6 education division cases. Emergency cases are discussed as soon as they are received, with a brief overview presented at the weekly acceptance meeting. The participation of each division facilitates a coordinated response to cases.

Variation of organisational cultures 221

The cases from the children's consultation division, which covers mental health and disability, are normally presented over five to ten minutes in groups, based upon the planned response. This includes groups where further psychological investigation or further medical investigations will be carried out. Individual cases are only highlighted in this meeting where the psychologist wants advice or to raise the possibility of abuse or neglect. Finally, the education consultation division cases are presented. These are presented individually, within about two minutes, and usually receive minimal feedback. Both the consultation and education divisions hold more detailed case meetings within the division.

The most significant decision taken at the acceptance meeting is whether to take a child into temporary care. This decision is made to protect the child, to facilitate further investigation, or for both these reasons. Most cases do not enter temporary care. Where required, cases where children do not enter temporary care are followed up by the caseworker, who is supported by their section and division head.

In the acceptance meeting, caseworkers lay out their planned course of action. This 'support policy' is often challenged or amended by senior management, with the underlying reasoning always explained. The act of refining or amending the provisional plans proposed by the caseworker informs not only how the staff proceed with the case in question but also how they respond to future cases.

The majority of the children's support division staff attend the majority of the ruling meetings and acceptance meetings. More senior caseworkers tend to present their cases first and then return to the office; junior caseworkers usually observe all cases. This allows them to learn from others' cases and the feedback given by senior managers on different 'types' of cases. More senior caseworkers, who have been through this process, receive less feedback on their cases than junior caseworkers do. This is one way that the senior managers shape the caseworkers' beliefs, or at the very least their actions, and build a coherent organisational culture.

There are two different types of aid objectives meetings in Teru. The first is carried out throughout the week and led by the children's support division head. This meeting is known in the Teru CGC as the 'division head meeting', the *kacho-kai*. For straightforward cases, for example, where the caseworker, clinical psychiatrist, and division head agree that the child should enter a specific CWI, the final decision is made at this meeting.

There is no specific paperwork for this meeting. The caseworker may use the consultation overview form, or less frequently, the simpler progress notes form. The supervising caseworker, caseworker's section head, supervising clinical psychiatrist, and division head must attend this meeting. Other staff, including the CGC head, emergency division head, children's consultation division head, and temporary care section head, attend as required.

For cases understood as more complex,[2] including all foster care placements, the division head meeting simply determines that the case should go to a 'full' aid objectives meeting. These begin at 1 p.m., with each case lasting from half an hour to one hour. There are usually four or five cases per week, though one week saw eight meetings. These meetings most frequently determine whether a child will enter care and the placement type. They are also convened for children in care where circumstances have changed or new information has come up – for example, a child in care who has been starting small fires, a child who has abused others or been abused while in care, or a child in care who may be returned home, despite concerns over further abuse.

The aid objectives meetings in Teru follow a set format. The caseworker first presents the case, using paperwork that is referred to but not read aloud. The caseworker states the meeting's objectives, reports on the child's situation, and briefly states their opinion.

In most cases, the clinical psychologist then presents their report, referencing detailed paperwork. This covers the child's IQ, any recognised or suspected diagnoses, and any behavioural and emotional issues. Where relevant, the temporary care section head then reports on the child, covering the child's educational level, 'lifestyle' (which includes dietary information), play, engagement with sports time in temporary care, and relationships and behaviour with other children and the staff. Where a child is in a BIWI or CWI, the caseworker presents a brief report from the institution. Where the child is in foster care the foster care section head gives this report.

Having covered the child's status, any remaining internal reports are given, including from the lawyer, and any external reports, most commonly by doctors on abuse, are presented by the caseworker. Following this, the caseworker concludes with their opinion on what should happen. Finally, the floor is opened for discussion. This is led by senior managers.

A characteristic of the meetings that will surprise alternative care scholars is the absence of the parent, child, and care provider from these meetings. I did not see any meeting in which the child or guardian took part. This relates to the limited legal authority that the CGC has to act without parental consent, which means that the CGC must present a unified and consistent front when engaging with the guardian.

In Teru, the seating plan was established by position, with the desks arranged into a square around the edge of the room. The CGC head sat on the top row of desks with the division heads next to him. The relevant section heads sat on the near and far sides, with the supervising caseworker and psychiatrist sat on the opposite side from the CGC head (see King, 2017: 330 for a visual representation). Where a placement was unclear, for example, whether a child should enter foster care or a CWI, staff responsible for each placement type attended the meeting. Where parental consent was not confirmed the lawyer would also attend. All aid objective meetings in Teru are chaired by the same section head from the children's support section.

The aid objectives meeting makes a final recommendation to a monthly meeting of a local authority subcommittee, which rubber-stamps the decision. In some local authorities, including Yuno, this monthly meeting is used to discuss one or two of the most challenging cases or cases that set precedent.

Extra-ordinary meetings can be held at any time. These are quickly convened and override senior managers' existing schedules. Here a decision is made whether an emergency response or intervention is required, and if so, which caseworker within the emergency assistance division will do it, when they will do it, and what support they will require.

Meetings in Irifune are also normally held on Wednesdays, though it is not uncommon for non-emergency meetings to be held ad-hoc. In Irifune, the acceptance meeting covers new cases and ongoing cases that are not yet ready for a ruling meeting, totalling around 10 to 20 cases per week. All alternative care cases are covered by Sections A and B of the consultation support division. These sections also have responsibility for the CWIs and some specialist institutions, with section C responsible for foster care, BIWIs, mental health welfare institutions, and the mental health of all children in care. All caseworkers attend their section's acceptance meeting, with the staff leaving after they present their cases. The cases are covered in similar length as in Teru.

The ruling meeting in Irifune is longer than in Teru. The caseworker first presents a summary of the case, which is followed by a summary from the clinical psychologist and, where relevant, by the temporary care worker. These reports are followed by a short discussion, primarily between the junior staff and with occasional input from senior managers; only the staff directly involved in the case attend the meeting. There are normally two to five meetings per week, held for cases where a decision is close to being made.

The aid objectives meeting in Irifune serves to confirm the decision made in, or after, the ruling meeting. The caseworker gives a three-minute report on the case. This is followed by a one-minute report by the clinical psychologist and a one-minute report by a temporary care staff member. The caseworker then states their planned course of action, which is pre-printed on the paperwork. Senior managers can then ask for further information or raise points. This is normally limited to confirming certain steps have been taken. In every case I saw, the final decision followed the caseworker's suggestion. As in Teru, only staff directly involved in a case attend this meeting. The aid objectives meetings in Irifune normally last about ten minutes and are chaired by a different caseworker each week.

There are several significant differences in how meetings are conducted in Teru and Irifune. The first is Teru's use of the division head meeting. This allows less time to be spent on straightforward cases, so that more time can be spent on more complex and 'borderline' cases in the full aid objectives meetings. The second is that the decision in Irifune is made more concrete in the ruling meeting, resulting in each case going through one less layer of discussion than in Teru.

224 *Variation of policy implementation*

The third difference is the role played by senior management. In each of the three meetings, the senior management in Teru plays a greater role in shaping discussion and decisions than they do in Irifune. The senior management in Teru have more experience to draw on and reference previous similar cases more frequently than the Irifune senior managers do. This experience allows them to speak with more confidence on the suitability of different placements.

The fourth difference is in who participates in and audits the meetings. In Teru, the majority of the children's support division attend the ruling meetings and the acceptance meeting. In their first few months, new caseworkers in Teru also audit other staff members' aid objectives meetings. This affords them the opportunity to learn from others' cases, not just their own. This amplifies the impact of the contributions of the senior management in Teru, as comments are heard by more staff than in Irifune, where caseworkers do not attend others' ruling meetings or aid objectives meetings.

The fifth difference is in how the responsibility for the decision is understood within the CGC. In Teru, the discussion is more detailed and decisions are understood as collective, often framed as 'we will try' x, 'let's do' x. In Irifune the caseworker's proposed plan is invariably the outcome. This difference is encapsulated in the fact that in Irifune the caseworker's 'provisional' decision is printed onto the form before the meeting, whereas in Teru it is handwritten on the form by each participant at the meeting's conclusion.

The discussion in the ruling meeting in Irifune is more detailed than in Teru, though this is still significantly shorter and less collaborative than the aid objectives meeting in Teru. The shorter discussion shifts the responsibility for the decision from the collective to the individual, which makes Irifune caseworkers more risk-averse than the Teru caseworkers. This impacts on the caseworkers' willingness to use foster care, for which the CGC is seen as being more responsible, and their willingness to challenge guardians' wishes. The emerging belief in Teru that institutional placements also carry risk is making the caseworkers more willing to accept the 'positive' risks associated with foster care.

In both CGCs caseworkers discuss cases prior to the formal meetings. One key distinction here is that in Irifune some of these discussions result in the elimination of the possibility of a foster care placement, a decision that in Teru is always made in the formal meetings. Following one meeting in Irifune, regarding an infant girl, I asked the foster care caseworker why foster care had not been discussed. The foster care caseworker responded that the caseworker had asked her informally if there were any suitable foster parents, and because there hadn't been, the matter was not raised in the meeting. In Teru this discussion is always conducted in a formal meeting. This ensures that beliefs on what is best in each case are always raised, even where they cannot be acted upon.

The forms used in Teru are longer and more detailed than those in Irifune: for example, the aid objectives form is one side of A4 in Irifune and two in Teru. In Irifune these forms are sometimes read verbatim; in Teru they are a reference point for the person speaking. There is also a considerable difference in the tone of meetings. In Teru the collective nature of the meetings, along with the manner in which senior managers work with section heads and caseworkers, means that meetings are open and friendly, with discussion encouraged. This is in stark contrast to the time limits set upon staff reports in Irifune's aid objectives meetings. On the one occasion in Teru where I saw real disagreement that was not resolved in the meeting, a training session was held at a later date to explore both positions and find common ground.

In Teru, meetings were unambiguous in terms of responsibility for future action, timeframe, and goals. These points were often left less defined in Irifune. It seems likely that the continuity in the chair of the aid objectives meeting in Teru, which contrasts with a rotating chair in Irifune, contributes to these differences in the tone of the meeting.

The informal input caseworkers receive from other staff also differed between Teru and Irifune. The consistent approach of senior managers in Teru has resulted in an organisational culture that evaluates foster care positively. This creates a positive feedback loop where experienced staff share these beliefs to newer caseworkers.

This positive feedback loop is fragile. In Teru, the shift to promoting foster care around 2003–2005 led to a decision to attempt to place children of all ages into foster care. A high placement breakdown rate for children over 14 years in the first few years did not lead to a decision to abandon foster care. Instead, a decision was made around 2009 to focus on younger children and, as support capacity developed, to expand to older children later.

Negative feedback loops are easier to fall into than positive ones. There are two main reasons for this. The first is that the move towards foster care challenges the status quo on its function and capability. Where a caseworker predicts and then sees failure in foster care it is more likely to harden their opinions than when they have doubts and sees one case of success. The second reason is related to the fact that the CGC is held more directly accountable when a placement into foster care breaks down than when one into a CWI breaks down. This is because the CGC is the service provider for foster care, in contrast to institutional care where it is the service regulator. In Teru, the stable and consistent approach towards foster care from senior managers has led the CGC to respond to placement breakdowns in foster care by developing more support capacity rather than by abandoning change.

This consistency in approach is made possible in Teru by the stability of the senior management. In Irifune the positive feedback loop is a lot weaker, with successful placements into foster care often attributed to luck.

Returning to the two cases of extreme neglect discussed in Chapter 6, the section head noted that she was

> really impressed by the results of this fostered child and I think that for kids like this a family-like environment might be best, but there was also some luck here in how the child and the foster carers clicked and if the child had been placed in another foster care placement they could have ended up being abused.

In addition to the reservations expressed here over foster care, this comment highlights the individual nature of caseworkers' attitude towards foster care in Irifune. Unlike Teru, where the senior managers use meetings to shape and unify caseworkers' beliefs, the Irifune section head's comments here were an individual opinion that had not been expressed in meetings. This limits the impact of individual cases on policy and practice change in Irifune, as well as meaning that new caseworkers receive different advice depending on who they speak to. This hinders the processes that led to the 'sea change' in attitudes towards foster care in Teru.

The differences in the meetings between Teru and Irifune are profound. While the format is uniform, the process in Teru promotes the use of foster care and allows senior managers to shape beliefs and practice at an organisational level. In Irifune caseworkers only learn from their own cases, which inhibits lessons learned from individual cases leading to policy or practice change at a CGC level. A discussion in a meeting in Teru on the lack of a suitable foster parent may lead to a concerted recruitment drive, whereas in Irifune this discussion often occurs outside the formal meetings and does not result in any change. The limited participation by senior management in Irifune in shaping responses to cases leaves caseworkers feeling individually responsible for decisions, which increases risk aversion and strengthens path-dependent responses. This is amplified by the lack of specialist social work knowledge in all CGCs, though the experience of senior managers, foster care caseworkers, and the lawyer means that Teru is less affected by this than the Irifune CGC is.

Perhaps the most important difference here lies in the staff's construction of the role of the CGC. Miwa argues that the most important factor explaining the low foster care rate 'is the lack of children available to be fostered' (2016: 10) and highlights that 'the approach of the CGC to parental consent can lead to more parents consenting to foster care' (2016: 11). The more collective approach to decision-making in Teru dissipates this responsibility, making caseworkers more willing to 'push' for foster care than caseworkers in Irifune. As noted in Chapter 6, the Teru caseworkers share best practice on how they have gained parental consent. The caseworkers' willingness to use foster care is also undoubtedly increased by the higher confidence in the Teru CGC in their ability to 'match' foster parent and child and to support them post-placement. Underlying all of these differences is the fact that the desire for change in the Teru CGC is strongly held by senior managers and across all levels of staff, whereas the desire for change in the Irifune CGC varies across each level of staff.

The 'Galapagos' metaphor Sano used in relation to Japan in the international context can be extended to the 'islands' of the local authorities within Japan. The limited extent of domestic practice and policy sharing mechanisms means that regional variation in policy implementation in alternative care is increasing, with the organisational culture of each CGC critical in determining the trajectory of this change in each local authority.

5 Knowledge acquisition, retention, and use in informing change

Teru's use of meetings to share knowledge and shape beliefs and practice is a response to a challenge all CGCs face: how to acquire, retain, and use knowledge to inform change. This issue, first raised by Ushijima and Yukawa (1975), is picked up by Miwa, who suggests that staff rotation means that CGCs 'don't have a sufficient system to develop specialist knowledge' (2016: 8). This section considers the other ways in which Teru has addressed this issue and compares these with practices in Irifune.

The first and most important difference is the length of service of senior managers in Teru. The CGC head has served in the same post for over a decade, the children's support division head has worked in the CGC for over 30 years, and the children's emergency division head for nearly 20 years. The clinical psychologists in Teru also serve particularly long terms, with postings of over ten years not uncommon. The Teru CGC also makes extensive use of contract staff in the foster care team, some of whom have been in their role for over ten years.

The senior managers' long postings allow a consistent approach to foster care, the development and retention of experience and expertise, and enables the CGC to execute a long-term vision to develop foster care service provision capacity. It also inhibits the negative feedback cycle that can occur when foster care placements break down, as well as strengthening the CGC in relation to both the local authority hall and the welfare institutions.

Continuity in the more junior staff, particularly within the foster care team, helps the CGC to address two important problems: the CGC's limited expertise in how to address specific childrearing issues faced by foster parents (Miwa, 2014), and the challenge staff rotation creates for foster parents in making a meaningful relationship with the CGC for support (Goldfarb, 2012; Ito, 2015).

The rotation of staff represents a third axis that must be considered in all studies of policy implementation in Japan – that of time. As well as the well-considered vertical divisions between siloed ministries and horizontal divisions over levels of government (Johnson, 1975), policy implementation in alternative care in Japan faces temporal divisions, which hinder the formation of coalitions to promote change (see Tsuzaki, 2003). These temporal divisions are a significant factor in explaining why policy change in alternative care is incremental.

The effect of these continual changes is amplified by the belief that those who cause the least disruption are the most likely to be promoted (Johnson, 1982). Tsuzaki notes that this is perhaps one reason why most of the reforming heads of CGCs have been clinical psychiatrists, who have a status independent of their government role (personal correspondence, 2015, January 7).

Irifune is a more 'typical' CGC, with senior managers changing position every one to three years and caseworkers changing position every two to three years. The longevity of senior management in Teru is contingent on continued support from the local authority hall, and several staff expressed their concerns that the CGC may change when these three managers leave.

The second difference between Teru and Irifune is how training is used to share knowledge and change practice. In Teru training for new staff lasts two weeks. There are also monthly training sessions where staff discuss issues, share best practice, or an external expert comes in to speak. During my fieldwork, this included a professor leading a hypothetical aid objectives meeting for a challenging case, and the head of a specialist institution for teenage girls with challenging behaviour lecturing on their approach.

The initial training for staff in Irifune is significantly shorter than in Teru and the ongoing training sessions have lower staff participation. The main difference between the ongoing training sessions in the two CGCs was that in Teru these directly led to policy and practice change at a CGC level, from structural changes in the allocation of resources to changes in daily practice. One Teru training session, which discussed an unresolved dispute that arose in an aid objectives meeting over the best way to manage a case between divisions, led to a change in the management of all similar future cases. Another provided guidance for caseworkers' in gaining parental consent for foster care.

The final form of training in both CGCs is the informal mentoring of new caseworkers by their more experienced colleagues. The limited nature of formal training means that new staff rely heavily on the support and experience of senior colleagues. Staff have a limited time to understand their role, to master what is expected of them, to determine what positive change they can affect, and to create and implement this positive change. This serves to strengthen path dependency. Where a CGC, such as Teru, is aiming to unify their approach to cases and create a coherent culture, the new caseworker is likely to receive informal mentoring in line with this culture. In Teru this helps to transmit norms on the goals of care, the functions of different types of care, and on the threshold above which a child cannot enter foster care over generations of caseworkers. In CGCs where the organisational culture is less uniform, such as Irifune, this informal mentoring is dependent on individual caseworkers' norms and will vary more widely. An integral part of this in Teru comes in staff auditing others' case meetings, which is far less common in Irifune.

CGC staff do occasionally have opportunities to learn from practice in other local authorities. National conferences, including the Japanese Society for the Prevention of Child Abuse and Neglect (JaSPCAN), and NPO training sessions, including the Osaka Association for the Promotion of Family Based Care (*Osaka katei yōgo sokushin kyōkai*), provide CGC staff opportunities to build personal connections with their peers in other local authorities. The Teru foster care section head noted that their relationship with foster care supervisors in two other local authorities had been invaluable in deciding how to respond to some of the more unusual and challenging cases they had faced. These connections must be created, and are thus limited to proactive staff.

The MHLW has engaged with limited attempts to share best practice across local authorities, most notably with the 2013 report on how Fukuoka City and Oita have increased their foster care rate (MHLW SC, 2013). There is also a national association of CGC heads, though this has limited input into national or local policy creation. Marginally more active is a network of the CGC heads of the 22 designated cities. Yet here too, the nature of this network means that local authorities with no interest in changing practice either do not engage or engage only superficially.[3]

Even where staff are experienced and do wish to change practice they are aware that they may be followed by a staff member with no relevant experience. This affects staff at all levels of government. A CGC foster caseworker and an MHLW bureaucrat both confided to me their fear of enacting radical changes that would leave their successor struggling. The caseworker expressed this succinctly, noting, 'I could do more, and change things a bit, but my boss told me that I should be aware of creating too much work or making it too hard for the person who follows me'.

There have previously been more formal mechanisms for policy and practice learning across local authorities, including an 'internship' wherein a CGC staff member spent several months in another local authority's CGC. During one training session for staff in Teru, the head of the children's emergency division explained how this system had contributed to the creation of Teru's emergency division and the decision for the emergency team to only manage the initial intervention, rather than also managing all subsequent support:

> In most CGCs they don't have an abuse specific team, but all the designated cities have one. I went to Osaka and Kyoto to learn from them before we set up this one. Osaka had 40–50 people [in their emergency team], Kyoto had 4–5 people, this was over a decade ago. In Kyoto the normal caseworkers worked with abuse cases. The emergency caseworkers dealt with the intervention and effectively acted as a support team. In Osaka the emergency caseworkers did the intervention and then took

on [all the following support work for] the case. I thought that the Kyoto team would build up specialist knowledge in abuse cases... In Osaka at the time the staff stayed for 10 years so were specialists, but we felt we couldn't do this in [Teru]. I wondered that if we copied Osaka we may end up with issues.

This scheme has long since been closed and change in Teru now often stems from CGC training sessions. The most recent change in organisational structure came in April 2015 with the creation of a new section, consisting of a section head and one caseworker, which focuses exclusively on reassessing the cases of children who have been in care for over five years. The creation of this section followed reflection on several case meetings where children had 'drifted', *zuruzuru*, and ended up spending much of their childhood in institutions.

The relationship between practice and practice change in Teru is reliant upon the senior management who connect issues raised in case meetings with policy and practice change. This contrasts with Irifune, where practice change is less connected to issues arising in the decision-making process on individual cases, and ongoing training plays less of a role in mediating between cases and practice or policy change.

The final area where Teru and Irifune differ in how knowledge is acquired, retained and used is connected to the relative specialisation of jobs in Teru. The emergency division in Teru is the most obvious example of this. In a monthly training session, the Teru Children's Emergency division head outlined the reasons behind this decision to specialise in tasks:

> For casework there is an internal problem. We have to support children, and we have to support the parents' needs. There are times when the needs conflict. We have to prioritise the child's needs here, and this may lead to opposition from the parents. This issue is most prevalent in abuse cases. The child's needs must come first. This makes a divide between support social work, and the abuse kind of work. So, we figured that supporting parents' needs cannot easily be done by the same person as who is supporting the child's needs.

This increased specialisation allows caseworkers to acquire more specialised knowledge than in CGCs, including Irifune, where caseworkers also manage emergency cases. The investment in Teru into developing capacity in the foster care support team, who work solely on foster care, the hiring of a full-time lawyer, and the outsourcing of initial investigation into 'light' abuse cases to an NPO, also allow the Teru CGC staff to develop particular skills and acquire more specialist knowledge than in Irifune, where CGC staff are more 'generalists'. Irifune's attempt to narrow and focus their workload by outsourcing foster care recruitment and training to a BIWI does speak of an effort to develop specialist knowledge in an organisation, though here this organisation is outside the CGC.

6 Conclusions

This chapter has outlined the mechanisms that create different organisational cultures in the Teru and Irifune CGCs. It first examined the decision-making process before looking at how differences in the length of service of the staff, staff training, and the degree of staff specialisation affect how knowledge is acquired, retained, and used to inform policy and practice change.

The different organisational cultures impact upon policy implementation, mediating the relationship between beliefs and resources. The Teru CGC head understands the 'sea change' in caseworkers' attitudes towards foster care as critical to the changes in policy implementation. Sabatier argues that the implementation of policy reform requires *'committed* and skilful officials' (1986: 23, emphasis added) – that is, caseworkers who are capable and who *believe* in the reform. In Teru this change came from caseworkers seeing better than anticipated outcomes for children entering foster care *and* this evaluation feeding into future practice.

This positive feedback loop was enabled by the attitude of the senior staff towards foster care and by the collective nature of the decision-making process dissipating risk. This facilitated, for example, slightly older children or children with slightly more complex needs being placed into foster care, and the gradual expansion of the threshold below which a child is seen as suitable for foster care. The feedback loop was amplified by caseworkers auditing other caseworkers' meetings, which allowed the active shaping of care plans by senior managers in individual cases to influence a wider audience.

The connection between individual cases and policy change is more direct in Teru than in Irifune. This is mediated by the active role played by senior management in individual cases and through ongoing training sessions, where policy and practice are discussed by all levels of staff. In Teru this involved changes in the allocation of resources, including the creation of the children's emergency division, employing a lawyer, and the decision to invest in developing the capacity of foster care service provision.

These changes were situated within the specific organisational culture of the Teru CGC. The Irifune CGC's decision to resolve the BIWIs being full by moving older infants to CWIs or returning them home (see Chapter 5) was made in a ten-minute meeting between two senior managers, the staff member responsible for BIWIs, and their section head. In a later discussion, the section head noted to me that 'in reality, a lot of infants who move from baby and welfare institutions to foster care have attachment issues', but this opinion was not raised during this meeting.

I do not mean to suggest that Irifune does not change their practice based on their experiences; to do so would be absurd. Like any organisation, the Irifune CGC changes their practice based on the knowledge that they have, their understanding of this knowledge, and the resources at their disposal. For example, the decision to outsource foster care recruitment and training to a BIWI was based on the CGC's understanding of their own resources and their beliefs on foster care. Another example of practice change in Irifune saw the adoption of a 'Common Sense Parenting' programme for some parents before a child is returned home, following concerns over the lack of support offered after care placements end. Despite this, it is fair to say that in Irifune, more than in Teru, the desire for change is less uniform and the path of change taken is often the one that offers the least resistance.

Notes

1 This mirrors Nagano (2012) on the progression of CWI careleavers to tertiary education, which found that the attitude of CWI staff and the 'organisational culture' of the CWI were of central importance (see also Nabekura 2004; Ogiso, 2010).
2 There are guidelines that distinguish which case has which kind of aid objectives meeting. These state five situations where a full aid objectives meeting must be held: where a child may be placed into a short-term therapeutic institution for children with mental health disabilities, a children's self-reliance support institution, a self-reliance assistance home, an institution for children with disabilities, or foster care; where a child will leave a BIWI, a children's self-reliance support institution, or a short-term therapeutic institution for children with mental health disabilities; where a child will return home from a CWI having been placed due to abuse; any case where a decision under Article 27.1, 27.2, 27.4, 28, 33.6, 33.7, or 33.8 of the Child Welfare Act will be cancelled; and where the case has been transferred to the CGC under the Juvenile Act.

There are two situations where a case should in principle have a full aid objectives meeting: where a child will return home from a placement in temporary care, made due to delinquency, development, or abuse; and where the children's support division has previously dealt with the case or the case has lasted for more than a year.

The guidelines list seven situations where a full aid objectives meeting can be held if necessary: to make a decision on a child returning home from temporary care; to review cases where a child has been in temporary care for more than two months; where a child may be placed into a CWI or an institution for children with disabilities; where a baby or infant may be placed into a BIWI; where a foster care placement will be cancelled; where a case may be referred to the classroom for school refusers or other related educational services; and 'other' cases, where discussion is necessary to make a decision.

The guidelines state that exceptions can be made for 'simple childrearing cases' where both parents are sick, or there are other 'pure', *junsui*, reasons where the guardian is absent.
3 Non-governmental groups also occasionally attempt to learn from practice in other local authorities (see Aizu Foster Parent Association, 2014), though these often have limited impact on practice.

References

Aizu Foster Parent Association. (2014). *Fukushima no satooya shien to jidō fukushi sokushin jigyō. Fukushima susumu fundo. Chōsa jigyō hōkoku-sho* [Fukushima forwards fund: The promotion of foster care and child welfare in Fukushima. Research survey report]. Fukushima: Aizu Foster Parent Association.

Aspinall, R.W. (2006). Using the paradigm of 'small cultures' to explain policy failure in the case of foreign language education in Japan. *Japan Forum*, 18(2), 255–274.

Bloom, H.S., Hill, C.J., & Riccio, J. (2001). Modeling the performance of welfare-to-work programs: The effects of program management and services, economic environment, and client characteristics. *Manpower demonstration and research corporation working papers on research methodology*. n.p.: MDRC.

Child Welfare Act. (1947). Act No. 164 of 1947, December 12.

Collier, D. (2011). Understanding process tracing. *Political Science and Politics*, 44(4), 823–830.

Coser, L.A. (1977). *Masters of sociological thought: Ideas in historical and social context*. New York: Harcourt Brace Jovanovich.

Dubois, V. (2010). *The bureaucrat and the poor. Encounters in French welfare offices*. Ashgate: Farnham & Burlington.

Evans, T. (2011). Professionals, managers and discretion: Critiquing street-level bureaucracy. *British Journal of Social Work*, 41(2), 368–386.

Goldfarb, K. (2012). *Fragile kinships: Family ideologies and child welfare in Japan.* (Doctoral dissertation). The University of Chicago.

Hill, M. (2013). *The public policy process*. London: Routledge.

Holliday, A. (1999). Small cultures. *Applied Linguistics*, 20(2), 237–264.

Ito, K. (2015). Satooya no shien nīzu to shien kikan ni motomeru yakuwari [Foster care support needs and clarifying the role of the foster care support agencies]. *Nihon Shakai Fukushi Gakkai*.

Johnson, C. (1975). Japan: Who governs? An essay on official bureaucracy. *Journal of Japanese Studies*, 2(1), 1–28.

Johnson, C. (1982). *MITI and the Japanese miracle. Growth of industrial policy, 1925–1975*. Stanford: Stanford University Press.

Kashiwame, R., Nakatani, S., Hayashi, S., & Amino, T. (1995). Jidōsōdanjyo no unnei bunseki [Analysis of child guidance centres' operations]. *Nihon sōgō aiiku kenkyū kiyō*, 32, 137–147.

King (Rivera King), M. (2017). *Child guidance centres in Japan: Regional variation in policy implementation and the family-bond.* (Doctoral dissertation). The University of Oxford.

Kurihara, N. (2011). Jidō fukushi-hō dai 28-jō tekiyō no genjō to kadai ni tsuite: jidōsōdanjyo no genjō to kadai [The current state and challenges around the use of Article 28 of The Child Welfare Act: The current state and challenges of the child guidance centres]. *Nihon Shakai Fukushi Gakkai*.

Lin, A.C. (2000). *Reform in the making: The implementation of social policy in prison.* Princeton: Princeton University Press.

May, P.J., & Winter, S.C. (2007). Politicians, managers, and street-level bureaucrats: Influences on policy implementation. *Journal of Public Administration Research and Theory*, 19, 453–476.

Meyers, M.K., & Vorsanger, S. (2003). Street-level bureaucrats and the implementation of public policy. In B.G. Peters, & J. Pierre (Eds.), *Handbook of public administration*. Thousand Oaks: Sage.

MHLW Specialist Committee for the Promotion of Placements into Foster Care (MHLW SC). (2013a). (*Zenkoku satooya itaku-tō suishin iinkai*). *Satooya-tō itaku-ritsu appu no torikumi hōkoku-sho ~ itaku-ritsu wo ōkiku zōka saseta Fukuoka-shi Ōita ken no torikumi yori ~* [Report on efforts to increase the foster care rate: The efforts of Fukuoka City and Oita Prefecture, which have greatly increased foster care placements]. 2015, February.

Miwa, K. (2014). *Satooya seido no chouki-teki doutai to tenbou* [The long-term dynamics and outlook of the foster care system]. (Doctoral dissertation). Tokyo Metropolitan University.

Miwa, K. (2016). Naze satooya itaku wa shinten shinai no ka? Satooya touroku-sha fusoku kasetsu to satooya itaku jidō gentei kasetsu [Why has family-based foster care not become more common in Japan? A lack of registered fostered carers and of children who are able to be fostered]. *Japanese Journal of Social Welfare*, 56(4), 1–13.

Miyajima, K. (2001). *Jidō gyakutai bōshi-hō shikōgo no jidōsōdanjyo to satooya seido no kongo ni tsuite* [On the child guidance centres and foster care system after the enforcement of the Child abuse prevention act]. Preliminary paper for dai 75-kai yōshi to satooya wo kangaeru kai kōjutsu-roku.

Murray, C. (2006). State intervention and vulnerable children: Implementation revisited. *Journal of Social Policy*, 35(2), 211–227.

Nabekura, S. (2004). Jidō yōgo shisetsu ni okeru hi gyakutai jidō no kyōiku wo ukeru kenri no shomondai mensetsu chōsa oyobi san'yo kansatsu wo chūshin to shite [The problems of the right to education for the ill-treatment child in the child welfare institutions: Based on the interview investigation and the participatory observation]. *Bungaku kenkyū-ka kyōiku senkō hakushikōkikatei zaigaku*, 26, 261–276.

Nagano, S. (2012). Jidō yōgo shisetsu de seikatsu suru kodomo no daigakunado shingaku ni kansuru kenkyū: Jidō yōgo shisetsu seikatsu keiken-sha e no intabyū chōsa kara [A study on university attendance of child foster care [alternative care] leavers: Through an interview analysis]. *Nihon Shakai Fukushi Gakkai*, 52(4), 28–40.

Ogiso, H. (2010). Jidō yōgo shisetsu jidō jiritsushien ni nyūsho suru jidō no genjo to shien shisaku no kadai [The current status of children in child welfare institutions and self-reliance support institutions and the challenges in support measures]. *Kikan shakai hoshō kenkyū*, 45(4), 396–406.

Preston-Shoot, M., Roberts, G., & Vernon, S. (2001). Values in social work law: Strained relations or sustaining relationships? *The Journal of Social Welfare & Family Law*, 23(1), 1–22.

Sabatier, P.A. (1986). Top-down and bottom-up approaches to implementation research: A critical analysis and suggested synthesis. *Journal of Public Policy*, 6(1), 21–48.

Saimura, J., Shibuya, M., Kashiwame, R., Shoji, J., Arimura, T., Aizawa, H., ... Yamamoto, T. (2004). Gyakutai taiō-tō ni kakaru jidōsōdanjyo no gyōmu bunseki ni kansuru chōsa kenkyū (2) [The analysis of actual quantity of works in child guidance centres (2)]. *Nihon-kodomo katei sōgōkenkyūsho kiyō*, 41, 129–174.

Saimura, J., Arimura, T., Kashiwame, R., Yamamoto, T., Nagano, S., Tsuruoka, H., ... Yokoyama, T. (2010). Jidōsōdanjyo no gyōmu bunseki ni kansuru kenkyū (1) [Time-studies and incident-studies about social work for child abuse cases in child guidance centres]. *Nihon-kodomo katei sōgōkenkyūsho kiyō*, 47, 181–191.

Saimura, J., Wada, I., Yamamoto, T., Ookubo, M., Nagano, S., Arimura, T., ... Kawamatsu, R. (2013). Jidōsōdanjyo jidō shinri tsukasa no gyōmu jittai haaku ni kansuru kenkyū [The analysis of actual quantity of works of clinical psychologist in child guidance centres]. *Nihon-kodomo katei sōgōkenkyūsho kiyō*, 50, 1–19.

Sandfort, J.R. (2000). Moving beyond discretion and outcomes: Examining public management from the front lines of the welfare system. *Journal of Public Administration Research and Theory*, 10, 729–756.

Tsuzaki, T. (2003). *Sōshiruwāku to shakai fukushi – Igirisu chihō jichitai sōsharu wāku no seiritsu to tenkai* [Social work and social service: The establishment and evolution of British local authority social work]. Tokyo: Akashi Shoten.

Ushijima, Y., & Yukawa, R. (1975). Jidōsōdanjyo ni okeru hantei no kinō oyobi kijun ni kansuru kenkyū [A study on the decision making function and standards of the child guidance centres]. *Nihon sōgō aiiku kenkyū kiyō*, 11, 305–331.

Note: Where the author(s) provided an English translation of their work I have given this translation, rather than my translation.

Part IV
Conclusion

8 Conclusion

1 Introduction

This book addresses the research question: what factors contribute to the regional variation in policy implementation on alternative care in Japanese child guidance centres? It does this by examining regional variation in the resources available to the CGCs, in the norms of those implementing policy, and in the organisational cultures of the CGCs.

Prior to examining regional variation, the book introduced the puzzle and research methods used, the Japanese alternative care system, and the CGCs. The book also introduced the values of those implementing policy, the family-bond.

The CGC has five kinds of *resources*: physical geography, political attention, the capacity of care providers (affected by the quantity, perceived quality, and the need for care), the capacity of the CGCs, also considered in terms of quantity and quality, and external support.

Both physical geography and political support varied between Teru and Irifune. The compact nature of Teru means that it is easier for the CGC to provide foster care services than in Irifune. Political support at critical moments in Teru has facilitated the development of foster care services, with ongoing support allowing the lengthy placements of three senior managers. This 'two-level' support for change, of bureaucrats and politicians, is not found in Irifune, where the CGC staff who want to promote foster care lack political support.

The limited research conducted on national policymaking on alternative care suggests that the 'two-level' model of change is potentially valid at the national level too. This model places importance on individuals with similar beliefs and goals occupying key positions in politics and the bureaucracy simultaneously. The emphasis on individuals in this model reflects the challenges posed by staff rotation to building stable coalitions. In my fieldwork notes, I reflected that attempting to form coalitions with constant staff rotation is like trying to do a jigsaw where the pieces keep changing shape. The national welfare institution associations do not face this issue, which contributes to their strength in relation to local and national authorities.

240 *Conclusion*

Further research is required to test this 'two-level' model in different policy contexts in Japan.

The capacity of care providers also varied between Teru and Irifune. Irifune has higher institutional capacity relative to population, while Teru has higher relative foster care capacity. The limited institutional capacity in Teru, coupled with the belief that the large-scale CWIs were not providing suitable care for children's diverse needs, triggered the decision to develop foster care capacity. Irifune has never reached the threshold where further capacity is required, and has sufficient institutional capacity that it can respond to concerns about abuse within one institution by using other institutions.

The CGC's evaluation of the quality of foster care is more important than their evaluation of the quality of institutional care. This is because the threshold for registering foster parents is low. This means CGCs must create internal mechanisms to determine which registered foster parents can be used. Further, the fact that CGCs are the service provider for foster care increases their responsibility for any issues here, which raises the threshold for 'acceptable' care.

The need for alternative care also varies across local authorities. This is affected by material conditions, including the child poverty rate, and by the local construction of the threshold at which a child should be removed from the family.

The capacity of care in Teru and Irifune mediated the impact that a change in need had on policy and practice change: the increased number of children entering care in Teru, which led the CGC to increase foster care capacity, had a greater effect than it did in Irifune, where surplus institutional capacity absorbed this additional need.

This interaction, between need and capacity, also impacts upon national practice change. As outlined in Chapters 2 and 5, the increased foster care rate between 2000 and 2010 relates to increased need, rather than coming at the expense of institutional care. It is possible that 2010 represents a turning point, as the increasing foster care rate after this point does correlate with a decrease in the number of children in institutions.

Regional variation in foster care service provision capacity is related to the capacity of the CGCs. Here the number, experience, workload, and degree of specialisation of the staff play a significant role in shaping policy implementation. Teru, which has over five staff members working solely on foster care, a lawyer, and three experienced senior managers, has considerably more CGC capacity than Irifune. Teru also has more support from external actors, including the foster care association and local NPOs.

The book next explored the impact of regional variation of the *norms* of those implementing policy on policy implementation. This focused on regional variation on the goals of care, the functions of different types of care, and the threshold until which a child is considered suitable for foster care. To understand the impact of these norms it is first necessary to understand the values on the family-bond of those implementing policy.

In Japan, the family-bond is constructed as singular and discrete: a child is understood as only being able to have one family-bond at a time. The creation of a new family-bond necessitates the destruction of the existing family-bond and removing a child risks destroying the existing or potential family-bond. Further, a child is only considered able to form a new family-bond until a certain age. There is slight regional variation in this age, with Teru using foster care as a proxy for adoption for older children than Irifune.

This speaks to one of the early questions that triggered this research, Japan's low rate of children entering care. The decision to place a child into care is made by weighing the risk to the child's family-bond posed by removing the child against the risk to the child posed by not removing the child. At its most extreme, this decision represents an evaluation of the risk of social death against that of biological death.

Concerns over destroying the family-bond by placing the child into care are amplified by the dearth of resources available to the CGC in facilitating family reunification. This relates to the high workload of CGC staff but is also affected by the limited support offered by the judiciary. In the absence of this support, the CGC's limited authority means that staff are often wary of contacting natal parents in case they decide to remove the child from care before the CGC considers this to be safe. This contributes to the difference between placing a child into care and leaving the child in the family being seen as a 'cliff edge', as well as to the lengthy duration of placements.

The limited judicial support relates to the judicial system's limited capacity, limited expertise, and belief that the goal of care should, almost without exception, be family reunification. Why the judiciary takes this position requires further research.

This construction of the family-bond means that regional variation in norms on the function of foster care plays a critical role in determining regional variation of policy implementation. Where foster care is understood as a proxy for adoption, with care based upon the creation of a new family-bond, it is not considered suitable for children for whom the goal of care is family reunification, who comprise the majority of cases. Conversely, where foster care is understood as semi-professional care in a family setting it can be used for children for whom the goal of care is family reunification. This finding contributes to our understanding of the first puzzle that inspired this research, Japan's low foster care rate.

Teru and Irifune differed in how they constructed the function of foster care. The challenges around gaining consent for adoption mean that both Teru and Irifune use some foster care as a proxy for adoption. Both local authorities also use some foster care as 'a boarding house' for older children. Where Teru and Irifune differ is in the amount of foster care that is constructed as 'semi-professional'. Teru is actively attempting to develop this kind of foster care, with a pilot 'therapeutic foster care' programme, the conversion of experienced foster parents into family homes, and by increasing support to raise the threshold until which a child can enter foster care.

These differences are visible in the images used for foster care recruitment in Teru and Irifune.

Teru and Irifune also differ slightly in the function ascribed to welfare institutions. In both CGCs institutions are used because they do not result in the creation of a new family-bond. The conclusion of Ren's case, in Teru, that it was 'better if he goes to a baby institution as he won't think of them as new family, but as staff' demonstrates how this lack of attachment is at times seen as being in best interests of the child. This echoes Goldfarb's description of Japanese welfare institutions as 'the space of waiting' (2012: 79).

This finding challenges MHLW literature describing a move from children being raised by their families to being raised by all of society (MHLW, 2010), which echoes the title of Goodman's seminal work 'Children of the Japanese State' (2000). Children in alternative care are children neither of the state nor of society. Children in welfare institutions are children of their families, in the temporary care of the state. Children in foster care are either in the same position or are children of a new family. The state only exceptionally takes on any of the parental rights when a child is in care. It is only where the goal of care is self-reliance that the child could be potentially be described as a child of the state, and even here the parent almost always retains the ability to determine the child's education, healthcare, and even their removal from care whenever the parents wish.

The difference in the function of the welfare institutions between Teru and Irifune is that in Teru the staff are starting to problematize this limbo, this liminal space. Concerns in Teru over attachment in BIWIs and the suitability of large-dormitory CWIs are concerns over the function of the institutions, rather than the quality of specific institutions. This has contributed to the willingness of the staff in Teru to take 'positive risks', placing children who would previously have entered institutions into foster care.

The Teru and Irifune CGCs also differ in how the goal of care is understood. In both CGCs determining the goal of care is a 'joint production process' (Meyers and Vorsanger, 2003: 246) between the CGC staff and the child's parents. The Teru CGC staff are more willing to challenge the natal parents' goals of care than the Irifune staff. Further, the Teru CGC places marginally more weight on the child's development as an individual, distinct from the family-bond, than Irifune.

Finally, the threshold above which a child is seen as too complex for foster care, which is largely determined by the child's age and the complexity of their need, also varies between Teru and Irifune. In Teru there is a drop in the number of children entering foster care at around nine years of age; in Irifune this occurs at seven years of age. This variation is linked to the greater capacity for foster care support in Teru than in Irifune and conscious attempts in Teru to expand this boundary.

The interaction of resources and norms are mediated by the *organisational cultures* of the CGCs. The organisational cultures of the Teru and

Irifune CGCs are distinct. This relates to and manifests in differences in the decision-making processes and in how knowledge is acquired, retained, and used to inform policy and practice change. Responsibility in the decision-making process is more collective in Teru than Irifune, where the individual nature of the decision-making process increases risk aversion. The organisation of meetings in Teru allows more stages of discussion than the organisation of meetings in Irifune does. The differentiation of two types of aid objectives meetings in Teru allows more time to be spent on complex cases, including those that may enter foster care.

In Teru, senior managers are engaged in the decision-making process, giving guidance and explaining their input. In Irifune, senior managers limit themselves to checking details, with the caseworker's provisional, pre-printed, decision being the outcome of every case I saw. The impact on the norms of CGC staff of the senior managers' input is amplified in Teru by caseworkers auditing other caseworkers' meetings, a practice which is less common in Irifune.

The Teru senior managers' approach is made possible by their unusually long placements. This has also helped Teru to deal with the problem of knowledge retention, and to connect knowledge from individual cases to policy and practice change. Stability in senior management helps Teru to minimise the impact of the constant rotation of other CGC staff, who are generalists and often begin with no specialist knowledge or experience.

The rotation of staff and the non-specialist nature of the caseworkers implementing policy distinguish this study from the majority of studies on street-level bureaucrats. These factors increase the importance of the caseworkers' values, here on the family-bond, and contribute to limiting change to being incremental in nature. Teru attempts to mitigate these factors with staff training, including the staff auditing the decision-making process of others' cases, and by connecting issues raised in the decision-making process to practice change. Again, the role of the senior managers is key here.

These practices in Teru have created a positive feedback loop of practice change, with informal mentoring and on-the-job training important in passing on norms on foster care over generations of caseworkers. There is concern among the Teru CGC staff that when the three senior managers retire the CGC's organisational culture may change.

The lack of stability or continuity in approach among senior managers in Irifune means that positive steps taken by one caseworker or foster care caseworker are isolated, and susceptible to being annulled or reversed by their replacement or by other staff. The Irifune CGC has engaged less with tackling knowledge loss or creating a unified approach to alternative care within their staff than Teru. This more disparate organisational culture serves to limit change in Irifune.

2 Contributions

This work makes contributions to the academic fields of street-level bureaucracy, alternative care, and Japanese studies. Taking first the theoretical body of work on street-level bureaucrats, this book explores how models based on professionals or semi-professionals apply to generalist bureaucrats. Drawing on a historical institutionalism in a sociological perspective approach, this book argues that the absence of professional norms increases the importance of the 'values' and 'norms' of those implementing policy, as well as the organisational culture of the institutions in which they work. Starting from values, rather than norms, is particularly important where there is little existing research in the field.

The second contribution to the street-level bureaucracy literature is the development of work on vertical and horizontal divisions in bureaucracy to include temporal divisions. The constant rotation of staff strengthens path dependency by impacting upon the ability of actors to form networks and coalitions. This tripartite framework may contribute to our understanding of why policy and practice change in other areas in Japan are incremental, particularly in fields where actors are generalists rather than specialists. Future research on other policy areas in Japan, and in other systems that have generalist staff in regular rotation, is needed to develop this concept.

The third contribution here is the exploration of an unusual power balance between street-level bureaucrat and the client. The ability of the natal parent to withhold consent and the limited judicial support available mean that here the street-level bureaucrats are not as powerful, and the 'clients' not as disempowered, as is often the case. This increases the 'co-production' of policy and leads CGC staff to rely on attempting to create role expectations in parents.[1]

The fourth contribution to this literature is the oft-overlooked consideration of the physical geography in which policy is implemented. The final contribution here is the structuring of findings and analysis into organisational context, value context, resources, norms, and organisational culture. This addresses Meyers and Vorsanger's (2003) call for better integrated political, individual, and organisational explanations, and takes into account May and Winter's (2007) argument on the importance of the role of management in integrating these explanations. Within this structure, organisational culture is seen as an important factor in explaining why differences in resources and beliefs occur.

This thesis also contributes a richly detailed description of the decision-making process in alternative care in Japan. This represents an important contribution to the comparative literature on alternative care, which often excludes Japan or seeks to explain it with an amorphous conceptualisation of *a* Japanese culture. Goodman notes that 'there is virtually nothing written in English, not only on the child welfare services but indeed on personal social services in Japan in general' (2000: 4). This work is the first ethnographic work on the CGCs.

Sano, the head of the Teru CGC, argues that one of the issues Japan has faced in developing foster care services is that it exists as a kind of 'Galapagos', removed from a global discourse on alternative care. This thesis seeks to imitate Darwin's *Beagle* by exploring this Galapagos and reporting outwards what is happening and why. This is done in the hope that comparative scholars of alternative care integrate Japan into this global discourse, and that actors in Japan will be aware of these new works and engage with them when creating and implementing policy and practice.

There are many things in this study that are likely to surprise scholars of alternative care: the lack of social work as a profession; the fact that decisions are made by generalist local bureaucrats; the continued use and scale of BIWIs; the CGC's inability to stop a child being returned to his mother, even in the case where the child had been locked in a room for seven years without stimulation and his sibling had been starved to death; the continued existence of CWIs housing over 150 children, even of those housing over 30 children; the fact that each caseworker has an average of 107 active cases (Saimura, 2008); the limited role of the judiciary and, perhaps linked to this, the absence of the child's voice and the lack of family participation in the formal decision-making process. The second contribution of this thesis to alternative care literature is explaining why at least some of these practices occur.

The third contribution to alternative care studies is the move past looking at Japan as a single case study and the recognition of domestic regional variation. As elsewhere, there is a tension between the devolution of authority and the right to equal services. To date, the MHLW has resolved this by taking the position that neither type of care is inherently better, and that different does not mean worse. Under this logic, the drive to promote foster care services has to be seen as diversifying the range of care available rather than as de-institutionalising care. Yet the MHLW's foster care guidelines state that foster care should be considered the default placement, with institutional care reserved for children in particular circumstances. This tension is yet to be resolved at a national policy level, which increases the space in which local authorities can exercise discretion.

Finally, here, this book poses a new perspective on one of the macro-themes running through alternative care literature – the nexus between care and control. One manifestation of this comes in discussions on the balance between child protection and state intervention into the family. This thesis offers an unusual perspective on this nexus, namely that the inability of the CGC to exercise control inhibits their ability to provide care that would allow the child to return to the family or to remain safely within the family. Without judicial support, the caseworker is unable to set parameters for parental involvement. This means that children often remain in alternative care for much longer than is necessary. In Japan, the lack of control is a significant barrier to providing appropriate care and facilitating family reunification.

The findings of the book also represent a significant contribution to scholars of Japan, informing understandings of the family-bond and of the interaction between the state and the individual. The account of the interaction of local and national authority, the diversity of practice between local authorities, and the feedback from local policy and practice up to national policy and practice also represent significant contributions.

There is a need for more detailed research into the roles of the police and the judiciary here, and on how the values, norms, resources, and organisational cultures of these institutions interact with those of the CGCs. There is also a need for further research to test the model of the family-bond offered here. This could involve work on the family registration system, informal joint-custody, or kinship foster care.

This book was not able to address policy and practice change over time. The three fieldwork sites have all chosen to increase their foster care rates through very different mechanisms: Teru by investing in the CGC and NPOs that can support it, Yuno by working with foster care specialists in welfare institutions, and Irifune by outsourcing some foster care services to a BIWI. A historical study tracing the interaction of norms, resources and organisational cultures in different local authorities would test the proposed 'two-level' change model and further clarify the relationship between national and local authority.

3 Policy implications

Works on alternative care in Japan often conclude with predictions of imminent change (Bamba and Haight, 2009a, 2009b; Goodman, 2000, 2012). Discussing a change in funding in CWIs, from being based on capacity to being based on the number of children in the CWI, Goodman posited that this increased competition would mean that 'after forty years of virtually no change, *yogoshisetsu* [CWIs] changed very rapidly during the late 1990s and look as if they will change even more rapidly at the start of the next decade' (2000: 179).

Yet there has not been a rapid change in the function of the welfare institutions since this point. There are still more children in large-style CWIs than in unit-style or community-based CWIs, and many CWIs still have 12 children in each dormitory room, with only a fractionally improved staff to child ratio from 2000.

Concluding this thesis faces the same challenge faced by earlier authors, namely that once again alternative care in Japan appears to be on the cusp of significant change. The 2016 revisions to the Child Welfare Act seek to promote foster care and adoption and move away from the large CWIs and BIWIs that dominate service provision (MHLW, 2016). Doi argues that 'if this revised Child Welfare Act is diligently observed, the alternative care system will drastically migrate from institutions to families' (2016). The key is whether these revisions will be diligently observed: after all, local authorities did not respond to calls to create a target of one-third of children in foster care with uniform enthusiasm, with two local authorities submitting plans to decrease their foster care rate.[2]

At the heart of this issue lies the tension between the desire to devolve authority and the desire of the central government to promote change in a uniform direction across local authorities. One way to ameliorate this issue, already under consideration by national policymakers, is to create a powerful national inspectorate for care providers and CGCs, a role that is performed in the UK by OFSTED.

Discussing alternative care in Japan, Goldfarb (2013: 166) states:

> Although legal and policy changes are certainly key in altering child-welfare practices, fine-grained cultural analysis is necessary in order to fully understand both the stakes of contemporary welfare practices, and the wide variety of beliefs and values that must be considered in any reform effort.

The research presented in this book points at 'beliefs and values' that any attempt to realise policy change must take into consideration to be successful. The first is the construction of the family-bond as discrete and singular. It is possible that this value will change, with the emerging issue of joint custody likely to influence discourse here, but this will take considerable time. Any attempt to increase the foster care rate must, therefore, begin with the semi-professionalization of foster care.

While well-intentioned, current efforts to gain childcare leave for all foster parents risk further shifting the function of foster care towards adoption. Where foster care is seen as a proxy for adoption, with care based upon a family-bond, it is only considered suitable for the few children for whom the goal of care is not family-reunification, who are considered young enough to make a new family-bond, and who do not have 'complex' care needs. On the other hand, where foster care is constructed as semi-professional care in a family setting, it is less of a threat to the existing or potential family-bond and can be used for children for whom the goal of care is family reunification, older children, and children with more complex needs.

There are several important steps towards the semi-professionalization of foster care. The first is to develop foster care service capacity. This could be in the form of not-for-profit organisations, as is the case with welfare institutions, or it could be in increased CGC capacity. Given the issues posed by staff rotation in CGCs, a hybrid of internal and external provision could provide local authorities with a suitable balance of control and expertise.

The second step is to create more stringent national criteria for foster parent registration so that CGCs can reject unsuitable applicants. This, coupled with investment into foster parent training, would allow CGCs to use all registered foster parents, rather than simply increasing the number of registered foster parents irrespective of their ability to foster or the CGC's ability to support them. The MHLW is attempting to develop some foster care service provision capacity in welfare institutions. While this is not impossible, in its current incarnation there are significant conflicts of interest, in both beliefs and financial incentives.

CGC staff must also have more accessible avenues to resolving cases where the parent opposes their preferred course of action, on removing the child, returning the child, and placement type. The most internationally accepted means of doing this is for the judiciary to decide where the parent does not give consent. Harada argues that to do this, Japan 'will have to overcome many challenges, both technical and philosophical, since our child welfare system has been operating without court authority for many years' (2010: 233). Given that this may take considerable time, there may be the need to create a stop-gap solution that affords caseworkers, senior managers or independent mediators greater power in these decisions.

Any solution here must address the challenges posed by staff rotation. One way this could be achieved would be to designate bureaucrats with enough experience as senior social workers and ensure they only rotate through positions that use their specialist knowledge. This senior bureaucrat could be given greater authority to resolve issues. A second, more palatable, solution would be to empower the subcommittee of the social welfare and public health committee with more legal powers. However this is achieved, this system must facilitate the cultivation and retention of expertise and experience.

Adoption should not be devolved from the judiciary, even as a stop-gap measure, as this is a permanent decision. The fact that adoption is only an option when the parent voluntarily cedes their parental rights means that some foster care will continue to be used as a proxy for adoption. A new category of 'long-term foster care' could be introduced to cater for all placements that are anticipated to last over three years and placements that cross this threshold.[3] To ensure placement stability, which is considered as critical by the CGCs, and to move towards achieving permanency, 'long-term foster care' placements would have to have some mechanisms to prevent the parent removing the child from care on a whim.

The introduction of 'long-term foster care' could be connected to a change in funding structure, with higher levels of financial support for foster carers in their first three years of fostering and a reducing scale after that point. This would also contribute to the creation of a class of more professional foster carers, who would focus on providing shorter-term placements.

My second policy recommendation, related to the first, is the introduction of a new term for foster parents. The Japanese for foster care, *sato oya*, literally translates as natal village parents. CGC caseworkers explained to me that the word *oya*, parents, is often an issue for natal parents. In an effort to redress this, and to distinguish foster care from adoption, Tokyo now uses the term *Yōiku katei*, [child] rearing home, which is less emotive. One Tokyo CGC head explained that 'in adoption you enter the same grave, you enter the family register. Foster care is more for care, so we created the name *yōuiku katei*' (interview, 2015).

If a 'long-term foster care' category was created, this could retain the term *sato oya*, perhaps with the prefix *chou-ki*, long-term. This would further increase the contrast between foster *carers*, used to promote family reintegration, and long-term foster *parents*, used as a proxy for adoption. This may also help caseworkers secure parental consent for foster care.

The third piece of policy advice that stems from this thesis relates to attachment and the dissemination of academic constructions of attachment to practitioners. If attachment theory were understood by practitioners as it is by academics, both those inside and outside Japan, the development of attachment to a foster parent would not be seen as a threat to the natal parent or to the family-bond. Under attachment theory, the child's ability to form a bond with an adult strengthens their capacity to do this with another adult. That is, forming a family-bond with a foster carer not only poses no threat to the family-bond, it could strengthen it. This means that the constructed limbo of welfare institutions is a limbo that does not need to exist. The gap between theory and practice here is likely to be magnified by the staff turnover and the generalist status of those implementing policy.

The importance of connecting practice to evidence extends beyond attachment. The aversion within the MHLW to conducting research on BIWIs and attachment disorders, for fear of stigmatising BIWI alumni, goes against the very idea of evidence-informed policy. This fear of being confronted with evidence, seemingly based largely on insecurity over the ability to readily respond to it, also leads to outspoken academics being excluded from MHLW committees, and a reluctance in the MHLW to meet with critics of the status quo, most notably HRW. This further inhibits anything other than incremental change.

It is possible that the continual rotation of staff within the MHLW, and indeed within local authorities, contributes to this insecurity. This apprehension is not limited to governmental actors. After one cautious response to a query on why they still run BIWIs, in which they acknowledged that they are 'aware of the UN Guidelines' (see Appendix 1), the Japanese Red Cross, which is the largest provider of BIWIs in Japan, stopped all communication with me for 'fear of adding fuel to the fire' (anonymised interview, 2014).

This caution over evidence exists even though some BIWI, CWI, and CGC staff believe some children are damaged by spending prolonged periods in BIWIs. One CWI staff member noted that 'children who have been in BIWIs have greater difficulties even than children who come from abusive households' (interview, 2014). Yet individuals are unable to act upon these concerns, turning their energies instead to improving the system they are working within. This concern, of being confined in a system with serious issues, was most concisely expressed by a senior manager in Teru, who stated with regret: 'I fear that all I am doing is moving children from abusive households to abusive institutions' (interview, 2014).

Achieving the stated goal of developing foster care service provision will require further reallocation of resources, as well as the establishment of up-front funds to develop new systems (European Commission, 2013; Fox and Gotestam, 2003; Mulheir and Browne, 2007; UNICEF, 2012; UNICEF and World Bank, 2003; UN Office of the High Commissioner for Human Rights, 2011; World Health Organization, 2010). At present, economy of scale means that for CGCs placing a child into a CWI is comparable in cost to providing a supported foster care placement. The higher cost of BIWIs, even than a well-supported specialist foster carer, means that these may be a sensible place to begin any de-institutionalisation programme. One pilot scheme attempting exactly this is occurring in Nagano, under the supervision of Kamikado (Kamikado, personal correspondence, 2017, April 30).

Local authorities often lack the resources, both fiscal and of expertise, to invest here.[4] The creation of a dedicated centralised team bringing together domestic and international experts on alternative care and the de-institutionalisation of care, along with the creation of a national fund for pilot programmes to evaluate the efficacy of de-institutionalisation, would greatly accelerate this process. While the position that local authorities are best placed to address local needs is a reasonable one, there is also sense in addressing shared problems in a coordinated manner to maximise the impact of available resources.

As a final suggestion, there is considerable scope to expand kinship foster care in Japan. The lack of enforceable legal authority means that CGCs are often cautious of kinship foster care as they cannot control the natal parents' access to the child. Creating a system with more control would open this care pathway up to more children.

I feel a little presumptuous making these policy recommendations: there are many experts within Japan who have devoted their lives to these issues, which I have only spent a decade or so on so far. My only defence against this charge is that by looking at this as an outsider I have had a different viewpoint from most. Here I take heart from Thelen's (1999: 386) observation:

> Institutions are socially constructed in the sense that they embody shared cultural understandings ("shared cognitions," "interpretive frames") of the way the world works... This means that even when policy makers set out to redesign institutions, they are constrained in what they can conceive of by these embedded, cultural constraints.

Further, I know that all of those who were gracious enough to host me during my fieldwork or grant me their time for an interview, or chat over coffee are doing their best within the system in which they work. When volunteering with CWIs, I was constantly humbled by the dedication of the staff to the children in their care, a dedication I also found in foster parents. Similarly, when researching with CGCs, I was deeply touched by the efforts of the staff to resolve incredibly challenging situations over which they had little concrete authority, and when interviewing bureaucrats and politicians, I was struck by their desire to improve the situation of the system they manage.

Yet, for too long alternative care in Japan has been a closed world, evolving in unusual directions like the birds of Darwin's Galapagos. The limit to this metaphor is that the birds in the Galapagos were perfectly adapted to their environment while the care provision in Japan does not represent the best possible care that a child in the third-largest economy in the world could have. My most fervent hope for this book is that it provides a different standpoint for those tasked with creating and implementing policy to re-examine their views; that it serves to stimulate change.

Notes

1 This creation of role expectations, in lieu of formal power, is also used by the CGC to attempt to shape the behaviour of care providers.
2 As noted in Chapter 4 (endnote), 2019 amendments to the Civil Code increased the age threshold for adoption to 15 years. This increases the number of children who are eligible for adoption, though further research is required on the implications of these changes on parental consent and the engagement of the judiciary with these reforms.
3 I have suggested a threshold of three years based on a study conducted in Fukuoka city. This found that 75 per cent of children in institutional care who are reunified with their families within three years of placement, with children who stay in institutional care for longer than three years are likely to remain in care until they age-out, at 18 years (Tokunaga et al., forthcoming)
4 The Nippon Foundation (2015) has created social impact bonds aimed at helping local authorities meet these transition costs but this is still very limited in scope.

References

Bamba, S., & Haight, W. (2009a). The developmental–ecological approach of Japanese child welfare professionals to supporting children's social and emotional well-being: The practice of mimamori. *Children and Youth Services Review*, 31, 429–439.

Bamba, S., & Haight, W. (2009b). Maltreated children's emerging well-being in Japanese state care. *Children and Youth Services Review*, 31, 797–806.

Doi, K. (2016). *Revised Child Welfare Act: The principle of family-based care now guaranteed by the law.* 2016, May 7. Retrieved from URL: https://www.hrw.org/news/2016/05/27/revised-child-welfare-act-principle-family-based-care-now-guaranteed-law (last accessed 2017, August 28).

European Commission. (2013). *Investing in children: Breaking the cycle of disadvantage.* Commission recommendation of 20.2.2013, C(2013), 778 final.

Fox, L., & Gotestam, R. (2003). Redirecting resources to community based services: A concept paper. *Social protection Discussion Paper No. 0311.* Washington: The World Bank.

Goldfarb, K. (2012). *Fragile kinships: Family ideologies and child welfare in Japan.* (Doctoral dissertation). The University of Chicago.

252 Conclusion

Goldfarb, K. (2013). Japan. In P. Welbourne, & J. Dixon (Eds.), *Child protection and child welfare: A global appraisal of cultures, policy, and practice*. London: Jessica Kingsley Publishers.

Goodman, R. (2000). *Children of the Japanese state: The changing role of child protection institutions in contemporary Japan*. Oxford: Oxford University Press.

Goodman, R. (2012). The 'discovery' and 'rediscovery' of child abuse (*jido gyakutai*) in Japan. In R. Goodman, Y. Imoto, & T. Toivonen (Eds.), *A sociology of Japanese youth: From returnees to NEETs*. London: Nissan Institute/Routledge Japanese Studies.

Harada, A. (2010). The Japanese child protection system: Developments in the laws and the issues left unsolved. *International Survey of Family Law*, Vol. 2010, pp. 217–236.

May, P.J., & Winter, S.C. (2007). Politicians, managers, and street-level bureaucrats: Influences on policy implementation. *Journal of Public Administration Research and Theory*, 19, 453–476.

Meyers, M.K., & Vorsanger, S. (2003). Street-level bureaucrats and the implementation of public policy. In B.G. Peters, & J. Pierre (Eds.), *Handbook of public administration*. Thousand Oaks: Sage.

MHLW. (2010). *Kodomo ~ kosodate bijyōn ~ kodomo no egao ga afureru shakai no tame ni* [Children and child rearing vision ~ In order to build a society overflowing with children's smiles].

MHLW. (2016). *Jidō fukushi-hō-tō no ichibu wo kaisei suru hōritsu-an shinkyū taishō jōbun* [Draft law amending part of the Child Welfare Act. Highlighting original and amended articles].

Mulheir, G., & Browne, K. (2007). *Deinstitutionalising and transforming children's services: A guide to good practice*. European Commission Daphne programme in collaboration with WHO regional office for Europe and the University of Birmingham UK. Birmingham: University of Birmingham (WHO Collaborating Centre for Child Care and Protection).

Saimura, J. (2008). Kore kara nihon ga susumibeki hōkō to wa [The directions the Japanese child abuse system should proceed toward]. In Tsuzaki, T., & Hashimoto, K. (Eds.), *Jidō gyakutai wa ima – Renkei shisutemu no kochiku ni mukete* [Current situation in child abuse – Toward the establishment of a collaborative system]. Kyoto: Minerva Shobo.

The Nippon Foundation. (2015). *Exploring "Social Impact Bond" structure in Japan. Nippon Foundation and Yokosuka City partner to promote special adoption*. Retrieved from URL: http://www.nippon-foundation.or.jp/en/news/pr/2015/13.html (last accessed 2017, August 22).

Thelen, K. (1999). Historical institutionalism in comparative politics. *Annual Review of Political Science*, 2, 369–404.

Tokunaga, S., Fukui, M., Saigo, M., & Nagano, S. (Forthcoming). A new era for child protection in Japan. In J.D. Berrick, N. Gilbert, & M. Skivenes (Eds.), *The Oxford handbook of child protection systems*. New York: Oxford University Press.

UNICEF. (2012). *Children under the age of three in formal care in Eastern Europe and Central Asia: A rights-based regional situation analysis*. (Amended 2013, January). Geneva: UNICEF.

UNICEF & World Bank. (2003). *Changing minds, policies and lives: Improving protection of children in Eastern Europe and Central Asia: Gatekeeping services for vulnerable children and families*. Florence: UNICEF & World Bank.

United Nations Office of the High Commissioner for Human Rights. (2011). *The rights of children under the age of three, ending their placement in institutional care.* n.p.: Regional Office for Europe of the Office of the United Nations High Commissioner for Human Rights.

World Health Organization. (2010). *Better health, better lives: Children and young people with intellectual disabilities and their families: Transfer care from institutions to the community.* EUR/51298/17/PP/3. Bucharest, Romania.

Note: Where the author(s) provided an English translation of their work I have given this translation, rather than my translation.

Appendix one
Email response from the Japanese Red Cross on BIWIs

Received 4 November 2014

Mr. Michael Maher King

Thank you very much for your continued understanding of the activities of the Japanese Red Cross. You wrote to us in English… however given that you understand Japanese we would like to reply to you from the office of the Welfare department, of the Relief and Welfare Division, which supervises the administration of child welfare institutions.

1. The reasons why the Red Cross runs baby and infant welfare institutions

    The Red Cross runs baby and infant welfare institutions under the Child Welfare Act, with the approval of the Ministry of Health, Labour and Welfare. We raise children who cannot be cared for by their guardians. Of the babies and infants who enter the Japanese Red Cross baby and infant welfare institutions, approximately 20 per cent are accounted for by sick and disabled babies and infants. Given that these babies and infants need medical services it is necessary to raise these babies and infants in cooperation with Red Cross hospitals. In addition, the costs for caring for babies and infants in these institutions are covered by government payments.

    We are aware of the UN Guidelines and the Japanese government policies corresponding to them, which you (Mr. King) mentioned in your email. However, until the foster care system is sufficiently in order in Japan, under the Red Cross's principles of humanity, in order to protect the lives of children whose guardians cannot care for them, we think that there is no choice but to raise babies and infants in baby and infant welfare institutions.

2. The Japanese Red Cross' plans to close baby and infant welfare institutions

    The Japanese Red Cross is actively engaged in driving forwards the foster care system. We have run salons and research meetings targeting people interested in becoming foster carers, and hosted meetings for foster carers peer exchange meetings. However, as we stated in point 1., given the reality that the foster care system is at present not sufficiently in order, and in order to protect the lives of sick babies and infants, and babies and infants with disabilities, for whom it is difficult to enter foster care, we think that it is essential to run baby and infant welfare institutions. Therefore, at present we do not have any plans to close baby and infant welfare institutions.

3 The number of children in the Red Cross baby and infant welfare institutionsThere are currently 235 babies and infants in the Japanese Red Cross baby and infant welfare institutions.

...

Yours Sincerely,
Japanese Red Cross
Head of Welfare Department, Relief and Welfare Division

Appendix two
List of prefectures for figures 1.2, 1.3, and 2.2

Hokkaido

1. Hokkaido

Tohoku

2. Aomori
3. Iwate
4. Miyagi
5. Akita
6. Yamagata
7. Fukushima

Kanto

8. Ibaraki
9. Tochigi
10. Gunma
11. Saitama
12. Chiba
13. Tokyo
14. Kanagawa

Tohoku

15. Niigata
16. Toyama
17. Ishikawa
18. Fukui
19. Yamanashi
20. Nagano
21. Gifu
22. Shizuoka
23. Aichi

Kansai

24. Mie
25. Shiga
26. Kyoto
27. Osaka
28. Hyogo
29. Nara
30. Wakayama

Chugoku

31. Tottori
32. Shimane
33. Okayama
34. Hiroshima
35. Yamaguchi

Shikoku

36. Tokushima
37. Kagawa
38. Ehime
39. Kochi

Kyushu & Okinawa

40. Fukuoka
41. Saga
42. Nagasaki
43. Kumamoto
44. Oita
45. Miyazaki
46. Kagoshima
47. Okinawa

Index

adoption: age threshold 126; demand for 128; family-bond 120; introduction of special adoption 40; lack of eligible children 128, 187; normal adoption 127; numbers 33; open *vs.* closed 120
Aiba, H. 192
Ainsworth, F. 5
alternative care: acclimatisation period 34; budgets and stability 47–50, 168; care and control 245; children raised by society 242; competition between care providers 147; contact with parents 192; creation of expectations on role performance 90; ethnic composition of children in 37; historical development 39–46; increase in number of children entering care and foster care 153; institutions or residential care 36; international context 3; Japan as Galapagos 215; local authority structure 65–66; lack of change 39, 64; lack of data 13, 38; lack of media attention 217; low rate entering care 121; numbers by care type 33; numbers in care relative to population 151; overview 39; placement changes 38; poverty on rate entering care 151; presence of parents by placement type 192; private providers and policy change 50; progression to tertiary education 38; quality of care providers 155; reasons for entering 37; role of judiciary 66–68; specialist counsellor for foster care support 43; spectrum of care 203
Arimura, T. 157
Aspinall, R.W. 217

baby and infant welfare institutions: absence of family-bond as a positive 113; age 36; as foster care provider 163; domestic concerns 157, 199, 249; domestic concerns (Irifune) 231; domestic concerns (Ministry of Health, Labour, and Welfare) 200; domestic concerns (Teru) 200; risk 224; role 49, 201–202; size 36
Baldcock, J. 104
Bamba, S. 121, 156
Bourdieu, P. 103
Browne, K. 36

careleavers 157, 185
case study: baby and infant welfare institution 200, 202; child welfare institution to foster care (Izumi) 165; family-bond (abuse - Ayame) 122; family-bond (abuse - Chiyoko) 122; family-bond (abuse - Daiki) 122–124; family-bond (abuse - Hideo) 122; family-bond (abuse - Kenji) 122; family-bond (age threshold - Natsuko) 129–130; family-bond (expectations - Haruto) 110–111; family-bond (familial love - Jiro and Ichiro) 110; family-bond (ibasho - Akemi) 109–110; family-bond (ibasho - Maiko) 109; family-bond (ibasho - Taisei) 109; family-bond (judiciary *vs.* child guidance centres) 124–125; family-bond (legal, blood, practice - Jinpei) 108; family-bond (legal, blood, practice - Sosuke) 107–108; family-bond (singular - Ren) 112–113; family-bond (singular - Yamato) 117; family-home *vs.* child welfare institution 202; foster care as lucky - Irifune 197–198, 226
child abuse: discovery of 40, 64, 151; impact on local policy change 48, 49;

recording when entering care 37; response of hospitals 65–66; response of police 66; response of schools 66; role of the judiciary 66–68; Suginami incident 49

child guidance centres: capacity 166; challenges in accessing children in need 89; change in staff attitudes 198; differences in organisation of Teru and Irifune 73–75; diversity of role 63; engagement with external actors 164; engagement with welfare institutions 165; and the family 63–64; foster care staff 79, 161; generalist staff 63, 160; lack of expertise on foster care 161; moral responsibility for abuse in alternative care 49, 158; narrow or wide staff responsibilities 165; organisation of 75; organisational cultures 216; role 63, 64, 226; role of judiciary 220; role specialisation 230; senior managers experience 165, 198, 215, 227; service provider *vs.* service regulator 161–162; staff 80; staff caseload 151, 153; staff differences in Teru and Irifune 80; staff experience 164, 215, 219; staff informal training 228; staff - lawyer 166; staff rotation 227; staff training 80, 228–229; typical day 218–219

child psychotherapy institutions: change of name 36; role 37

child self-reliance support institutions: role 36

Child Welfare Act: recent revisions 41, 44, 188

child welfare institutions: absence of family-bond a positive 109; abuse in 204; abuse scandals 155; age 36; as foster care provider 163; domestic concerns 157, 199; large *vs.* small 155; layout 36; as neglectful 110; risk 224; role 201; size 36

childrearing: as challenging 158–159

Collier, D. 215

Davis, K.C. 10

decision-making process: acceptance of care provider 160; acceptance meeting 82–83; aid objectives meeting 85–88; children's voice 89, 185, 222; clinical psychologist 222; consultations 80; disability 49; family-bond and removing a child from their family 105; goals of care 185; informal discussions 224; Irifune 223; overview 80, 206; parental consent 66–68, 88, 166, 185, 226; placement stability 186; placement type 182; positive risk 187; regional variation (Teru and Irifune) 223–227; role of judiciary 66–68, 86–88, 124–125; role of mediation 103, 131; ruling meeting 83–85; summary of the stages 80–89; Teru 220–223; the family-bond and removing a child from their family 105

deinstitutionalisation of care: abuse scandals 4; child development 4; domestic arguments 4; external pressure 4; financial considerations 4; international trends 4; United Nations Conventions on the Rights of the Child 4; United Nations Guidelines for the Alternative Care of Children 4

disability: influencing decision-making process 49; leading to vulnerability 122

discretion: definition 10; exercised by generalist staff 76

Donahue, J.D. 50

Dubois, V. 217

family: normal-enough 112; role in welfare state 63

family registration system: the family-bond 118–120

family-bond: age threshold 126; familial love 110; foster care 121; ibasho 109–110; in other countries 106; legal, blood, practice 107–108; overview 105–106; protecting the image of 206; risk of destroying 105, 122–124; Singular and discrete 112; summary of components 107

family-homes: contact with parents 192; contested role 192–193; introduction of 41; role 201

foster care: age threshold 128, 189, 205; as a boarding house 190–191; child contact with parents 191; child guidance centre concerns 158; child guidance centre evaluation 158; child-rearing leave 192; for children child welfare institutions want to leave 191; confusion with adoption 39, 188; contested role 193; discretion in use of

Index 261

registered foster parents 72; family-bond 121; giri-giri foster parents 72; lack of eligible children 150, 226; LGBT 199; as a proxy for adoption 188; registration 158; role 192, 205; role (Irifune) 194–196; role (Ministry of Health, Labour, and Welfare) 193; role (narrow) 199; role (Teru) 196–197; role of welfare institutions 44; as a safety valve 147; Teru pilot scheme 197; types of 33
foster care associations (local) 162
Foster Care Guidelines 43, 45
foster care rate: domestic explanations of Japan 6; international explanations of Japan 5; issues with official foster care rate 39; Japan in international context 4; regional variation in changes to 45; as a resource to the child guidance centres 156; staff attitudes 198
foster care service agencies 163, 165

Geertz, C. 104
Genograms 113
Gilbert, N. 183
goals of care: international context 182–185; judiciary 87, 185; Ministry of Health, Labour, and Welfare 184; the three goals 185
Goldfarb, K. 64, 106, 118, 120, 188–189
Goodman, R. 40, 64, 242

Haight, W. 121, 156
Harada, A. 67
Hayashi, H. 11, 158
Hayes, P. 72
Hendry, J. 86, 125
Hertog, E. 119
Hill, M. 70, 78
Hirada, M. 164
Holliday, A. 217
Human Rights Watch 87, 157

Ishii Juuji 4

Japanese Red Cross: running baby and infant welfare institutions 249, Appendix 1

Kamikado, K. 250
Kashiwame, R. 4
Kawamatsu, R. 187
Key Assets 43

koseki seido *see* family registration system
Krogness, K.J. 118, 119
Kubo, K. 88
Kumasaka, Y. 192
Kurihara, N. 219

Lipsky, M. 10, 77
lobbying: by national welfare institution associations 150

Mashaw, J. 78
Matsumoto, I. 151
Matsumoto, T. 11
May, P.J. 216
Maynard-Moody, S.W. 182
Mehrotra, V. 127
Meyers, M.K. 143
Ministry of Health, Labour, and Welfare: perceived role 69; relationship with local authorities 69; technical guidance to local authorities 70
Ministry of Justice 90
Miwa, K. 6, 148, 150, 226
Miyajima, K. 158, 188
mother and child living support institutions: role 37
Mulheir, G. 36
Murata, K. 161
Musheno, M.C. 182

Nagano, S. 157
New Vision of Alternative Care 44–45
The Nippon Foundation 16
non-profit-organisations: Teru 162

Ochiai, E. 107
Omori, H. 121

Parsons, T. 77
policy and practice recommendations: attachment theory and practice 249; centralised expertise 250; child guidance centre knowledge 168; evidence-based 249; foster 'parent' 207, 248; foster care funding structure 248; foster care provider system 168, 207–208; funding structure 249; increase registration threshold 207; issues around parental consent 248; kinship foster care 250; long-term foster care 207, 248; national inspectorate 247; new categories of

foster carers 207; role of judiciary 248; semi-professionalization of foster care 207–208, 247–248
policy change supported by two-levels 146, 239–240

regional variation of policy implementation: child guidance centres 10; child guidance centres willing to challenge parents 186–187; continuity of approach 159; decision-making process 206–207; decision-making process (Teru and Irifune) 223–227; devolution of power and ideals of equality 9; evolution in isolation 161; foster care age threshold 205; foster care function 182, 192–199; foster care - luck or planned 197–198; foster care rate 7; foster care role 241; generalist staff 76; Japan as Galapagos 72, 227; knowledge acquisition, retention, and use in informing change 227–231; negative feedback loops 159, 225; physical capacity of care providers 146; physical geography 144; placement stability 186; political attention 144; positive feedback loops 225; practice learning at local not national level 167; the right to equal provision of welfare 9; role of different placements 187; senior managers experience 198; staff experience 165; use of meetings 186
rights: children's rights *vs.* parental rights 63, 106

Sabatier, P.A. 231
Saimura, J. 79, 161

self-reliance assistance homes: role 36
sexual exploitation of children 89
Shirai, C. 107
SOS Children's Villages 43
specialist counsellor for foster care support 163, 164
street-level bureaucrats: beliefs 182; definition 10; generalist bureaucrats 244; organisational culture 216; power balance with clients 78; resources 143; staff rotation 244

temporary care: placements not recorded as alternative care 38; role 38
Tenri-kyō 129
Thoburn, J. 5
Tokunaga, S. 126
Tsuzaki, T. 5, 6, 63, 147, 160

United Nations Convention on the Rights of the Child: ratification 40
United Nations Guidelines for the Alternative Care of Children 4
Ushijima, Y. 219

Vision for Children and Childrearing 43, 199
Vorsanger, S. 143

Wada, I. 9
Winter, S.C. 216

Yamamoto, T. 38
Yukawa, R. 219

Zeckhauser, R.J. 50
zuruzuru 201, 230

Lightning Source UK Ltd.
Milton Keynes UK
UKHW022040030422
401046UK00004B/31